G000298746

PALS

The 11th (Service) Battalion (Accrington) East Lancashire Regiment

WILLIAM TURNER

Additional research
FERGUS REED

Pen & Sword Books Limited

This book is dedicated to the memory of those men who served in the Service Battalion known as the 'Accrington Pals'.

First published in **1987** by Wharncliffe Publishing Limited

Second impression **1992**
Third impression **1998**
Published by Leo Cooper
an imprint of
Pen & Sword Books Limited
47 Church Street, Barnsley
South Yorkshire S70 2AS

© William Turner 1987, 1992, 1998

ISBN: 0-85052-360-5

Printed by Yorkshire Web, Barnsley

Front cover: The Hindle brothers, Clarence (standing) and John, members of X (District) Company.

Also available in the same series:

Barnsley Pals: The 13th & 14th (Service) Battalions (Barnsley) The York & Lancaster Regiment *by Jon Cooksey*
Sheffield City: The 12th (Service) Battalion (Sheffield) The York & Lancaster Regiment *by Paul Oldfield and Ralph Gibson*
Liverpool Pals: A History of the 17th, 18th, 19th & 20th (Service) Battalions The King's (Liverpool Regiment) *by Graham Maddocks*
Leeds Pals: A History of the 15th (Service) Battalion The Prince of Wales's Own (West Yorkshire Regiment) *by Laurie Milner*
Salford Pals: A History of the 15th, 16th, 19th & 20th Battalions Lancashire Fusiliers *by Michael Stedman*
Manchester Pals: The 16th, 17th, 18th, 19th, 20th, 21st, 22nd & 23rd Battalions of the Manchester Regiment *by Michael Stedman*
Birmingham Pals: The 14th, 15th, & 16th Battalions of the Royal Warwickshire Regiment *by Terry Carter*
Tyneside Irish: 24th, 25th, 26th & 27th (Service) Battalions of the Northumberland Fusiliers *by John Sheen*
Tyneside Scottish: 20th, 21th, 22nd & 23rd (Service) Battalions of the Northumberland Fusiliers *by Graham Stewart and John Sheen*

Below: A group of 'X' (District) Company Pals on active service in France.

Contents

Foreword 7

Introduction 8

1. Come back this afternoon 13

2. And we be brethren 37

3. Croeso i Gymru! Welcome to Wales! 65

4. Some Battalion! Some Colonel 79

5. An eastern interlude 103

6. We captured Serre three times a day 117

7. God help the sinner 137

8. The Aftermath 169

   Epilogue 185

   Appendix
   1. Personae 193
   2. Correspondent's Reports 197
   3. Report on Operations 198
   4. Battle Report 12th Y.& L. July 1st. 200
   5. Peltzer letter 201
   6. Appreciation messages 202
   7. Casualty lists 203
   8. Hometowns of July 1st casualties 209
   9. Total Battalion casualties 1916 - 1918 210

Nominal roll 211

Decorations 243

Officers Monthly Army List 247

Name index 248

Photo postscript 249

Selected Bibliography 252

Acknowledgments 254

*And away went
another, a red
horse; its rider was
allowed to take peace
away from the earth
and to make men slay
each other; he was
given a huge sword.*

Revelation 6 verse 4
(Moffatt Bible)

PAL
Slang or low colloquial
Romany English: 'Phal' — brother, friend
Sanskrit: Bhrator — brother
Websters International Dictionary 1961

Below: The industrial town of
Accrington at the turn of the
century.

Foreword

Martin Middlebrook

I've been there, a most striking place, a sad place — Serre! The front line trench from which the 11th East Lancashires attacked on the first day of the battle of the Somme is still there, a grassy zig-zag, clearly a trench, just on the edge of a wood up a farm track. The 11th East Lancashires were, of course, the Accrington Pals. Unfortunately, the place where their old front line trench is to be found is now called the Sheffield Memorial Park. But the Sheffield unit did not attack from this stretch of front line. Their sector was a short distance to the north, but post 1918 Sheffield established their Memorial Park nearer the track up which the visitors would have to come. Accrington must have been asleep and made no protest.

In many ways the Accrington Pals were typical of Kitchener's New Army of volunteers in 1914, but that local enthusiasm seems to have had a harder time in getting its Pals Battalion accepted by the War Office. Bill Turner's book will describe the difficulties. In the post-war period, Accrington could not seem to stir itself to provide any memorial at the place where the Pals suffered so terribly on the Somme.

An Accrington man has produced a different type of memorial, a well researched history of the Pals which deserves wide circulation and support, not only in Accrington but further afield. I congratulate Bill Turner and most willingly commend his work.

Introduction

Above: Mr Tom Bullough, Chairman of Directors of Howard & Bulloughs, a family firm founded in 1856.
A.O.& T.

Below: An artist's view of Messrs. Howard and Bulloughs Ltd, Globe Works, Accrington, as featured in a 1914 advertisement. Notwithstanding some artistic licence the works was large enough to employ over 4,000 men and boys.
A.O.& T.

Accrington, East Lancashire, in the high hot summer of 1914 was a town of 45,525 people. A town famous for textile machinery, bricks and its football team. Howard and Bulloughs, makers of textile machinery, sold and installed thousands of machines, world-wide, every year. Seven collieries and thirty-two cotton mills completed the industrial basis of the town's economy.

Accrington was a prosperous town. The Borough Treasurer presented 'the most gratifying report on our financial position in thirty years an excellent state of affairs.'[1] In contrast the Medical Officer of Health spoke of general mortality and infant mortality rates higher than the national average with 'too many preventable deaths.'[2] In a 'prosperous' town there were many poor, the margin separating working people from want and hunger desperately narrow. Accrington, as other industrial towns in Britain in 1914, had its bad housing and poverty but its parks and open spaces, along with easy access to open countryside, helped to make it a comparatively pleasant town. It had a considerable civic pride in its good reputation and achievements.

On June 27th, 1914, one of the cotton mills closed for six weeks because of lack of orders, putting five hundred men and women out of work. The closure came as no surprise. Orders for cotton cloth weaving had been falling for many months as part of a general decline in the British cotton industry. Other mills announced the extension to two weeks of the annual one weeks, unpaid holiday. The news added to the cotton workers' growing fears about the future for themselves and the industry.

Engineering workers in the town were also restless for a different reason. In early June, 1914 simmering unrest by the skilled employees about low wages at Howard and Bulloughs culminated with a formal request for a ten per cent increase in wages.[3] Saturday June 27th arrived with no reply from the employers. Feelings ran high, nothing it seemed could prevent a strike. The employees decided on a final dead-line of July lst.

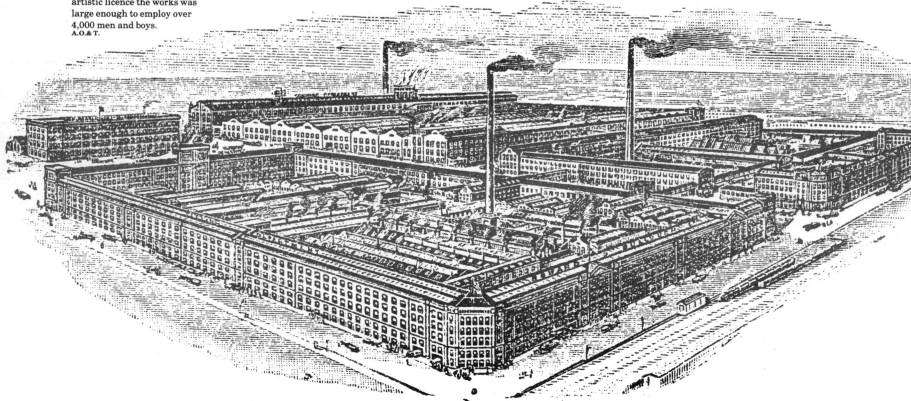

Left: Groups of engineers from Howard and Bulloughs discuss the strike outside Accrington Market Hall.
A.O.& T.

Below: Franz Ferdinand, Archduke of Austria, heir to the Austrian throne from 1889, with his wife Sophia and children.
B.C.P.L.

Meanwhile, on Sunday June 28th, whilst East Lancashire enjoyed the hottest day of the year, in Sarajevo, Bosnia, the heir to the throne of Austria-Hungary, Archduke Franz Ferdinand along with his wife died, the victims of an assassination plot. Balkan quarrels meant little to most in Accrington so the news received but passing interest the following day. At the Empire Picture Palace, the week's film, 'A King in Name Alone,' coincidentally shared its opening night with the news, the film was proclaimed as a 'strong drama set in South Eastern Europe showing the secret springs of intrigue and plot to overthrow a dynasty.' The real-life attempt to overthrow a dynasty gave the film a measure of publicity.[4] Concern, however, centered more on Wednesday July 1st.

The day dawned bright and full of promise, yet in the early afternoon the hot weather broke with a tremendous thunderstorm. Floodwaters swirled into the Howard and Bulloughs machineshop and stopped production. At 5.30 p.m. six hundred skilled engineers, their final dead-line ignored, walked out on strike. The strike had bitter beginnings. Everyday following when the works opened and closed, mounted police stood by as crowds of hostile strikers jeered and jostled non-strikers. One week later the works closed. Almost 4,000 semi-skilled and unskilled men and boys were prevented from working, 'locked out' by the closure. July had begun badly for Accrington and district.

GREAT LOCK-OUT AT HOWARD AND BULLOUGH'S.

Entire Works Closed Down.
Over Four Thousand Men Idle.

THE ENGINEERS AND THEIR CLAIMS.

QUESTION OF UNEMPLOYMENT BENEFIT:
Insurance Officer's Decision Yesterday.

The fears that the strike of the engineers employed at Messrs. Howard and Bullough's,

The average wages for piece workers was about 37s. per week, but whereas some might earn £2 or more others would not get more

non-unionists and will thus be thrown on their own resources. From information available it would appear that quite one half of the workmen are unorganised, these being mostly the section who come under the description of unskilled labourers. The Gasworkers and General Labourers' Union claim to have 1,100 members who will be entitled to lock out pay amounting to 10s. per week, the benefit being a high one, as the subscription is only 3d. per week. The members of the A.S.E. who are out on strike and primarily responsible for the impasse number 600 and they will receive £1 a week whilst on strike. Other workmen are members of the following unions: Grinders and Glaziers; Plate Mounders, Ironfounders, and Sheet Metal Workers. These will probably aggregate from 300 to 400 so that leaves over 2,000 non-unionists.

INSURANCE REFEREE'S DECISION.

We are informed that the Insurance Officer for the district, whose headquarters are at Warrington, visited Accrington yesterday and considered the claims for unemploy-

cotton industr is to be mast manding tha should work i pear to hav machines tha to complete tl customers. ' close down v manage your the nuisance lence, and th 'peaceful' pi letting them is that those trouble do no sands of the their work. phenomenon the new type.

A report of holders of Me including a st Company. Mr ing of the we

STOC

9

On July 18th, one week before the annual holiday, the six hundred skilled engineers collected their first strike pay of £1 each and 1,100 labourers ten shillings each from their respective Trade Unions. Three thousand not in a Trade Union had no income. On the same day a second cotton mill closed for an indefinite period, leaving five hundred more cotton workers with an income of only ten shillings a week.

On Summer Sundays many enjoyed a stroll in the public park and to listen to regular band concerts. In Oak Hill Park in Accrington, on the day after the cotton mill closure announcement, the band of the Scots Guards played. Seats near the bandstand cost three pence. Those who could not afford this (by now there were many) sat on the nearby grassy slopes and put what they could into a collection box. Hundreds basked in brilliant sunshine listening to music by Wagner, Tchaikovsky, Massenet and Gilbert and Sullivan. 'The final waltz,' the new 'Destiny', by William Baines, was a particular favourite. As they listened none of the audience had a notion of the significance the tune would have for them in the near future.

Four days later, on July 23rd, by which time the murder of the Archduke at Sarajevo was but a memory for most in Accrington, Austria delivered an ultimatum to her neighbour Serbia. Austria considered Serbia's reply, with its one major reservation, as a rejection. Serbia objected to the demand that Austro-Hungarian police be allowed into Serbia to conduct the inquiry into the assassination. On July 25th both Austria and Serbia mobilised their armies.

These changed developments were as yet unknown in Accrington. July 25th was holiday Saturday and in spite of the recent troubles, railway bookings exceeded the 1913 record. The station quickly filled with families on their way to the popular resorts. Six crowded trains left for Blackpool, three for Morecambe, three for Scarborough and the Yorkshire coast. Most people were bound for the 'two shillings per person per night, supply your own food,' boarding houses. The wealthier and more adventurous left for London, Dover and the Continent. A one week tour to Bruges and the Ardennes cost £5.

ES, TUESDAY, JULY 28, 1914.

l to try conclusions with they would have preferred , and to have risked defeat h. Accrington are still nd they are blessed with ssession of no mean im- ount it an advantage to eral of their rivals for the

* * *

congratulate J. Hargreaves, is selection to play with d eleven against a Preston n on August 6th and 7th. t the last two seasons made a batsman, and is just the t the County club officials n the ground staff, for he attributes which, if de- ke him a first class bats- al prowess quickly enabled first class footballer, Joe, called, migrating to Brad- rington Stanley.

* * *

ion and receiving home at ttage Homes is to be form- ursday by Mr. Edwin Cun- the Building Committee and the Board. The building,

Bullough's Dispute.

NO OFFICIAL NEWS OF RE-OPENING.

Umpire's Decision Not Given.

There is no new feature to report regarding the strike and lockout at Messrs. Howard and Bullough's Works. The workers are awaiting with considerable interest and anxiety the decision of the Umpire as to the payment of unemployment benefit under the National Insurance Act, the umpire having to decide between the Chief Insurance Officer for the district and the Court of Referees, who came to different conclusions on the point. Up to last evening inquiries elicited that the Umpire's decision had not been communicated to Accrington.

It will be remembered that the Chief In- surance Officer ruled against the men's claim on the ground that the works are closed in consequence of a trade dispute. The deci- sion was appealed against by the Gas- workers' and General Labourers' Union, and, as stated in Saturday's "Observer and

ON THE BRINK OF WAR.

Austria's Demands Upon Servia.

THE INTERNATIONAL SITUATION.

Europe yesterday stood on the brink of a great war. Austria had broken off diplo- matic relations with Servia; Russia threatened to come to the support of Servia; and in that way Germany and France would in all probability enter the conflict. The position of Great Britain was that of work- ing towards peace.

Yesterday the situation was regarded as being a trifle easier. It is announced from Rome, without confirmation, that Sir E. Grey has induced Austria to extend the time

Austria, both are t and if Russia an any one of the thre the combined armi

FRANCE

The Dual Allia Russia is suppose in 1895, but it w August, 1897. The once been modifie that France shall of Russia in a Fra that France is n proviso is so worde under what circu be extended or wi

HOW BR

The Triple Ent the Entente Cord tween this country position of this European conflagra Mr. Asquith in th March 24, 1914. I how far Great Bri obligations, Mr. A If war arises l there are no which will restri of the Governm decide whether o participate in a

On the same day Russia mobilised her forces in support of Serbia. Germany upheld Austria's firm policy towards Serbia in an attempt to deter Russia from taking action. On July 27th France informed Russia of her complete readiness to fulfill her alliance obligations in the event of a dispute with Germany. France stopped all Army leave and recalled her troops from Morocco and Algeria.[5]

Above: A group of ladies from Plantation Street, Accrington, ready to leave for a trip to the seaside.
Author's collection

In Accrington, however, the holiday spirit prevailed. Charabanc trips to Windermere and Morecambe were popular. A pleasant ride through the countryside to Blackpool complemented by a stroll on the Promenade could be had for six shillings return. The first editorial reference by the 'Accrington Observer' to the situation in Europe took a particularly local line, "It is most unfortunate black and forbidding war clouds should be spreading over Europe, Accrington, exports vast quantities of machinery to Russia, Germany, Austria and France. One needs no far seeing eye to realise the state of affairs should war come upon us." With no thought that Great Britain would be involved, the editor continued, "How a great European war would affect our insular land fills us with apprehension."[6]

The apprehension was justified for on August 1st, the day Accrington holidays ended, Germany declared war on Russia. Accringtonians returned home to the news of a War Office request to the local St. John's Ambulance Brigade for volunteers for a British Expeditionary Force if such service be required. Holiday leave for the Lancashire Constabulary was suspended. By Sunday news worsened; three local people arrived from Paris with news of soldiers crowding the streets, banks closed and an air of war fever. They had been ordered by French police to return home immediately.

All day Sunday in Accrington there were unprecedented scenes as huge crowds in tense excitement gathered outside the newspaper offices waiting for news. In the afternoon another large crowd watched an order posted outside the Central Post Office calling on Army Reservists to prepare to join their Regiments.

On the Verge of War.

GRAVE SITUATION in EUROPE

Martial Law in Germany: "A State of War."

PREPARATIONS IN RUSSIA.

GERMAN LINERS NOT TO SAIL.

The European situation is to-day exceedingly grave, and it is feared that war may break out at any moment.

A profound sensation was created yester-

STOCK EXCHANGES CLOSED.

In London, Manchester, and

measures.

The number of men aff small proportion of the wh

10,000 MEN AFI
FOR SPECIAL SERVIC

A military corresponden The War Office order call paratively few Territorials contract with the State to military service in the Un created some excitemen circles, although inquirie quarters of units fail to c tion concerning it. But i in the circumstances t reticence should be observ

The Army Council lay s ment that this latest and military move is only measure, but the surprise so great if the Army r ordered to hold themselve any emergency, for it wou more natural proceeding.

POLICEMEN'S HOLIDA

The members of the T

Above: Sir Edward Grey, Liberal M.P. for Berwick on Tweed 1885 to 1916 Foreign Secretary 1905 to 1916.

Many in the crowd, anxious for the future, held a strong desire for peace. Most non-conformist churches sent telegrams to Herbert Asquith, the Prime Minister; to Sir Edward Grey, the Foreign Secretary; and to Harold Baker, the Liberal M.P. for the Accrington Division, asking them "to avoid any step which may depart from our strict neutrality."[7] By this time the British Cabinet decided any violation of Belgium's neutrality would oblige Britain to intervene. The same Sunday evening an ultimatum demanding passage for German armies to pass through Belgium', convinced them that Britain needed to join France and Russia in the coming conflict.

war on France. The following day Britain served on Germany an ultimatum, expiring at 11 p.m. calling on her to withdraw from Belgium territory.

In London, as the time-limit approached crowds gathered in Trafalgar Square "singing and dancing and displaying marked tendencies towards mafficking."[8] The 'Accrington Observer' still had hopes for peace. Its editorial, written for publication on August 4th, reviewed recent events in Europe and concluded "One would fain hope these point to a state of readiness which may dispel the threatening shadows and enable Britain to stand by, a mere spectator of a clash of arms the like the world has never seen."[9] The crowds in London made it clear attitudes were changing.

The anti-war element resisted to the very end Britain's entry into the conflict, in their view, "binding commitments ought not to bind."[10] The pro-war group had no doubt Britain's vital interests at heart and demanded British intervention, quite apart from French expectations. The fear of a victorious Germany turning to confront Britain, plus an acute sympathy for 'little Belgium, convinced them that Britain needed to join France and Russia in the coming conflict.

At 11 p.m. on August 4th, the ultimatum remained unanswered, Britain and Germany were at war. The locked-out engineers, the unemployed cotton workers, and now the remaining citizens of Accrington and district saw a future of more foreboding and uncertainty. None in Accrington, nor indeed any in Britain, Europe or the Empire, had an inkling of the price to be paid for victory.

ED.—"TIMES" - 1866. } AMALGAMATED
    "OBSERVER," 1887. } 1892.

TUESDAY, AUGUST 4, 1914.

'k to th' beginnin' an' book deawn
vanted.
ooa, an' then aw towd Billy as he
set up a Quareyum uv his own i'
Hey an' charge sooa mich a heyd
d.
me a quare look, an' ses drily loike,
think as it's allus best to humour
? Id saves a lot o' trubble."
t th' bottom o' th' Quareyum Billy
r shall wey gooa neaw, Harry?"
k wey'll gooa an' hev a look at th'
ts neaw," aw ses.
weel, lecad on: theaw kno's th'
Billy.
(Mooar Next Week.)

HOW BRITAIN STANDS.

SIR EDWARD GREY EXPLAINS THE SITUATION.

Neutrality of Belgium to be Maintained.

Women, and the Vote.

By Ada Nield Chew.]

he north-west gale had rioted
-onst. The sea was grey and
the waves dashed ever more de-
up to the low sea wall. The
es answered the onslaughts of
ith constant protest; the flowers
n bowed their heads and drooped
ed before the charging attacks.
iothing for it but to remain in-
s one wanted to be blown away.
ening, however, the wind grew

FRENCH PORTS TO BE PROTECTED.

Navy Ready for Emergencies.

GERMANY'S ULTIMATUM TO BELGIUM.

A survey of the European situation in the light of yesterday's news from the Continent and Sir Edward Grey's momentous statement in the

COMMUNICATIONS CUT OFF.

All communications with Germany have

Brit

SIR

To Inte

Belgian

Of the
statement
Commons
Edward (
Rising
Edward s
that the
for peace
but to pr
To-day it
Europe
Russia ai
war upon

Introduction Notes

1 Accrington Observer and Times (Hereafter A.O.T.) 27.6.14.
2 Report on Health and Sanitary Conditions, Borough of Accrington, Year Ending December 31st, 1913.
3 The application was to bring the rate up to 36 shillings per week, the rate paid for comparable work in other textile machinery works in Lancashire.
4 A.O.T. 27.6.14.

5 See 'Origins of the First World War', L.C.F. Turner P.104.
6 A.O.T. 1.8.14.
7 E.G. Cannon Street Baptist Church and others. A.O.T. 4.8.14.
8 See 'Britain in the Century of Total War', A. Marwick P.50 (quote from Daily News, August 5th, 1914).
9 A.O.T. 4.8.14.
10 'Britain's Moral Commitment to France, August 1914.' T. Wilson, article in 'History', Vol. 64, No. 212, October, 1979.

Chapter One

Come back this afternoon

In Accrington, in the first few days after Britain's declaration of war, the excitement intensified. The grave anxieties of the last days of peace gave way to a patriotic enthusiasm for war as every day excited crowds gathered eager for any news, outside the Town Hall, the Post Office and the newspaper offices.

On Wednesday August 5th over five hundred Special Reservists, those alerted the previous Sunday, left Accrington on special trains. All the previous day and through the night, well into Wednesday morning, the Post Office remained open to pay each man the three shillings allotted by the War Office as expenses. Thousands of people clapped and cheered as the Reservists marched through the town to the railway station. In the station they bade their private and family farewells, then started their journey to their various depots and thence active service.

The same evening over fifty of the Accrington Company of the North East Lancashire Squadron of the League of Frontiersmen attended a meeting in the Territorial Drill Hall, Argyll Street. The meeting presided over by the Squadron Commanding Officer Captain A. G. Watson of Clayton-le-Moors, unanimously agreed to advertise in the 'Accrington Observer and Times' an offer to instruct volunteers for active service in musketry and drill. The Frontiersmen had long awaited this moment.[1]

In 1914 Accrington had few military traditions and associations, unlike neighbouring Blackburn and Burnley which had permanent barracks and strong links with the East Lancashire Regiment. In spite of its large population Accrington rated just one company of the 5th East Lancashire Regiment Territorial Force. The nine Officers and 140 men of the Accrington Company, returned from Caernarvon on Monday August 3rd, recalled a week early from their annual camp. On Thursday August 6th at 8 a.m. the Company left Accrington for the Battalion H.Q. at Burnley, five miles away. In spite of the

Below: In the early days of the war crowds filled the streets of every town in Britain to watch the departure for active service of Reservists and Territorials. Here on August 5th, 1914 an immense crowd gathers to watch the local Reservists parade on Burnley Cattle Market before they march to the railway station.
Lancashire Library, Burnley District

Above: G' Section, 1/2 Field Ambulance RAMC (Burnley) 42 East Lancashire TF on the platform at Barracks railway station, Burnley. L.L.B.D.

early hour a crowd of several hundreds gave them an enthusiastic farewell as they left the Drill Hall and marched through the streets. The Battalion's intended later destination was to be Ireland, to relieve Regular troops for active service.

The following day a quiet, hushed, crowd watched a third march through the town. A hundred men of the Accrington St. John's Ambulance Corps were en-route for Netley Military Hospital, Southampton. Their special train was already laden with colleagues from Colne, Nelson and Burnley as it steamed into the station. The subdued mood did not last, any momentary doubts soon pushed aside. Many townspeople echoed the *Accrington Observer and Times,* which, now hopes for peace gone, stated "We were one of a host of newspapers which worked up to the eleventh hour for peace. War is a miserable way of settling differences. Now that England (sic) has drawn the sword in defence of our interests, we join shoulder to shoulder with the rest of the country and pray that God will defend the right." In common with many others the *Accrington Observer and Times* transferred its aversion to war into a support which was to become almost a crusade.[2]

The man who held the sword in defence of 'England's' interests was Lord Kitchener of Khartoum. On August 5th Lord Kitchener, as Commander in Chief of the Army, entered the Cabinet as Secretary for War. Kitchener's national prestige alone guaranteed him a place. Ever since his service in the Sudan, Egypt and in South Africa, the British people felt an admiration for him which verged on hero worship. Thousands of young men copied his broad martial moustache in their desire to look manly and inspiring. "Wearing its bushy magnificence with an air of power, tall and broad-shouldered, he looked like a Victorian image of Richard the Lionheart except for something inscrutable behind the solemn blazing eyes."[3]

Kitchener immediately disagreed with the Government, War Office and Cabinet view of a short war. He believed it far more likely to last at least three years and not won at sea as many thought but only after many bloody battles on the European continent. A powerful Germany, bent on world domination, would concede defeat only when beaten to the ground. Great Britain's contribution could not be limited to her small Regular Army. Kitchener proposed at once to raise a New Army of at least a million

Below: Men of the St. John's Ambulance Corps at the Ambulance Hall, Accrington, before entraining for Netley Military Hospital, Hampshire. A.O.&T.

men. In his view the professional Regular Army would be too small and too precious to risk in a long war, and the Regular Army Special Reserve too small to maintain it in the field. Kitchener held, unjustly as it proved, the Territorial Force to be untrained amateurs who even if they were to volunteer for overseas service, would still be unfit to replace Regular troops. He undoubtedly thought the same about the National Reserve which existed to provide replacements for the Territorials. Although all the Cabinet had doubts about his proposal, in the end, Kitchener's ability as a professional soldier to appeal to the interest and sympathy of civilians, the knack of getting civilians with him instead of against him - as other professional soldiers were prone to do - proved his greatest asset.

Kitchener's first appeal for 100,000 volunteers went out on August 7th, 1914. From that day his recruiting poster appeared on every hoarding and in every shop window. The martial moustache, the magnetic eyes and the pointing finger demanded the attention of every man in the country.

Left: Field Marshall Lord Kitchener on August 5th 1914 was appointed Secretary of State for War, the first serving soldier to hold the post. He was drowned on June 5th, 1916 when HMS Hampshire, in which he was travelling to Russia, sank after striking a mine.
B.C.P.L.

Top: Burnley Borough Police reservists leaving the Police Station with the Chief Constable seeing them off.

Bottom: Men of the 5th East Lancashire Regiment (Burnley) Territorial Force, 42 (East Lancashire) Division outside the Drill Hall awaiting orders. Along with the 4th Battalion (Blackburn) they served in Gallipoli.

L.L. Burnley District

The Territorials, however, were more enthusiastic and anxious to serve than Kitchener gave them credit. In East Lancashire at least, they preceded him by one day. On the morning of Thursday August 6th, Colonel Richard Sharples, an Accrington solicitor and Commanding Officer of the National Reserve Battalion of the 5th East Lancashire Regiment, called an emergency meeting of the Officers in the National Reserve Club in Burnley Barracks. The meeting, immediately and unanimously, requested the Lancashire county Territorial Association to obtain permission from the War Office to form a battalion of infantry, "not less than 600 strong, with further necessary sections for signalling, machine-guns and cyclists, etc. A guarantee fund was promised towards such necessaries as may be required if the battalion were formed."[4]

The resolution anticipated by one day not just the recruiting posters, but a letter from Lord Kitchener to the Lords Lieutenants of Counties and Chairmen of Territorial Force County Associations on August 7th, inviting their co-operation in raising the first 100,000 men. Col. Sharples and his fellow officers' individual offer to recruit and pay for a volunteer battalion received no support from the County Association, his idea over-taken by Kitchener's recruiting campaign. The original idea of an East Lancashire raised and trained battalion of volunteers must go to the credit of Col. Sharples. Although unsuccessful, the idea nonetheless stayed in Col. Sharples' mind.

At the outbreak of war ex-regular Company Sergeant Major Renham of Blackburn, retired after 27 years service, re-enlisted to the Colours. On Monday August 10th, newly promoted Lieutenant, he became Recruiting Officer for North and East Lancashire. He at once installed a recruiting Sergeant and staff into an office hurriedly converted from an empty cafe in Union Street, Accrington. When the recruiting office opened its doors men rushed to volunteer. Encouraged by families, employers and even magistrates, lured by prospects of regular pay and allowances and afraid the war might be over soon, men flocked to the Colours. 250 such enrolled in the first week. Indeed the press of volunteers often forced the recruiting staff to close the office door periodically in order to peacefully enroll those already inside. By the end of the month Lt. Renham and his staff gained more than five hundred recruits for Kitchener's first and second 100,000. A good beginning.

At the War Office on August 27th Kitchener

Left: Sunday, August 9th, the 5th East Lancashire Regiment T.F. attended St. Peter's, Burnley. Lord Shuttleworth, the Lord Lieutenant of Lancashire takes the salute.

Below: Accompanied by the Mayor of Burnley, Alderman Sellers Kay, Lord Shuttleworth inspected the men.
L.L.B.D.

17

received a proposal from Lord Derby that he wished to raise a battalion of 'Comrades' in Liverpool. Kitchener accepted, stipulating only that the battalion should subsequently be taken over by the War Office and enjoy no special privilege other than the men be kept together. Lord Derby's offer helped resolve three important recruiting considerations: firstly, to take the strain of the rush of volunteers off an understaffed and inadequate War Office recruiting organisation; secondly, to co-ordinate and expand isolated efforts by local authorities and individuals to assist recruiting; thirdly, and most importantly, to sustain the energies of the British public in the urgent task of attracting men to the New Army, while at the same time providing for their requirements until the hard-pressed War Office could assimilate the new recruits.

In Liverpool on Friday August 28th, Lord Derby put to the young men of the city's commercial interests his proposals to raise a comrades battalion. By Friday September 4th a Brigade of four infantry battalions had been formed of four thousand volunteers. Clerks from the White Star and Cunard Lines, the Cotton Association, the Stock Exchange, brokers from the fruit, wool and sugar trades, insurance and bank workers, formed separate platoons or squads within their battalions. Later the War Office allocated them the titles of the 17th, 18th, 19th and 20th (Service) Battalions, The Kings (Liverpool) Regiment but the men always regarded themselves as the 1st, 2nd, 3rd and 4th 'Liverpool Pals.'

Lord Derby's success excited the imagination of mayors and corporations of many towns in Great Britain. The idea of citizens of the same town recruited, equipped and serving together greatly appealed to their patriotism and civic pride. "The Mayor and Corporation generally constituted themselves recruiters for their towns, and the inhabitants took a personal interest in the rapid raising of their own battalions, business men lent their warehouses as stores, orderly rooms and drill-halls, and spent much time and money in perfecting the organisation for the purchase of supplies or the erection of huts to shelter the men."[5]

There were other, smaller, sections of the public who raised 'local' battalions. In Glasgow the Tramways Department formed most of the 15th (Service) Battalion, Highland Light Infantry, the Glasgow Boys Brigade, most of the 16th (Service) Battalion. In Grimsby the headmaster of a local grammar school started recruitment of the 10th (Service) Lincolnshire Regiment (the Grimsby Chums). Sheffield raised a battalion representing the 'City and University of Sheffield' the 12th (Service) Battalion York and Lancaster Regiment. Following quickly on their rival, Liverpool, the clerks and warehousemen of Manchester formed the 16th, 17th, 18th and 19th (Service) Battalions The Manchester Regiment. There were many such examples.

These purely local efforts in recruiting, equipping and housing their own units were without precedent for a population unused to the idea of general military service. The War Office, to ease its own administrative burdens, limited its involvement to the issue of 'directives,' i.e. general directions on the standards to which all units should work. The system adopted was reminiscent of the old 'Commission of Array.'[6] Sanction was given to some local authority or magnate to raise a body of men; they were given wide latitude in the appointment of officers; were to undertake all administrative burdens in connection with the new units; were

Below: Naval and Marine reservists say goodbye to their wives and children. Note the traditional dress of the female mill workers - clogs and shawl. L.L.B.D.

to be responsible for their training and military efficiency until such time as the War Office should be prepared to take them over and fit them into the general, national, Army. It was a very elastic system, but one which worked well.[7]

In Accrington, as elsewhere, the thought of joining a 'Pals' battalion commended itself to many. Immediately it became known 'Pals' battalions were recruiting in Manchester, many Accrington men, as individuals or in groups, left the town to enlist. One group of sixteen League of Frontiersmen, deciding 'giving instruction in musketry and drill' in Accrington not nearly exciting enough and, anxious to stay together, on Wednesday September 2nd enlisted in the 2nd City (17th Service) Battalion, The Manchester Regiment.

The *Accrington Observer and Times* picked up the story from the "depressed sixteenth" who was 'plucked' (failed his medical).[8] In their haste to enlist, the sixteen did not know that the Mayor of Accrington, Councillor Captain John Harwood, J.P., had anticipated their idea by two days.[9] On Monday August 31st he had telegraphed the War Office offering to raise half a battalion of troops and even then awaited a reply.

The reply came Saturday morning, September 5th. In the meantime, Captain Harwood had an anxious wait. Every day, local men no less keen and enthusiastic, and ideal material for his own half battalion, enlisted in the town or elsewhere, in regiments of their choice. As the week passed by Harwood knew his ambition of raising Accrington's own half battalion presented enormous difficulties. If to him, an intensly patriotic man, the unthinkable were to happen and he failed, he also faced a direful loss of prestige and reputation, both of himself and the town he represented.

That Saturday morning a dismayed Harwood learned that Army policy demanded a full battalion or none at all. In a mood of either optimism or unrealism the Army Council, supported by the War Office, apparently believed a town as small as Accrington, some forty five thousand people, could raise a thousand men in the same time that much larger cities required. In spite of the patriotic spirit of his fellow citizens, Harwood knew he faced a formidable task, one indeed that might prove impossible. To raise a thousand man battalion quickly in competition with the local recruitment for the Navy, the Territorials and Kitchener's first 100,000 seemed a daunting prospect.

Harwood had to move quickly for since he had telegraphed the War Office some three

Above: Boy Scouts at Burnley prepare for their task of guarding telegraph lines, canals and railways. During a period filled with rumours of German spies and sabateurs the East Lancashire Boy Scouts gave their services as runners at recruiting stations and drill halls. At Rishton newly enlisted men marched to the railway station en-route for Accrington led by the local Scout Band.
L.L.B.D.

19

TOWN HALL & BLACKBURN ROAD ACCRINGTON.

Above: Accrington circa 1914. The Town Hall was erected in 1851 as a memorial to Sir Robert Peel (a local man.) It became the municipal offices and Town Hall in 1878. The outside stalls of the Market Hall (1879) are centre. The Cash Clothing Company's shop is on the corner of Peel Street (left) and Little Blackburn Road.
Trevor Adams

hundred Accrington men had enlisted. He already had the support of Captain Watson of the League of Frontiersmen who knew of his decision to telegraph the War Office on August 31st. He therefore invited Watson to his home, Whalley House, Accrington on Sunday September 6th. He also invited Colonel Sharples (who four weeks before had suggested raising a local battalion of Territorials) and two of his fellow officers, Captain G. N. Slinger, an Accrington solicitor and Captain P. Broadley a Clayton-le-Moors businessman.

By inviting Watson and Broadley it is clear Harwood intended to increase his area of recruitment. Watson's role as Commanding Officer of the North East Lancashire Squadron of the League of Frontiersmen had obvious advantages, as also the prestige and standing of Sharples, Slinger and Broadley in their local communities. Harwood had an important contact at the War Office itself in Harold Baker, who had been Liberal M.P. for Accrington Parliamentary Division since 1910 and Financial Secretary to the War Office in 1912-13. On the outbreak of war Baker was appointed a civilian member of the Army Council.[10]

Harwood and his military colleagues believed that by joining forces, helped by Baker's influence and support, there would be no difficulty in raising a full battalion. Fears of failure could be allayed. The meeting agreed Harwood should immediately send a telegram to Lord Kitchener, and one to Baker, offering to raise a full battalion. They now envisaged, not an Accrington Pals Battalion, but an Accrington and District Pals Battalion, a tripartite undertaking, the municipality, the military and the League of Frontiersmen.

On Monday morning, September 7th, Harwood received a reply from the War Office. In the afternoon, in his capacity of Mayor, he formally presided over an Accrington Town Council meeting. Modestly concealing his recent hard work and anxieties, he told them he had just received authorisation from the War Office to raise a full battalion in Accrington and dis-

20

Far left: The Right Hon. Harold T. Baker, Liberal M.P. for the Accrington Parliamentary Division 1910 - 1918.
The Division included the townships of Clayton-Le-Moors, Church, Great Harwood, Rishton and Oswaldtwistle.
A.O.& T.

Left: Councillor Captain John Harwood, J.P. Mayor of Accrington fron November 1912 to November 1915.
L.L. Hyndburn District

trict. The Council "received the cheery news with much enthusiasm and gave Harwood their congratulations and good wishes for success." The *Accrington Observer and Times,* the following day, made the news public and outlined the War Office conditions in detail.

Readers of the report might have got the impression recruitment for the battalion would centre on Accrington and district only, i.e. the municipal Borough of Accrington and the neighbouring district Councils of Clayton-le-Moors, Church, Oswaldtwistle, Rishton and Great Harwood. However, before the week passed, the area of recruitment extended well beyond these local boundaries. Whilst Harwood awaited his reply, Lord Kitchener, in guidelines to raisers of New Army battalions, issued September 4th, gave permission for Territorials (through their County Associations) to help train, house and feed new battalions until taken over by the War Office. Kitchener also asked local Territorials to help in the selection of temporary officers and non-commissioned officers. "Candidates for commissions are advised to apply through their local T.A."[12] This was good news for Harwood. He could now use his contacts with the local Territorials officially. As it happened, a not so local Territorial came to Harwood.

On Tuesday September 8th, the day the news broke, Harwood received a telephone call from a Captain J. C. Milton of Chorley, a small market town eighteen miles west of Accrington. Milton offered to raise 250 men in Chorley for

the Accrington Battalion. In less than five minutes conversation, Harwood (who forty years earlier had married a Chorley girl and had lived in the town) cheerfully agreed, his final words to Milton "If your lads are as good as my wife, they'll do." Even before recruiting started in Accrington, Harwood had 250 men. It was an excellent beginning.

The agreement ended a difficult week for Captain Milton. Whilst Harwood awaited a reply from his first telegram to the War Office, Milton, a Chorley solicitor, Town Councillor and Captain in the Duke of Cornwall's Light Infantry National Reserve, had been involved in his own negotiations with the War Office to get permission to raise a company of volunteers in Chorley after succeeding, he found that an agreement to attach them to the 5th Loyal North Lancs Territorials at Bolton been withdrawn. An attempt to attach his 'Chorley Company' to the Kings (Liverpool Regiment) failed. Hence his telephone call to Accrington.

In Burnley the same week other moves were made. On Thursday September 3rd the North East Lancashire Squadron of the League of Frontiersmen held a meeting in a local hotel. About fifty "middle-class men" attended.[14] Lt Robinson of the 5th East Lancs Territorials, and also a Frontiersman, read to the meeting a letter from Colonel Driscoll, the Commandant of the London Squadron. Col. Driscoll had offered the War Office the immediate services of the Frontiersmen but had been told the offer would

Above: Colonel Paddy Driscoll. He became the Commanding Officer of the 25th (Service) Battalion (Frontiersmen) Royal Fusiliers on its formation, February 12th, 1915.
Author

not be considered until Kitchener had raised his 100,000 men. Captain Watson, as Squadron C.O., explained League policy in the meantime was to persuade young men to volunteer for the New Army and help in training. In this way the Frontiersmen would convince Kitchener of their worth. Watson also told the meeting of Harwood's telegram offering to raise half a battalion. They at Burnley, he added, could at least form an East Lancashire Battalion. Such were Watson's ambitions at the time.

In September, 1914 and after, army recruiting contained many anomalies. Too many calls competed for attention and the demands of one group competed with those of another. The Regular Army conflicted with Kitchener's New Army appeal, the Territorials had their own ranks to fill. Even then, the Territorials needed 2,500 men as reserves for the East Lancashire Division.[15] An advert on September 2nd in the Burnley Express asked for five hundred volunteers from that district alone. Watson and the Frontiersmen therefore had a problem. They did not wish to be accused of taking volunteers away from the Territorials. At the same time they knew Kitchener would be more likely to look favourably on Driscoll's offer of the Frontiersmen as a body, if they proved themselves capable of recruiting and training other volunteers throughout the country. It was there-fore prudent for Watson and his men to recruit for Kitchener and not for the Frontiersmen.[16]

The individuals at the meeting had to decide how they could best serve their country as Frontiersmen. They had three choices: to join Driscoll's London Squadron; to join the Territorials; or to help form a local Kitchener battalion. To join Driscoll was chancy at best, even if the offer were accepted, the East Lancashire men had no guarantee they would stay together as a separate group. In common with many of the British public at the time they held a poor opinion of the ill-trained 'Saturday afternoon soldiers' of the Territorials. They knew at least if they formed a Kitchener battalion they would stay together. Watson clearly decided for them by announcing a 'Pals Company' enrolment and drill meeting to be held the following Tuesday September 8th, at Keighley Green Mill, Burnley. (Keighley Green Mill, like so many cotton mills in Burnley stood closed for lack of orders.)

The Burnley Express gave its considered support "The local League of Frontiersmen have taken the initiative and suggested the formation of companies of Pals and have offered to drill them. This Pals movement is a grand idea and as Lord Kitchener wants such companies of friends you can depend on them being made useful."[17]

With this publicity and encouragement over

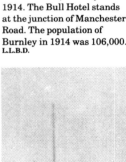

Below: A quiet day in St. James' Street, Burnley circa 1914. The Bull Hotel stands at the junction of Manchester Road. The population of Burnley in 1914 was 106,000. L.L.B.D.

Left: Chorley circa 1914, a general view of Market Street looking north towards towards Preston. The Town Hall Clock Tower is seen in the middle left. Chorley had a population of approximately 30,000 in 1914.
L.L. Chorley District

Below: King William Street, Blackburn, circa 1914, looking towards Library Street showing the Market House with its Clock Tower. The Market and Tower were built in1845 and were demolished in1964. Note the coal-fired hot potato cart, a common feature of Blackburn town centre until the 1950's. In 1914 Blackburn's population was 133,000.
L. L. Blackburn District

a hundred men turned up on September 8th. Quartermaster Sergeant Riley of the Frontiersmen described recent developments in Accrington and the conditions laid down by the War Office. He told the audience that 'the Accrington men' (Harwood and Sharples) had, since the meeting on September 3rd, asked the Frontiersmen, through Captain Watson, to help provide a Burnley Company for the Accrington Pals Battalion. (It is more likely Watson changed his mind about forming a full battalion from East Lancashire and opted to assist Harwood instead.) Q.M.S. Riley invited the meeting to support the 'Accrington men' and asked for a show of hands. At least sixty agreed. On this optimistic note the sixty remained behind for a preliminary course in drill by Sgt. Barrow of the Frontiersmen. As well as Milton and Chorley, Watson and Burnley could now confidently assure Harwood and Accrington of help to raise another company of the four required for a complete battalion.

In spite of the meetings and publicity, the Mayor of Burnley, Ald. Sellers Kay, expressed no interest. His fellow citizens, as newspaper correspondence showed, hoped however, Burnley could still raise a full battalion — a Burnley Pals Battalion. Raising a company for Accrington — a town half Burnley's size — affronted Burnley civic pride, and considered only a beginning of what Burnley could really do. The *Burnley News* supported both views — "In the army all are pals which may be an argument against the Pals Battalions being formed just now, but there is another side — if men form friendships in the citizen life and their friendships continue in times of war a better spirit is felt. Who can be a coward when a pal is looking on? — We welcome the formation of as many companies as the War Office will accept from Burnley and district."[18]

Accrington, Burnley and Chorley, in their different ways prepared themselves for the task of raising the Battalion. Harwood, confident of success, authorised Lt. Robinson in Burnley and Captain Milton in Chorley, to recruit a company of 250 men in each town. Next, on September 10th, Harwood called a meeting at Accrington Town Hall of the Chairmen of the district councils in the Accrington Parliamentary Division, i.e. Clayton-le-Moors, Church, Oswaldtwistle, Rishton and Great Harwood. They readily accepted his suggestion to open recruiting stations for the Battalion in their respective townships. Recruits were to travel to Accrington to be medically examined and attested.

Harwood's plans had been well publicised in the local *Northern Daily Telegraph* stimulating interest in the Battalion in Blackburn, the newspaper's home town. Although a much larger town, with its own 4th East Lancs. Territorial Battalion, the interest shown by Blackburn in the Accrington battalion delighted Harwood.

With the Mayor of Blackburn's agreement, Harwood placed appeals for volunteers for a 'Blackburn Detachment' of the Battalion on placards throughout the town and arranged for a recruiting station to open.

With these arrangements made, Harwood travelled with Colonel Sharples and Captains Broadley, Milton and Watson, to Chester to meet General Sir William Mackinnon, K.C.B. the Officer Commanding, Western Command. At this meeting the War Office directions on recruiting and maintaining the Battalion were agreed. The new battalion, as an additional battalion of the East Lancashire Regiment, designated the 7th (Service) Battalion (Accrington) (subsequently changed to 11th). The meeting ended, the party hastily returned home to submit to the waiting presses of the local newspapers a recruiting advert for an 'Accrington and District Kitchener Pals Battalion.'

In his edition the editor of the *Accrington Observer and Times* wrote the first of many editorials supporting Harwood, commending him for his "energy and initiative" and testifying his confidence in the "patriotism and sense of duties animating the young men in this town."[20]

Except in Chorley the recruiting stations opened on Monday afternoon September 14th. On the first day eight stations recruited a total of 104 men, hardly a satisfactory reflection of 'the patriotism and sense of duty animating the young men.'[21] On Tuesday, opening hours were 10 a.m. to 5 p.m. and a further 124 enlisted. On Wednesday 99 joined the ranks. There were, however, many more willing than those who passed the 'medical'. Most who were 'plucked' did not meet the War Office standard height of 5ft 6in and 35in chest measurement. "Generations of starving in the damp mills and workshops of Lancashire had hardly been conducive to the production of a race of giants. There were many disappointed men in those days, and scathing were their comments on the 'Whitehall Brass Hats' who dared to think Lancashire patriotism could be measured in inches."[22]

Clearly, these standards offended local pride and decreased local enlistment and the district cheered an immediate War Office adjustment of minimum requirements to a height of 5ft 3in and 34in chest measurment. The disappointed could try again. Recruiting increased to 628 by Saturday September 19th; by Tuesday 784; by Thursday September 24th the recruiting stations of Burnley, Accrington and district closed, their targets met.

Reaction to the idea of a Pals battalion had been patchy in the townships surrounding Accrington. Great Harwood showed little interest and provided only a dozen or so recruits. In contrast Rishton, smallest of the five townships, responded well. On the first day, the 19 who enlisted at the recruiting station in the Conservative Club, marched to the railway station to

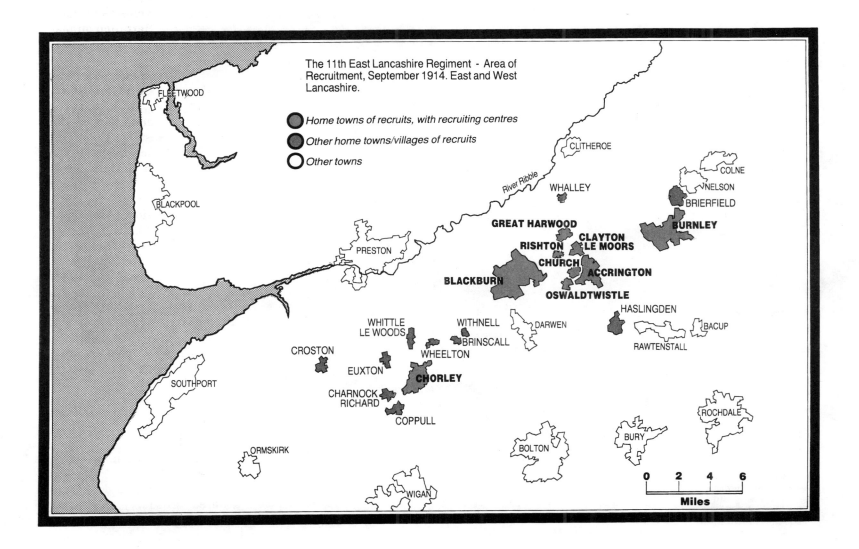

The 11th East Lancashire Regiment - Area of Recruitment, September 1914. East and West Lancashire.

⬤ Home towns of recruits, with recruiting centres
⬤ Other home towns/villages of recruits
◯ Other towns

take the train to Accrington for their medical and attestation. Hundreds lined the streets to see them off. Although not repeated in later days, Rishton's enthusiasm for the Pals remained, with a total of 68 villagers enlisting.

As noted, in the Summer of 1914 East Lancashire suffered from a recession in the cotton industry. In September in Accrington alone more than 7,000 cotton workers were unemployed or working only part-time. Six hundred families were on relief. Each day over seven hundred children were fed at Accrington Town Hall under the terms of the 1906 (Provision of Meals) Act. Howard and Bulloughs were still closed after ten weeks, with little prospect of a settlement despite the war. 4,500 men and their families lived on strike or lock out pay of £1 or ten shillings a week.

The poverty induced many men and boys to join the Army. Pay and billeting allowances amounting to £1 1s. a week was a particular attraction to join the Accrington Battalion. Although the initial patriotism inspired in August remained, as did the expectation of the war

being over by Christmas, poverty also remained as a spur to recruitment for the Battalion. In those circumstances, to be a solider in the company of one's friends and to be paid for staying at home with one's family, was a combination which could hardly be resisted.

Those better placed financially had another consideration. Although by 1914 gradual reforms had improved the Regular Army, the public idea of an army recruited from social misfits and the very poor died hard. Now, in September 1914 Lord Kitchener himself, almost a demi-god in many British eyes, appealed to men to join a specially created New Army. The personal stamp of Lord Kitchener made the New Army an opportunity, for 'decent' citizens to join a respectable army.

In Accrington every day every type of man and boy crowded outside the temporary medical and attestation centre in the Sunday School of Cannon Street Baptist Church, in nearby Willow Street. In this crowd stood George Pollard. At sixteen years, three months, tall for his age he looked at least nineteen.

Above: Burnley children wait for their free meals. In the Summer of 1914 there was much unemployment in the cotton industry. Mills closed down for weeks at a time or worked part-time. At town halls throughout East Lancashire hundreds of children received a free meal a day. Under the terms of the 1906 Necessitous Children (Provision of Meals) Act, the Government paid the costs. L.L.B.D.

Above: Pte. George Pollard

"On Tuesday morning September 15th, I went with my friend Ernie Place for our medical at Willow Street School. The doctor asked me to expand my chest. I didn't quite understand what he meant so I just stood there. He measured me, then told me I'd failed. Ernie, nineteen on September 4th, passed his medical. I was so disappointed I'd failed I went home at once and told my father what had happened. He said, 'Take your jacket off and expand your chest.' He made me expand my chest a few times, then measured it with a tape. He said, 'What's that doctor talking about, you've got a 35in inch chest. You should have been taken in. Go down and tell him.' (I'm not sure whether he was super-patriotic or just trying to get rid of me!) On Thursday the 17th, I went back to Willow Street, this time I passed, so I went into the Pals. At that time I was serving my apprenticeship at Howard and Bulloughs. The dispute was a prime reason why so many joined up. As an apprentice my wage was 10/6d a week. Because of the dispute I got nothing. When you joined up you got 21/- a week. First thing they did at home was to send for the 'club-chap' (insurance collector) and put me in for a shilling a week. I've got the same policy today." (1984).

The scene inside Willow Street Sunday School as men stood in queues awaiting medical inspec-

tion occurred in thousands of similar centres throughout the country. Edgar Wallace described a typical scene. "Our would-be recruit found himself ushered brusquely into a large square apartment equipped with a weighing machine, a scale for measuring height, a wash-bowl and two tables, at one of which sat a clerk busily filling up the attestation forms containing particulars of the recruits physical appearance, his trade, relatives and measurements. The examination is brief, yet thorough. Heart and lungs tested by stethoscope and judicious tapping. His chest is measured, his exact height and weight recorded. His teeth are inspected, then the crucial test of eyesight, a quick examination for varicose veins and other infirmities, then, with a quick nod he is dismissed. The medical officer signs the attestation form and the recruit is hurried to another room where half a dozen men who have passed their medical are awaiting their turn. The Recruiting Officer distributes a few New Testaments to the waiting recruits. "Take the book in your right hand say after me, 'I swear',

'I swear', repeats the recruits

'To serve His Majesty the King'

'To serve His Majesty the King', say the recruits, —

— and the oath proceeds.

"His heirs and successors ..... and the generals and officers set over me by His Majesty the King, his heirs and successors, so help me God!"[23]

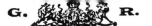

G. R.

ACCRINGTON & DISTRICT

KITCHENER PALS BATTALION

Men of Lancashire your **King and Country Need You,** and call for your help in this terrible struggle for the very existence of the Empire.

All parts of the **EMPIRE** are responding nobly to the Nation's call.

Shall **ACCRINGTON AND DISTRICT** be left behind ?

The Town and District have through the Mayor of Accrington offered a Battalion for the Army to serve as a "**PALS**" Battalion during the War.

This offer has been accepted by the War Office and Army Council, and it now remains for you men of Accrington and District to fill up the ranks at once, **250** men from Chorley and District have, with the official sanction of the War Office, offered to join this Battalion, and have been accepted, and will be known as the "**Chorley Pals'**" Companies of "**The 7th (Accrington) Battalion of the East Lancs. Regt.**

Offers of Companies have been received from Blackburn and Burnley, also men from Clayton-le-Moors, Great Harwood, Rishton, Church and Oswaldtwistle, so no doubt the **1,100** men required will soon show their loyalty by joining its ranks.

Men between **19** and **35** years of age are eligible, and Special Ex-Noncommissioned Officers up to **50** years can be enrolled.

The men after being sworn in will have a Special Uniform, will draw the usual Military Pay and Billeting Allowance, amounting to 21/- per week, and be billeted at their own homes, where possible, while being trained in Squad, Company, and Battalion Drill, also Class Firing and Musketry Instruction.

All further information can be had at the various recruiting stations in Accrington, Clayton-le-Moors, Great Harwood, Rishton, Church, Oswaldtwistle, Burnley, Blackburn and Chorley.

JOHN HARWOOD,
Mayor of Accrington.

R. HINDLE,
Mayor of Chorley.

MARK J. WHITTAKER,
Chairman U.D.C., Clayton-le-Moors.

DOUGLAS H. HACKING,
Chairman U.D.C. Rishton.

JOHN BURY HOLT,
Chairman U.D.C. Church.

THOMAS NOBLE,
Chairman U.D.C., Great Harwood.

JOHN RILEY,
Chairman U.D.C., Oswaldtwistle.

God Save the King.

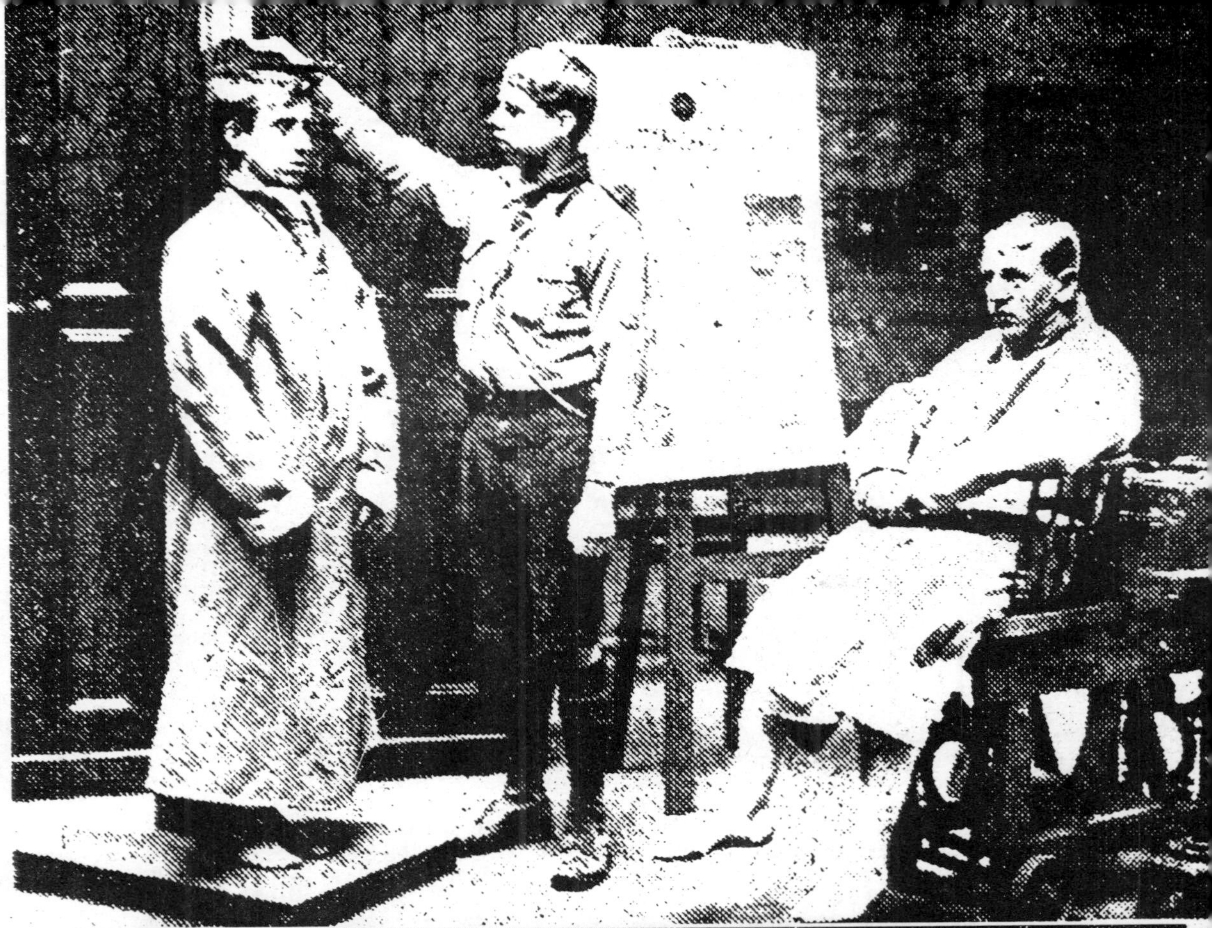

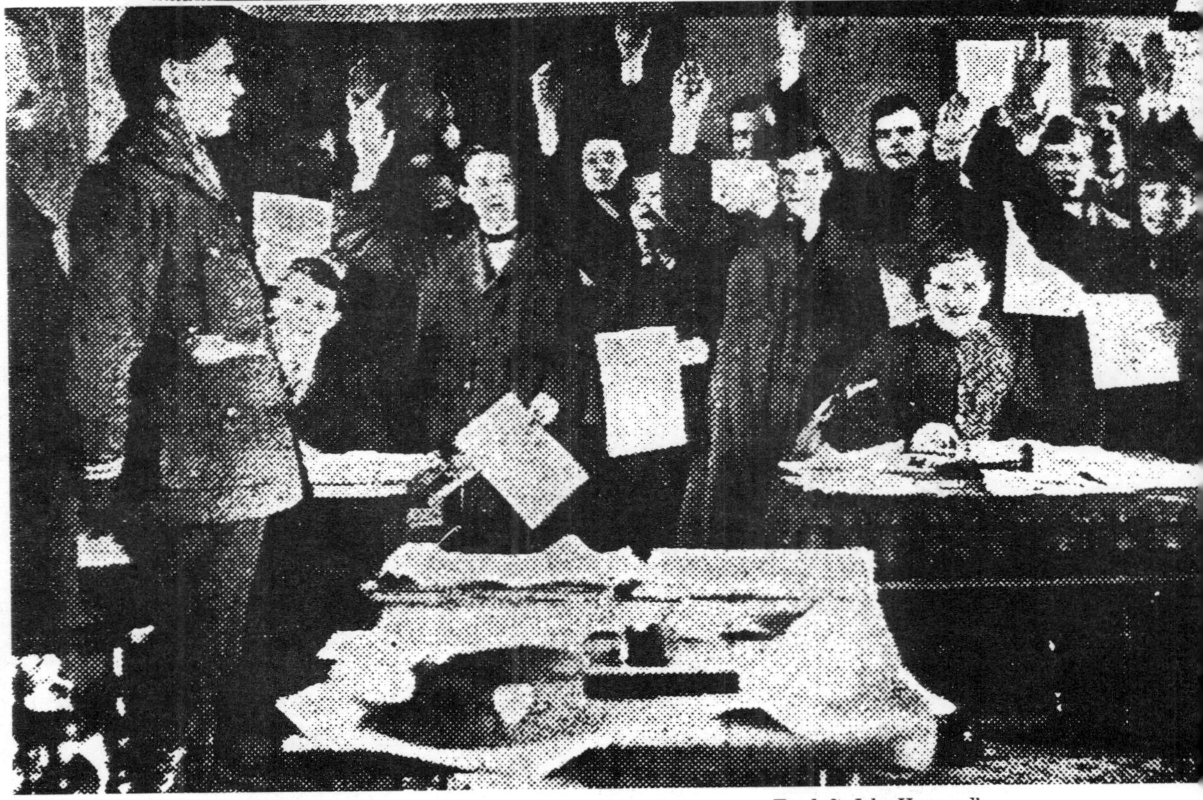

In Accrington, the oath taken and the book kissed, the men and youths, after no doubt congratulating themselves and each other, went to the Town Hall to collect their first day's service pay.

Lt. Robinson opened recruiting at the Territorial drill hall in Bank Parade, Burnley on Monday September 14th, knowing he already had 97 men towards his target of 250. (37 more had joined the Frontiersmen's group since September 8th.) The local newspapers still tried

Far left: John Harwood's first advertisement for recruits, September 12th, 1914 which appeared in the Accrington Observer & Times.
Top: Recruits in Burnley have their medical. One man's height is being measured by a Boy Scout acting as an orderly, whilst another would-be recruit sits in a weighing chair.
Below: After passing their medical the recruits take the oath of allegiance to the Crown.
L.L.B.D.

G. R.

ACCRINGTON AND DISTRICT
KITCHENER "PALS" BATTALION.

Men of Lancashire, Your King and Country need you, and call for your help in this terrible struggle for the very existence of the Empire.

All parts of the Empire are responding nobly to the Nation's call.

SHALL ACCRINGTON & DISTRICT BE BEHIND?

The Town and District have through the Mayor of Accrington offered a Battalion for the Army to serve as a "Pals" Battalion during the war.

This offer has been accepted by the War Office and Army Council, and it now remains for you men of Accrington and District to fill up the ranks at once; 250 men from Chorley and District have, with the official sanction of the War Office, offered to join this Battalion, and have been accepted, and will be known as the "Chorley Pals" companies of the Accrington Battalion of the East Lancashire Regiment.

Offers of Companies have been received from Blackburn and Burnley; also men from Clayton-le-Moors, Great Harwood, Rishton, Church, and Oswaldtwistle; so no doubt the 1,100 men required will soon show their loyalty by joining its ranks.

Men between 19 and 35 years of age are eligible, and special ex-non-commissioned officers up to 50 years of age can be enrolled.

The men, after being sworn in, will have a special uniform, will draw the usual military pay and billeting allowance, amounting to 21s. per week, and be billeted at their own homes, where possible, while being trained in Squad, Company, and Battalion Drill; also Class Firing and Musketry Instruction.

All further information can be had at the various recruiting stations

ACCRINGTON HEADQUARTERS—TOWN HALL.
RECRUITING OFFICE ....WILLOW STREET.
CLAYTON-LE-MOORS ...MECHANICS' INSTITUTE.
GREAT HARWOOD .....COUNCIL OFFICES.
RISHTON ....CONSERVATIVE CLUB.
CHURCH ....COUNCIL OFFICES.
OSWALDTWISTLE ... .TOWN HALL.
CHORLEY ....DRILL HALL.
BLACKBURN ....PRESTON NEW ROAD.

JOHN HARWOOD, Mayor of Accrington.
R. HINDLE, Mayor of Chorley.
MARK J. WHITTAKER, Chairman U.D.C., Clayton-le-Moors.
DOUGLAS H. HACKING, Chairman U.D.C., Rishton.
JOHN BURY HOLT, Chairman U.D.C., Church.
THOMAS NOBLE, Chairman U.D.C. Great Harwood.
JOHN RILEY, Chairman U.D.C., Oswaldtwistle.

GOD SAVE THE KING.

Right: H. D Riley, J.P. of Hawks House, Brierfield, Burnley. In 1905 he founded the Burnley Lads' Club for working class boys. The Lads' Club had a library, reading room and evening education classes, as well as football, cricket, boxing and athletic teams.
Author's collection

to keep hopes of a Burnley Pals Battalion alive. Reporting the efforts of Lt. Robinson, the *Burnley Express* speculated whether "there is still some chance of a Burnley Battalion" and suggested the Mayor chair a public meeting "to raise the requisite number of men."[24] The public meeting never occurred, it was evident therefore the idea should be dropped. Meanwhile recruitment for the Burnley Company started in earnest. Within a day or so Captain Raymond Ross of the National Reserve, East Lancashire Regiment, in civilian life the Burnley Borough Analyst, took over from Lt. Robinson as recruiting officer, with Robinson (now Captain) becoming temporary Officer Commanding, Burnley

Company. Q.M.S. Riley and Sgt. Lancaster of the Frontiersmen remained with Captain Ross.

Recruiting figures rose slowly during the week, but by Friday September 18th, 56 men had enlisted, making a total of 153. On Saturday, however, an advertisement appeared in the *Burnley Express*:-

ACCRINGTON PALS BATTALION
A meeting of Burnley Lads Club
Old Boys will be held in the Club on
TUESDAY NIGHT at 8.45 to consider the
formation of a LADS CLUB COMPANY
in connection with the above Battalion
all past members of the Club are invited.
H.D. RILEY, Hon. Sec.[25]

On Wednesday morning September 23rd seventy 'Old Boys' of the Lads Club, with H. D. Riley himself, joined the Burnley Company. Athough not enough to form a separate Lads Club Company, the numbers ensured Ross met his target by Thursday, September 24th.

Left: The old Court House and Police Station, Keighley Green, Burnley. In 1914 the building was the club house of the Burnley Lads' Club. L.L.B.D.

Some Lads Club members did not, of course, wait for the meeting at the Club. Will Marshall, a 21 year old weaver in Burnley, with his friends Ben Ingham and Arthur Brunskill, enlisted on September 17th.

"Ben, Arthur and myself heard they were forming a Pals Company at the Drill Hall, so in order that we could keep together we decided to enlist with them. My parents expected me to join up, but they didn't mind so much because I went with my friends. Naturally, they were a bit upset at the thought of me going to the war".

The Frontiersmen originally intended to recruit a company of "business young men, such as bank clerks, shop assistants and clerks." In the event a "great diversity of trades and professions" including cotton manufacturers, cotton buyers, surveyors architects and solicitors enlisted.[26] The Burnley Lads Club members and Old Boys, mostly manual workers from poor families, helped to make Burnley Company truly representative of the town.

"Miners, mill-hands, office-boys, black-coats, bosses, school-boys and masters, found themselves appearing before Mr. Ross and the medical officer. Young men who should have been tied to their mothers' apron-strings took home their first service pay — 1/9d in coppers — and nearly broke their mothers' hearts. Men of mature age, patriotic or sensing adventure or escape from monotony were ready to have a go at anyone who should pull the lion's tail. The thing was done! 250 men of good spirit and willing in body assembled at the Drill Hall to be patiently told how to 'form fours.'"[27]

On Thursday, September 24th, Harwood appointed Captain Ross, his recruiting job complete, as Officer Commanding Burnley Company.

In contrast, the Chorley Pals Company idea got the Mayor's support from the beginning. When Milton returned from his visit with Harwood to Chester on September 11th, he arranged with Alderman Ralph Hindle, the Mayor for a recruitment meeting to be held in Chorley Town Hall on Monday evening September 14th. The meeting came to be one of the most extraordinary ever held in the Town Hall. The Mayor presided over the largest, noisiest and most enthusiastic assembly seen in Chorley for decades. The audience, in a constant patriotic fervour, sang to patriotic airs played by the North Lancashire (Chorley) Band while awaiting the speeches to start.

On the platform with the Mayor were a score of local dignitaries, Captain Harwood as Mayor of Accrington and raiser of the Battalion, Colonel Sharples as newly appointed Officer Command-

Above: Pte. Will Marshall

29

Left: Members of the Burnley Lads' Club in camp at Landudno, North Wales. They have just finished erecting the dining marquee. H. D. Riley is seen fourth from the left, back row. Most of the youths in this picture and those below later enlisted with H. D. Riley in the Burnley Company of the Pals.
Mrs. Beint

Left: A group at Llandudno pose before a newly erected bell tent.
Mrs. Beint

Left: Burnley Lads' Club Harriers team 1911 - 1912. Will Marshall is seated fourth from the right, front row.
Mrs Beint

Above: The recruiting office at 17 Market Street, Chorley. Sergeant Buchanan, on the left, is with Sergeant Brady. Sergeant Buchanan's son in complete uniform in miniature stands between. Note the poster 'Remember Scarborough' - this refers to the bombardment of the seaside town by German battle cruisers on December 16th, 1914. 86 men women and children were killed and over 400 injured.
L.L.C.D.

ing, Captain Milton and Captain N. Holt of the Chorley Company, 5th Loyal North Lancs. Territorials. The Mayor told the meeting of Milton's hopes to form a Chorley Company. "I hope we will not fail in the attempt. We are all very proud so many of our young men have responded to the call of their King and Country. We must, however, admit there are still a large number lounging about the streets smoking cigarettes who ought to come forward". To loud cries of 'hear', 'hear', he continued, "I would remind them one day the war will be over and if they have not taken their part, they must not expect to share in the honour and glory".[28]

Harwood made no apologies for coming to Chorley to plead for the Pals Company. Continuously interrupted by cheers and laughter he told them, "Nearly half a century ago I robbed Chorley of the finest girl in the town. My wife and I have been 'Pals' together for 48 years, and finding her in Chorley has made me highly respect the town. I am now pleading for a Chorley Company to defend the Empire — I am sure you will rally to the banners, so that Kitchener gets the men he wants in order to punish Germany for so audaciously declaring war against the world." He sat down to ringing applause.[29]

Milton detailed recent happenings. Ten days previously he visited the War Office to request permission to form his own Pals Company. "On Saturday morning (September 5th) Lord Kitchener agreed to my request. He told me, through his Secretary, that Chorley should be highly honoured as the only town in England to have official sanction to form a Company and not a Battalion! Arrangements were made for their attachment to the 5th Loyal North Lancs. Regiment at Bolton, but later this was withdrawn. I felt, to use a vulgar phrase, I was in the soup. I made an attempt to get an attachment to the King's (Liverpool Regiment) this proved impossible. I then had a private intimation I might get an attachment to the Accrington Battalion. In less than five minutes Captain Harwood agreed." Speaking of his visit to Chester the previous Friday, Milton continued, "We had a wonderful day! We got a Colonel (Sharples), a bank account for an unlimited amount, and four Captains. No man in England could say he had such an experience as that!" He then announced recruiting would start the following morning (Tuesday, September 15th) at 9 a.m. at 17 Bolton Street, Chorley. "There is no doubt it is the duty of young men to give up home and profession, as I have done. I know also you would

Right and below: Many and varied were the nationally produced advertisements design to encourage or shame men to enlist in 1914. Both these appeared in the local newspapers of East Lancashire in September 1914.
(See also pages 34, 35 and 36.)
A.O.& T.

WHAT IS <u>YOUR</u> ANSWER TO YOUR COUNTRY'S CALL?

"The day" has come for <u>you</u>, young man—the great day of decision! Will you fight for your King and Country, or will you <u>skulk</u> in the safety your fathers won and your brothers are struggling to maintain. England awaits your answer at the nearest recruiting office. <u>GO</u>!

NOW THEN, <u>YOU</u>.

Look here, my lad, if you're old enough to walk out with my daughter, you are old enough to fight for her and your Country.
At any Post Office you can obtain the address of the nearest Recruiting Office.

Left: Battalion Headquarters set up in an unused shop, number 5 Whalley Road, Accrington. On the left CQMS J. Hindle, on the right Sgt. J. Bridge.
J. Trengove

"One morning I was called to the Orderly Room and informed that I should have to start work there as things were so busy. I received my first stripe, of which I must add I was rather proud, a drawback being that having no uniforms we could not wear the stripes. I was however receiving the remuneration of such rank 1/6d (7p) per day, quite an increase to my bob' (5p). I was placed in charge of the Mayor's Imprest Account, which I might add, was no small job."
J. Bridge

rather be led by a Chorley officer than by one you have never seen nor heard of."[30] Milton, at this moment the most popular man in Chorley, sat down to a standing ovation.

In another contrast to Burnley, the Territorials in Chorley initially disapproved of the idea of a Pals Company in the town. However in the national interest and the belief there were enough recruits for everyone, differences were soon reconciled. Captain Holt told the audience of his promise, 'to look after the drill hall and any new recruits,' to the Loyal North Lancs. Territorials leaving Chorley soon after war broke out. "When I saw the advertisement for this public meeting I first thought the men from Accrington were poaching on my preserves and I protested to Col. Sharples and the East Lancashire Regiment H.Q. at Preston. It was however agreed poaching was not the intent and the Territorials would not be robbed of a single man. Men are needed for both Kitchener's Army and a Territorial reserve battalion in Chorley and I am confident Colonel Sharples, Captain Milton and I can work together to help us all to achieve our aims. I hope many of you will join Captain Milton in the morning."[31] With these generous words Holt and the Chorley Territorials cleared the final obstacle for Milton.

Strong, if not prosaic support came from the *Chorley Weekly News*.

"*Chorley has been given the exceptional honour of forming a company of Pals. It would be an ungrateful circumstance if it were abused by any signs of slackness. The pay of £1 1s. is extraordinarily good — and the new separation allowances — wife 12/6d, 2/6d for each child — improve it even more. To be billeted at home should greatly influence the influx of desirable recruits and be an inducement to shop assistants, clerks, etc. to join.*"[32]

Chorley, at least shared with Burnley, the idea of a Company made up of 'business young men'.

Some thirty men gave their names to Milton before the recruiting office opened on Tuesday morning. By the following Tuesday another 123 volunteered. One of these was sixteen year old James Snailham.

"*I was working at Swansey Printworks in my home village of Whittle-le-Woods. I wasn't a bad footballer for my age. I'd played regularly in men's teams so I knew I was as strong as they were. When I heard about the Pals forming I decided to go because a few other lads I knew were joining. I also knew you could play football in the army — I must have been an innocent! But I was patriotic as well and I wanted to do my bit. On September 7th I walked three miles from Whittle-le-Woods to Chorley and the recruiting office. Doctor Rigby, the medical officer said 'How old are you son?' Not thinking, I said, 'Sixteen, Sir,' He looked at me for a while, then said, 'Come back this afternoon when you are a bit older.' I took the hint, went back in the afternoon. 'How old are you son?' He said, 'Eighteen, Sir.' He passed me A1. I then had to go home and break it to my mother, I'd joined up.*"

Milton did not wait for men to come forward.

Above: Pte. James Snailham

A Soldier
of the
KING.

AFTER the War every man who has served will command his Country's gratitude. He will be looked up to and *respected* because he answered his country's call.

The Regiments at the Front are covering themselves with Glory.

Field-Marshal Sir John French wrote in an Order of the day,

"It is an Honour to belong to such an Army."

Every fit man from 19 to 38 is eligible for this great honour. Friends can join in a body, and serve together in the same regiment.

Rapid Promotion.

There is rapid promotion for intelligence and zeal. Hundreds who enlisted as private soldiers have already become officers because of their merits and courage, and thousands have reached non-commissioned rank.

Enlist To-day.

At any Post Office you can obtain the address of the nearest Recruiting Office. **Enter your name to-day on the Nation's Roll of Honour and do your part.**

GOD SAVE THE KING.

He busily organised recruiting meetings in the surrounding villages. On Monday, September 21st, he spoke to a crowded meeting at Croston Parish Hall and promised to return on Saturday the 26th with Dr. Rigby and Lt. Beale the recruiting officer. On Tuesday he went with the M.P. for Chorley, Sir H. F. Hibbert, to Brinscall. Here Milton made a characteristic speech, "Berlin is on the Spree and if we are on the spree at the finish, say sometime next spring, we would not be in for a very bad time. At this moment we have recruited 153 'boys' and there are still vacancies. So come along!"[33]

It worked. On Friday, September 25th, with 190 men, Milton suspended recruiting in Chorley and the surrounding villages. The formation of the Blackburn Detachment, to be part of Chorley Company, changed his original target of 250 to 200 men. Fifty would-be recruits left their names for a Reserve. Ten men from Croston, accepted on Saturday the 26th, completed Milton's ambition of forming his own Chorley Pals Company. Although, for a Chorley man, not the ideal of the Loyal North Lancs. Regiment, the good reputation of the East Lancashire Regiment, and Harwood's local associations, were some compensation. Milton, with a shrewd feel for publicity, made a statement in the local newspapers expressing his gratitude to the people of Chorley and the local newspapers, for their encouragement and support in raising the Company. There began a fond and close relationship between the town of Chorley and its 'Company'.

Compared with such cities as Liverpool's raising of 4,000 men in five days and Newcastle's raising of a 'Pals's Battalion in 24 hours, the ten days to form the Accrington 'Pals' Battalion was markedly slow. It was still, however, a very creditable piece of organisation to raise 1,000 men over a wide area of East Lancashire, an area already well recruited by Regular, New Army and Territorial Battalions, using nine recruiting stations covering four towns and at least twelve villages.

On September 19th, Lord Kitchener appealed for ex non-commissioned officers of His Majesty's Forces to re-enlist at once for service as drill instructors. These men were to form the nucleus of trained, experienced men intended to shape these ex-clerks, ex-shop assistants, ex-weavers and ex-engineers into a unified body of trained soldiers.

"Those in the battalion with any previous military knowledge were very few and only one or two had any knowledge of active service. Under such conditions the moulding of this mass of raw material into an organised fighting unit was a heavy task and required the enthusiasm and whole-hearted co-operation of officers, non-commissioned officers and men to carry to through."[34]

From September 24th in Accrington and Burnley, and September 25th in Chorley, this 'heavy task' began.

DADDY, WHY WEREN'T **YOU** A SOLDIER DURING THE WAR?

IN YEARS TO COME *YOU* MAY BE ASKED THIS QUESTION.

Join the Army at once, and help to secure the glorious Empire of which *your* little son will be a citizen.

NOTES

1. In 1904 Captain Roger Pocock, an ex-Canadian Mounted Policeman, explorer and adventurer, convinced war with Germany was inevitable, formed the 'League of Frontiersmen'. Its members came from those 'interested in Good Fellowship, Mutual Help and service to the Empire in case of war'. By 1914, throughout the British Empire, the Frontiersmen were organised into local semi-military squadrons, with each member providing uniform, mount, equipment etc. at his own expense.
2. A.O.T. 8/8/14.
3. The Guns of August, Barbara W. Tuchman, New English Library 1965 p 224.
4. A.O.T. 8/8/14.
5. Raising and Training the New Armies, Captain B. Williams Constable 1918 p17.
6. From the 13th century onward, Commissions were appointed by the Crown to 'array' the able-bodied men of each shire between 15 and 60 and to select the best men for the Kings' service. Each shire was responsible for mustering and equipping the men, who then passed into the Kings pay. From the mid 16th century 'arraying' became one of the principal functions of Lord Lieutenants of the County and the Shire levies were the direct ancestors of the Militia of the 19th century. (Steinbergs' Dictionary of British History, Edward Arnold 1970 p 20).
7. The Kitchener Armies, V. W. Germains, Peter Davies 1930 p 103.
8. A.O.T. 5/19/14.
9. John Harwood held the honorary rank of Captain. As a young man in the cotton trade in India he held a commission in the Cawnpore Rifles.
10. The Army Council was a War Office committee under the Secretary of State for War. It acted as an advisory body on general policy and military matters.
11. A.O.T. 8/9/14.
12. W.O. 159/18, Public Record Office.
13. Chorley Guardian (Hereafter C. G.) 12/9/14.
14. Burnley Express (Hereafter B. E.) 5/9/14.
15. The East Lancashire Territorial Division, the first to volunteer for overseas service, embarked for Egypt on September 10th, 1914. The Division (subsequently the 42nd) played an heroic role in the Dardanelles campaign.
16. The War Office eventually accepted Driscolls' offer of a Frontiersmen Battalion. Known as the 25th (Frontiersmen) Battalion Royal Fusiliers, it served in East Africa from May 1915 to the end of 1917.
17. B.E. 5/9/14.
18. Burnley News (Hereafter B. N.) 9/9/14.
19. A.O.T. 12/9/14 and Accrington Gazette (Hereafter A. G.) 12/9/14.
20. A.O.T. 12/9/14.
21. Of the 104 enlistments, Accrington took 52, Rishton 19, Clayton-le-Moors 8, Church and Oswaldtwistle (combined) 3, Great Harwood 4, Blackburn 4 and Burnley 14.
22. Unpublished manuscript 'History of the Accrington Pals', H. Crossley, Accrington.
23. Kitcheners' Army and the Territorial Forces, E. Wallace, George Newnes 1916 p 12.
24. B.E. 12/9/14.
25. B.E. 19/9/14.
26. Ibid.
27. Unpublished typescript 'History of 'Z' Company', F. Sayer & P. Crabtree, Burnley.
28. Chorley Weekly News (Hereafter C. W. N.) 19/9/14.
29. Ibid.
30. Ibid.
31. Ibid.
32. Ibid.
33. C.W.N. 26/9/14.
34. 'The History of the East Lancashire Regiment' 1914-1919 Littlebury Bros., Liverpool 1936 P520.

N.C.O's and MEN
who have won the
VICTORIA CROSS

BATTERY-SERGT.-MAJOR (NOW SECOND-LIEUT.) G. T. DORRELL, "L" Battery, Royal Horse Artillery.

SERGEANT D. NELSON (NOW SECOND-LIEUTENANT), "L" Battery, Royal Horse Artillery.

CORPORAL C. E. GARFORTH, 15th (The King's) Hussars.

BOMBARDIER E. G. HARLOCK (NOW SERGEANT), 113th Battery, Royal Field Artillery.

LANCE-CORPORAL C. A. JARVIS, 57th Field Company, Royal Engineers.

LANCE-CORPORAL W. FULLER, 2nd Battalion, Welsh Regiment.

LANCE-CORPORAL F. W. HOLMES, 2nd Battalion (The King's Own) Yorkshire Light Infantry.

PRIVATE S. F. GODLEY, 4th Battalion, Royal Fusiliers.

PRIVATE G. WILSON, 2nd Battalion, Highland Light Infantry.

DRIVER J. H. C. DRAIN, 37th Battery, Royal Field Artillery.

DRIVER F. LUKE, 37th Battery, Royal Field Artillery.

There is room for your name on this Roll of Honour.

THESE HEROES would never have won the VICTORIA CROSS by staying away from the RECRUITING OFFICE. They enlisted for their Country's sake, and fought as only brave men do.

Is *your* name to be known from one end of the world to the other as one of the Empire's *bravest* sons?

ENLIST TO-DAY.

The more men we have, the sooner the war will end.

At any Post Office you can obtain the address of the nearest Recruiting Office. Enter *your* name to-day on the Nation's Roll of Honour, and do *your* part.

GOD SAVE THE KING.

Chapter Two

And we be brethren

The 7th (Service) Battalion (Accrington) East Lancashire Regiment was part of Lord Kitchener's Fourth New Army, (K4). Four companies, each with four platoons, made up the Battalion.[1] 'A' Company, composed mainly of Accrington men and 'B' Company, men from the 'Districts' i.e. Clayton-le-Moors, Church, Oswaldtwistle, Rishton and Great Harwood were to train in Accrington; 'C' Company in Chorley and 'D' Company in Burnley. The fifty men of the Blackburn Detachment of 'C' Company were to train in Accrington. Kitchener's directive of September 4th ensured the T. A. drill halls in Accrington, Burnley and Chorley were available, with officers such as Captain Robinson and Lt. Cockshutt of Burnley T.A., together with some senior N.C.O.'s to temporarily assist with training.

Candidates for commissions with the Battalion, however, went directly to Harwood. Twenty year old Tom Rawcliffe decided to leave the Accrington Company of Frontiersmen and enlist in the Battalion. His father, a Clayton-le-Moors cotton manufacturer 'had a word' with his friend Harwood.

"I went to the Town Hall first thing next morning. It was just like applying for a job on the Corporation. I had a short interview with the Mayor (Harwood) and Colonel Sharples. They must have liked me — I was in as a second-lieutenant, temporarily gazetted, of course."

The War Office, still limiting its involvement to the issue of directions, allowed Municipalities — "£7 per man to provide two suits of clothing — if they undertake to do so," paid no doubt from Miltons' sanguine 'bank account for an unlimited amount.'[2] Knowing he had to provide for a thousand men for at least the next six months Harwood had no time to lose. Whilst still recruiting he advertised in the local newspapers for tenders to be submitted, by Septem-

Above: 2/Lt. Tom Rawcliffe

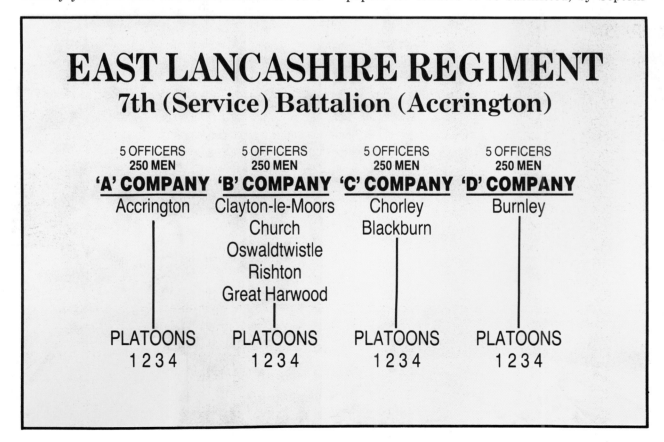

EAST LANCASHIRE REGIMENT
7th (Service) Battalion (Accrington)

5 OFFICERS 250 MEN	5 OFFICERS 250 MEN	5 OFFICERS 250 MEN	5 OFFICERS 250 MEN
'A' COMPANY	**'B' COMPANY**	**'C' COMPANY**	**'D' COMPANY**
Accrington	Clayton-le-Moors Church Oswaldtwistle Rishton Great Harwood	Chorley Blackburn	Burnley
PLATOONS 1 2 3 4	PLATOONS 1 2 3 4	PLATOONS 1 2 3 4	PLATOONS 1 2 3 4

In 1914 the chief industries of the towns of East Lancashire were cotton weaving, mining and engineering. Many of the Pals worked in these industries before enlisting.
Right: Labourers at a Burnley cotton mill load woven cloth for delivery to the major warehouses of Manchester.
Below right: Two weavers (left and centre) pose with a tackler (loom mechanic) before a typical 'Lancashire' loom.
L.L.B.D.

Above: A group of miners underground at Duxbury Hall Colliery, Chorley. Note there are no safety helmets. There is however a Davy Safety Lamp on the leg of the miner in the foreground.
Right: The pit-head and loading stages of Duxbury Hall colliery.
L.L.C.D.

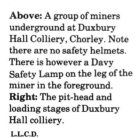

ber 22nd, from local firms to supply 'clothing and accessories' for the Battalion. The clothing included great coats, jackets and trousers in Melton blue and accessories ranged from kit-bags, toilet-requisites and eating utensils to socks, braces and towels.[3]

"Tailors tendering for uniforms will be expected to measure and fit every man individually, guaranteeing a perfect fit."[4]

With no time wasted after recruitment either, every morning newly enlisted men from Accrington and district assembled in the T. A. drill hall and marched to a public open space, Ellison's Tenement, a short distance away, to be introduced to the intricacies of Company drill. R.S.M. Stanton, a 60 years old, who had answered the call for retired N.C.O.'s, instructed them.[5] George Pollard enjoyed this period.

"I was in my element. We paraded on the 'Tenement' every morning and afternoon. There were some, of course, who arrived for the afternoon parade after being in the pub at lunch time. We only had our civilian clothes to wear. Every day large crowds watched us parade, with so many not working there wasn't much else for them to do. We weren't used to marching so it was a bit of a shambles sometimes, especially when the Sergeant Major ordered 'about turn!' and some carried on marching! This always amused the onlookers of course and we became the daily entertainment for many. My platoon (Number 4, 'A' Company), did its physical training in Milnshaw Park (a small public park nearby) and here, as well as on route marches through the streets, crowds always watched us."

The drilling and marching in public quickly brought comments from the onlookers. The first of many letters to the local newspapers complained about 'the giggles of idle women and frivolous girls mixed with the sneers of supercilious men' and suggested a guard to be put round Ellison's Tenement to keep onlookers away. The ragged clothing worn and shoes and clogs of some marchers became noticeable, "- a man must be obtuse indeed if he did not

Above: Pals awaiting orders to dismiss. On parade on Ellisons Tenement, Accrington on September 24th 1914.
"After forming fours a tremendous number of times, I presume on account of not doing it to the satisfaction of Major Slinger, we marched on to the Tenement. We continued forming fours. 'Right, left and about turning' until we were dismissed. Thus I received my first dose of military training."
J. Bridge

39

TENDERS.

THE OFFICER COMMANDING THE

ACCRINGTON BATTALION EAST

LANCASHIRE REGIMENT,

Asks for TENDERS to be submitted to this office not later than TUESDAY NEXT, the 22nd inst., for the following Regimental requirements.

CLOTHING

Great Coats.
Boots and Laces.
Caps, special pattern, blue or grey
Drawers, woollen.
Jackets, blue or grey serge
Trousers, blue or grey serge.
Putties, drab.
Cardigan, waistcoats or jerseys.

NECESSARIES.

Kit Bags.	Forks.
Braces.	Spoons.
Hair Brushes.	Housewife.
Shaving Brushes.	Razors.
Tooth Brushes.	Shirts (flannel).
Combs.	Socks.
Knives.	Towels.

Cloth will be provided by the Officer Commanding for Great Coats and Uniforms. Tailors Tendering for the Uniforms and Great Coats will be expected to measure and fit every man individually, guaranteeing a perfect fit. Samples of uniform can be inspected at the Town Hall.

R. SHARPLES, V.D.,

Col., Commanding.

---

feel what little self-respect he has is being lost by this public exhibition of poverty. I suggest these men are withdrawn and drilled while the rest are marching."[6] Harwood and Sharples — and the men concerned — of course ignored the suggestion. Clearly, so early in its existence, the people of Accrington felt the Pals belonged to them, and with characteristic bluntness would never hesitate to praise or reprove them in print.

The first formal parade of the "Battalion" was a great success. 'A' 'B' and 'D' Companies assembled on Ellison's Tenement at 4 p.m. on Saturday September 26th. ('C' Company, and its Blackburn Detachment, with Harwood's blessing stayed at home). With 'Accrington Old Band' at its head, the three Companies, led by Sharples, marched in a more or less military formation, four abreast, through the streets to the Town Hall. There the Band halted and played as the men, dressing in an assortment of smart or shabby clothes with headgear of either straw-boaters, trilbys or flat caps, marched past as Harwood took the salute. Thousands lined the streets as the Pals, rejoined by the Band, marched by a circular route around the town, back to Ellison's Tenement.

The sight and sound of over seven hundred men, albeit in civilian dress, gladdened the heart of Harwood. He had raised a full Battalion for his town (although the compromises of Burnley and Chorley could not be ignored) and he had beaten his larger neighbours, Blackburn and Burnley. Accrington had already achieved distinction as the only non-county borough in the Country to raise a full battalion for Kitchener (not strictly true, the recruiting area was not solely in the town) Accrington enjoyed this prestige with much larger cities as Sheffield, Glasgow, Leeds, Manchester, Belfast, Cardiff etc. The legend of 'little Accrington' raising a thousand men had been born.

Harwood took the salute of 'his' battalion with all his hopes and ambitions realised. The Accrington newspapers, enthusiastic from the beginning, took a great interest in the 'daily doings' of the Battalion. The *Accrington Observer and Times* in editorial and feature columns attempted to dub the units 'Accrington's Own.' This did not catch on — Pals was easier to say perhaps, and of course Burnley and Chorley would not have agreed. Nevertheless, local newspapers chose to refer to the Pals as belonging to Accrington alone, with only rare references to the neighbouring towns. The *Observer and Times* enthusiasm continued unabated. An edition carried a typical vignette: "I met a fellow of my acquaintance who is engaged in business in the town. 'Well, I enquired, how is business in these uncertain days?' 'Oh,' was the reply, 'I'm not much concerned with business just now, I've joined the Pals, and now my chief end in life is drilling and marching.' 'And what does your mother think?' 'Oh,' she's quite proud of me, in fact . . . she was the recruiting sergeant."[7]

Not all Accrington businessmen became so free from care. Those hopeful of a share of the advertised clothing contracts were very troubled. Hardwood's purchasing policy had showed more of an eye for a bargain than support for local tradesmen. The first public protests, by a local bootmaker about the ordering of five hundred pairs of boots from a national wholesaler came in early October. At the same time, local tailors also learned of Harwood's singular business methods.

It seemed Harwood, in a gentlemen's agreement, promised local master tailors the clothing contracts on condition they cut their prices to the minimum. Nevertheless, he later told them he was about to accept a much lower tender from a Leeds firm of multiple tailors. Loud protests from the local tailors were met by Harwood's offer to grant them part of the contract at the multiple's price. This the locals could not meet. Profits and wages already were pared to the bone. In spite of private meetings and public protests Harwood awarded the contract to the multiple tailors. The economics of multiple tailoring and the business acumen of Harwood, combined to defeat local partialities. Although Mayor, Harwood gave no concessions to his businessmen ratepayers.

The resultant bad feeling and recriminations persisted in Accrington for many months. The high esteem for Harwood diminished among the town's tradesmen. He had broken a gentlemen's agreement, but worse still, allowed some three thousand pounds to go out of the town — a town desperately in need of work and wages. The quarrel also caused the issue of the blue uniforms to 'A', 'B' and 'D' Companies to be delayed until the early days of December.

No such problems arose at Chorley. Captain Milton, in a shrewd move, arranged with Harwood for 'C' Company's clothing to be supplied locally. More mindful perhaps of good public relations, Milton appreciated the extra business would give a needed impetus to local trade. Approving this, the *Chorley Guardian* on September 19th asked Chorley tradesmen to return the favour by encouraging their employees to join

ACCRINGTON SERVICE BATTALION
EAST LANCASHIRE REGIMENT.
———
A BATTALION PARADE and ROUTE MARCH
will take place
On SATUURDAY NEXT, the 26th inst.,
through the town and district, accompanied
by the
ACCRINGTON OLD BAND.

By Order,
R. SHARPLES, Col. Commanding.
———
RECRUITING.
MEN STILL REQUIRED, Chest and Height Measurements Reduced to 5 feet 3 and upwards, and 34 inches and upwards.

Above: On Saturday September 26th, 1914 the new battalion (except for 'C' [Chorley] Company) parades through Accrington.
Authors collection
Left: The advertisement for the parade placed in the Accrington Gazette on September 19th, 1914.

the Pals. The Chorley-made uniforms were ready by the middle of October. A national shortage of brass buttons delayed their appearance in public until November 15th.

The blue melton uniform, although admired by the local population, was not particularly popular with the men. To them, the private soldiers dress of blue tunic, with red piping on collar and cuffs and blue trousers, looked suspiciously like a tram-drivers uniform. The N.C.O.'s, although adorned by wide gold stripes of rank on tunic sleeves, wore blue, peaked, 'tram-drivers' caps. The forage cap 'special army pattern,' of the private soldier needed adjusting with great care and skill for it to remain on the head. Weeks of wear and tear of civilian clothes in cold, wet weather made everyone pleased to get something — even though con-

Right: A group of regulars at the Commercial Hotel, Chorley, celebrate enlisting.
L.L. Chorley District

Below: A group from St. Chad's Roman Catholic Church Wheelton, near Chorley pose in the new uniforms.
J. Garwood

N.B. Pte. Wilfred Ellison (1st left rear) was to be the first Chorley Pal to die in active service. He died in France of untreated appendicitis on May 25th, 1916. (See page 124)

sidered a stop-gap until the coveted khaki arrived. Chorley Company at least, with uniforms much better made with much better material, endured them with more grace than the Accrington and Burnley Companies.

Meanwhile training continued in the three towns. The newly issued training manual, 'Infantry Training (4 Company Organisation)' became required reading for ex-regular N.C.O., instructors and raw subalterns alike. The recommended six months training syllabus consisted of forty-two hours per fortnight on physical training, squad drill, musketry and lectures supplemented by regular route marches. The hours per fortnight increased gradually to fifty five and included platoon and company drill, field work (day and night) and entrenching as well as longer route marches. "The object to be aimed at in the training of the infantry soldier is to make him a better man than his adversary in the field of battle; — The preliminary steps necessary for the efficent training of the soldier are:-

i) the development of a soliderly spirit;
ii) the training of the body;
iii) training in the use of rifle, bayonet and spade."[8]

From the beginning officers, N.C.O.'s, and men set about putting these principles into practice with lots of enthusiasm, energy and not a little lightheartedness and hilarity.

Above: 'C' (Chorley) Company parade for inspection outside the Technical College (now Chorley Library) in Union Street on Saturday December 19th, 1914. They are wearing the new melton blue uniforms for the first time. **Authors collection**
Left: Lance Corporal James Henry Woods 'C' (Chorley) Company.

The training in the winter months of 1914 and early 1915, formed the character of the Battalion. In this time all ranks strengthened existing friendships and made new, often life-long ones. The officers were already well known to most men, as sons of employers or men in public life. Some private soldiers, family men with sons as old as the younger subalterns, were not inclined to take seriously the orders of these callow youths, particularly when already acquainted with them in civilian life. There was no strong discipline in the manner of the Regular Army. The bases of spit and polish could hardly be imbued in men wearing civilian clothes who went home to their families in the evening. The Accrington Battalion shared this attribute with many other Kitchener Battalions. "In those great volunteer armies, discipline was a matter of the natural respect of the men, and their willingness to learn. The officer who found himself in charge of a thousand men had no means actually to enforce discipline — he would have been lynched if he had tried. But with any officer of any common sense, no need for enforcing discipline arose — at least no need opposed to that of the general instinct of the men themselves."[9] The Accrington Battalion, officers and men, wished to be soldiers, friends, volunteers together in their own home town company. The pride and expectations of their home towns bonded them together and formed their distinct qualities.

Full time training took over only gradually. For many, domestic and social routine changed little. Colonel Sharples, even after his official appointment, on October 16th, as Lieutenant Colonel (temporary) of the Battalion, visited his solicitors' office most mornings. Major Slinger (now Second in Command) and Captain Milton, as solicitors; Captain Watson as a General Practitioner; and Captain Broadley, in his family printing business; only gradually wound up their business affairs as training proceeded. Only Captain Ross, as an employee of Burnley Corporation, immediately served full-time with his Company. These six officers however with the sprinkling of ex-regular army N.C.O.'s, were the core of experience of the Battalion. Its junior officers were completely inexperienced as yet.

Left: On parade on Ellison's
Tenement. Note the newly
constructed tram depot in the
background. In wet weather
the Pals used the building as
a drill-shed.
A. O. & T.
Below: 'A' (Accrington)
Company, along with an
assortment of children and
spectators, march along
Queens Road, Accrington.
A. O. & T.

On November 4th, Harwood and Sharples published their official list of officers. Local families prominent in the area's business and social life were well represented.[10] Harwood's wide powers had allowed him to appoint as officers the relatives of business associates and magisterrial colleagues. He saw such appointments as an extension of the authority and leadership which their public standing had given them.

This belief rationalised their appointment as officers. It is therefore not remarkable to see how closely the social structure of the Accrington Battalion mirrored the social structure of the town. Whatever the reasons for their appointments these youthful officers integrated into the battalion. Without exception their enthusiasm and readiness to take on any task quickly earned them the friendship and respect

Above: 'D' (Burnley) Company drilling on Bank Hall Meadow, Burnley.
L.L. Burnley District

Right: The newly appointed officers of 'D' (Burnley) Company. (Left to right) Capt. R. Ross, Lieut. J.V. Kershaw, Lieut. F.A. Heys and Lieut. H.D. Riley.
L.L. Burnley District

of the N.C.O.'s and men.

In Burnley training quickly settled down. The Company soon found the T.A. Drill Hall too small so for most of their early drill practice they used nearby Bank Hall Meadow."Here in the atmosphere of a Sunday School field day, in the fresh air and sunshine, blossomed the family spirit of the Company. A big crowd, all in little groups clumsily trying to learn squad drill from army training manuals."[11] As sections and platoons were formed men with qualities of leadership became N.C.O.'s. Anyone with service in the Regular or Territorial Army, Boy Scouts or indeed anyone who volunteered, gained promotion. On October 1st the Company moved to Burnley Barracks and Lt. Riley and Lt. Heys

took over from Captain Robinson and Lt. Cockshutt of the T.A.

The Burnley Company spirit of irreverent enthusiasm soon evolved. Section rivalled section in keeness and platoon rivalled platoon. In contrast they responded only slowly to the strictures of the training manual. "The jigsaw was piecing together and now able to form itself into a square of four lines, each double. 'Platoons,' we heard them called. 'Platoons!' I thought those bloody things were for crossing rivers on!"[12]

Elementary military discipline did not come easily, "discipline was politely requested, by all, 'The salute must be given to all officers.' 'What! off the parade ground?' Many of the Company walked around street corners in town to avoid that salute, just shyness, said some. 'Not bloody likely!' said others. It was a long time before saluting came freely and in good style, but the leaders were men of understanding who had confidence and hopes for the best."[13]

The Company, however, did begin to take training seriously. As early as September 21st seven mile route marches became routine. A typical week, for men in civilian clothing, was punishing by any standard. Starting Monday, November 16th, a 22 mile route march to Blackburn and back; Tuesday, drill parade, then baths parade at Burnley Public Baths; Wednesday, drill parade and a seven mile route march; Thursday, a 22 mile route march to Hebden Bridge and back; on Friday, drill parade and a five mile route march. Not surprisingly, they quickly gained a reputation for fitness and excellence in sports. The *Burnley News* commented on the number of excellent swimmers in the Company. "A few of the leading members of Burnley Swimming Club are in the ranks, and with members of Burnley Lads Club, this accounts for the good swimming to be seen at the Public Baths."[14]

Their keeness and proficiency in marching also became known. Captain Ross bet the Accrington Company his men could march to Accrington and back in three hours. "Like a flash they were off, all on foot except Sergeant Kay, who drove his ambulance in the form of a motorbike and side-car, and saved his wind to sing 'Cock-Robin.' 'Good luck, Bobby McGregor' and 'Tatty, will you go,' etc. With the Captain in front and Ernest on his bike, blasting his songs into the ears of anyone showing signs of wearying, 'D' Company did it. The bet was won. Each man's share of the bet was a bun and a bottle of pop."[15]

The daily routine of the two Accrington Com-

Above and below: 'D' (Burnley) Company drilling and marching on Bank Hall Meadow. Note (above) several Territorials temporarily attached to the Company to assist with drilling.
L.L. Burnley District

DEPTH 4'3"

Above: Visits to the Public Baths made a change from route marches and drilling. Here a group of Burnley Pals pose for the camera.
L.L. Burnley District

panies was no less arduous with the same combination of drills, marches and swimming. They also had their compensations. On the evening the Burnley bet was won, the Accrington Companies made a night march to Burnley. Tom Rawcliffe:

"We assembled outside Colonel Sharples' office in Avenue Parade at 8 p.m. He looked us over, then sent one or two home who had already had a pint or two. We set off for Burnley. It was a pitch black, moonless night and on the open road half way there, there were no lights at all. An order by Captain Slinger to halt went unheard by 'A' Company which disappeared into the darkness ahead. Moments later I heard, 'Where the hell are 'A' Company, Lt. Rawcliffe?' Don't know, Sir, somewhere round the corner, I should say. 'Well damn well catch them up then!' However, we didn't, but we all got to Burnley Barracks about the same time. What a welcome! Burnley were a most hospitable crowd beer and sandwiches galore. Perhaps a bit too much for some. We put one or two officers into taxis to get them home, and then we left to march to Accrington. Some of the men weren't really capable of walking and we were a bedraggled, but happy, lot when we got back home."

The following day, the Accrington and Burnley Companies, with the Blackburn Detachment, were formally inspected by Colonel R.J. Tudway, C.B., D.S.O., of No. 3 District, Western Command. During the inspection, so the story went, Colonel Tudway asked an Accrington man, 'Did you ever drill before?' He replied, honestly, 'Yes Sir, I worked at Howard and Bulloughs.' Colonel Tudway, when asked his opinion of the men, told the parade they would be pefectly capable of taking the field abroad in three months time. Whether this reply reflected Colonel Tudway's honest view of the Battalion's qualities is conjectural, but his words encouraged all in the Battalion. In six weeks a mob of men, unversed in military methods, had been shaped into an acceptable sort of order, enhanced by a quickly established camaraderie. The approbation of Colonel Tudway gave confidence to all in the Battalion.

The Accrington Companies were becoming the source of a fund of stories in the town. In bitterly cold weather in late November, night exercises took place on the moors between Accrington and Burnley. The *Observer and Times* reporter, attached to 'A' Company, wrote, "The manoeuvring was reasonably well done and Accrington can rest assured every effort is being made to make the Battalion an efficient fighting unit. Comical events, of course happened.

Wandering inhabitants were captured, trying to get through the lines and in one case, a relative with a small Lancashire Hot Pot for one of the defenders was seized. It is hoped the savoury and welcome dish reached its rightful owner."[16]

The evening lecture in the T.A. Drill Hall became another element in the development of the men's soldierly spirit and a source of other stories. The lectures were given by officers who themselves had scant knowledge of the subject. The men saw lectures as a relaxation rather than a serious part of training. Often their own views about the subject helped shape the lectures into a battle of wits.

Lt. Rawcliffe underwent the 'ordeal.' "A typical week's lecture started on Monday with Lt. Roberts on the subject of 'Belgium.' Unfortunately someone unknown changed the slide sequence on the magic-lantern. His description of Bruges Cathedral accompanied by a slide of a steamer entering Antwerp harbour produced great hilarity. On Tuesday, Lt. Ramsbottom, as O.C. Battalion Scouts lectured to a rapt audience on 'Scouting.' On Wednesday, Colonel Sharples and Captain Slinger (christened by the men, ever ready to apply a nickname, Mick and Mack, the crosstalk comedians) gave a joint lecture on 'Co-operation in Warfare.' I gave my lecture of 'The History of the British Army,' on Thursday, and because of my habit of standing with my hand tucked into my belt, I was quickly dubbed 'Napoleon.' They didn't care if you heard them either! We officers didn't bother, it was without malice. They didn't always win the battle of wits. In his lecture on shells and explosives, Lt. Bury (Flash Harry, because of his smart dress) was asked, 'Sir, what would happen if we were in a trench and a Lyddite shell dropped in?' 'You would never know, replied Harry, but your friends would read about it in the paper the next day.'"

As in Accrington and Burnley, training for the Chorley Company was a combination of squad, platoon and company drill in the mornings and field exercises or route marches in the afternoons. Lieutenants Gidlow-Jackson and Rigby gave the evening lectures assisted by the Accrington officers. Chorley Company visited almost all the neighbouring villages on their route marches and often combined the visit with a social event. On November 28th the Company marched seven miles to Croston, to be entertained to a potato-pie tea in the Wesleyan School by the villagers. The Company gave a drill display and played football against a village team, then marched back to Chorley leaving the ten Croston members to go home. A fortnight later, at Eccleston, five miles from Chorley, the Company attended a social and

SOME OFFICERS OF THE "PALS" BATTALION.

SUB-LIEUT. S. HAYWOOD.
(Photo, Moffitt.)

SUB.-LIEUT. H. BURY.
(Photo, Sunbeam Studio, Blackpool.)

LIEUT. A. B. TOUGH.

LIEUT. W. CHENEY.
(Photo, Tattersalls, Accrington.

Although not yet gazetted, information has been received from the War Office that those recommended locally as officers of the Accrington and District Battalion will be accepted. Photos of other officers of the Battalion will appear in due course.

dance in the National School before returning to Chorley.

Whilst equal to the Accrington and Burnley Companies in their cheerful enthusiasm and dedication, the Chorley Company retained a more formal association with the town. Milton clearly believed in involving the Company in local social life and the townspeople reciprocated. The town's civil and religious leaders, from the beginning, cared for the welfare of the Company. As early as September 20th weekly public church parades were held for C. of E. and Roman Catholic members, with Non Conformists attending their own chapels.

A service at St. Georges C. of E. on October

Above: Placed in the Accrington Observer and Times, September 26th, 1914.

Right: Major G.N. Slinger,
Second-in-Command and
acting Adjutant of the
Battalion.

without a uniform, whilst a Terrier already has a uniform? Married men have to keep a wife and family on the paltry sum of three shillings a day (21 shillings per week.) Understand we receive no separation allowances. So what have the Pals got? Nothing, except a small testament from St. George's Church. Again, is he aware the East Lancashire Pals Battalion is one of the worse paid in the country? How is it a married man in the Salford Pals (15th Service Battalion,- Lancashire Fusiliers) gets 3/11d per day (27/6d per week) and those in the Manchester City Battalions, 7/6d for using their own overcoats? Men in Kitchener's army in the South of England are compensated for clothing, wear and tear, whilst we receive nothing. How would you like to pay your own rail fare to go to your training, as a few of the Pals have to do?"[19]

Public airing of the Chorley Company's grievances worked. Harwood, as paymaster of the Battalion reacted quickly and in the same week, the Chorley married men received 3/11d per day with back pay, for the weeks the correct pay scale had been in existence. It is a minor mystery why, when the pay-scales were already in force, Harwood had not voluntarily paid his men. The Territorials also benefited. The same week, 134 shirts, 132 mufflers and 506 pairs of socks were sent to Sussex by the Chorley Ladies Committee.

Burnley Company shared Chorley's grievance over pay. Some men, disappointed with their pay and also anxious for active service, took their complaints to Mr. P. Morrell, Burnley's M.P. On February 10th, 1915 Mr. Morrell raised the matter in the debate on the Army Estimates in the House of Commons. Referring to married men in local battalions who were billeted at home, he stated, "Many left excellent jobs in civil life and they are still receiving payment which compares very unfavourably with their civilian wages, and also with the pay of men training away from home. A soldier away from home pays his family 3/6d per week plus a separation allowance of 17/6d making £1 1s. per week. A man at home receives £1 1s. per week pay and billeting allowance. He gets 6/5d for light and fuel, so his wife has to keep him in everything on 6/5d per week. These men suffer from a double sense of grievance. They are willing to earn less than in civil employment, but they are receiving less than they would if they were away from home. They joined entirely from the highest motives and all they ask is to be sent away or have terms of service which corresponds with those who are away from home." Unfortunately, Mr. Morrell's question came too late. Two weeks later the Battalion left home and qualified for the separation allowance.

4th typified the spiritual concern for the men. One hundred and thirty six of the Company were each presented with a small, inscribed testament. The text of the service 'For we be brethren.' A month later, at St. Mary's, each Roman Catholic member received a prayer book, a rosary, 'a soldiers guide book' and a medallion inscribed, 'Our Lord, Mount Carmel.'[17]

In early November, the three Chorley officers' wives set up a comforts fund for the Company and made a public appeal for gifts of socks, mufflers, body-belts, etc. News of the appeal disquieted several local Territorials then serving in Sussex. One wrote to the Chorley Guardian appealing for a similar comforts fund. He added "The men in the Pals are lying at home at night and do not feel the cold as we under canvas do. The only cry is for the 'Chorley Pals.' We are all fighting for one King, so why not let us chaps have the same honour as the Pals they seem to have it all at present."[18]

A week later, an indignant 'One of the Pals' outlined some of the disadvantages of being a Pal. "Does he know we have been ten weeks

The criticism of the Chorley Company comforts fund did not affect the people of Chorley. Three weeks after their first appeal the officers wives advertised for furniture and other articles for a jumble sale and auction to be held in the Town Hall. A total of 1,079 articles was donated, making it necessary to divide the auction into three sections:- furniture, farm produce and clothing. Over seven hours of bidding and 'knocking-down' bought £85 14s 11d for the fund. The ladies were pleasantly surprised. In spite of the poverty in the town, people had responded very generously. In the same week 460 children had free meals in the Town Hall. Only four of Chorley and district's forty cotton mills were working full-time. By a special irony, on New Year's Eve 1914 the Canteen Committee of Chorley Town Council decided the Pals pay increase brought them above the minimum income of 26/- per week, so their children no longer qualified for free meals.

Two days after the C. of E. members received their Testaments, the Chorley Company received their first rifles. Two hundred, fifty per company, were allocated to the Battalion in early October. The Lee Metfords, relics of the South African War and before, were unfit for firing so were for drill purpose only. It also meant lectures on the elementary theoretical instruction in musketry of the Training Manual could now begin.

Chorley Company attended voluntarily, lectures of a different sort. When war was declared, Miss K. Knight, a French teacher at a Chorley school, as her patriotic duty taught French free of charge, to local servicemen. She offered her evening classes to the newly formed Chorley Company and from then on each evening taught the men elementary French. Phrases thought to be useful whilst on active service 'Do you know which way our soldiers have passed?' 'Madam, I want something to eat as I am very hungry' were taught. French speaking Belgian refugees and wounded soldiers helped with practical exercises. Miss Knight became a staunch friend and advocate of the Chorley Company and is still remembered with affection for her concern for them and their families. She died in 1948.

Christmas 1914 provided the first break in training along with the first opportunity for relaxation and entertainment. Celebrations started on December 19th, when the Accrington N.C.O.'s, repaid the Burnely N.C.O.'s, for their hospitality a short time before, with a concert and supper in the Old Black Bull. On December 23rd a more formal concert took place in Accrington Town Hall. Harwood spoke to a hall filled with 'men and officers of the Battalion, officers wives and a few lady friends.' He spoke of his pride in them and his confidence that they would do their duty in a manner which would bring credit to themselves and the town. A concert followed of which all the entertainers except one, were men from the Battalion. The evening closed with the presen-

tation to each man of two pairs of socks, with the officers also receiving a khaki silk handkerchief, the gift of Mrs. Sharples. The socks, twelve hundred pairs, were provided by the Accrington Pals Comforts Fund set up by Col. Sharples' daughter and the officers' wives.

In Chorley, Miss Knight arranged two Christmas celebrations, the first, for her French class, on December 16th, the second, for all the Chorley Company on December 22nd. Local tradesmen supplied free food and drinks, and the Company members, with a few wounded Belgian soldiers, entertained with songs and monologues. The whole Battalion, in all Companies, appeared to have a wealth of musical talent in the ranks.

In the three main towns church parades and services were held. In Accrington, while the Roman Catholics went to Sacred Heart Church, four hundred men marched to St. John's C. of E. Baxenden. Here the Reverend Mills, concerned as many were, for the moral and spiritual welfare of the men, appealed to them to keep themselves pure and sober. "They had the chance of a lifetime in going to the front", he told them, but, " no man disregarded God when he was in the trenches with shells or bullets shrieking about him. It was then they needed religion, and plenty of it, but if they were right in their Christian faith, he had no doubt they would do great deeds."[21]

It might be said, Harwood lost an opportunity to unite at least socially, the four Companies of the Battalion at Christmas 1914. For over three months, the Accrington Companies, with the Blackburn Detachment; the Burnley Company and the Chorley Company trained quite separately, albeit to the liking of individualists such as Ross and Milton. For them the opportunity had come to form and train their own company. Understandably, they were not in-

Below: The Men's Class of a Roman Catholic Church pose with their priest before the camera.
J. Garwood

51

It is the duty of every able bodied man to defend his Country in her hour of need. Your Pals are calling for you. Will you respond?

The atrocities committed on the Women and the Children must be avenged.

Remember what has happened before may happen again and your own kith and kin may be the Victims.

Will you take your share in the noble work of fighting for your Country and your homes, your Brothers and your Sisters?

Men of Burnley, will you join the proposed

BURNLEY PALS BATTALION

OF THE

EAST LANCASHIRE REGIMENT?

The Committee of the Burnley Volunteer Training Corps have undertaken to Register the names and addresses of all those who wish to join a Burnley Pals Battalion.

To ensure the success of the proposal leave your names and addresses at the Offices, 2, St. James Row, Burnley, during the Hours of 12 & 2 p.m. and 6 and 9-30 p.m. next week.

1,000 NAMES WILL MAKE IT GO.

clined to share their company with anyone, however senior. The resulting quality of their companies showed their success. Harwood supported this view in a speech on his re-election as Mayor on November 9th, 1914. He had refused a War Office offer of £10,000 with which to build a barracks for the Battalion in Accrington. He believed the men would be better looked after at home, and so was content that the advantages of separate companies outweighed the disadvantages. Nevertheless, he knew Christmas 1914 would likely be the only one the Battalion would spend at home and the only opportunity to gather the whole Battalion together. In speeches, conversations etc. Harwood always referred to the two Accrington and District Companies as 'the Battalion,' so it is not surprising Accrington people believed this to be so. (Only the two Accrington and district companies were present at the 'Battalion' concert on December 23rd.) Happy in their semi-independence, the Burnley and Chorley Companies seemed not to hold any ill-will.

Burnley Company's part in civic life never achieved the prominence of Accrington's or Chorley's. They had no Mayor sufficiently interested to give them prestige, no Miss Knight to work on their behalf. Burnley had 106,000 population, the 'Company' but a small fraction of those who had enlisted. One Company of Pals in an Accrington battalion still rankled in a few hearts in Burnley. The weeks before Christmas saw an attempt to form a Burnley Pals Battalion. Letters in the *Burnley News* demanded the Mayor form such a battalion.[22] The Mayor kept a diplomatic silence, leaving the enthusiasts to call their own public meetings. In spite of strong support by the local newspapers the idea, within a week or two, languished and died, killed by the realisation that official War Office sanction for raising Pals battalions ceased in September. The idea of Burnley's own Pals battalion ended when sixty men who met weekly at Briercliffe, near Burnley to drill and Burnley Pals by name only, disbanded at the end of the year, their ranks reduced through enlistment. Although some Burnley folk did not like the idea, the Burnley Company of the Accrington Pals, was the only Pals unit in the town.

The Burnley Company, carefree as always, were too busy training to bother. In a night attack on Townley Hall (a 17th century house, set in acres of parkland) arrangements for 'casualties' to be inflicted were made. "After the first rush it was good to see what good marksmen the imaginary enemy really were. Half the defenders, evidently tired by their walk through town, died peacefully and were fast asleep ere the shouts of the attackers had echoed through the woodland."[23]

On December 10th, 1914 the Fifth Army (37th to 42nd Divisions) was formed by the War Of-

Opposite page: The attempted Burnley alternative to the Accrington Pals. This advert appeared in the Burnley News on November 28th, 1914.
L.L. Burnley District

Left: A group from No. 4 Platoon 'A' (Accrington) Company in Milnshaw Park, Accrington. Three were killed, one died of wounds and at least nine were to be wounded on July 1st, 1916. At least two in the Pals were only fifteen in 1914. One, Pte. Frank Bywater, stands third from left, back row.

fice. As a result the 7th (Accrington) Service Battalion became officially designated as the 11th (Accrington) Service Battalion, East Lancashire Regiment, and became part of 112th Infantry Brigade, 37th Division. The full complement of a New Army Battalion was now thirty officers and 1,350 men, including a new reserve company of five officers and 250 men. The War Office requested Harwood to recruit these at once. Recruitment for the new company designated 'E' started in Accrington, Burnley and Chorley on December 8th, 1914 and ended January 26th, 1915.

The existence of 'E' Company meant some necessary re-organisation, four months had been hardly long enough for the ex-regular N.C.O.'s to train many junior N.C.O.'s. Miracles enough had been performed in getting the Battalion to its present standard. However, several barely-experienced lance-corporals and privates were promoted and transferred to 'E' Company to impart their military skills to the new recruits. At the same time, following Lord Kitchener's recent recommendations that future commissioned officers should come from the ranks, five N.C.O.'s and privates were gazetted temporary second lieutenants. It so happened, four of them had a similar social background to those officers already serving:- Sgt. Williams, the son of a prominent businessman; Cpl. Ruttle, (on business in Japan when war broke out, he hurriedly returned to Accrington to enlist) the son of a local doctor; Pte. Slinger, son of Major Slinger; Pte. Whittaker, the nephew of Alderman Whittaker, Chairman of Clayton-le-Moors District Council. The exception was Lance Cpl. Kenny, a member of a theatrical touring company in Accrington in September 1914, and

among the first to volunteer. The Battalion, now fully part of the New Army and up to full strength, was impatient to leave for active service. There was still some time to wait, meanwhile the mundane tasks of training continued.

At the end of 1914, both the Blackburn Detachment and the Burnley Company became involved in controversy. On November 26th, passengers on the 7.55 a.m. Blackburn to Accrington tram complained of overcrowding. Many of the Blackburn Detachment used the tram, free, to attend morning parade in Accrington. Because of the complaints Blackburn Corporation decided men in uniform must pay tram fares. (How this would solve the overcrowding problem was not made clear.) The Blackburn men at once boycotted the tram service. Each morning, after assembling at the tram terminus, they marched the five miles to Accrington and marched back to Blackburn in the evening. The

Below: Many Pals were family men. Pte. Ernest Kenyon, age 37, of Accrington with his wife and young family. Before enlisting Pte. Kenyon was a calico-printer at Broad Oak works, Accrington. He was killed in action on June 23rd, 1916.

Right and below: Calico printing was one of the chief industries of Accrington in 1914. A large group of employees from Broad Oak Calico Printing Works enlisted in the Pals. Pte. Kenyon (see previous page) was one of those presented to His Majesty King George V and Queen Mary when they visited the works on their Royal visit to Accrington on July 9th, 1913.
A. O. & T.

BROAD OAK WORKS, ACCRINGTON.

A PORTION OF BROAD OAK WORKS.   [*Photos: E. V. Ward, Manchester.*

SOAPING AND DRYING DYED MATERIALS.

sight of 'Kitchener's volunteers' having to march ten miles a day for the sake of a 4d tram fare each, incensed many of the public. Comparisons with Accrington's free transport for five hundred men were made and in the face of such bitter criticism, Blackburn agreed to a special free tram for the Detachment, leaving at 8 a.m. and returning at 6 p.m. The boycott quickly ended. An arduous day's training was quite enough without having a ten mile march added to it.

Only Blackburn had transport problems. The Accrington Companies, although some walked from their homes, travelled by tram from Church, Oswaldtwistle and Clayton-le-Moors. (The Rishton and Great Harwood men came by train from Rishton). From October 19th, when the fourteen week dispute at Howard and Bulloughs ended (one of the very few in the country to continue after the commencement of the war) the trams became much more crowded as over 3,000 men and boys returned to work. Sharing the journey were 300 ex-employees, now serving with the Battalion.

As the Blackburn controversy ended a different one began in Burnley. On the evening of December 3rd, Captain Ross and the Burnley Company were invited to attend free, the Palace Theatre, Burnley. The men, in their blue uniforms for the first time, were in high spirits. Even before the show began they entertained the rest of the audience with music-hall songs and encouraged the audience to join in the choruses. Understandably, the 'military evening' went down well. Encouraged, Ross arranged a visit to the nearby Empire Theatre. Here the professional musicians were on strike and had appealed to the public to stay away. Their protests about Ross's 'strike-breaking' reached Mr. Arthur Henderson, Leader of the Labour Party, the Central Parliamentary Recruiting Committee and Colonel Sharples himself. Mr. Henderson formally protested to the War Office against troops being paraded at places of entertainment at which there was a trades dispute, and angry Burnley trade unionists threatened not to help with future army recruiting.

Colonel Sharples hastily visited the Burnley Company and the theatre finally arranging a 'truce' in that groups of men could not go but individuals could. The strikers final words were, "we have no objection to that if a Pal did not take another Pal with him "[25] Ross's action, from

Below: Messrs. Howard and Bulloughs Globe Works, Accrington. 'Bulloughs' as it was known in Accrington had a world-wide reputation as manufacturers of textile machinery. In normal times the street would be filled with men and boys as they made their way to and from work.

Above: Men of the Blackburn detachment outside the Territorial Army Drill Hall in Accrington in September, 1914. The uniformed N.C.O.'s are ex-regular soldiers who re-enlisted to act as drill instructers.

Right: A group of the Blackburn detachment in Milnshaw Park, Accrington, October 1914.

the best of motives the entertainment of his men succeeded only in bringing the Company, and the Battalion, to the unflattering notice of the War Office and threatened recruiting in the town. Even worse, in the eyes of some of his men, he had ended the type of night out they thoroughly enjoyed.

During those winter months the Battalion lost three men. Pte. Robert McGregor of Rishton drowned in the Leeds and Liverpool Canal in Rishton on November 9th. At the inquest the Coroner advised the jury, the deceased had 'drowned himself whilst temporary insane.' The jury disagreed and brought the more open verdict of 'Found Drowned." "The Coroner stated, 'That's not in accordance with the evidence.' The jury foreman replied, 'I say it is, we knew him personally.' "[26] How much the jury were influenced by McGregor's membership of the Pals, is of course, conjectural. In Chorley, Pte. George Milton died at his home, of pneumonia, on February 1st, 1915. In Blackburn, Pte. John Brierley died at his home, also of pneumonia, the following day. Both men were buried with full military honours. Undoubtedly, the exceptionally cold, wet weather of January 1915, added to the rigours of trench digging, night exercises and route marches.

Times, however, were changing. After an inspection by Colonel Mackenzie of 112th Brigade on January 6th, 1915, speculation began about the Battalion leaving home. Inoculations against typhoid and the news of a plan to billet the Burnley and Chorley men in Accrington being abandoned added conviction. Further news of an inspection to be held on February 16th, by Major General E. T. Dickson, Inspector of Infantry, led everyone to conclude the Battalion's imminent departure.

By this time, for some townspeople the novelty of troops in the town began to pall and attitudes were changing. Many local men had been on active service for some time. The 1st Battalion, East Lancashires, went to France on August 22nd, 1914; the 2nd Battalion in November. The 4th and 5th Territorial Battalions had been in Egypt since September. Chorley's 1st Battalion, Loyal North Lancs, had also been in France since August 13th. Both 1st Battalions suffered heavy casualties and every week the local newspapers published disturbing letters from wounded men. Inevitably resentment arose; 'Fred Karno's Army'; 'Petted Pals'; 'Harwood's Babies,' were bestowed by those who believed they had 'played at soldiers' enough. Many of the men, sensitive to the criticism, wanted to go to the Front. As expressed by Burnley's M.P., some had left good jobs to be less well paid than those away from home, so none were keener for active service.

In Chorley 'One of the Pals' wrote to the *Chorley Guardian* on January 30th, protesting against the, "insulting remarks of some Chorley

Left: Private Walter Briggs of Accrington in the Melton blue uniform.

inhabitants regarding the Pals not being drafted away we are all anxious to do our bit." Support for the Pals came from the trenches. Bombardier Storey told a relative, "the man who comes out to France needs to be fully trained and then he needs his wits about him. So if perchance you hear any more unpleasant remarks about Kitchener's Army please inform the bounders of the reason".[27]

Sometimes the men themselves, in their irreverent enthusiasm, encouraged the critics. Lt. Rawcliffe:

"Sometimes we were not serious enough about the whole job. We Accrington officers lunched daily at the Station Hotel and one day we drank the health of some newly promoted second lieutenants. Time passed, of course, and when we eventually got to Ellison's Tenement, a couple of hundred yards away, for the afternoon parade there were no soldiers there! Can you imagine it? We stopped passers-by to ask 'Have you seen the Pals?' Which way did they go?' It seemed the Sergeant Major got fed up waiting for us and marched the whole lot off! We were a bit like Fred Karno's Army at times, but nobody was happier!"

On Tuesday, February 16th, 1915, the day of Major General Dickson's inspection, resentment and speculation vanished, the 'bounders' were to be satisfied. The formal inspection over and the General departed to Chorley, Harwood made

Below: Major-General E.T. Dickson, Inspector of Infantry 1914-16.

Below: The Mayor of Accrington, Councillor John Harwood, J.P. with the Officers of the 11th East Lancs. Regiment (The 'Accrington Pals') February 1915.

Top Row (left to right) 2/Lt. J. Ramsbottom; 2/Lt. G. G. Williams; 2/Lt. W. Slinger; 2/Lt. C. D. Haywood; 2/Lt. H. Ashworth; Lt. C. W. Gidlow-Jackson; 2/Lt. F. Bailey; 2/Lt. W. R. Roberts. **Second Row** Mr. W. J. Newton (Accrington Borough Surveyor); 2/Lt. C. Stonehouse; 2/Lt. T. W. Rawcliffe; 2/Lt. J. V. Kershaw; Lt. A. B. Tough; 2/Lt. H. H. Mitchell; 2/Lt. J. C. Shorrocks; 2/Lt. E. Jones; 2/Lt. W. G. M. Rigby. **Third Row** Lt. Campbell (R.A.M.C.); 2/Lt. F. A. Heys; 2/Lt. L. Ryden; 2/Lt. F. G. MacAlpine; 2/Lt. F. Birtwistle; Lt. T. J. Kenny; 2/Lt. T. Y. Harwood; 2/Lt. M. E. Whittaker; 2/Lt. J. H. Ruttle; Lt. H. D. Riley. **Front Row** Hon. Capt. and Q.M.G. Lay; Capt. W. H. Cheney; Capt. H. Livesey; Capt. R. Ross; Major G. N. Slinger; The Mayor, John Harwood, J.P.; Col. R. Sharples; Capt. J. C. Milton; Capt. P. J. Broadley; Capt. A. G. Watson; Lt. A. Peltzer.

Above: No. 7 Section, Blackburn Detachment, outside the Drill Hall, Accrington, February 1915.

58

the long-awaited announcement. He knew, he told them, they were anxious to leave the town and go into training elsewhere. "Now, he could say they were going, in a week's time, to one of the brightest places on God's earth, Caernarvon! (Cheers) 'The Battalion, at the suggestion of Colonel Sharples, agreed to march through the centre of the town to give the townspeople an opportunity to see how well they looked.' "[28]

A departure as early as February 23rd meant farewell parties had to be quickly organised. Chorley Company had two. At the first, a tea and concert, Milton (now Major) presented on the men's behalf a leather travelling bag, with initials embossed, to Miss Knight. The second, in the Town Hall with the Mayor, the Town Council and many local employers and dignitaries present, was a more formal affair. In an evening of speeches in which the keynote was patriotism and devotion to duty, Milton, in keeping with his theme of spending War Office money in the town, said £742 12s. 2d had been spent with local tradesmen. He had also paid £5,276 8s. 9d in pay and allowances. Every single item of the Company's equipment had been bought and paid for locally. He saw this as a small reward for the way Chorley treated them. The *Chorley Weekly News* commented, "The good wishes of the whole community will go with the Pals, the hope being they will remem-

ber the eyes of their native town are on them at all times."[29]

Smaller townships bade their own farewells. Alderman Whittaker (Lt. Whittaker's uncle) and Mr. J.H. Rawcliffe J.P. (Lt. Rawcliffe's father) entertained the Clayton-le-Moors members of the Battalion to a tea and concert in the village Mechanics Institute, and each man received a pipe and an ounce of tobacco. Similar presentations took place in clubs, churches and chapels up to the eve of departure. Eight members of Oswaldtwistle Conservative Club received a hundred cigarettes each. Nine members at Rishton Conservative Club each got a pipe and tobacco and a khaki handkerchief with the flags of the Allies printed on them in colour. In Accrington, at Whalley Road Primitive Methodist Chapel, Ptes. Passmore, Proctor and Glover each received a Bible. "One would have thought the Pals were to sail straight for France and the trenches such was the fuss and palaver. Churches were crowded for valedictory services, at which sermons concentrated with extraordinary Christian unity on the dangers to the soldiers morals, rather than his life."[30]

The official arrangements for Tuesday, February 23rd were for 'A' and 'B' company to leave Accrington at 9.15 a.m. 'E' Company and the Blackburn Detachment at 10.15 a.m. First parade 6.30 a.m. on Ellison's Tenement to transport

Below: 'A' (Accrington), 'B' (District) and 'E' (Reserve) Companies paraded in the St. John Ambulance Drill Hall for official photographs before leaving for Caernarvon (now Caernarfon) on February 23rd, 1915. Below are 3 and 4 Platoons 'A' (Accrington) Company.

ACCRINGTON BATTALION.
East Lancashire Regiment.
Every officer, non-commissioned officer, and man should see next Saturday's "Observer," with splendid photogravure group of the officers.

Accrington Observer & Times

OUR NEW SEASON'S
CANTERBURY (N.Z.) LA:
HAS ARRIVED.
Ours is the first consignment
England for 1915.
ARGENTA MEAT Co., L
3, MARKET PLACE,
Accrington.   Tel. 276.

No. 3,308. Established—"TIMES" 1866. "OBSERVER" 1887. AMALGAMATED 1892. TUESDAY, FEBRUARY 23, 1915. REGISTERED AT THE GENERAL POST OFFICE AS A NEWSPAPER. One Halfpenny.

The "Pals" Departure.

THIS MORNING'S SEND-OFF.

ACCRINGTON'S "AU REVOIR."

Full List of Officers and Men.

Amid the hearty good wishes and "Godspeed" of the whole community, the men of the Accrington and District "Pals" Battalion leave to-day (Tuesday) morning for their new training quarters at Carnarvon.

As is stated in fuller detail in to-day's "Observations" column, the first train leaves Accrington at 9-15 a.m., and the second at 10-15 a.m. The first contingent will parade at the Accrington tram shed at 8-15 a.m., and march to the station, and the second contingent will leave in ample time for the later train.

The Burnley and Chorley companies will travel by a third special train leaving Burnley at 11 a.m. and Chorley at 12-5 p.m.

The Battalion will no doubt be given a most enthusiastic send-off. It is stated that of the mills are to suspend work until the departure of the "Pals," and many will be glad to avail themselves of opportunity to show their admiration for rington's Own," and to participate in neral "au revoir."

OFFICERS AND MEN.

COMPLETE LIST OF NAMES.

following is a full list of officers, non-commissioned officers and men of the is "Battalion, to use the official title, (Service) Battalion, East Lancashire ment:—

OFFICERS.

Colonel R. Sharples, V.D. (in command)
Major G. N. Slinger (Acting Adjutant).

(full regimental name lists continue across multiple columns for A Company, B Company, C Company, D Company and E Company)

AFTER THE CHURCH PARADE.

Accrington "Pals" Battalion on the Market Ground on Sunday, after the Church Parade to St. John's, Accrington.

SECTIONS OF THE ACCRINGTON "PALS"

(Photos, G. Howarth.)

CALLED AWAY.

[BY BARNLEY RIGG.]

They're going you, going to leave us;
that speed them on their way.
A smarter lot of soldiers
no man saw for many a day.

TO THE PALS—"AU REVOIR."

[The Mayor, addressing the "Pals," said he would bid them au revoir, but not good-bye.]

Au revoir. How shall we say it?
Shall dark forebodings, shadowy forms of fears yet unborn,
And hope and dauntless courage strive,
And so bedim the sight,
That o'er the plain of battle's gloom
We see not the dawn of light?

Au revoir. How do we say it?
When the storms fiend rides the seas in rage
And gd ships beckon help? Then, courage high,
Which needs the less, and which the more,
To battle in the lifeboat, or to wait
And watch upon the shore?

Au revoir. No women's tears or men's grief voice can hide nor pride.
With the calm of steadfast purpose
And strengthened heart and arm, we part.
Sturdy sons of battle they, and wistful watchers we,
Shall join the world's triumphant song
Of Freedom—yet more free.
1915.   E. VEEVERS.

luggage etc., to the railway station, then breakfast at home and parade again at 8.30 a.m. At 9 a.m. headed by Slinger (now Major) and a fox terrier mascot, 'A' and 'B' Companies marched to the station. En-route, the crowds, lined six or seven deep, were surprised and disappointed to see there was no band. Several of the men taking matters into their own hands, started playing 'Tipperary' on concertinas or mouth organs. The march rapidly became more informal as men responded to the cheering crowds and shook the hands of friends. At least one man broke ranks, kissed his child and returned to his place. On the station approach mounted police forced a way through the crowd for the men to reach the station platform.

Promptly at 9.15, 'A' and 'B' Companies left for Caernarvon, the men leaning out of the carriage windows to return the farewells of the crowd and Harwoods civic party. At Church and Oswaldtwistle station, half a mile up the line, crowds, including school children given the morning off, waved Union Jacks and cheered them on their way. An hour later the second

Top: 1 and 2 Platoons 'A' (Accrington) Company.
Below: Two Platoons of 'B' (District) Company.

Above: 'C' (Chorley) Company on parade in the Territorial Army Drill Hall, Devonshire Road, Chorley in February, 1915. Col. Sharples, Commanding Officer, on extreme left front row.
L.L. Chorley District

train drew away to more farewells. After its departure the crowds waited in vain as it turned out for the advertised march of a second contingent not realising they had watched the whole contingent march past at 9 a.m. A misleading newspaper announcement had caused the crowd to believe that the two contingents would march separately to the station. The good humour of the crowd helped compensate for the disorganised manner of the leave-taking. "The event smacked of a public holiday. Many of the workshops and mills granted leave of absence, at other large works the employees took matters into their own hands and left without consent. It was a striking tribute to the Battalion that such a large crowd (estimated at 15,000) should assemble."[31]

Burnley fared far better. At 10 a.m. the Company, led by Ross (now Major) and the bugles and drums of the T.A. Depot Company marched from the Barracks to the Town Hall. In the first civic recognition of the Company, the Deputy Mayor, Alderman Keighley, said "Burnley is proud of those who have volunteered to serve their King and Country in this hour of greatest need. I congratulate you on your smart appearance and wish you every success."[32] The formalities over, the Company marched through crowded streets to the railway station. They were given a 'good send-off' by the people and in true Burnley Company style they responded. "Plenty of cheers and tears and most of the men felt a fondness for their smoky old town for the first time. They sang cheerfully along

Standish Street, but why it was 'Wash me in the water that you washed your dirty daughter', is past understanding. There were songs more appropriate, but there is no accounting for taste."[33] As the train drew away many men had mixed feelings, although good to be away, many left families to a world of anxiety and uncertainty.

As the crowds in Accrington finally dispersed and those in Burnley gathered outside the Town Hall, the Chorley Company attended their private civic send-off in the T.A. Drill Hall. It was a celebration almost, the Chorley North Lancs Band played light music, and good humour abounded. The Mayor, in his speech, spoke inevitably, about his concern for their welfare away from home, then Mr. R. E. Stanton, a local businessman, in a mock-serious ceremony, formally presented to Milton a small terrier as a Company mascot. Milton, calling the dog Ned, after its donor, promised on behalf of his men to be 'kind to the pet.' He then called for 'three cheers' for the Mayor and Corporation of Chorley, followed by three cheers, amidst much laughter, for Ned. The Mayor thanked the men, amongst more laughter, on behalf of the dog.

At 11.20 the Company with Lt. Rigby and Ned at its head, marched to the railway station to the music of the Chorley North Lancs band. Although cold and wintry, with a light snow drifting down onto an overnight fall, crowds lined both sides of the route. Many in the crowd recollected it was fifteen years to the day since active service volunteers from Chorley had left for the South African war. All those men came safely home. It seemed a good omen. At the station a large crowd, including children excused from school, watched the Company march onto the platform. As they waited, the men, in a carnival mood, sang songs to entertain the crowd. The train, carrying Burnley Company, arrived at 11.50. Five minutes later, to the cheers of the crowd, to the sound of fog detonators on the line and the strains of 'Auld Lang Syne,' Chorley Company left for Caernarvon.

In Accrington the recriminations started, letters to the newpapers complained bitterly about the missing band and charged that its absence devalued the men and disgraced the town. All the local bands quickly pointed out they had always offered their services free for route marches, parades, etc., and each time were turned down by Colonel Sharples. For his own reasons he kept to his 'no bands' policy on February 23rd. He might have reconsidered if he had known how deeply local people were affected that morning and in the days to follow. The controversy soon fizzled out, the Pals were gone and life had to continue.

The three towns settled back to normal life. All knew Caernarvon, in billets, did not compare with the trenches, but it did mean a step nearer active service and the Front.

Left: 2/Lt. W. G. M. Rigby, accompanied by Ned the mascot, leads 'C' (Chorley) Company up Chapel Street, Chorley, on the way to the railway station en-route to Caernarvon on February 23rd, 1915.
L.L. Chorley District
Below: 'C' (Chorley) Company marching along Chapel Steet, Chorley on their way to the railway station, February 23rd, 1915. Note the light snow fall on the ground.
L.L. Chorley District

Above: Wives and dependents are now eligible for a separation allowance of 17/6d (87p) per week. Here wives in Burnley queue in the rain for their allowance books.
L.L. Burnley District

Right: 'C' (Chorley) Company on the march to the railway station (see preceding pages).

NOTES

1. A New Army Battalion consisted of four companies, 250 strong. Each company divided into four platoons, each platoon into four sections. The Battalion was commanded by a lieutenant-Colonel, with a Major as Second-in-Command. An Adjutant (Major) was responsible for administration, food, clothing, etc., Each company was commanded by a Major, assisted by a Captain; each platoon by a subaltern (Second Lieutenant) assisted by a Sergeant; each section by a Sergeant or Corporal assisted by a Lance Corporal.
2. See WO 163/44/M63 + M22 P.R.O.
3. Blue melton cloth, the traditional material for policemen's, firemen's and tram-driver's etc., uniforms was in plentiful supply compared to khaki cloth.
4. Accrington Gazette (Hereafter A.G.) 12/9/14.
5. As a youth R.S.M. Stanton served with the U.S. Army in General Custer's campaigns against the Sioux Indians. Later, in the Connaught Rangers he fought in the Zulu and South African Wars. He retired as C.S.M. in 1905. He died on March 2nd, 1915.
6. A.G. 26/9/14.
7. A.O. 3/10/14.
8. Infantry Training (4 Company Organisation) General Staff. War Office, H.M.S.O. 1914 Page 1.
9. The Kitchener Armies Page 141.
10. Typical examples include:- H. Livesey, Blackburn engineering firm director (Harwood was Chairman of the Company); A. Peltzer, the son of Howard and Bulloughs Company Secretary; A.B. Tough, the son of Accrington Medical Officer of Health; W.R. Roberts, M.D.; H.D. Riley, secretary and founder of Burnley Lads Club and J.P.; J.Ramsbottom, son of a leading building contractor; H. Bury, son of a Church chemical manufacturer and J.P.; T. Harwood, grandson of Captain Harwood; F.G. MacAlpine son of Sir George MacAlpine, colliery and brickworks owner, past Mayor and J.P.; J. Heys, son of a Burnley cotton manufacturer and J.P.
11. History of Z Company Page 2.
12. Ibid Page 2.
13. Ibid Page 3.
14. B.N. 21/11/14.
15. History of Z Company Page 4.
16. A.O.T. 28/11/14.
17. Genesis, Chapter XIII Verse 8 'and Abram said unto Lot, Let there be no strife, I pray thee, between me and thee, and between my Lordsman and thy herdsman, for we be brethren'.
18. C.G. 21/11/14.
19. C.G. 28/11/14.
20. Hansard, 5th Series, Volume LXIX, 10/2/15.
21. A.O.T. 15/12/14.
22. B.N. 28/11/14.
23. History of 'Z' Company Page 4.
24. The 24th (Service) Battalion, Manchester Regiment (Oldham Pals), 11th (Service) Battalion, South Lancashire Regiment (St. Helens Pals) and the 11th (Service) Battalion, Border Regiment, (The Lonsdales) made up the rest of 112th Brigade.
25. B.E. 30/12/14.
26. A.O.T. 21/11/14.
27. C.G. 6/2/15.
28. A.G. 20/2/15 (N.B. Modern spelling Caernarfon).
29. C.W.N. 20/2/15.
30. History of the Accrington Pals Page 30.
31. A.O.T. 27/2/15.
32. B.N. 24/2/15.
33. History of 'Z' Company Page 6.

Chapter Three

Croeso i Gymru! Welcome to Wales!

Four days before Harwood announced the departure of the Battalion to Wales, Mr. R. O. Roberts, Town Clerk of Caernarvon received a telegram from Western Command Headquarters, Chester.[1] This requested him to find accommodation, as soon as possible, in hotels, boarding houses and private homes for 36 officers and 1350 men of the 11th (Accrington) Service Battalion, East Lancs Regiment. One exhausting week later, on February 18th, the Town Clerk reported to Western Command that his staff, helped by Captains Broadley and Peltzer (who had arrived during the week), had completed a billeting canvass with accommodation guaranteed for the Battalion.[2]

Caernarvon townspeople heard the news with pleasure and relief. They had been badly affected by the decline in the slate industry, now here was a chance of an income by keeping soldiers, if only for a few weeks. Up to that time Caernarvon had been the only North Wales resort not full of troops. Since December, 1914 three Infantry Brigades of Lloyd George's Welsh Army Corps had been billeted in the neighbouring and rival resorts of Llandudno,

Rhyl and Colwyn Bay.[3] Caernarvon felt particularly pleased that its troops were from the East Lancashire Regiment, for they were already a familiar sight in the town. The week before the outbreak of war, the 5th East Lancashire Territorials, of which 'E' Company came from Clayton-le-Moors, and 'F' Company from Accrington, attended their annual camp at Coed Helen, across the River Seiont from the town. They had been in camp just one week before being recalled home. Also for the townspeople, a full Battalion in billets was a vast improvement financially, over Territorials in a tented camp.

So with pleasant expectancy the Mayor, Town Council, the Town Clerk, and a large crowd, were at the station to greet three trains bearing the Battalion. The Pals were in holiday mood singing and cheering, as the carriages pulled in late in the afternoon of Tuesday, February 23rd, 1915. Intermittent showers of snow and sleet, falling on a layer of overnight snow, ensured the briefest of civic welcomes before the men of each company, led by special constables, marched off to their billets. In accordance with the Town Clerk's instructions to land-

"After much embracing between husbands and wives, mothers and sons sisters and brothers we were bound for Caernarvon. Things were awfully lively in our compartment, due I suppose to the free intoxicants, which had been freely offered to the departing Pals. Therefore time passed very quickly, and in the afternoon we were being dismissed to our respective billets. Straight at the bottom of this street. i.e. marked by a cross, is where we were billeted."
J. Bridge

Right: The party on the photo were billeted together. Back row: Sgt. Folan; L/Cpl. Secker; C.S.M. Hey; Cpl. Hodgson. Middle row: L/Cpl. Ashworth; Cpl. Cassidy. Front, Sgt. Bridge.
J. Bridge

Far right: Officers from Accrington pose on the steps of the Officers Mess, the Royal Hotel, Caernarvon.

ladies, a hot meal awaited the men.

In the wintriest of conditions, 'A' company assembled in Bangor Road, just off Castle Square.

"The specials, with an officer, took men from each platoon off to billets. Sixteen, including my friend Pte. Place went to a large boarding house. they were lucky there. The owners had a lovely daughter! (Later, I used to call to see if the lads were going out, but I couldn't get them away from the place!) Pte. McGoughlin and myself went two doors away to the finest confectioners in Caernarvon. We were lucky as well. To get to our room we went through the shop, past trays of pies and cakes. We could just put our hands in and help ourselves. It was marvellous! We were always hungry." Pte. Pollard.

Others fared less well. Pte. Marshall billeted in a house with several others, "It was so crowded we slept two to a bed. The landlady was a mean, miserable woman and the food was poor. We posted lookouts and raided the larder when she was out." Contrary to the War Office regulation, 'bed for each man,' many men shared double beds. In less than two hours all the men were settled in, the officers' horses stabled, the officers' Mess established in the Royal Hotel, and Battalion H.Q., set up in Caerau, Church Street.

Once settled in many immediately wrote home.

Letters and postcards were delivered in hundreds of East and Central Lancashire homes in the days following. On February 25th, the Mayor of Chorley read a letter from Major Milton to the Town Council meeting, "My Dear Mayor, you will be glad to know we arrived safely and all are very comfortable the puppy Ned is very happy and is already quite the Regimental pet." After thanking the Mayor again for the civic farewell, Milton promised to keep him 'posted of our doings' and enclosed a book of views of Caernarvon.[4]

The *Observer and Times* was equally concerned to keep its readers informed of the Battalion's 'doings' and conversely the Battalion was anxious to hear news from home. Caernarvon newagents soon received plentiful supplies of the newpaper and it appointed a 'Caernarvon Correspondent.' He first interviewed Major Slinger, who sent a formal message on behalf of the Accrington Companies thanking the town for the generous treatment received whilst training and also for the hearty send-off on February 23rd. He ended, "It is the wish of all ranks to do credit to the Mayor, the district from which they emanate and to their King and Country."[5] Other reports were less formal. Pte. Johnson of 'B' Company wrote to Councillor Whittaker, "Caernarvon is a home from home but we can't get used to the 'twang.' They keep saying we must learn Welsh, but I don't think we could if we stayed here forever. Tell everyone the Clayton Pals are the liveliest in Caernarvon and keep looking after our wives and daughters!"[6] (A reference to a promise made at the farewell party on February 20th).

Carnarvon from Eagle Tower

On Wednesday morning, February 24th, hundreds watched the Battalion parade in Castle Square. For the first time in the Battalion's existence all five companies were together, the scene made more memorable by the impressive backdrop of Caernarvon Castle, the sea, and the distant mountains of Snowdonia. The contrast to the smoky atmosphere of Ellisons Tenement and the streets of Burnley and Chorley could not be greater. For Major Ross came the honour of taking the first Battalion drill in the five month life of the Battalion.[7]

In the afternoon, the separate companies went on route marches as an introduction to the Welsh countryside. It seemed, apart from the scenery and the novelty of billets, things were to continue much as before. Another novelty was the guard duty in Caernarvon Castle. Pte. Snailham went on guard the first night.

"It was the first guard I ever did in the Army. For me, a seventeen year old, it was an exciting experience. We looked out from the Castle towards the sea in the darkness watching out for the German submarines which were rumoured to be in the Menai Strait. We took it very seriously, of course, but however hard we tried we never saw any!"

On Saturday, Major (temporary Lieutenant-Colonel) A. W. Rickman, arrived to take command of the Battalion from the acting Commanding Officer, Major Slinger. Colonel Sharples, then sixty five years old, had quietly and without fuss, just started the customary twenty six days leave prior to retirement.

A professional soldier, Rickman rejoined the 3rd (Special Reserve) Battalion, Northumberland Fusiliers on August 4th, 1914. On February 20th, 1915 he was posted to the General Base Depot, Southampton, as Adjutant. Six days later, he was appointed Commanding Officer of the 11th East Lancs, to join them immediately. The day after he arrived in Caernarvon, on Monday March 1st (St. Davids' Day) another memorable day for the Battalion, he introduced himself to his new command on Battalion parade in Castle Square.

Lt. Rawcliffe watched from his position in front of his platoon in 'B' Company.

"I'll never forget that day. We were brought up to attention as Colonel Rickman rode up the street towards us. He had to pass a motor-lorry parked outside a shop. This narrowed the street and his horse shied. We all thought it was going through the shop window, Colonel Rickman beat the horse hard with his stick (it wasn't a riding-crop, but an ash walking-stick) to make

"This is Castle Square where we paraded each day — as our Commanding Officer we received Lt. Col. Rickman and after a short period under his command the Battalion underwent a considerable change. Officers and men realised we now had a 'head' — this being easily discernible to anyone who saw us on parade."
J. Bridge

Below: Caernarvon Castle

67

Above: 'D' (Burnley) Company on parade in Castle Square, Caernarvon on the morning of the takeover by Lt. Col. Rickman on March 1st, 1915. The Battalion was later given the day off.
Below: Lt. Col. A. W. Rickman. His horse 'Ben' remained with him on active service throughout the war. Only he could handle the horse.

it pass the motor-lorry. We saw a real display of strength and will-power. What an entrance! I thought, we're in for it now!"

1,380 pairs of eyes were on Rickman and his horse. His entry into their lives left a never to be forgotten impression. Pte. Pollard remembered:

"We were all in our blue uniforms. Our new C.O., came on parade riding a hunter. It was wild and skittish, rearing up on its hind legs but he kept it under control. He was very smart, a true professional. We were looking at a real soldier for the first time. We knew he would sort us out."

It seemed to some cynics the hunter reared on its hind legs only when Rickman wished it. If Rickman intended to impress with his horsemanship and determination he succeeded. It left a lasting effect.[8]

Other lessons were learnt that day. Pte. Marshall:

"The Colonel noticed a young soldier who happened to have his belt on upside down, and had him brought to the front of the parade. This sort of thing was unheard of before. After that his mates made sure the lad was properly dressed before going on parade."

Nevertheless, the new Colonel had other qualities. After his inspection he gave the N.C.O.'s and men the day off.

Rickman quickly initiated several changes. Major Slinger again became Second in Command. Captain Peltzer became Adjutant. Companies 'A', 'B', 'C', 'D' and 'E' became 'W', 'X', 'Y', 'Z' and 'R'. One platoon of the Blackburn Detachment transferred to 'Y' Company, the second to 'Z' Company. This brought both Companies to full strength. He ordered buglers each day to sound the various calls, 'Dismiss,' 'Standfast,' 'Alarm,' 'Charge' and 'Continue,' 'because you must be conversant with these before you cross the water.' 'Reveille' sounded to awaken the men for the 6.45 parade. It is doubtful whether the people of Caernarvon appreciated bugle calls in the streets in the early hours of every morning. The battalion pace of life sharpened, discipline appeared. The training programme became more rigorous with Swedish Drill (Physical Training) from 6.45 a.m. until 8 a.m., then breakfast, with a second parade at 9.15 a.m. followed by training until 12.30 p.m. Training continued from 2.15 p.m. until 5.30 p.m.

Although not unexpected, the men took some time to get used to the new regime. Pte. Will Cowell of 'Y' Company, wrote to his wife, "The weather is grand here, but they are starting to put us through it. We do as much before breakfast as we did all day in Chorley."[9] Pte. Earl Whittaker of 'Z' Company, told his sister, "We will not do so much dodging here as we have got a new Colonel and he is very 'strick' " (sic).[10] As some compensation for his 'strickness,' Rickman stopped Saturday parades and encouraged all kinds of sports particularly cricket, football and cross-country running. He also let it be known, as some already knew to their cost, that he frowned on heavy drinking. This programme of 'work hard — play hard' established Rickman as a competent and fair-minded commander in the Battalion's eyes.

Caernarvon Town Council, as concerned as others about the Battalion's moral and spiritual welfare, arranged for the Glanymor Mission Hall of the Moriah Chapel to be available for sing-songs and smoking concerts, etc. The Council's Pavilion Assembly Rooms at the Battery were also made ready, and the Guild Hall opened for Sunday evening concerts for the troops. Independently many chapels and churches, Welsh and English speaking, prepared to entertain the men with concerts both sacred and secular. The Y.M.C.A. in Bangor Street provided writing materials, books, magazines and newspapers free, with tea, coffee, cakes and biscuits provided by the Ladies Auxiliary at a small charge.

On Saturday, February 27th, hundreds of the men attended their first social event in the Pavilion a flag day and fete in aid of the National Fund for Welsh Troops, a movement initiated by Mrs. Lloyd George.[11] A dance held in the evening attracted many more. It was, of course, the first Saturday since leaving home. The fears for the men's morals, once away from Church, Chapel and family were becoming more real. On February 21st, at a valedictory service at St. John's C. of E. Accrington, the Revd. Wilkinson had made an impassioned appeal to his congregation. "When away from home in Caernarvon you will come in contact with dangers of which you will have been barely aware there is, particularly amongst younger women and girls, a fascination for the soldier. This hero worship, for such it is, brings them confidently to your side. Do not take advantage of them. Let them retain a noble opinion of the British soldier, both as a gentleman and a hero."[12] For many soldiers from Accrington and

district this dance seemed a good opportunity to test the Revd. Wilkinson's assumptions.

Weekly church parades for seven hundred 'C. of E.'s' and three hundred Roman Catholics began at once. Non-conformists went as individuals to the English Wesleyan Chapel or the numerous Welsh chapels. At the latter, for the benefit of the newcomers, services were partly in

Left: Pte. Earl Whittaker and his family.
Below: Lt. Col. A. W. Rickman of the Northumberland Fusiliers. With the exception of short breaks when he was wounded (twice) and temporary secondments to Brigade, he was to command the Battalion throughout the war.

"During my stay in
Caernarvon I had a few good
motor trips with my friends.
The day I took this we had a
beautiful run through the
Pass of Llanberis through
Betws y Coed to Llandudno.
Had tea there then on to
Conway and here I took the
photograph. If this was part of
soldiering there would be no
occasion for conscription, but
it is not — worst luck."
J. Bridge

English. The friendly response and co-operation of the men to such welcoming gestures set the scene for the remainder of the stay in Caernarvon.

Sport also became a social event and as early as March 1st a Battalion boxing tournament in the Pavilion attracted hundreds of local people. The star attraction Pte. 'Kid' Nutter,[13] beat an out-classed Pte. Baker in the third round of a six round contest. Football matches between Officers and N.C.O.'s, between Companies, and between an 'X' Company team and Caernarvon F.C., entertained large crowds. Company and platoon billiard teams played teams from social and political clubs. Roller-hockey became the vogue. A Battalion team beat a Caernarvon team 3-2 at the Pavilion. Unfortunately for the Battalion sporting reputation, crowds gathered to watch a challenge race on roller-skates between a local man and a member of 'X' Company, left disappointed when the latter failed to turn up.

The men were more successful as artistes and entertainers, they quickly gained a reputation for their singing and musical talents. They provided much of their own entertainment at Glanymor Mission Hall, Castle Square Chapel and the Y.M.C.A., which soon became the most popular meeting place, where nightly sing-songs were accompanied inevitably by the concertina. These sing-songs, together with the more formal weekly concerts, were arranged and compered by Pte. Tom Coady.[14] From the day the Battalion arrived Pte. Coady and Mr. Isaac Edwards, President of the Y.M.C.A. entered into a partnership which ensued the success of the Battalion's social life in Caernarvon. Here Pte. Coady formed the Battalion Concert Party and Glee Club. Both, with Edwards' help gave regular concerts in the town and in local hospitals. These concerts along with the sporting events, created a warm relationship between Caernarvon and the Battalion remembered with pleasure in the years to come.

There were other interests, one of these being the sea front. For some the only previous sight of the ocean had been on occasional Sunday School outings to Blackpool or Morecambe. Some men found it pleasurable to walk along the Slate Quay to watch the boats enter and leave the harbour, while others tried their hands at fishing or rowing. The antics of the amateur rowers were watched with alarm by the locals. The Vicar of Christ Church, whilst commending the general behaviour of the men, said, "We cannot praise the rowing of the East Lancs. The specimens we have seen as oarsmen are more suited to ornamental ponds than the sea."[15]

A 10 p.m. curfew formed part of Rickman's new strictures. The curfew, plus his known response to heavy drinking, undoubtedly helped men to keep fairly sober. But there were others with an eye on the Battalion. At the North Wales Temperance Federation Executive meeting in Bangor, the Caernarvon delegate reported, "the East Lancs' behaviour was excellent, with drunkeness very rare."[16] Another, somewhat dubious, compliment came from a Caernarvon Congregationalist minister. From his pulpit he declared, "I doubt very much if there is another class of people with so few drunken wastrels as these Lancashire Pals."[17]

Not all was amity, however. A Pal wrote anonymously to the Caernarvon and Denbigh Herald, "Will you allow me to protest against the snobbishness of people who have warned their girls not to be seen talking to a soldier? We have sisters ourselves and we resent the evil-minded insinuations." The editor commented, "Perhaps the complaint is well founded.

Below: Pte Tom Coady

Some girls do go dizzy at the sight of a uniform, but some Caernarvon people, as the correspondent says, are intolerably snobbish."[18]

A week later Isaac Edwards endorsed the newspaper's guarded agreement when the letter became the subject of debate at a meeting of the Wales Division of the Y.M.C.A. He asked the meeting to discourage any deprecating of the association of girls with soldiers. He believed if men were treated honourably they would react honourably to whosoever they met. There is no record of the audiences reaction but some Caernarvon girls doubtless continued to go 'dizzy,' and some soldiers continued to be pleased that they did.

Caernarvon's social life notwithstanding, the Battalion's main purpose was to progress from the Company training it began in Accrington, Burnley and Chorley. Rickman followed up the new energies he had infused into the men and immediately started an intensive programme of battalion training. After morning parade on Castle Square each day, the Companies marched a quarter of a mile to the 52 acre field of Coed Helen (recently rented by the War Office for £105 per annum.) With a view over Menai Strait to Anglesey in the west and the mountains of Snowdonia in the east, the training ground was magnificently sited. The fresh sea breezes and the warm spring sunshine were especially invigorating.

The familiar, unending squad, platoon and company drill still continued, with and without rifles. The Training Manual stressed, 'every man should be well grounded in bayonet fighting,' so although with only one rifle between six men bayonet training started. "We constantly practised charging straw-filled sacks suspended from a frame they called it 'killing Gerries.' (Pte. Pollard) Most disliked bayonet practise however. To follow the dictum of a 'a spirit of aggression and alertness' the men constantly and self-consciously charged and 'killed the Gerries.' Although thought a useless exercise by many, in retrospect, bayonet practise did make men quickly and energetically respond to shouted commands. Discipline and smartness visibly improved.

Route marches were taken in the afternoon. Although no longer than they were used to, they were more frequent and in full equipment. The Caernarvon countryside greatly impressed the men, Pte. Pollard particularly.

"It was a world of difference to what we were used to in Accrington. We went through open country, with the hills as a backdrop, and saw pheasants, grouse and plovers, when most of us had only seen ducks before. It was marvellous to go out in it everyday and the distances didn't trouble us."

Officers too were getting tougher. Lt. Rawcliffe:

"'X' Company were on an eight mile march and 2/Lt. Robinson, on horseback, led his platoon. The men, as always, were singing on the march. His platoon chose to sing a ditty with the irreverent refrain of, 'and a little child shall lead them.' Robinson, only

"The place marked with a cross was our training ground. The lads look rare and fit, due no doubt to the healthy air, early morning physical training on the promenade and constant training in the field (see left) which runs parallel to the Menai Straits."
J. Bridge

Coed Helen from Eagle Tower, Carnarvon

Right: Specially printed postcards were for sale in Caernarvon. Left: Posted to his wife Polly by Pte. W. Cowell of Chorley. Right: Posted to his sister, Doris by Pte. S. Rollins of Chorley.

Don't be Alarmed, the Accrington Pals are on guard at Carnarvon.

For gootness sake go back ! Here kom der ACCRINGTON PALS

nineteen and young-looking, said nothing. Back at Coed Helen he asked Captain Broadley, 'X' Company Commander, not to dismiss his platoon. He then turned and said, 'You lot will do another march and a little child shall lead you! He did, another eight miles, on foot this time, of course. The rest of the Company enjoyed the joke and cheered them on their way."[19]

The former easy-going attitude towards field training now gave way to more structural work up to Battalion level. They practised, on Coed Helen and in the open countryside, delivering and receiving infantry assaults, the pursuit, assuming the offensive from the defensive and retirements.[20] To this end men were instructed in reconnoitering and observation by out-post and standing patrols. One N.C.O. and four men from each Company became scouts with specialist skills of map reading, distance judging and compass reading. Another specialist group was the signallers who practised with semaphores on 'moving station' work.[21] This had its own dangers. Moving often meant trespassing on land owned by angry farmers, or being chased by angry bulls.

Instruction in night observation and listening techniques and in orientation prepared the Battalion for night exercises. Some lessons learned in France were beginning to be applied, with a new emphasis on entrenching work. On Coed Helen 'W' Company dug a series of trenches.

At night 'X' Company defended them from attack by 'Y' Company. 'Z' Company later relieved the occupants and thus the exercise was repeated until each Company played a different role.

The entrenching work and exercises, although in conditions far from the front-line horrors of France and Flanders, were the nearest to reality the Battalion experienced in their training at Caernarvon. After November 1914, at the end of the first battle of Ypres (October 12th to November 11th) the mobile war in Belgium and France turned into stalemate with a continuous line of trenches from the Belgian coast to Switzerland. The Battalion was actually taught battle tactics, entrenching apart, which were already obsolete. The Training Manual used by its inexperienced officers and South African War veteran N.C.O.'s alike, clearly stated: "The essential to success in battle is to close with the enemy, cost what it may. The action of infantry must be a constant pressing forward and as the enemy fire is gradually subdued further progress will be made by bounds from place to place until the enemy can be assaulted by bayonet."[22] The Battalion endlessly practised this role in the Welsh countryside never to put it into action in the 'real world' of the Front. They were not alone in this, for many other battalions in Kitchener's Army were engaged in similar training in camps all over Britain.

Rumours of a move for the men began to flourish in Accrington and Caernarvon as early as the middle of March. Two events helped the rumours along. On March 16th, Brigadier General McKenzie formally inspected the Battalion on Castle Square. He pronounced himself pleased with the appearance and bearing of the Battalion. Rickman, no doubt also was pleased at the first test of his command. Three days later the Battalion marched, in full equipment, ten miles to Penrhyn Park, Bangor, for a Brigade inspection. Again, perhaps predictably, McKenzie expressed himself satisfied at what he saw.[23]

Shortly before his inspection, McKenzie informed Harwood by letter of his intention to move 112 Brigade, early in April, to Belton Park Camp, Grantham, Lincolnshire. The 11th East Lancs were to be at full strength of 1,100 all ranks. This news, of course, proved the rumours true. Harwood caught the first train to Caernarvon to spend the next two days with the Battalion, taking his leave of many individual officers and men. On Sunday, March 21st, as guest of honour at a civic concert in the Guild Hall, Harwood spoke generously of Caernarvon's kindness and hospitality, adding tactlessly perhaps, in the presence of Companies from Burnley, Chorley and the smaller townships, of Accrington's debt to Caernarvon 'for taking such good care of its sons.'[24]

Harwood returned home convinced, with everyone else, of the Battalion's imminent departure for Grantham and the Front. A capacity audience at a 'farewell' grand concert in the Guild Hall on April 4th, heard the Caernarvon Choral Society and several of the Battalion give a programme of songs. One man, a light tenor "sang 'The Holy City' as well as any local singer ·could have sung it." This was praise from a town famous for its fine singing.[25]

Meanwhile preparations were made for leaving. Men transferred from the reserve to the regular companies and vice versa. Pte. Cowell, who stayed with 'Y' Company, wrote, "They have been sorting us out here. Those who are not so well up in their drills or those who do not seem strong enough for the Front have to go with the reserve company to Heaton Park, Manchester, for another six months training. Old 'Donnelly' ('Y' Company's ex- regular C.S.M.) is going with them".[26]

The re-organisation, with its transfer of the young and the old, and those 'not so well up in their drills' unsettled many. Groups, closely knit since September 1914, broke up. One could also be a good soldier but too young. Pte. Snailham left 'Y' Company.

"They came round asking our ages. I was just two weeks turned seventeen.I was sent to see the Colonel and he told me I was too young for active service, so into the Reserve I went. I was bitterly disappointed."

Pte. Pollard 'got away with it'.

"The sergeant said, 'How old are you, Pollard?' I looked him in the eye and said, 'Twenty,' I wasn't seventeen until July, so I stayed where I was."

Many of the veteran N.C.O.'s (Donnelly et al) went into 'R' Company to continue training recruits. An advance party of twenty five men went to Grantham on April 6th only to return the following day with the report that the camp was not ready and unfit for habitation. The leaving preparations came to a halt the farewells had been premature.

This gave Rickman valuable breathing space and so training continued, although as always handicapped by lack of specialist equipment. Rickman, believing it better to get the equipment immediately than wait for a War Office

Left: Posted by Pte. W. Cowell of Chorley (Note the word 'will' added by hand).

C.T.H.

The 11th East Lancs. Will Fight to a Finish"

73

Above: The Signalling Section taken in Caernarvon Castle in May 1915. Pte. O.T. Duerden stands on the extreme left. Fifth from the left is Pte. S. Challen, sixth is Pte. R. Bradshaw. Seated far right is Pte. H. Bury.

Right: Pte. Percy Martin, age 16, of 'W' (Accrington) Company in his newly issued hat and jacket. He is still wearing the blue Melton trousers.

issue, asked Harwood to help. Harwood, unable to provide anything 'on the rates' asked the public for subscriptions.[27] Within two weeks, from donations and the sale of jewelry etc., Rickman received £125, the first of many similar donations.

Other equipment, this time officially issued, arrived. At long last each man received the coveted khaki uniform complete with leather equipment, the blue melton uniform retained as second-best. Enough rifles, although still worn out Lee Metfords, arrived for each man to have his own. The men were delighted, the Front seemed closer than ever. Apart from the 'luxuries' of trench warfare, the non-specialist equipment of the Battalion was complete. With the new equipment and probably because of it, came rumours again of a move to the Front. In the event they were to stay five more weeks.

By now changes were coming quickly. Seven newly gazetted second-lieutenants arrived, the first 'non-locals' in the mess. 2/Lt.'s Haywood and Gidlow-Jackson left on transfer to the R.F.C. and Royal Engineers respectively. Other officers were promoted in a general re-shuffle. As part of this Rickman asked Harwood to raise an extra fifty men in Accrington for 'R' Company. These brought the Battalion again to full complement. Now only nominally the responsibility of the Raiser, the Battalion progressed from its disparate, happy-go-lucky beginnings into a competent, confident unit of Kitchener's Army.

At a second brigade inspection at Penrhyn Park on April 26th, Major General Dickson, Inspector of Infantry gave the news of the Battalion's transfer to 94 Infantry Brigade, 31 Division.[28] This meant a move to Rugeley Camp, Staffordshire in the very near future. On May 10th, orders came to move on Thursday, May 13th, with 'R' Company, Major Slinger in command, to go to Chadderton, near Oldham, on the same day.

With three days to prepare, there was no time for a second civic farewell. A number of dances and social events were hastily arranged for Tuesday and Wednesday evenings. These and Rickman's extension of the curfew until 11 p.m. enabled everyone to make his own sort of public and private farewell. Rickman, for the second time, formally thanked the Mayor and town of Caernarvon for the kindness and hospitality extended to his men. The Mayor, again, assured the Battalion it had Caernarvon's warmest wishes for its future welfare and success.

Home town scenes were repeated as the Battalion left on May 13th. 'W' 'X' and 'Y' Companies paraded in Castle Square at 7.20 a.m. Despite the early hour hundreds of townspeople were present as they, with Rickman at their head, marched to the railway station. The men,

as always on the march, singing popular songs,- interspersed with the chant 'Are we downhearted?' with the shouted answer 'No!'[29] Crowds blocked the station approach, and reminiscent of Accrington, police forced a way for the men to enter. 'Z' Company, led by Major Ross, left Castle Square at 8.30 a.m. before an even larger crowd to the sound of the concertina and mouth-organ playing 'Alexander's Ragtime Band' and 'Tipperary.' Two hours later 'R' Company left for Chadderton. Even as they assembled in Castle Square they sang 'Till we meet again' and as they marched off, many pleased the crowd by shouting 'Good Bye' in Welsh 'Yn Iachffarwel!'

As the flags and handkerchiefs were waved, in the crowd there were girls seeing boyfriends for the last time, some by choice perhaps, certainly some by the fortunes of war. Others awaited their return and marriage.[30] Landladies watched their charges leave for harder billets, many sorry to lose new family friends. As the trains drew out, the Battalion left Caernarvon as it arrived boisterously cheering and singing music hall songs.

Before the Battalion's arrival in February, it

FOUR HAPPY "PALS."

A snapshot of four Accrington "Pals" taken at Carnarvon. They are, left to right: Private Walter Dewhurst, Private Reggie Clayton, Private Fletcher, and Corporal Jackson Hindle.

Below: Lt. Col. Rickman and Adjutant Captain A. Peltzer with the Battalion N.C.O's in Caernarvon Castle, April 1915.

Above: Part of 'Y' (Chorley) Company on parade in Castle Square.
Right: Many friends were made by the Pals whilst they were in Caernarvon. Here Pte. Ernest Kenyon poses with his landlady and her son.

would have not been thought possible that the sojourn of troops would have induced such feelings of affection the townspeople now felt. The outspoken, jovial, rough and ready Lancashire men had quickly endeared themselves to Caernarvon. Town and troops were genuinely sorry to part. As the trains steamed towards the hutted camps of Rugeley and Chadderton the men took the first of many nostalgic looks at their Welsh hosts. In this, and future times, talk often turned to landladies, their 'Welsh Mothers.' Not all stories were complimentary, most concerned food,"How do you like your eggs boiled?' 'One hard, one soft,' the hint was never taken there was always just one egg on the plate." "We're having fish tomorrow,' visions of cod steaks or turbot were dashed by a solitary kipper put before us." 'Mothers' had their own stories — a dish of tinned apricots intended for the second course had been left on the sideboard while two Burnley men were having a stew. When the landlady came in to remove the plates, the dish lay on the table empty. The two Pals said, "Eeh, thanks, Missus, we've never tasted pickles like that in us lives."

Only once did the copybook get seriously blotted. Unreported in Accrington, 15234 Sgt. Edwardson, a South African War veteran, was publicly stripped of his stripes for drunkenness. Several days later, in Caernarvon Magistrates Court he was fined 20/- with costs, for theft of a bicycle.[31] As Pte. Edwardson he was now en-route for Chadderton.

"Well, all good things come to an end and at last we received orders for our move to Rugeley. We paraded on good old Castle Square amid a crowd of people and marched to the station. Major Slinger (now Reserve Company) seemed very upset at leaving the boys with whom he had been connected so long. I could see many a long face at having to leave such comfortable billets."
J. Bridge

Above: 'W' (Accrington) Company prepare to leave.
Below: 'W' (Accrington) Company leave Castle Square for the railway station.

NOTES

1. The municipal borough of Caernarvon, administrative centre of the county of Caernarvon, population (1911 census) 9, 119, was situated at the broader south western end of the Menai Straits. The 13C. Castle, in 1911 scene of the Investiture of Edward, Prince of Wales, dominated the town. By early 1915 decline in the local slate industry caused severe unemployment in the area.

2. War Office regulations decreed men should not be billeted in licenced premises and homes of 'substantial' house holders utilized where possible. Homes in 'poorer' districts were to be avoided. Rates of 3s 4½d (17p) per head, per day were payable. Not every landlady volunteered. Any vacant room was taken.

3. The First Brigade of four battalions of Royal Welsh Fusiliers based at Llandudno; the Second Brigade of four battalions of the Welsh Regiment at Rhyl; the Third Brigade of two battalions, South Wales Borderers and two battalions of the Welsh Regiment at Colwyn Bay. Artillery Brigades were at Pwllheli, Criccieth and Portmadoc.

4. C.G. 27/2/15

5. A.O.T. 27/2/15

6. Ibid

7. One interested spectator, a sixteen year old office boy, William Hamilton-Jones was, in November 1917 as 39369 Pte. Hamilton-Jones, posted to the Battalion in France.

8. Colonel A.W. Rickman was born at Leicester in 1874, son of Lieut. Gen. W. Rickman. Educated at Winchester College, he was gazetted to the Northumberland Fusiliers and served with the 2nd Battalion in the South African War (1899 to 1902). He received the Queen's South Africa Medal (3 clasps) and the King's South Africa Medal (2 clasps). He lived at Alnwick on retired pay (Captain) from March 1909 to August 1914 when he rejoined the 3rd (S.R.) Battalion at Newcastle.

9. Postcard to Mrs. P. Cowell, Chorley.

10. Postcard to Miss A. Whittaker, Burnley.

11. David Lloyd George, Liberal M.P. for Caernarvon since 1890 and Chancellor of the Exchequer in the Asquith Liberal Government of the time. In September 1914 he proposed the recruitment of the Welsh Army Corps, with formal authority given by the Army Councilon October 10th.

12. A.O.T. 23/2/15 and Caernarvon and Denbigh Herald (hereafter C.D.H.) 26/2/15.
N.B. 9th December, 1985, the organ at St. John the Evangelist's Church, Accrington, was dismantled for sale to a church in Australia. On a wooden panel near the old manual bellows was found to be inscribed, in indelible pencil, 'Pals in church 21st February 1915'. Underneath, in a different hand was written, 'Toke (sic) in action at Sir (sic) July 1st 1916. Heavy casualtys (sic).'

13. Pte. Harry 'Kid' Nutter, 'X' Company, of Rishton, age 18, an ex-miner, was a well known bantam weight boxer in Lancashire. He had fought Jimmy Wilde, the 'Welsh Wizard', to a draw over twenty rounds.

14. Pte. Tom Coady, 'R' Company, of Oswaldtwistle, age 33, an ex-dental mechanic. He was a popular singer and comedian in Accrington and district before the war, best known for his impersonations of George Formby, Senior, a music hall favourite.

15. Christ Church Monthly Magazine, March 1915, quoted in C.D.H.12/3/15 and B.E. 17/3/15

16. C.D.H. 26/3/15

17. Quoted in C.G. 27/3/15

18. C.D.H. 19/3/15

19. See Isaiah Chapter 11, Verse 6

20. See Infantry Training Manual, Section 10

21. Outpost patrols sent out to obtain information and return quickly. Standing patrols remained in one place and observed the enemy. Moving station work a group in a fixed station (H.Q.) with a second group a mile and a half distant signalling by semaphore. After each message the group moves on and signals again.

22. See Infantry Training Manual, Section 121

23. Not all 112 Brigade were present. Although the 11th South Lancs and the 24th Manchester Regiment were billeted nearby in Bangor and Llanfairfechan repectively, the 11th Border Regiment were still at Blackhall Racecourse, Carlisle.

24. A.O.T. 27/3/15

25. C.D.H. 9/4/15

26. Postcard to Mrs. Cowell, Chorley.

27. A.O.T. 10/4/15 Letter: 'To the Editor, The O.C. desirous of having the Battalion fully trained before proceeding to the Firing Line, has written to me as Raiser, asking for the following: Four Mekometers (Range Finders); one set Armourers tools; eight periscopes; one electric lamp and signalling buzzer; one field telephone; sixteen pairs of binoculars; ten Morris Tubes; sixty four police whistles. Estimated value 100 to 125. The O.C. thinks it will be better for the Battalion if they learned the uses of the above at once for this purpose I will be glad to receive subscriptions J. Harwood (Mayor)'.

28. In April 1915 the original Fifth New Army (37 42 Divisions) became the Fourth New Army, its Divisions re-numbered 30 35. (See Army Council Instruction 96, April 1915). The 11th East Lancs was one of several Battalions transferred to other Divisions. They joined the 12th (Service) York and Lancaster Regiment (Sheffield City), then based at Redmires, Sheffield; 13th (Service) York and Lancaster Regiment (1st Barnsley) and the 14th Service York and Lancaster Regiment (2nd Barnsley), both based at Silkstone, Barnsley, in 94 Brigade.

29. A catch-phrase made popular by Shaun Grenville, a noted comedian and music-hall artist (1884-1968)

30. As far as is known four men returned to marry local girls. One, Pte. J. Walton of Burnley, married Miss Mollie Owens, secretary of the Y.M.C.A. Ladies Auxiliary.

31. C.D.H. 30/4/15

Right: The advance party which went to Grantham on April 6th, 1915 only to return to Caernarvon the following day.
A. O. & T.

The above is a special snapshot taken in the Accrington "Pals'" new lines at Belton Park, Grantham, and is of the advance party preparing for the arrival of the Battalion. The group includes (left to right)—on the ground—Privates C. Glover, J. Baron and C. Harling. Second row (seated)—Sergt. Lang, Privates Gibbons, Barton, Bates and B. Dean. Third row (standing)—Sergt. Kay, Privates R. Almond, W. Whittington, Lance-Corpl. Ashley, Sergt. Swallow, Privates Shackleton, G. Clayton, H. Bower, Pioneer-Sergt. Hughes and Sergt. Lyons. Top row—Privates R. Baxter, Needle, Ratcliffe, G. Yates and Horsfield. The men, who were snapshotted before one of the hutments, all hail from Accrington and immediate district.

Chapter Four

Some Battalion! Some Colonel!

In August 1914, only 175,000 men could be accommodated in military barracks. By December 1914, over a million had enlisted and accommodation problems became acute. 800,000 men were housed in hired buildings and billets and mustering men from billets scattered over wide areas, as in Caernarvon, was irksome and inefficient for training at Battalion strength and impossible at Brigade and Division. In the winter of 1914 and the spring of 1915, therefore, dozens of hutted camps were hastily erected throughout the British Isles, each camp designed to house an Infantry Division (18,000 men).

In addition to new camps in the established military encampments of Aldershot, Catterick and Salisbury Plain large open spaces in non-military areas were used, e.g. near Ripon, Yorkshire; Kinmel Park, North Wales and Prees Heath, Shropshire. Two others, Rugeley and Brocton Camps, were on adjacent sites on Cannock Chase, the ancient Royal hunting forest in Staffordshire. Rugeley Camp's first occupants were the newly formed 94 Brigade, 31 Division.[1]

Moving in on May 12th, 1915, the advance party of the 11th East Lancs. Battalion found, as at Grantham, nothing ready. Many huts were roofless with no lights and no water within half a mile. With a dozen or so civilian joiners to help them, the advance party laboured a day and a night to make the thirty-man huts, the offices, stores and stables at least habitable. In the afternoon of May 13th, after a four and a half mile march from Rugeley station in pouring rain, the Battalion arrived to a welcoming lit coke-stove in each completed hut — and little else. At 8 p.m. the men ate a supper — the only meal of the day — of corned beef, bread and butter. Their tea, with neither sugar nor milk, was drunk from basins, jugs and whatever could be borrowed or stolen. Beds were just a straw palliasse on a board and trestles, with three blankets. The ablutions were in the open air, the camp a sea of mud, and chaos reigned supreme. The pleasures and comforts of Caernarvon were already but a dream. The realities of army life had begun.

Fine weather and drying winds quickly made camp life more bearable. Fatigue parties spent the first weeks improving roads, paths, and the water supply. Rugeley Camp and the Battalion along with it, rapidly took shape. Together as a unit for the first time since its formation, the Battalion specialist groups were organised. The regimental police, the transport, medical and

"We had been marching about an hour, but it seemed more like a day, when we saw 'Hutments'. It might have been land in the middle of the ocean by the way the lads stared at it. We arrived absolutely wet through and we anticipated a drink of hot tea but alas nothing doing. It was the first taste we had of camp life and I can assure you it was a bitter pill to swallow."
J. Bridge
Below: Men of 'Z' (Burnley) Company at Rugeley Camp. Note the civilian workmen.

Above: A group of 'Z' (Burnley) Company at Rugeley Camp. Of these men five were killed or died of wounds and seven wounded on July 1st, 1916.

Right: Pte. J. Walton (second left, standing) of 'Z' (Burnley) Company with friends at Rugeley Camp.

THE Z C II⁵ E.L.

Above: No. 7 Hut 'Z' (Burnley) Company. Cpl. Holt (first right standing) in charge. Pte. Davy is third right standing.

sanitary sections came into being. Regimental cobblers and tailors were busy. The cookhouse, most important of all in most men's eyes, started from scratch.

Men volunteered, or if necessary were appointed as Sergeant Cooks, past experience not essential. Sgt. Clegg of 'W' Company, an ex-weaver, volunteered. Sgt. Kay of 'Z' Company, the motor-cycling corporal of early Burnley days did not. With the benefit of a short course in cookery they had the task of providing meals for hundreds of men. Their efforts were not always appreciated. "Some believed Sgt. Kay's mind was still concentrated on internal combustion engines — but he was the persevering type and when one considers the cooks he had, it is a wonder anyone survived to tell the tale."[2]

Others, including Pte. Marshall, took matters much more seriously. "Things were badly organised. Trouble started one day when we were very short of food. Some of us in 'Z' Company refused to parade at dinner-time in protest. We were then given a good meal. Later we were paraded and given a long lecture by the C.O. He told us we could have been shot for disobeying orders. A voice from the rear rank said, 'Tha cor'nt do thad, tha'd shoot all your best sowdgers!' With that, the matter ended."[3]

The social and sporting activities of the Battalion continued. Pte. Coady, now in 'W' Company, with A.Q.M.S. Jack Hindle of Accrington, re-formed the Concert Party and Glee Club. A regimental Institute opened, with gifts of books

and games from Burnley townspeople. Inter-Company football matches began. The Battalion football team (seven of whom were Burnley Lads Club members) with great pleasure consistently defeated the Yorkshiremen of the three York and Lancaster Battalions in the Brigade. Pte. Birch of 'X' Company whilst on home leave (fifty per Company per week) borrowed 'for the duration' the instruments of a local comic band. He re-formed the band on the returning train. The Battalion first knew of the existence of the 'Pals Comic Band' when it marched into camp at 2.30 a.m. playing 'The Bluebells of Scotland.'[4]

Training continued Caernarvon style — still limited by lack of specialist equipment — with Brigade exercises confined to continual route-marches. In the hot, dry, early summer of 1915, these tested the fortitude of many. As training progressed there were operational changes. On May 18th, the Battalion formally transferred from Western Command to join the three York and Lancaster Battalions in Northern Command.

Training intensified after the transfer. With no ammunition for the rifles, the bayonet remained the main weapon. The battalion learned how to form section, to advance and deploy in section, then push home a mock attack against one of the York and Lancaster battalions with the bayonet. At night the exercise was complicated by the total darkness on the open lands of Cannock Chase. Exercises often ended in total confusion as even sections lost touch with each other.

"Here we received our Brigade training. Route marching with the fullest of real training and at the finish moment, including attack and defence manoeuvres all along the moors. With so many troops passing over the heather the dust rose in clouds and when the lads returned they were covered in dirt. The lads settled down to real training and at the finish they became to somewhat like Rugeley Camp."
J. Bridge
Rugeley Camp, 1915.

Right and centre: General views. **Below:** Parade ground and offices.

The battalion helped build an assault course made up of a series of belts of barbed wire and low hurdles. With the bayonet at the ready the men charged down the course, bridging the barbed wire with planks. After clearing the hurdles they charged and bayoneted 'Gerry' — still a bag of sawdust. Although the enemy had changed these were still the tactics of the South African War.

Three weeks after the transfer, on May 31st, every available man paraded for the acceptance of the Battalion by the War Office. The Army Ordnance Department first closely inspected the camp, equipment, clothing, stores etc. of the Battalion. The 'camp-correspondent' of the Accrington Gazette later described the acceptance ceremony. "All the officers and men were on parade, and after expressing his satisfaction in all he had seen, and with the smart appearance and bearing of the men, the War Office representative ceremoniously walked down the lines and touched one man in each platoon on the shoulder, thus formally claiming them as soldiers of His Majesty the King."[5] From that moment Harwood became officially free of the responsibilities, however nominal by then, as Raiser of the Battalion.

These developments convinced the men they were fit to go to the front. News also of a War Office request to Harwood, although not now officially connected with the Battalion, to raise a second reserve company of 250 men, convinced the men they were to go.[6] Ever since the formation of the reserve company in December 1914, there had been a common belief in the Battalion they would need a second reserve company before the Battalion went abroad. With this news the men were convinced and many wrote home, prematurely, for what they thought was the last time.[7] In spite of their own beliefs however, the men needed more training before they were fit for active service — their time at the front was yet to come.

With the Battalion an official part of the New Army, Rickman continued his efforts to make 'his' Battalion at least the best in 94 Brigade. Although tolerant of the 'Comic Band' for its entertainment value, he knew, as a regular soldier, a Regimental Band would be a more dignified acquisition. A good Band would be a prestigious possession, a morale booster and an entertainer. At the sugestion of Sgt. Ashmead of 'W' Company, a well known local bandsman and instructor to the Battalion's buglers, Rickman contacted Harwood and within days a com-

Above: The Rt. Hon. David Lloyd George. In July 1915 he became Minister of Munitions. B.C.P.L.
Below: 'The Comic Band'. Men of 'X' (District) Company dressed in the uniform of 'The Village Pirate Band'.

'W' (Accrington) Company at Rugeley Camp.

Top left: Company officers. Left to right: Lt. T. Y. Harwood, Capt. A. G. Watson, 2/Lt. H. Ashworth, Capt. H. Livesey and 2/Lt. H. Brabin.

Top right: Orderly Room staff. Back row left to right: L/Cpl. Haywood, Sgt. J. Bridge. Front row: L/Cpl. Jackson, Cpl. Aspinall and Sgt. Hodgson.

Above left: Pte. C. Glover (second right) with friends.

Right: Pte. V. Wardleworth (second right) with friends.

Below: A more formal group including Pte. Harry Wilkinson (second left back row) and Pte. W. Clarke (fourth from left front row).

plete set of instruments, some new, some borrowed from Howard and Bulloughs Works Band, were provided by Sir George MacAlpine, and a group of anonymous donors.[8]

Twenty serving ex-bandsmen were anxious to join, with no lack of volunteers to fill the remaining places. Sgt. Ashmead, as an ex-Territorial skilled marksman, unfortunately was almost immediately posted to the School of Musketry, Hythe, as an instructor. Rickman therefore invited Mr. 'Joe' Whitworth of Chorley, to be his bandmaster, with the honorary rank of Lieutenant.[9] After a little practice, the 11th East Lancs Regimental Band, the only band in the Brigade, proudly led the Battalion on the next Brigade route-march. "One moment it seems Col. Rickman was lamenting he had no band; almost immediately afterwards he had a band leading his men on the march."[10]

Such developments firmly established the Battalion as a tightly knit unit. Men extended their loyalties from 'their' Company to 'their' Battalion and 'their" Commanding Officer. Brigade exercises and sports promoted a friendly inter-battalion rivalry and a loyalty to 'their' Brigade.

As the Battalion improved in confidence and effectiveness, some thought the label 'Pals' gave an impression of 'Saturday afternoon soldiers' and so should be dropped, but most disagreed. Kitchener 'Pals' battalions, as a whole, had already gained themselves a good reputation. In contrast to the 'happy-go-lucky' impression of some, the Kitchener volunteers were turning out to be of a surprisingly high quality.[11] For the 11th East Lancs. admittedly, compared to conditions at the front, the happy-go-lucky impression may have been reinforced by the mixture of training and recreations at Rugeley Camp as Rickman continued his policy of using as much sport as possible to supplement training.

Left: 'W' (Accrington) Company at Rugeley Camp. A variety of headgear is a feature of this group. Pte. C. Glover stands first left.
Below: Sgt. J. Rigby stands in the doorway. Pte. H. Bloor is second left back row.

'Z' (Burnley) Company at Rugeley Camp.

Right: The group includes Pte. J. Power (with arms folded front row) and Pte. L. Bentley (in doorway, left, with monkey on his shoulder). Pte. Bentley wrote to the Burnley News on May 29th, 1915 requesting help in obtaining a replacement for the monkey when it was accidentally killed.

Centre: Sgt. A. K. Entwistle (second night middle row) with some of his men.

Below: Names not known. A chalked sign on the hut side states 'Sweeny Todd, Barber. Rag-time or slow time. Next Please 2/6d (12p) each. Boston Barred.

On May 14th, 1915 after the British setbacks at the battle of Festubert the shortage of shells on the Western Front had been revealed to the public.[12] The resulting 'shell scandal' contributed to the fall of the Asquith Liberal government on May 17th.[13] David Lloyd George became Minister for Munitions in the new Coalition Government, with his first task to re-organise the munitions industry to meet the demands of the war. Already the one fifth of male workers in engineering serving in the forces meant a major shortage of skilled labour.

The 11th East Lancs had many such skilled engineers in its ranks. Most were ex-employees of Howard and Bulloughs who enlisted when the works closed in September 1914. In July 1915, many of these were interviewed by Ministry of Munitions inspectors under the 'Bulk Release Scheme' and returned to Howard and Bulloughs as munition workers.[14] Others, as on July 12th, 1915, were drafted in small batches, direct to shipyards in the North East. At least 150 men, mostly from 'W' and 'X' Companies, left the Battalion under this Scheme.

In Accrington meanwhile, Harwood attempted to recruit a second reserve company. A detachment of fifty men from Chadderton, with the band of the 10th (Service) Lancashire Fusiliers, toured the area 'buttonholing every young man they met.' They had little success. In one disappointing week they enlisted just twenty-nine men — a sharp contrast to the heady weeks of September 1914.[15] Clearly a second full scale recruiting campaign to get the second reserve company and also replace those lost to munitions work was urgently needed. The opportunity soon came.

As early as the first week in June, Rickman had been endeavouring to move the Battalion to South Camp, Ripon, in the West Riding of

Yorkshire, for a musketry course. He intended to march the Battalion from Ripon to East Lancashire, accompanied by the band, over a period of eight or nine days and then recruit

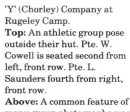

'Y' (Chorley) Company at Rugeley Camp.
Top: An athletic group pose outside their hut. Pte. W. Cowell is seated second from left, front row. Pte. L. Saunders fourth from right, front row.
Above: A common feature of many group photographs was the symbols of kitchen fatigues. Pte. L. Saunders (in shirt) stands in the doorway.
Left: A similar group with Pte. S. Rollins third from right back row.
J. Garwood

Right: A group of the Reserve Company at Chadderton Park Camp, near Oldham, Lancashire. After the recruitment of the second Reserve Company to replace those released for munitions work in the summer of 1915 they became the 12th (Reserve) Battalion. Note the mascot — the seven-year-old son of a Sergeant.

Centre: A group of 'X' (District) Company. Back row: Cpl. Duckworth, Ptes. J. Grimshaw, E. Kenyon and C. Hindle. (brother of J. Hindle, see front cover photo). Front row: Ptes. E. Culley, L. Kenyon and J. Hindle. Of this group one was killed in action on 20th June, 1916 and one on 23rd June, 1916. Two were killed in action and three wounded on 1st July, 1916.

Below: Blank postcards as kept by Pte. W. Cowell of 'Y' (Chorley) Company.

"Time passed on and I at last heard we were about to make a move. I remember quite well parading at 3.30 a.m. one morning and marching to Rugeley Station. It developed into a beautiful morning and the lads were awfully jolly at the prospect of marching through Accrington again. People were peeping from behind the blinds, it being too early for them to be up"
J. Bridge

I am Thinking of You at Rugeley

RUGELEY CAMP.

There's an isolated, desolated spot I'd like to mention,
Where all you hear is "stand at ease," "quick march,"
"slope arms," "attention."
It's miles away from anywhere, by Jove, it is a rum un,
A man lived there for 50 years and never saw a woman,
There's lots of tiny huts all dotted here and there,
For those who live inside them I have offered many a
prayer ;
It's mud up to your eyebrows, it gets into your ears,
But into it you have to go without a sign of fear ;
There's soldiers living in the huts, it fills my heart with
sorrow,
With tear-dimmed eyes they say to me, its "Rugeley
Camp" to-morrow.
Inside the huts live rats, they say as big as any goat,
Last night a Soldier saw one " trying on his overcoat."
For breakfast every morning it is just like mother
Hubbard,
You "double " round the hut three times and dive into
the cupboard.
Sometimes they give you Bacon, sometimes they give
you Cheese,
Which "marches" up and down your plate, "slope,
arms " and "stands at ease."
At night you sleep on straw and boards, just like a herd
of cattle,
And if perchance you should turn round, your bones
begin to rattle,
And when you hear "Reveille" blown, it makes you feel
unwell,
You knock the Icebergs off your feet and wish the Bugler
in Hell,
Now when the War is over, and we've captured Kaiser
Billy,
To shoot him would be merciful and absolutely silly,
Just send him up to "Rugeley Camp" among the rats
and clay,
And let the Crown Prince watch him as he slowly
fades away.

in the area for a few more days. Authority for the move did not arrive until mid-July so the idea had to be dropped. The campaign, therefore, had to be conducted on the way to Ripon, not from it. With this intention the Battalion left Rugeley at 4.20 a.m. on July 30th, by train to Chorley. With them travelled Pte. Joseph Bell, who only four weeks before returned as Cpl. Bell from Accrington under escort, absent without leave.[16]

At Chorley, the Mayor, delighted Chorley was the first home town to welcome the full Battalion, accorded the men 'a right hearty Lancashire welcome' at a civic reception. With Lancashire candour he asked Rickman to take back with him "the shirkers on the street-corners" and asked the Battalion to "do its utmost to get the war over as soon as possible — we are all miserable and want it to end." He then asked Rickman to give Chorley Company a day's holiday "when it is convenient."[17] The next morning the Battalion marched seven miles to the Royal Lancashire Agricultural Show at Witton, near Blackburn. Here, as the main event of the day, they gave a drill display. Lt. Rawcliffe, newly promoted, led his platoon in a display of Swedish Drill (Physical Training). After an hour or so of entertaining and being entertained, they marched two miles into Blackburn and were allocated to billets for the overnight stay. Pte. Pollard and others, succumbed to the temptations of home.

"It was a beautifully sunny Saturday afternoon. After we were dismissed in Blackburn, we Accrington lads strolled on the Boulevard (the main tram terminus in front of the railway station) for a while, just to let the girls look at us, you know, and then caught the tram to Accrington and home. We came back to Blackburn the following day, then marched back to Accrington. The whole town turned out to see us".

The whole town did indeed turn out. An estimated eighteen thousand lined the streets as John Harwood took the salute at the march-past in front of the town hall, the Battalion back in its 'home' town for the first and only time as a complete unit and for the first time in khaki. Six months training and discipline had made a tremendous improvement in their bearing, physique and self-esteem. They were proud in their belief that they were one of the best of the 'Kitchener' battalions and considered themselves the equal of any in the British Army. With the same old spirit they sang the same old songs. "It brought blushes to the faces of the young ladies out walking with their fellows when the massive choir blasted forth, 'Hello, Hello, Who's your lady-friend? Who's the little girlie by your side?' as they passed by on the road"[18].

The Battalion stayed three days in Accrington

Above: 'Y' (Chorley) Company in Commercial Street, Chorley on the recruiting visit on August 1st, 1915.
L. L. Chorley District.
Left: Major Milton and 'Y' (Chorley) Company in Coronation Park, Chorley. Note the mascot dog lying down.
Below: The Mayor of Burnley, Ald. Sellers Kay, addressing the parade on the recruiting visit to Burnley on August 4th, 1915.
Over page (left): The recruiting advert in the Accrington Observer & Times, July 1915.
Over page (right): A family snap of Pte. A. S. Edwards (fourth from left) as 'Z' (Burnley) Company march through Accrington on the recruiting visit.

G. R.

Accrington "Pals" Battalion.

(11th Service Batt. E. L. Regt.)

War Office has sent orders for the 6th Depot Company (Reserve) of

250 MEN TO BE RAISED AT ONCE.

It is hoped that Accrington and Burnley boys will fill up the ranks as soon as possible.

Recruits accepted at any Recruiting Office.

Height from 5ft. 2in., and chest measurement from 34 inches.   Age, 19 to 40.

Full Army Allowances, including Separation Allowances to families.

Khaki Uniforms and full Kits provided on joining Reserve Companies at Chadderton Camp.

RALLY ROUND THE FLAG.

GOD SAVE THE KING.

for a programme of recruiting marches, drill displays and evening band concerts in the local parks. At a dinner given by Harwood and his associates for Rickman and his officers, Rickman spoke of his gratitude that he, a stranger who had never even been to Lancashire, had been supported so loyally by his Lancashire troops. He was very moved by his acceptance by the men, by his reception in the town and 'absolutely astonished' by the great number of people who had greeted them so warmly. This reception given to Rickman by the town, more than anything else, helped turn a formal association into a deep and lasting friendship sustained throughout the long, hard years of the war.

At Burnley, the civic reception committee were delighted the Battalion should visit the town on the first anniversary of Britain's entry into the war. The enthusiasms of Chorley and Accrington were repeated as the Battalion entered the town. Several thousands watched as the Mayor welcomed them in the Market Square, the jealousies and apathy of September 1914

long forgotten. The speeches ended with the Mayor's hope that the Battalion would enjoy itself in its evening in Burnley (free tickets to the Empire Theatre were available) and the men again were allocated billets. Once again scores of 'we Accrington Lads' decided to forgo that pleasure, and went again absent without leave, back home. The following day Thursday, August 5th, 1915 the Battalion reached South Camp, Ripon.

As a public relations exercise the Battalion's visit home was a triumph. As a recruiting drive it was an abject failure. In Chorley just four joined the Battalion from a total of eleven of the Mayor's 'shirkers' who enlisted that week. In Accrington, Rickman admitted results 'had not been good'. Time and events had faded the euphoric enthusiasms of 1914. Since then the Territorial Battalions of Chorley, Blackburn and Burnley had suffered the disasters of Festubert and Gallipoli.[19] Local military hospitals were overcrowded with the wounded of France and Belgium. Alarming letters from survivors of heavy fighting filled the newspapers. War-time restrictions, food shortages and higher prices were beginning to add to the problem of poverty. The shell-scandal, with Harold Baker's involvement, affected public morale and convinced many the war was going badly wrong.

The demand for munition workers, with their high wages, for a war which was not going to end for some time, also affected recruiting. Old style recruiting marches seeking out 'likely young men' in a crowd watching a parade could not compete with the Munitions Work Bureau, which in Accrington during the Battalion's re-

cruiting visit, enrolled a hundred workers. Also those already in employment, particularly in the cotton-mills, were loth to enlist because employers in 1915 would not assure them of their jobs after the war.[20] It remained also that those with good health, patriotism and a sense of adventure had already enlisted for Harwood in 1914.

Twelve months later however, Harwood's ability and experience were still required by the war Office, as they made clear in their formal letter of thanks for raising the Battalion. The opening compliments were somewhat diminished by the broad hint of his continuing responsibility to provide recruits.[21]

By that time, recruiting had become a national and a political matter. In October 1915, as a

Top: The scene in Accrington as the Pals were dismissed from parade on August 2nd.

Above: John Harwood, Mayor of Accrington and raiser of the Battalion takes the salute from Lt. Col. Rickman as the Pals march past the Town Hall.

"We dismissed on the market square, and permitted to go to our homes, a privilege much admired. On Monday we had to parade for a route march through the District, i.e. Rishton, Great Harwood and Clayton-le-Moors, but I received orders that I, along with Sgt. Kay, had to proceed to Ripon that afternoon. Three o'clock saw myself in the side-car of Sgt. Kay's motor-bike speeding along to Ripon."
J. Bridge

starting to lie outside the range of the Battalion's military duties, the men settled down at Ripon.

Ripon, the ancient market town between the Vale of York and the hills and pastures of Nidderdale and Wensleydale, in 1915 became a military town, with its normal population of 7,000 swollen to 47,000. South Camp was one of several on the town's outskirts. In contrast to Rugeley, the sun shone on the Battalion as it arrived, the huts were electrically lit, the recreation rooms, stores, stables and offices, etc., ready for use. The men looked forward to an enjoyable stay in what many believed to be the finest scenery in the North of England.[22]

Men were again allowed leave, and the return to military life came harder for some than others. Pte. H. Riley of Clayton-le-Moors, Ptes. Tom Winchester, Jack O'Connor and William Pye of Church, Pte. John Winter of Accrington and Pte. Thomas Iddon of Chorley, needed to be brought back under escort. In Rickman's farewell speech in Accrington, he spoke proudly of there being only one man absent from the final Battalion parade. Pte. Iddon was that man. Whilst absent without leave, Pte. Iddon had been drunk and disorderly (damaging a policeman's uniform) and fined 14/- 'for a disgraceful exhibition for a man in uniform.' There is unfortunately no record of how he fared before his inevitable appearance before Col. Rickman.

Returning home from Burnley had its difficulties. Pte. Marshall started the journey with a group.

last attempt to make a voluntary system work, Lord Derby introduced a scheme by which men of military age 'attested' their willingness to serve when called upon. The scheme failed, therefore in January 1916, Asquith introduced conscription for single men, followed in May by universal conscription. So, as recruiting was

Left: Members of 'W' (Accrington) Company have tea at South Camp, Ripon. Below: 'W' (Accrington) Company practice aiming on the rifle range at Wormold Green.

"Some of the lads went for a drink when we changed trains. They missed their connection so were late back to camp. They told the Company Commander they were returning for the train when a band on the station played, 'God Save the King', and as they stood to attention, the train left without them! The Company Commander didn't believe them, of course, but they got away with a reprimand."

It became fashionable for relatives to visit the camp at weekends as Ripon lay only about three hours by train from East Lancashire. Pte. Glover's father, from Accrington, more fortunate than most, could visit both his sons — Clarrie at Ripon, and Willie, ten miles away at Masham with the 158 (Accrington and Burnley) Howitzer Brigade in 34 Division.[23] L/Cpl. Bradshaw's father described Sunday afternoons at South Camp, "The whole area is crowded with visitors. The huts are comfortable and clean and the situation is dry and healthy."[24] Not all agreed. Pte. Marshall:- 'Our huts were crawling with earwigs. We all slept with our cap-comforters on for protection.'

Apart from this, most men remembered their eight weeks at Ripon with pleasure. 'W' and 'X' Companies 'christened' a brand new rifle range at Bishop Monkton, four miles away. They were able to relax, walking in the countryside or swimming in the River Ure, as the other Companies fired their part of the course. 'Y' and 'Z' Companies in their turn then relaxed as the other two Companies fired the next course, and so life went on for all. The complete firing course on ranges with targets at 100 yards to 600 yards took four weeks. Everyone, officers,

N.C.O.'s, cooks, sanitary men, etc. became proficient to some degree. Col Rickman, who also fired, considered the course results with their high percentage of first class shots — as very satisfactory indeed. The results were remarkable as the rifles were worn-out Lee Metfords. Most men enjoyed the course for they found it individually more satisfying than trench-digging and bayonet-charging dummy 'Gerries.' The results were so consistently good there was more

93

"We were usually on parade by 4.30 a.m. and marched to the range, usually returning about 5.30 p.m. Rations were issued in the field; to which I did full justice, although the tea was always smoked, which I understand is quite unavoidable."
J. Bridge

Below: Captain H. D. Riley leads his men of 'Z' (Burnley) Company on the march through Ripon on the way to the rifle range.

than a suspicion of a 'fiddle'. After all, in a 'bulls-eye' a pencil made the same sized hole as a bullet. No one cared very much — the results were too good for morale.

The Battalion was taking shape. The transport section became fully equipped with the delivery of forty four mules for drawing the new field kitchens and ammunition wagons. The unbroken mules were a problem from the beginning. Six hundred arrived by rail at Ripon. Men from 34 Division (also based at Ripon) unloaded them only to find they were for 31 Division. Minutes later another train load of six hundred mules arrived for 34 Division. In a station yard full of squealing, kicking mules, Lt. Bury, O.C. Battalion Transport, and his men, selected their forty four mules from the confused mass and got them back to camp. Lt. Rawcliffe watched them arrive—and leave.

"Poor Harry Bury! Mules are fractious beasts at the best of times, but these were devils. They were no sooner in the compound, when they broke out and headed for the open countryside. They scattered in every direction, with Harry and his men after them! Some went up to four miles away. It took days to round them up again. It was hilarious for us of course — we hadn't to catch them!"

By the Summer of 1915 the Battalion was used to inspections by the 'top-brass' but two at Ripon gave Rickman particular pleasure. On August 11th, Major Gen. Sir A. Murray K.C.B., D.S.O., Deputy Chief of the Imperial General Staff, told Rickman "I have inspected tens of thousands of troops in Kitchener's Army but I have never seen a smarter, better turned out Battalion. A great deal of trouble has been taken and I am delighted."[25] Rickman, understandably, shared his pleasure in Battalion Orders, that, 'We are some battalion.' A few days later Major Gen. R. Wanless O'Gowan, G.O.C., 31 Division, added to the Battalion's high opinion of itself when he told them he, as an ex-East Lancashire man (he had served with the 1st Battalion) had expected them to be smart and they had exceeded his expectations.

These compliments specially pleased Rickman. On his responsibility alone, he at forty one, a comparitively young Commanding Officer, had to bring the Battalion to active service standards. He achieved much in his six months without the help of a single officer or N.C.O. with recent battle experience, although he was not to know that the 'active service standards' were unrealistic for trench warfare.

Rickman's responsibilities did not distance him

from his men, his reputation for kind hearted autocracy being enhanced on the day of the G.O.C.'s inspection. Pte. Fisher was eighteen. "We had just come off parade and a telegram awaited me at the Company Office. My mother had died, I was only a lad and was in tears. The C.O. came in, very stern and formidable, and to my utter surprise, said very softly, 'My boy, try to compose yourself.' He then turned to the Sergeant and literally roared, 'Take that man's name and send him home immediately!"

After the G.O.C.'s inspection, 31 Division prepared to move to Salisbury Plain, always considered a staging post for the Front. With 94 Brigade the first to go, the Battalion immediately got one week's home leave. Smarter, fitter, better nourished than the 'Harwood's Babes' of the year before, men in their hundreds visited the photographic studios of East Lancashire, some alone, some with friends, some with wife and children for the final 'keepsake to remember me by.' An air of finality spread — this was 'it' — the 'Pals' were going to the Front. In an effort to supply the Battalion with appropriate material, a thousand sand-bags were hurriedly made by the officer's wives or girlfriends of the Pals Comforts Committee. "The process of daubing the sand-bags with irregular patches of green and brown, said to render them invisible to the enemy, was not undertaken by the ladies, however."[26]

By a sad coincidence, as Accrington streets were crowded with men on leave, two of the reserve company died from illness.[27] As leaves ended there came sadness also to many homes. This time no cheering thousands 'saw the Pals off' as they caught the special trains to Ripon. The crowds round the station approach were subdued and tearful as families and friends bade their farewells. Many were convinced that their men were bound for Gallipoli to share the fate of the Territorials.

On Friday evening, September 24th, the Battalion left Ripon for Hurdcott Camp, Salisbury Plain. After an uncomfortable twelve hour train journey, via Sheffield, Leicester (tea served at 3 a.m.) and Cheltenham, they reached Wilton at 8.30 a.m. A five mile march in pouring rain on roads ankle deep in mud brought them to yet another new hutted camp — Rugeley all over again, with Ripon but a dream. The camp stood unfinished, with no lights, no tables to dine on, no cookhouse, the ground a quagmire — and bloody miles from anywhere.'

Hurdcott Camp lay on the southern edge of Salisbury Plain, seven miles from the Cathedral city of Salisbury. The nearby villages of Burford St. Martin, Fovant and the town of Wilton had few recreational facilities. In the event, the men had little free time to visit these places as the Battalion entered its busiest phase so far. Almost at once brand new Short Magazine Lee-Enfield rifles and Lewis light machine guns were issued. Equipment for signallers, bombers and medical staff appeared. It became clear the previous slow pace of life caused by lack of materials and equipment was to be made up by intensive training. Now that almost all equipment had arrived the military organisation and structure of the Battalion was complete.

Pte. Sayer of 'Z' Company, now one of 16 bombers in the Company, described a typical day at Hurdcott for the specialists.

"Early morning cup of tea and a biscuit was followed by physical training in loose dress. After a good breakfast, 9 o'clock 'fall

"We started on our march to camp wondering what sort of a place we were going to now. It was a weary march after travelling all night. The mud was ankle deep but we arrived about noon quite ready for a good feed. The camp was a new one and therefore very clean."
J. Bridge

Below: L/Cpl. Brigg's permanent pass.

Left: A wounded veteran of the front pays a visit to friends in the Blackburn Detachment at Hurdcott Camp.

(ORDERLY ROOM STAMP.)

11th (SER.) BATTALION
EAST LANCASHIRE REGT.

Letter "W" or

Captain......................Company.

PERMANENT PASS.

No...
has permission to be absent from his
Quarters from............till................
except when on duty.

Recommended.................................
Comdg "W" Company

....
Comdg .11th (Ser.) Bn. East Lancashire Regt.
.........................191

Gale & Polden, Ltd. Aldershot. 2070-w. REGD. PASS.

Above: 31 Division Sports Day on October 21st, 1915. Here the 'Pals' cross-country run team, mostly Burnley Lad's Club members, line up for the start.

Far right: A card posted to Miss Ada Woods from 'Will' (surname unknown) November 1915.

in,' had everyone on parade. Col. Rickman was a stickler for discipline and transgressors were 'for it.' Specialists marched off to their own jobs and the Bandsmen became stretcher-bearers. The Sanitary Squad enjoyed their buckets and spades. The Water-Cart team — what they did nobody really knew and were best left alone with their tanks of water and tins of chloride of lime. The Lewis-gunners and signallers were rather high-brow — they were 'brainworkers' and dignity was the acquisition. In contrast were we burly Bombers, housed in two separate huts, whether for our own welfare or the peace of mind of the rest is not known. The Police under 'Ow'd Nick' were near the general factotums, the Pioneers. Hidden away in nooks and crannies were the Officers servants, Mess waiters, Grooms, Cobblers, Tailors, Orderly Room staff and sometimes Detention men and Prisoners. Dinner was usually a big meal, then training until tea at five. Then the evening off unless there were manoeuvres or guard duty."*

Although the Battalion Concert Party and Glee Club entertained in the Y.M.C.A., and the Regimental Band gave regular concerts, inter-Battalion and inter-Brigade sporting rivalries were still encouraged. The tempo of training contrasted greatly with anything before. Manoeuvres and field exercises came before all else as 31 Division made its final preparations for active service in the last four months of 1915.

New, tough, instructors fresh from the trenches of France appeared and training became more relevant to battle conditions. Crowded days were spent digging trenches and laying barbed wire. The bombers practised clearing 'enemy' trenches with the new Mills bomb. Lewis gunners learned just how many different ways a Lewis gun could jam in action (reputed to be twenty seven). Battalion, Brigade and Divisional manoeuvres tested the organisational skills of transport, cook-house and signal sections. Ten days training at Hurdcott contrasted completely with the same period at Rugeley (see Appendix 2 (b)). 'Bloody miles from anywhere' or not, after a strenuous day in the field Hurdcott felt like home to everyone.

A Soldier's Letter to his SWEETHEART.

From ....

At FOVANT.

✚✚✚✚✚✚✚✚✚✚✚✚✚✚✚✚✚✚
MIZPAH.
✚✚✚✚✚✚✚✚✚✚✚✚✚✚✚✚✚✚

" May the LORD watch between thee and me when we are absent one from another "

Sweetheart, when the day's work is over,
 And from drilling I am free;
Sitting alone on the hillside,
 My thoughts are ALL of thee.
I'm not much good with a pen, dear,
 For the gun is now my line;
So I send you *Fond Love* by this Postcard,
 As I thought perhaps you might pine.
When Old England's Cry for soldiers,
 Sounded through our dear homeland;
'Twas Duty's Call—and I obeyed it,
 I *knew* that *you* would understand.
As I sit here fondly dreaming,
 I picture your sweet dear face;
Helping, cheering on the weary,
 Round about the dear old place.
Our " Boys " are doing well, dear,
 And it's "rumoured" we're soon to go;
With your sweet face to cheer me,
 I will bravely meet the foe.
Thoughts of *YOU* come flocking to me,
 Gives me bliss—without alloy;
Looking forward to a future,
 Peaceful future—full of joy.   *Copyright.*

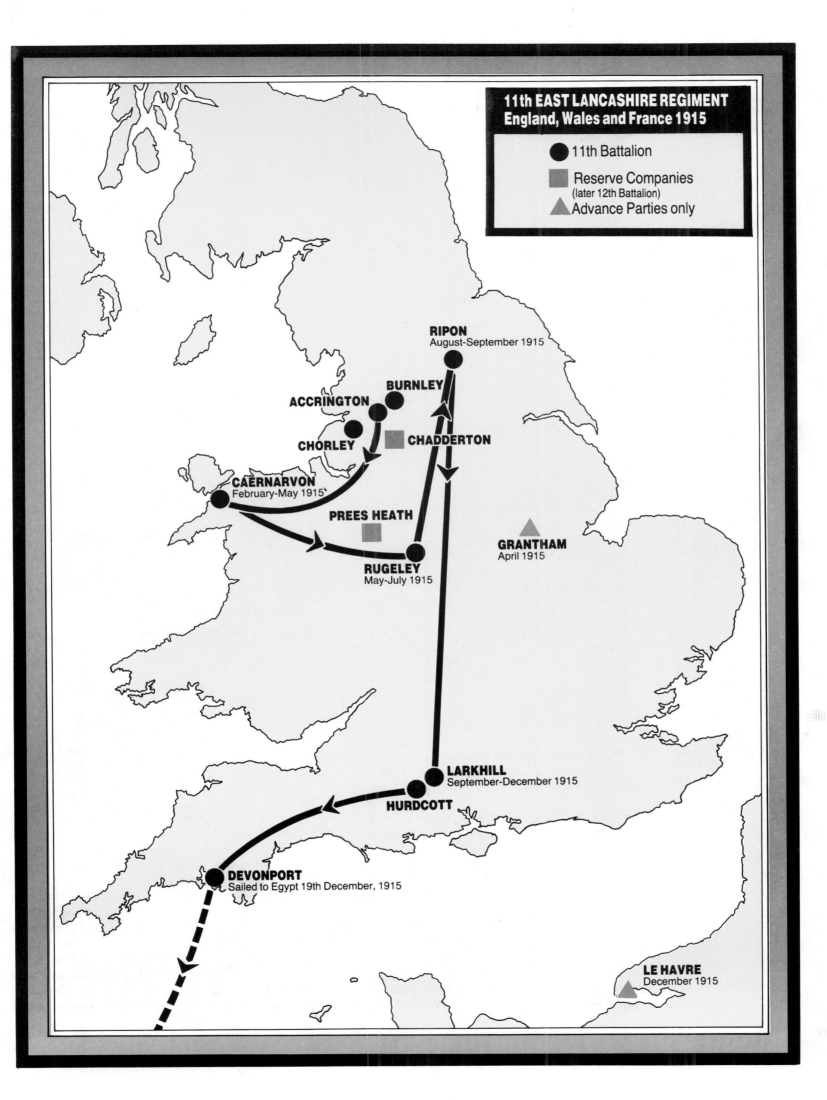

**11th EAST LANCASHIRE REGIMENT
England, Wales and France 1915**

● 11th Battalion
■ Reserve Companies
(later 12th Battalion)
▲ Advance Parties only

RIPON
August-September 1915

BURNLEY

ACCRINGTON

CHORLEY

CHADDERTON

CAERNARVON
February-May 1915

PREES HEATH

GRANTHAM
April 1915

RUGELEY
May-July 1915

LARKHILL
September-December 1915

HURDCOTT

DEVONPORT
Sailed to Egypt 19th December, 1915

LE HAVRE
December 1915

Thoughts of home entered the minds of many with the realisation that their time in England was limited. Many had saved up the money, or wired for it from home, to have a final forty eight hours leave. Others, Lt. Rawcliffe in Accrington and L/Cpl. Race in Burnley amongst them, got extended leaves to get married. Lt. Rawcliffe returned to find that there had been a 'to do.'

"Jack Ruttle and George Williams (both Lieutenants) had decided to shave off their moustaches. On morning parade Col. Rickman saw them. 'You've shaved off your moustaches', he roared, 'Yes, Sir', 'Get off my parade and don't come back until they've grown again!' The lads were in a real dilemma. How on earth could they stay off parade for days on end? Old Rickman soon relented, of course, his bark was always worse than his bite."

By now the October 'Indian Summer' changed to a wintry November. Days of heavy rain alternated with severe frosts. Mettle was tested as nights with temperatures as low as minus ten degrees of frost were experienced. Letters home pleaded for tins of cocoa and OXO cubes to be sent — quickly. Other nights were spent in trenches deep in 'slutch' (mud) as rain poured on 'defender' and 'attacker' alike. On bright, clear nights young officers tested newly acquired skills in astronomy by setting courses for route-marches by the stars — luckily, always successfully.

On November 16th, the Battalion marched fifteen miles to Larkhill Camp, in the centre of Salisbury Plain, to take their final firing course. At Larkhill, no preparations for their arrival had been made — no food, no bedding, no coke for the stoves. The Battalion seemed fated to arrive at places unprepared to receive them. Chaos reigned for five hours — from 2 p.m. to 7 p.m. — until all were settled in. L/Cpl. Bradshaw wrote "God only knows how we would have gone on but for Col. Rickman. At 7 p.m. he had not taken his full pack off. He was everywhere. He is 'some' Colonel."[29]

When finally underway, the firing course turned out to be even more enjoyable than that at Ripon. Everyone felt infinitely more satisfied to fire his own personal rifle, the rifle he had to take and use on active service. The Lewis gunners, though, did not share the same sort of feeling towards their light machine-guns, but they also passed their proficiency tests and formed into permanent teams.[30] After sixteen days the Battalion returned to Hurdcott Camp with a feeling of readiness for the Front and a great anxiety to be there.[31]

More new equipment arrived, but to the men's disappointment the new haversacks, valises and straps were the 'old fashioned' leather, rather than the canvas webbing more generally in use. For the Lewis gunners of 'W' and 'X' Com-

"Well, this place was about the limit. Inches deep in mud the hutments were filthy, the blankets similar and rats, mice etc., abounded. I took all my belongings and my bed into the Orderly Room, which I might add was the warmest place in the whole camp, so during my stay I made myself very comfortable."
J. Bridge

panies, 'the best machine-gunners in the Brigade,' came eight pairs of binoculars bought with £10 raised by an auction of jewellery by officers' wives in Accrington.

Officers were posted in — and out. Major E. L. Reiss, on active service in France since November 1914, reported as Second in Command. Amongst a batch of new subalterns came 2/Lt. Wilfred Kohn, son of a family friend of Rickman, whom Rickman had promised to 'take under his wing.' 2/Lt. Rigby of 'Y' Company was the senior of several men who volunteered for transfer to the newly formed Machine Gun Corps. A final batch of men were transferred to munitions work.

Company Commanders combed out their unfit and less than soldierly members for transfer to Prees Heath. A replacement draft of twenty four men from Prees Heath arrived in late November. A delighted Pte. Snailham came with them.

> *"I saw on Company orders the Battalion required men, so I appealed to my Company Commander to be allowed to go. He knew I was seventeen but he granted my appeal. I came, not to my own Chorley Company, but to 'Z', Burnley Company, but I didn't mind, I was glad to be back."*

On Monday, November 29th, 31 Division received orders to move to France on Tuesday, December 7th. The waiting was over! At once a frantic rush for forty-eight hour passes arose, with Accrington Post Office inundated with telegrams asking for money for the fare home. Many 'straining at the leash' to get to France suddenly felt a desire for the 'great day' to be delayed for just a week, the better to say goodbye to those at home.

Pte. Glover, as one of the Battalion advance party, had no such opportunities. The advance party were informed at 11 p.m. on Monday of their departure for Le Havre at 6.30 a.m. on Tuesday. While they were there, however, the order for the Division to move was cancelled. The day after, Pte. Glover with family souvenirs of Le Havre and a sense of anti-climax, returned with a disconsolate advance party to Hurdcott Camp.

While the advance party were away Pte. Snailham was very busy.

> *"They suddenly realised our draft hadn't fired the musketry course, so we were rushed off to Larkhill. We knew we had to pass to go on active service. We fired our course in the most dreadful wind and rain imaginable. It was a farce. We couldn't see the targets, let alone hit them. By a miracle — or a fiddle — we all passed with good marks!"*

With the recall of the advance party, rumours abounded about the Battalions future destination. These were partly answered by the issue of solar topees and puggarees — it was to be the East, but no one knew where or when. The 'when' came sooner than expected. With embarkation leave arranged and a special train for East Lancashire steaming up ready in Wilton station, a Divisional Order arrived for the recall of officers, N.C.O.'s and men already on leave and all future leave cancelled. Bad as this was, at least the Battalion escaped the fate of the 12th, 13th and 14th York and Lancaster Regiment who were almost in Sheffield when their trains were stopped, engines coupled to the rear, and the trains brought back.

"I'm Thinking of YOU Everyday."
At FOVANT CAMP. —— *A Soldier's Letter.*

I haven't had time to sit down and write,
  And thought perhaps you might grieve ;
So I send you this card just to say I'm alright,
  And longing to see you again when on "leave."

When the Empire's Call for more men to fight,
  For her Honour—in me caused a thrill ;
I felt fight I must or else I should "bust,"
  So on Salisbury Plain—I'm hard at drill.

The work it is stiff, for we're "at it" all day,
  And sometimes half of the night ;
But we're hardening to it and getting quite fit,
  And thank goodness for "grub" we're alright.

My duty calls me as this picture shows,
  To the Front where the fightin' is done ;
And when *Fovant Camp Boys* get grip on the foe,
  There's no letting go till they've won.

So cheer up, my dear, tho' parted we are,
  And though I'm so far away ;
My loved ones are ever *first* in my thoughts,
  I'm thinking of YOU everyday.

At "Duty's Call."   *From*   (Copyright)

Following this disappointment the Battalion had a final inspection by Brig. Gen. G. T. C. Carter-Campbell, O. C. 94 Brigade. For the second time in four months, Rickman said how proud he was of his men and from the whole Battalion only one man was absent. (Meanwhile at Church Magistrates Court, Pte. Thomas Grundy, absent since November 28th, was remanded for escort back to camp, — and, no doubt, an interview with Rickman.) [32]

On December 2nd, 31 Division received orders to embark for Egypt on December 6th. 94

Above: Another card to Ada from 'Will'. "Dear Ada, just a line hoping you and all at home are well. Dear Ada I did not know they would alter our leave. I will try to come on Thursday if I can get off."
Below: Three Burnley 'mashers' names unknown, at Hurdcott Camp.

Above: The Battalion leave camp on the rehearsal march on December 10th, 1915. Leading are the Pioneer Section carrying axes.
N.W. Film Archives

Far right: Postcard from Pte. A. T. Lomax. "Dear Mother, I am glad you are all well. If father is in Liverpool on Monday or Tuesday he might see some of our Division leaving there. Their colours are red and white chevron just below the collar on the back and are wearing sun-helmets. We expect to leave on Thursday but don't know where we will sail from." Abel.

Brigade to embark between December 18th and 28th. With this news, the men, confined to camp for the past week, were allowed out for short intervals. Those with relatives in the 'Howitzers' went to Bulford, others went sight-seeing in Salisbury. This leisure time ended on December 10th, when the Battalion rehearsed its move from camp. Each man was heavily laden, with all his possessions, in Field Service Marching Order complete with solar topee. The transport section, with mobile stores, kitchens, etc. accompanied them. The march ended in disaster, because all maps of the district had been handed in, consequently the Battalion lost its way. An intended three miles march became ten miles. In pouring rain the roads became churned into ankle-deep mud and when at last they returned to camp the men were completely exhausted. [33]

As embarkation time approached a busy Rickman found time to ensure the different Comforts Funds of Accrington, Burnley and Chorley were spent wisely and fairly. For some reason the Accrington fund lagged far behind those of Burnley and Chorley (each of which had almost £300 in the kitty). Reminding Harwood of this, Rickman optimistically wrote, "As soon as I know what they (the men) are likely to require I will let you know. I think it is better than having things sent which are not wanted." [34] The men decided on tobacco, cigarettes and writing-paper but in the event Rickman ordered that these would come only after Battalion specialist equipment needs.

The Battalion hourly expected to receive its detailed orders to move. At last on Wednesday, December 15th, orders came to embark on Sunday, December 19th. At once, a flood of farewell postcards, letters and telegrams went to hundreds of homes. To Harwood from Rickman,

a letter:- "Just a short line to tell you we embark on Sunday. The men are well and in good spirits. Thank you for all you have done. Goodbye and Good Luck." Harwood wired in reply, "To Lt. Col. Rickman, officers, N.C.O.'s and men, wishing you God Speed, Good Health and a safe return." [35] To the Mayor of Chorley from Major Milton, a telegram:- "Chorley Pals wish you and all the inhabitants of Chorley farewell and prosperity."[36]

Farewells made, the final march of the Battalion in England took place in the quiet, early Sunday morning hours along the empty roads and sleeping streets of Wilton and Salisbury. There were no cheering crowds, no songs to

With Loving Greetings

To My Truest of Pals.
" MY MOTHER. "

May the LORD watch for ever between me and thee
  When we are absent one from the other ;
Are the words that I send with heart full of love,
  To the best of dear pals My MOTHER.

For King, Queen and Country we're fighting,
  " Honour and Right " is our watchword true ;
Tho' " Might " at first seemed to hold the sway,
  Naught shall conquer the Red, White and Blue.

Twas some time since that I left my loved home,
  To answer old England's cry ;
The parting was hard, and tho' she tried to be brave,
  There was a tear in my dear mother's eye.

" God bless you ", said she, " God bless her," say I,
  For of mothers' no man had a better ;
And while I'm at FOVANT or when I go to the Front
  She knows I shall never forget her.

So, cheer up, Dear Mother, my Truest of Pals,
  Tho' at parting your heart may feel sore,
We will all look forward with hearts full of hope
  To true happiness when peace comes once more.

From .... " FIT AND READY."

bring blushes to the cheeks of young ladies, as they silently entrained at Salisbury station for Plymouth and Devonport. At Devonport, Company by Company, the Battalion boarded the T.S.S. 'Ionic.' The Battalion War Diary recorded the figures. "Twenty nine officers, including one R.A.M.C. and one Roman Catholic Chaplain, plus 956 O.R.'s." (Two officers and forty seven O.R.'s [the transport section] boarded the T.S.S. 'Huanchaco' at Plymouth). [37]

As the men awaited the 'Ionics' departure they bought hundreds of postcards of the ship for a final brief message home. Pte. Cocker of Accrington wrote. "Dear Wife and child, Goodbye until I return. We set sail today, Sunday." Pte. Cocker, with all the other writers, was not to know that the postcards were taken along on voyage and not sent home until passed by the censor, Lt. H. Ashworth in Pte. Cocker's case — this was on January 16th, 1916. The carefree days of 'Camp Correspondent' were now replaced by the exigencies of censorship, although pictorial views of Egypt were soon to arrive at many homes in East Lancashire.

At 5 p.m. the 'Ionic' moved off to The Sound to await its escort of destroyers. As the band of the quayside farewell party played 'Auld Lang Syne,' Rickman's thoughts could only be guessed at as he viewed the end of one phase in his — and the Battalion's — life, and the beginnings of another. He was a soldier too experienced to be afraid for himself, but certainly he must have felt afraid for the future of his men. Few had little idea of what lay ahead, simply to go abroad being adventure enough. A letter to Harwood expressed his thoughts, "You have given me a big charge in the men's lives. I only hope I shall be able to help them in the life that's before them." [38]

After the lonely and exacting task of producing a Battalion the equal of any in Kitcheners' Army although admittedly not perfect — (not many Battalions could get lost on a three mile route march) Rickman had the more exacting task of leading his Battalion through its longed-for active service.

Above: The 12th Reserve Battalion was left behind at Prees Heath Camp, Shropshire. With them were Lt. T. Y. Harwood (grandson of John Harwood), back, 2/Lt. Goodall, left, and 2/Lt. Standring, right.
Left: The 12,232 ton White Star Liner T.S.S. 'Ionic', a sister ship of the ill-fated 'Titanic'.

NOTES

1. Described also as 'Cannock Chase', 'Penkridge Bank', 'Penkridge Bank', confusion exists about the actual name of the camp. Both 'Rugeley Camp' and 'Penkridge Bank Camp' postmarks were in official use during the war. (See Great War Camps on Cannock Chase, C. J. Whitehouse and G. P. Ibbotson).

2. History of 'Z' Company Page 8.

3. The Army School of Cookery, which had been gradually raising the standard of cooking in the 'old' Army, unfortunately disbanded at the beginning of the war. However, schools of instruction in the home Commands and close supervision of the Quartermasters-General quickly improved the quality of the meals and supplies of food were mostly adequate. (The 'Z' Company protest was an isolated, domestic affair).

4. The 'Comic Band' of an Accrington engineering works played in carnivals, charity parades, etc. Its instruments were washboards, bin-lids, tin whistles, etc. The 'Pals Comic Band' subsequently played in many Battalion concerts raising money for Accrington charities. An unofficial 'duty' was to play 'Home Sweet Home' and similar ditties, as batches of men went on leave thereafter.

5. A.G. 5/6/15
   N.B. At Rugeley Camp, L/Cpl. Russell Bradshaw, the son of an Accrington draper and close friend of John Harwood, became 'Camp Correspondent' for the Accrington Gazette. He kept his unofficial post, in spite of later censorship, for over three years. In a letter to the author in November 1983, Mr. Bradshaw said, "It's a wonder I didn't get shot for some of the news I sent!"

6. In May 1915, 'S' Company became, at Chadderton Camp, Depot Company of the Battalion. The 11th Battalion, therefore, alone in the East Lancashire Regiment, had the privilege of its own Depot. The War Office request increased its establishment to two Companies and they became the 12th (Reserve) Battalion. In October 1915 the 12th Battalion moved to Prees Heath Camp and in September 1916 became 75th Training Reserve Battalion, 17th Reserve Brigade.

7. Pte. Coady wrote a poignant farewell letter to his friend Isaac Edwards in Caernarvon. For some reason it appeared in the Accrington Observer and Times on June 12th, 1915, 'Dear Mr. Edwards, It looks as if we will be in France before long. I do not care how soon, I joined the Army to fight Germany and I am pleased I did so. When I go into battle I know the game because I am in the hands of God and whatever will be my fate I won't grumble. If I get killed I hope to go where there are no battles. — Yours Tom Coady.'

8. It is highly probable the group included the several businessmen, magistrates and civic leaders whose sons were serving in the Battalion.

9. Mr. J. Whitworth, former conductor of the 4th Loyal North Lancs (Territorial) Band and the North Lancs (Chorley) Band. From September 1914 to February 1915 the latter band led the Chorley Company on their civil marches and church parades. Several former bandsmen were serving in 'Y', (Chorley) Company.

10. A History of the Accrington Pals Page 72.

11. As early as January 1915, Lloyd George, in a memorandum for the War Council of the Cabinet, described the Kitchener Army — "In intelligence, education and character it is vastly superior to any army ever raised in this country". (See Lloyd George: Twelve Essays, Ed. A. J. P. Taylor Page 99).

12. Many in Chorley Company lost friends and relatives at Festubert. The 1/4th Loyal North Lancs (Territorials) lost 10 officers and 250 men, killed, wounded or missing.

13. H. Baker, Accrington's M.P. was one held responsible for the shortage of shells and was replaced, on June 19th, as Financial Secretary of the Army Council by Mr. H. W. Forster, M.P. He was, however, immediately, in the June King's Birthday Honours list, appointed a Privy Councillor.

14. The Bulk Release Scheme consisted of a call by the Ministry of Munitions to all skilled men within 'non-barred' units, i.e. units which had not undergone advanced training or did not require skilled men. (See 'Arms and the Wizard', R.T.Q. Adams Page 96).

15. One recruit was Arthur Riley. A single man, he returned from Pawtucket, Rhode Island, U.S.A. in 1915 to his parents' home in Accrington to enlist. He was the town of Accrington's first fatal casualty in France when he died of wounds, April 30th, 1916.

16. Pte. Bell, an ex-reservist, by coincidence, served with Col. Rickman in the South African War. He was killed in action on July 1st, 1916.

17. C.W.N. 31/7/15.

18. History of 'Z' Company Page 9.

19. The 1/4th and 1/5th East Lancs Territorials had suffered severe losses in Gallipoli since May 1915. In late August, Burnley received news of the loss of thirty six men of the 2/2nd East Lancs Field Ambulance on the troopship 'Royal Edward' sunk in the Mediterranean with the loss of 861 lives.

20. Put as a reason when not one man responded to a recruiting appeal for the reserve company in Oldham (admittedly not a traditional East Lancashire Regiment recruiting area) in September 1915. (See Oldham Chronicle, 4/10/15).

21. War Office, London 18/7/16. Sir, I am commanded by the Army Council to offer you — their sincere thanks for having raised the 11th Service Battalion East Lancashire Regiment (Accrington) of which the administration has now been taken over by the military authorities. The Council much appreciate the spirit which prompted your assistance and they are gratified at the successful results — which added to the Armed Forces of the Crown, the services of such a fine body of men. — I am to add that its (the Battalion) success on active service will largely depend on your efforts to keep the depot companies up to establishment. — I am, etc. B. B. Cubitt, Secretary. (A.G. 21/7/15).

22. By the end of the month the whole of 31 Division assembled at Ripon: i.e.
   92 Brigade: 10th, 11th, 12th and 13th East Yorkshire Regiment;
   93 Brigade: 15th, 16th, 18th West Yorkshire Regiment and 18th Durham Light Infantry
   94 Brigade: 11th East Lancs Regiment.
   12th, 13th and 14th York and Lancaster Regiment.
   In addition were Artillery brigades, Engineering and Transport Companies, Pioneers, etc. (See Order of Battle of Divisions, Part 3B, History of the Great War, H.M.S.O. London 1945).

23. On January 14th, 1915 the War Office requested John Harwood to raise a Howitzer Brigade, Royal Field Artillery, in East Lancashire. Recruitment ended after four weeks.

24. A.G. 11/9/15.

25. B.E. 14/8/15.

26. A.O. 21/9/15.

27. Pte. Sam Ollerton, aged 20, a single man, died at his home in Accrington and buried in Accrington Cemetery.
   Pte. Fred Hacking, aged 22, a single man, died at his home in Oswaldtwistle and buried at Immanuel Church.

28. A.G. 20/11/15.

29. There were sixteen Lewis gun teams, four per Company. Pte. Pollard completed his course and became No. 6 in his team. The rest of the team were:- Cpl. Sam Smith, Ptes. Harry Kay, Tom Carey, Walt Greaves and Harry Wilkinson, all from Accrington.

30. Only four days were spent firing, the rest spent on 'butt duty' for other Battalions in the Brigade. Many men used their free time to visit relatives and friends in 158 (Accrington and Burnley) Howitzer Brigade, R.F.A. coincidentally, from September 1st, at Bulford, two miles away.

31. Northern Daily Telegraph 4/12/15.
   Other plans went awry. At the same court Thomas Duckworth of Clayton-le-Moors, fined 6/- for having a fox terrier dog without a licence, told the court his son, Pte. Thomas Duckworth, asked him to keep the dog as a mascot for the Battalion. Pte. Duckworth, of course, was unable to collect.

32. On hearing the news of the impending embarkation, Harwood arranged for a cine-photographer to film the Battalions' departure for showing in local cinemas. The cameraman however, filmed the men leaving camp on the rehearsal march. It is fortunate he did not film the return.

33. A.G. 11/12/15.

34. A.G. 25/12/15.

36. C.G. 25/12/15.

37. 11th East Lancs Regimental War Diary, December 19th, 1915. The War Diary, started December 18th, 1915 continued until March 3rd, 1919.

38. A.G. 11/12/15.

Chapter Five

An eastern interlude

By the autumn of 1915, the British High Command recognised that the Dardanelles campaign had failed. After the landings at Anzac Cove and Cape Helles on April 25th, the assault against the Turks turned into one of the most arduous and costly operations of the war. Whatever advantage had been gained by a landing at Suvla Bay on August 6th had been lost by the second day and the enemy lines remained as impregnable as ever.

On October 11th, 1915, Kitchener asked the Commander of the Mediterranean Expeditionary Force for estimates of the losses which might accompany a withdrawal from the Dardanelles. The Commander, Gen. Sir Ian Hamilton believed such a step 'unthinkable.' Four days later, on his recall to London, Kitchener informed him a fresh unbiased opinion from a 'responsible' commander was desired.[1] Hamilton's successor, Lt. Gen. Sir Charles Monro subsequently reported the British forces could be held down indefinitely. The lines had no depth, Turkish fire impeded all communications and approaches from the sea and deployment of fresh troops for offensive operations could not be concealed from enemy observation. Even a break-through would yield little military advantage, for an advance up the Gallipoli peninsula to Constantinople was now out of the question. Monro therefore advised that troops 'locked up' on the peninsula be given more useful work elsewhere. Such a withdrawal presented tricky strategic and political problems.

Both Monro and Lt. Gen. Sir John Maxwell, Commander of the Force in Egypt, considered withdrawal from Gallipoli would have grave effects unless Britain struck hard at Turkey elsewhere. One consideration was to use more troops for a landing at the Gulf of Iskenderun, near Alexandretta, now Iskenderun, on Turkey's border with Syria. The purpose being to cut and hold the Turkish railway to Palestine and Mesopotamia. Another consideration was for the Allied armies in Mesopotamia and Macedonia (Salonika) to be reinforced.

As the withdrawal would give Moslem Turkey tremendous prestige with Moslems and Arabs in the near East, Egypt, with her vital Suez Canal, and now restless under a British protec-

torate, became a grave concern. The loss of the Suez Canal would be a disaster almost comparable with the loss of the Armies of the Western Front, so defence of the Suez Canal was an absolute necessity.

In Palestine, Turkish troops were massing, railways and water supplies were being extended and aerodromes built. In the minds of British generals came a vision of Turkish troops, fresh from their 'victory' at Gallipoli sweeping through the Sinai Desert to the banks of the Suez Canal. With this, and the proposed landing at Alexandretta in mind, a further eight divisions were necessary to continue the British campaigns in the Near East. Two for the Alexandretta landing, four for Salonika and two — 31 Division and 46 Division — for the defence of Egypt. By November 19th, 1915, however, the Prime Minister and the War Committee decided against the Alexandretta landing and for an alternative, stronger defence of Egypt and the Suez Canal.

On the night of December 18th, 1915, as the 11th East Lancs were marching silently from Hurdcott Camp in England, the last of the British and Anzac troops embarked, as silently, from Suvla Bay and Anzac Cove. On January 8th, 1916, British troops successfully evacuated Cape Hellas, leaving Gallipoli and the Dardanelles in control of the Turks.

As 1915 ended the War Committee re-formed the troops freed from the Alexandretta operation

Above: Lt. Gen. Sir Charles Munro

Above: Lt. Gen. Sir John Maxwell

Below: A Turkish shell exploding on 'V' Beach near the ship 'River Clyde' during the evacuation of Gallipoli.
Barnsley Chronicle Picture Library

Above: Cpl. Walter Todd

Below: Malta, a view of Grand Harbour from the Saluting Battery looking towards Isola Point and French Creek.
Barnsley Chronicle Picture Library.

and from Gallipoli, together with 31 and 46 Divisions already en-route, into an Imperial Strategic Reserve to be based in Egypt under the command of Lt. Gen. Sir A. Murray. The War Committee had decided that France was to be the main theatre of war and Gen. Sir W. Robertson, Chief of the Imperial General Staff, told Murray that as the situation in the East became clearer, no more troops would remain there than absolutely necessary. "You should therefore be prepared to detach troops from Egypt, when and if the situation makes this advisable."[2]

Meanwhile, the men of the 11th East Lancs Regiment, not knowing, nor caring much about war strategy and the role of 31 Division, were enjoying their sea voyage. Rumours about their destination were rife. Was it to be Mesopotamia, Salonika, or — heaven forbid — garrison duty in India? Most, however, were convinced they were bound for Gallipoli. After all, men reasoned, the East Lancs. Territorials were there, 'they' (the High Command) were bound to put the 'Pals' with them.

A stormy passage through the Bay of Biscay brought the Ionic to Gibralter on December 23rd for further orders and to collect two destroyers as escorts. On the way to Malta, Christmas Day celebrations started with a dinner of stewed mutton, potatoes and peas, served in Army tradition by the officers. The choice of afters limited to a bottle of beer or sixpence. Songs and recitations by the Concert Party and a selection of seasonal music by the Regimental Band followed dinner. Two days later, the Ionic, with her escort, sailed into Grand Harbour, Malta for a two day stay.

Only officers were allowed ashore. Disgruntled at the freedom allowed the officers, scores of men clambered down ropes and hawsers into Maltese bumboats and bribed their way ashore. The bars and nightspots of Strait Street (the famous, or infamous 'Gut') were the main attraction for most. A few, such as Pte. Cowell, went further afield sight-seeing and buying postcards and souvenirs. Lt. Rawcliffe and some of his fellow-officers legitimately visited the Opera House, "where we suffered the indignity of being asked to leave for being too noisy!" Corporal Walter Todd, of 'W' Company, went ashore to Hospital and remained there when the Ionic sailed. There then began for him a desperate struggle with the military authorities to allow him to rejoin the Battalion.[3]

For some reason the Ionic sailed the most dangerous part of her journey, through the eastern Mediterranean, without her escort. All men wore life-belts continuously and there were con-

stant boat drills. Just a few hours out of Malta, Pte. James Wixted, of 'X' Company died of Siriais (heat exhaustion) and was buried at sea with full military honours on December 30th, the first battalion member to die on active service.[4]

The following morning, with the Ionic SSE of Crete, an enemy submarine suddenly appeared five hundred yards away on the port side. As lookouts gave the alarm and klaxons sounded, the ship quickly turned, leaving a torpedo to pass a hundred feet astern. According to the War Diary for December 31st, 1915, "all troops were at boat stations in three minutes," and the Ionic charged full steam ahead to safety. Pte. Marshall, sitting on a spar watching a boxing competition, saw the wake of the torpedo travelling towards the ship.

"After the ship swung round we (part of 'Z' Company) were ordered to line the starboard side of the ship and told, 'If you see a torpedo or a periscope — fire at it!' Of course, we all grumbled, 'How the heck can we damage a torpedo or a periscope with a rifle bullet!' Nevertheless two hours passed before we stood down".

Pte. Pollard missed everything.

"I was in my hammock reading when the hooter went for boat-drill — or so I thought. (My section of fifteen men shared a raft, to be thrown overboard, if necessary, with us to follow. Trouble was, I couldn't swim). I rushed up the stairway but took a wrong turn and found myself on the wrong deck. By the time I got to my boat-station the rest of the section were waiting. Lt. Ashworth my platoon commander said, 'As usual, last! Get your boots and socks off!' 'I said, 'What for?' 'You'll know soon enough, you'll be in the bloody water!' We stood there, our boots hung around our necks, for over an hour before 'stand down'."[5]

Twenty-four hours later the Ionic passed the Ras-el-Tin lighthouse to enter Alexandria harbour. While the ship lay at anchor the men watched, with a host of mixed feelings the arrival of the survivors of the S.S. Persia, which had been sunk in the area of Ionic's escape, very probably by the same submarine. The Persia had gone down in five minutes, with the loss of 334 lives. The men also watched, with some alarm, some of the Ionic's ballast cargo of high explosive shells being unloaded.

With a celebration of their escape in mind, many more men decided to have a night out in Alexandria, officers or no. Against explicit orders, over a hundred men made a concerted rush down the gang plank, brushed the guards aside and headed for the town. This time the indulgencies over a few men in Malta could not be repeated and a furious Rickman ordered the arrest and confinement to ship's quarters of all involved. There is no record of any further pun-

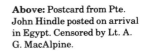

Above: Postcard from Pte. John Hindle posted on arrival in Egypt. Censored by Lt. A. G. MacAlpine.

"A parade was called at 6 a.m. for his burial. The ships engines stopped thus everything being perfectly quiet, the ship's bell rang once and Pte. Wixted was placed in the sea. I never saw anything so sorrowful." **J. Bridge**

Above: Pte. James Wixted

Left: A German U-boat of the U38 class. By coincidence the U38 was launched at Kiel on September 9th, 1914, the same day John Harwood and his colleagues at Chester gained formal War Office directions for forming the Pals Battalion.

Right: The landing stage at Port Said. The disembarking point of the 'Ionic'.

"Here our berth had been filled as they presumed we had been sunk, as a matter of fact a cable had been despatched to the White Star Line to this effect, but we were pleased to be in a position to prove this incorrect."
J. Bridge

Below: Two views of 'X' (District) Company going ashore at Port Said. Lt. Col. Rickman is standing on the floating platform.

ishment, but it is clear this was the first, and only time, any significant group tarnished the good relationship Rickman had with his men.

After four days the Ionic continued her journey to Port Said where the Battalion disembarked on January 5th, 1916. By nightfall all were encamped under canvas near the Railway Station, together with the rest of 94 Brigade. All rumours faded away, they had arrived.

The Imperial Strategic Reserve's twelve divisions confronted but one Turkish division bivouacked a hundred miles away on the eastern edge of the Sinai Desert. Kitchener's remit to Murray on the role of the Reserve included, "You should maintain as active a defence as possible — to ensure no formed bodies of the enemy come within artillery range of the Suez Canal. Every care must be taken small hostile parties do not reach the Canal and interfere with its navigation."[6] The 11th East Lancs, with the rest of 94 Brigade and 31 Division, put to work to carry out these instructions.[7]

At first the Battalion's duties were undemanding camp guards with occasional guards of honour for visiting dignitaries. Piquet patrols in the narrow streets of Arab Town in Port Said were less so. Ideas of a 'romantic East', based on childhood Bible illustrations quickly changed in the noise and squalor of the aptly named Rue Babel. Not all Port Said however was Arab Town. There were several quiet squares and tree-lined boulevards in the French style. Pte Cowell wrote to his wife, Polly "I went to church here on Sunday and although it is such a far-away country it was glorious to hear Mass said as it is at home." Always optimistic about getting home, he continued, "I don't think we will see any fighting here — so it is only a matter of time and then home once more."[8]

Occasionally, despite Kitchener's remit, small hostile parties peppered ships on the Canal with rifle bullets. Aimed primarily at ships' pilots, a successful shot could cause a ship to run aground and perhaps block the Canal. Conse-

quently a fifteen man section of troops travelled on each ship as lookouts. Parties sailed from Port Said to Suez and returned by train. This became the most popular duty in the Battalion. Pte. Snailham's section was one:

"A lot of us were only lads. I was still only seventeen and not worldly-wise. When we got to Suez, the ship's captain, a Swede, said 'Thank-you, boys. Would you care for a night-cap?' I replied, not knowing any different, 'No thanks, we don't wear them!' A quick kick on the ankle by Walt Smith, an old soldier, soon educated me!"

At the Battalion camp at Port Said a short time later Pte. Snailham happened to walk past Rickman.

"The Colonel looked at me, passed on, then called me back. I wondered what I'd done wrong. He said, 'What are you doing here?' 'I thought you were in the Reserves because you were under age.' (I was amazed how he remembered me — a private soldier — from ten months before at Caernarvon.) I explained how I joined the Battalion on Salisbury Plain. I thought, 'This is it, back to England I go.' He looked at me for what seemed at age, then said, 'You shouldn't be here, you know, but we can't do anything about it now.' He then dismissed me. I'm sure he knew I would have been broken-hearted to be sent back".

Rickman's reason for allowing Pte. Snailham

Above: The empty desert through which much of the Suez Canal passes. At this point in February 1915 a surprise attack by Turks using flat-boats was repulsed by British forces. One of the boats still lies on the water's edge.
Barnsley Chronicle Picture Library

Left: Port Said railway station. The Pals were encamped half a mile away behind the station.

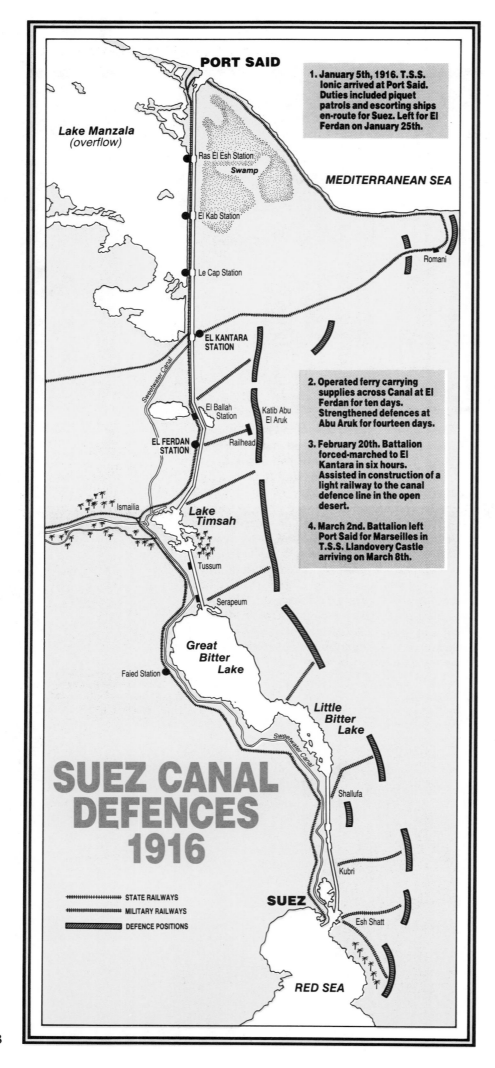

PORT SAID

Lake Manzala
(overflow)

Ras El Esh Station
Swamp

El Kab Station

MEDITERRANEAN SEA

Le Cap Station

Romani

EL KANTARA STATION

El Ballah Station

Katib Abu El Aruk

EL FERDAN STATION

Railhead

Ismailia

Lake Timsah

Tussum

Serapeum

Great Bitter Lake

Faied Station

Little Bitter Lake

Shallufa

Kubri

SUEZ

Esh Shatt

SUEZ CANAL DEFENCES 1916

+++++++++ STATE RAILWAYS
····················· MILITARY RAILWAYS
▨▨▨▨▨ DEFENCE POSITIONS

SUEZ

RED SEA

Sweetwater Canal

1. **January 5th, 1916. T.S.S. Ionic arrived at Port Said. Duties included piquet patrols and escorting ships en-route for Suez. Left for El Ferdan on January 25th.**

2. **Operated ferry carrying supplies across Canal at El Ferdan for ten days. Strengthened defences at Abu Aruk for fourteen days.**

3. **February 20th. Battalion forced-marched to El Kantara in six hours. Assisted in construction of a light railway to the canal defence line in the open desert.**

4. **March 2nd. Battalion left Port Said for Marseilles in T.S.S. Llandovery Castle arriving on March 8th.**

to stay will never be known, but he clearly had the authority — indeed an obligation — to return from active service anyone under eighteen.

In spite of the easy duties, life in the windy, sandy, tented camp at Port Said soon became miserable. No pay, 'we were stony-broke;' no mail, rumoured lost at sea; and a reduction in rations, added to the misery. On January 23rd, however, the 6th (Service) East Lancs Regiment of 13 Division, moved into the next camp. These survivors of Gallipoli had left leaving over two hundred dead mates behind and many were sick and exhausted. Although glad to be among friends and relatives most, with nerves shot,

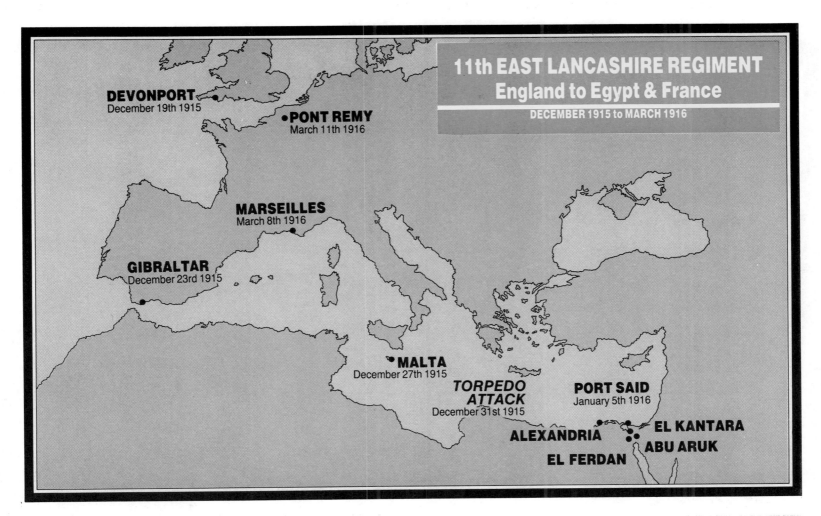

11th EAST LANCASHIRE REGIMENT
England to Egypt & France
DECEMBER 1915 to MARCH 1916

DEVONPORT
December 19th 1915

PONT REMY
March 11th 1916

MARSEILLES
March 8th 1916

GIBRALTAR
December 23rd 1915

MALTA
December 27th 1915

TORPEDO
ATTACK
December 31st 1915

PORT SAID
January 5th 1916

ALEXANDRIA

EL KANTARA
ABU ARUK

EL FERDAN

were reluctant to talk about their experiences. Their appearances — gaunt, emaciated, burnt by the sun, told its own story. Pte. Pollard's uncle Joe was something of an exception. An ex-regular, 'old sweat', he seemed remarkably unaffected. "After enthralling us all with his adventures, he borrowed the little money I had 'for a drink or two'. He offered to apply for me to go with him in the 6th Battalion, but I declined, I thought I'd better stay with my mates!" Pte. Connor, however, did transfer to be with his brother.[9]

The reunions were cut short on January 25th, by a move south to 94 Brigade H.Q. at El Ferdan, on the west bank of the Canal. Starting at 4 a.m. they journeyed in open railway trucks, with innumerable halts and delays, in pouring rain, to reach El Ferdan at 12.30 p.m. Their baggage and tents arrived six hours later. It took another six hours to make camp and settle in. The Battalion had the task along with the 12th York and Lancaster Regiment operating from the east bank, of transferring men, horses, stores and food across the Canal. They used a heavy, flat-bottomed ferry, pulled by teams of sixteen men hauling on two chains which lay on the Canal bed. It was arduous work for men with empty stomachs. Dates or figs, on bread with no butter, with one loaf between seven men became the rule for tea. A few Huntley and Palmers biscuits and a little stew and po-

Above: 'X' (District) Company digging in near Port Said.
Left: The open carriages of the Egyptian State Railway train to El Ferdan.
Barnsley Chronicle Picture Library

Opposite page: Lt. Col. Rickman at Port Said.

109

were pleased to be in a position to prove this incorrect. We had been at Alexandria 4 days when I received orders I had to disembark, much to my regret, as I was loathe to leave the lads I had been with so long, but orders in the Army have to be obeyed. and in accordance therewith went ashore. I watched the ships away, the Band played "Old Lang Syne" and when the ship was out of sight, I turned to the carriage I had engaged and proceeded on my way to General Headquarters where I was to report for duty. Thus ended my connections with the 11th (S) Bn East Lancs Regt bound for a place still unknown, and I sincerely hope I shall see them all again soon. Thus I parted from my Regiment on the 4th Jany 1916.

J B Bridge
OR Lst 11th East Lancs

Above: The concluding pages of James Bridges notebook (see page 106)
Top right: Setting up camp at El Ferdan. Captain Livesey knocking in a tent peg.
Centre right: Lt. Ryden and an unidentified officer.
Right: 'X' (District) Company N.C.O's supervise the loading of the chain operated ferry at El Ferdan.

Above: 'X' (District)
Company men watching the
Monitor H.M.S. M15 passing
along the Suez Canal from
Port Said to Ismalia. (The
M15 was to be sunk by the
U38 on November 11th,
1917).

tatoes for dinner. When sacks of raisins or dates and crates of corned beef and biscuits were
unloaded from ships onto the ferry, Pte. Marshall and his companions, ever hungry, could
not resist the temptation;

> *"Crates were 'dropped' and broken, and the
> contents pushed into the sand, to be re-
> trieved at night. Someone on guard duty
> usually helped us find what we'd hidden!
> We finally got 'sacked' from that job —
> they said we stole more than the natives!"*

By now the mail arrived, not as feared, lost
at sea. The men received a weekly allowance
of four packets of cigarettes or two ounces of

tobacco and gradually supplies of legitimate
food improved. The camp lay on ground rising
from the bank of the Canal and rest-days were
pleasantly spent watching the variety of Canal
traffic — stately Nile sailing dhows and dahabie-
has bringing stone from Suez; troopships en-
route to and from the East, and Royal Navy
gunboats and destroyers on patrol. No-one, however, mourned the end of their ten-day stint
at El Ferdan when news came of a move to
Abu Arak on the outer-most point of the Canal
defence line, seven miles into the Sinai Desert.

At Abu Arak, a mere huddle of small, poor
dwellings in the arid desert, 'W' and 'Z' Com-

Above: An officer's servant (name unknown) hangs out the washing.
Top right: An officer's servant (name unknown) enjoys a quick shave.
Right: Captain Peltzer and Major Milton share a joke.
Far right: Quartermaster Captain Smith.
Below: Part of the camel train taking supplies from El Ferdan to Abu Aruk.
Below right: Members of 'Z' (Burnley) Company with an Egyptian camel drover. Pte. James Walton first right.

Left: 'X' (District) Company Orderly Room (left) and signal section at Abu Aruk. **Below:** The interior of Lt. Rawcliffe's tent at Abu Aruk.

panies constructed strong-points of trenches and barbed wire. Digging trenches in the soft sand proved easy. Revetting trenches with wattle, hurdles and tarpaulins grew to be a frustrating and confounding task. They better enjoyed escorting pairs of camels dragging 'gates' across the front of their sector to smooth out the sand, to be followed later by the 'dawn patrol' to examine the cleared area for the footprints of intruders. Meanwhile 'X' and 'Y' Companies in turn, collected water supplies and materials from El Ferdan. At Abu Arak, with water restricted to one pint per man per day, the food at least improved. This didn't stop Pte. Marshall and his 'Z' Company colleagues, still hungry, paying a penny each for chappatis from the Indian troops of their cavalry screen.

After fourteen days, on February 20th, the Battalion marched six hours northwards alongside the Canal to El Kantara, thirty miles south of Port Said. The men arrived exhausted in the heat of mid-day; their baggage and tents followed, eight hours later. They seemed fated, as always, to arrive at unprepared destinations. Despite the poor beginnings, El Kantara proved an enjoyable break and for a few days everyone relaxed. Many had a welcome dip in the Canal and some joked, 'I'll just swim to Africa and back.' Pte. Pollard, with the Ionic torpedo incident in his mind, vowed to his friend Pte. Harry Kay he wouldn't go back 'over there' (across the Mediterranean) until he learned to swim.

"We cut open sacks of emergency rations, ate the food, and from the sacking made swimming trunks (we would have been shot if anyone found out.) The Canal, at that point had a waist deep shelf about two yards wide. On this shelf, with lessons from Harry, I learned to swim. I was then quite satisfied."

The railway junction of El Kantara was an important link in the defence of the Suez

Above: A group of 'Z' (Burnley) Company men at El Kantara. Pte. W. Peart in front centre.
Far right: Lt. Henry Mitchell.
Below: A group of 'Y' (Chorley) Company men at El Kantara. Pte Ormond Fairweather first left front row.

Canal. From here the Battalion now constructed a light railway to Hill 108, a point in the outer defence line in the Sinai Desert. More arduous than El Ferdan and without its compensations, the men laboured to dig cuttings and build embankments. Tragically, on February 23rd, Lt. Harry Mitchell of 'Z' Company, was seriously injured in an accident and died two days later.[10] L/Cpl. Bradshaw and the signallers had other work.

> "We had an easy but boring job. From a tower near the railway station we kept watch for, by day, a heliograph, by night, a green lamp, situated far out in the Sinai at an outpost watching the Turks. Any message by heliography or the lamp turning red, we were to report to H.Q. Not a thing happened."

By mid February, it came clear the Turks were unlikely to risk an attack on the Suez Canal across the Sinai Desert. The British High Command therefore decided by April 1916, (the beginning of the dry season) that three divisions could defend the Canal instead of the present twelve.[11] As the situation in the East cleared, more troops could be spared for the

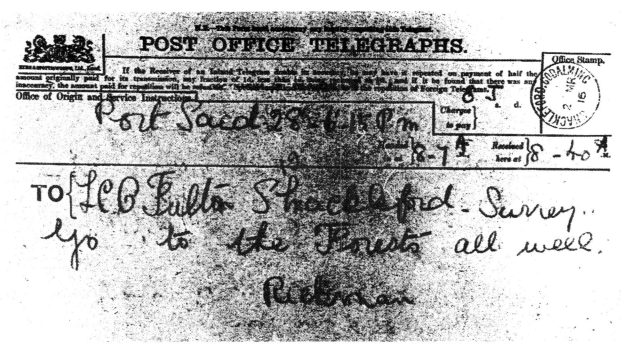

POST OFFICE TELEGRAPHS.

Left: Before leaving England Lt. Col. Rickman arranged a coded message with his fiancee so she would know of his impending return. This telegram was the signal for her to prepare for their wedding. (They were married within a month).

Below: A page from Fred Sayer's "Soldiers Small-Book" with the mosquito that bit his wrist, embedded into page 12.

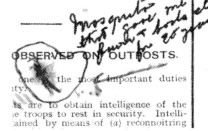

Below: The 'Llandovery Castle', 11,423 tons, launched in 1914. The sinking of the 'Llandovery Castle' on June 27th, 1918 was to be regarded as one of the worst atrocities of the war. She was sailing in the Atlantic as a hospital ship when she was torpedoed without a warning by the U-86. The U-boat then rammed or sank by gun-fire all expect one life-boat. 234 men and women died. I.W.M.

more important campaigns in France and Belgium.

As early as December 6th, 1915, at the second Allied Military Conference at Chantilly, held to discuss Allied operations for the coming year, Great Britain and France in a joint enterprise with Russia and Italy, decided to deliver simultaneous attacks with maximum forces on their respective fronts, 'as soon as circumstances were favourable,' probably in the Spring of 1916. By February 1916, this changed to June or July for a joint British and French attack astride the River Somme, where both forces met. After the Chantilly Conference the British High Command readied their full strength in men and munitions in preparation for the great offensive, with the ruling principle to place every possible division, fully equipped, in France by Spring. This released divisions in the Imperial Strategic Reserve, amongst them 31 Division, for France and the 'Big Push.'

46 Division was the first to leave and sailed from Egypt on February 4th, 1916. On February 26th, 31 Division received its orders to embark for France. Three days later the 11th East Lancs Regiment got two short days notice to leave Port Said on March 2nd. In a letter to Harwood, Rickman described the speed of events. "We came in very hurriedly, handed in all camp stores, transport vehicles, horses and mules. (The transport drivers had already gone ahead with Lt. Bury.) We did a pretty quick embarkation leaving ('El Kantara' was deleted by the censor) by train at twelve noon and sailing five hours later."[12] The Battalion left behind Pte. William Baron, ill in hospital in Port Said; he later died on March 25th, 1916.[13]

The voyage on the T.S.S. Llandovery Castle was comfortable and uneventful. For the men, after three months of hard sand, the hammocks 'felt like feather beds.' Officers had the luxury of a large lounge, a library and a smoking room. Pte. Cowell, optimistic as always, wrote to Polly his wife "I am expecting to be with you before long, as I am going to where — (censored), — so the chances of getting home will be a lot better."[14] Pte. Sayer of 'Z' Company did not enjoy the voyage. On February 29th a mosquito had bitten his wrist. 'It was caught in the act then picked up and enmbedded in my small-book.' After three days at sea his hand had swollen to twice its size and he had a fever. This fever, unknown to Pte. Sayer, was to recur at intervals for the next twenty years. The Llandovery Castle entered Marseilles harbour on the afternoon of March 8th. At 9 a.m. the following morning, two hours after disembarking, the Battalion entrained for the 'Front.'[15]

The Battalion arrived in France fit, confident and high in morale. In spite of grumbles about trench-digging, outpost duties and poor food, they had 'rested' away from the rigours of a

Right: Aboard the 'Llandovery Castle' March 2nd, 1916. Lt. Col. Rickman (with his back to the camera talks to Lt. Ryden (left), Capt. Riley (centre) and Capt. Watson.

European winter. Egypt added to their life-experience and so they were tougher and more self-assured in consequence. They compared themselves, more realistically than in England, with Regular, Territorial and other Kitchener Battalions, and felt equal to any. Seeing the state that the 6th Battalion were in after Gallipoli gave them a glimpse of what war could do to men but paradoxically this spurred them on to want to 'do their bit.' Their 'esprit de corps' formed by the pre-war friendships, in which Lord Derby and Lord Kitchener had such faith, made the Pals, in their own opinion at least, the equal of any one. This belief shaped their loyalties and attitudes. Pte. Marshall described an illustration of this.

> *"We were at El Kantara and marching past a Regular Army camp. Two men were strung up on a gun-wheel in the sun (i.e. Field Punishment No. 1, one hour each morning and evening.) 'Potty' Ross, ('Z' Company Commander) said, 'That's what happens if you misbehave.' The reply came back, It won't tha' knows, if you did that to any of us, t'others would cut him down!"*

Captain Ross' remark may or may not have been serious, but the reply was.

Although in reality still poorly trained for their new role, all officers and men of the Battalion were glad to be in France, glad to be on their way to what they had so readily enlisted to do so long ago.

NOTES

1. History of the Great War, Military Operations, Gallipoli, Volume II Appendix 17, Page 69 Heinemann 1932.
2. History of the Great War, Military Operations, Egypt and Palestine, Note II pp 99 — 100 H.M.S.O. London 1928.
3. On January 17th, 1916, Cpl. Todd wrote from Ghain Tuffieka Convalescent Camp, Malta, to A.Q.M.S. Hindle in Egypt. "I am the voice of one crying in the wilderness. What a bleeding hole! I had hopes to get to the Battalion direct from hospital, but the C.O. said such movement must be done through Convalescent Camps and one must be classified either: I.H. (Invalided Home) L.C. (Lines of Communications) or A.S. (Active Service). I cornered the M.O. and told him I wanted to go A.S. to Egypt. After an administration of brandy, he recovered and said I was the only one who ever asked for that. He put me down A.S. straight-away. So far, so good. Yesterday a draft of Colonial troops (I.H.) left for Australia. I tried to get a passage with them as far as Egypt without success. I have written to Capt. Watson (now the Battalion Medical Officer) asking him to ask for my release as soon as possible. One of the staff here says he can easily get me I.H. on the next draft. All N.C.O's and W.O's seem to work that job alright. If the Captain writes the C.O. here, I think I shall escape such a fate". (Cpl. Todd got to Egypt on the eve of the Battalions' departure for France on March 2nd, 1916).
4. 15835 Pte. James Clarence Wixted, of Accrington, aged 24, a single man, is commemorated on the Helles Memorial, Gallipoli, Turkey.
5. The 'torpedo incident' caused some bitterness in later years. In 1918, the War Office decided members of the Battalion did not qualify for the 1915 Star because 'they had not served on the establishment of a unit in a theatre of war during that year'. Many considered a torpedo being fired at them qualified them. Two formal appeals failed. As late as April 1935, Major Proctor, Accrington's M.P., told the first Annual Reunion of the Battalion 'he would not let the matter rest'. There is no record, however, of any further action, or applications to the War Office.
6. The only enemy submarine known to be in the area was the U38, commanded by Captain Valentine, later listed as a war criminal for shelling and machine gunning survivors of torpedoed ships. From December 27th, 1915, to January 4th 1916 he sank

five British, including the 'Persia', and several allied ships with the loss of over 500 lives. The U38 survived the war. She was surrendered to France February 23rd, 1919 and broken up for scrap at Brest in 1921.

7. History of the Great War, Military Operations, Egypt and Palestine, Note I pp 98-99.
8. 31 Division with 11 and 13 Divisions, became part of XV Corps formed in Egypt on January 12th, 1916. XV Corps was responsible for No. 3 (Northern) Section, (El Ferdan to Port Said) Canal Zone Defences.
9. 18103 Pte. John Connor of Oswaldtwistle, aged 40, sailed with the 6th Battalion on February 13th, 1916, to Mesopotamia. He drowned crossing the River Tigris on April 10th, 1916. He is buried at Amara War Cemetery, Iraq.
10. Lt. Henry Harrison Mitchell of Blackburn, aged 29, a single man and a former insurance broker in Blackburn. He is buried in Port Said War Memorial Cemetery. Major Ross wrote to Lt. Mitchell's parents:- "I have had the pleasure of being his Company Commander from the very first, and a better Lieutenant and comrade I could not possibly have wished for. His men were devoted to him and I can assure you we all feel his loss very greatly. He is the first officer in the Brigade to give his life for his country and we shall always hold his name in honour and reverence."
11. History of the Great War, Military Operations, Egypt and Palestine, Note II pp 170-174.
12. A.O. 18/3/16.
N.B. Rickman, using a pre-arranged code, informed his fiancee in England of his departure. His telegram, dated March 2nd, 1916, said simply, 'Go to the florists. All well. Rickman'.
13. 15478 Pte. W. Baron, 'X' Company, was married and lived in Rishton. He is buried in Port Said War Memorial Cemetery.
14. Postcard, Egyptian scene, dated March 8th, 1916. Written at sea, posted Huppy, Northern France, March 12th, 1916.
15. 31 Division was the second of five divisions to leave Egypt for France during the first quarter of 1916. The men of 31 Division firmly believed that they left Egypt in order of military efficiency. Only the experienced 46 (North Midland) Division (Territorials), who left on February 15th, were deemed to be better than they.

Chapter Six

We captured Serre three times a day

The train was old, draughty with wooden seats and the men were squashed tightly into the carriages. It travelled slowly through the fresh green countryside, passing through Orange, Lyons and Dijon, stopping only for the men to exercise and eat. "The rations were served at rather longer intervals than our stomachs were accustomed." (Cpl. Bradshaw) An extra 'brew' of tea became more welcome as the train drew northward into colder weather. Pte. Pollard's colleague, Pte. Tom Carey, an ex-railway fitter, showed the rest of the squad (when the train-driver wasn't looking) where to drain the hot water from the engine. Cold nights and overcrowding made sleep impossible as they passed through Reims, Amiens and Abbeville. Pte. Sayer suffered more than most. He still had not been able to get treatment for his poisoned hand. He was in constant agony. At last, at 11 a.m. on March 11th, fifty hours from Marseilles, came the end of the line at Pont Remy, Picardy.

Suffering from the cold and incongruously wearing pith helmets, the Battalion marched six miles to their billets of barns, outhouses and cottages in the village of Huppy. Immediately, several of 'Z' Company complained to Major Ross about the filthy lice-ridden straw and the rats scuttling about on beams overhead. His reply came, "You're in France now, my lads, so you had better get used to it." After all the longing to come to France, they already dearly missed Egypt and the warmth of her sun. Several men including Pte. Marshall, entered hospital in Amiens suffering from frost-bite. At long last Pte. Sayer's hand was treated, only now his miseries increased. The poison in his system produced a crop of boils on his neck and face.

Luckier men went on leave. Captain Watson of 'W' Company, returned to Accrington where his 'sun-tan was much admired.' Rickman went to Godalming to marry his fiancee, who had 'gone to the florists' as part of the wedding preparations. He took with him as a wedding present a silver tray inscribed with the names of the thirty five officers of the Battalion. Pte. Cowell, still hoping, wrote to Polly on March 24th, "It has been snowing heavily since last

night and Billy Gladstone isn't half as cold as we are. I am expecting to see you before long — they are doing their best to get us home. Tell your mother to start making that potato-pie." Cpl. Bradshaw wrote, with less confidence, "only two per Company (ten per Battalion, including H.Q.) are ballotted when a leave train is despatched, so it will be 1917 before some of us arrive home.[1]

Others busied themselves in the new routine. Pte. Coady and C.Q.M.S. Hindle re-organised the concert parties, ex-members of Miss Knight's

Below: X' (District) Company at Marseilles boarding the train for Picardy and the Front.

Top left: Lt. Colonel Rickman and his wife.
Top right: AQMS Jack Hindle.
Bottom left: Pte. Will Cowell and his wife.
Bottom right: Captain A. G. Watson.

118

Above: Lt. General Sir A. G. Hunter-Weston (holding map) with his staff officers.
IWM

French classes from 1914 Chorley days got the chance to say in French, "Madam, I want something to eat, as I am very hungry," and so dined on 'oeuf et pommes frites et cafe avec' in Huppy's only cafe. Others 'scrounged' — and sometimes bought — eggs from farmhouses to supplement their meagre rations. Keeping warm and clean became a preoccupation, now that everyone was infested with body-lice. 'Chatting' (finding and killing lice and their eggs) was a new social pastime.

On March 1st, 1916, as 31 Division was enroute for France, General Sir Henry Rawlinson, as Commander of the newly formed Fourth Army took over a fifteen mile length of the Third Army sector,[2] from the River Somme to Hebuterne. On its arrival, 31 Division went into VIII Corps (Lt. Gen. Sir A. G. Hunter-Weston G.O.C.) then in Fourth Army Reserve

with Corps H.Q. at Marieux, five miles S.E. of Doullens. As more Divisions joined VIII Corps, 31 Division, at the end of March, moved nearer the Fourth Army sector.[3] Each Battalion moved independently through the French countryside towards the Front. The journey of the 11th East Lancs took eight days, marching through Longpré, Vignacourt and Beauval to Bertrancourt for a five day stay. Then, on through Courcelles to Colincamps, thirteen kilometres north of Albert and two kilometres behind the line.

As the Battalion approached Colincamps the undulating countryside reminded some of Salisbury Plain on a smaller scale. Here, however, the houses in the villages en-route were gaunt ruins, with few people left to watch them pass by. The narrow, winding roads crawled with motor-lorries and horse-drawn waggons laden

NORTH SEA

River Waal

River Maas

HOLLAND

River Rhine

GERMANY

Zeebrugge

ANTWERP

Ostend

COLOGNE

Ghent

Dunkirk

River Yser

Passchendaele

River Schelde

BRUSSELS

Aix-la-Chapelle

Ypres

Menin

River Lys

St. Omer

Bailleul

Messines

River Schelde

BELGIUM

Liege

Hazebrouck

Armentieres

LILLE

Lillers

Neuve Chapelle

Mons

Namur

Huy

La Bassee

Charleroi

Bethune

Loos

Valenciennes

River Sambre

Lens

St. Pol

Douai

Arras

Cambrai

Maubeuge

Doullens

Le Cateau

Serre

Givet

Bapaume

River Moselle

AMIENS

Albert

Peronne

River Oise

Neufchateau

River Somme

St. Quentin

Guise

Trier

Ham

Mezieres

Sedan

LUXEMBOURG

Saarburg

Montdidier

La Fere

Virton

LUXEMBOURG

Lassigny

Laon

Longuyon

Noyon

River Aisne

River

Thionville

Compiegne

Soissons

Briey

River Oise

RHEIMS

METZ

Senlis

River Ourcq

VERDUN

Chantilly

Chateau Thierry

River Marne

Morhange

Epernay

Chalons

St. Mihiel

PARIS

Pt. Morin

River Ornain

Bar-le-Duc

Gd. Morin

Toul

Nancy

FRANCE

River Marne

River Meurthe

Charmes

Epinal

River Moselle

Inset map

Serre • Bapaume

Beaumont Hamel

Thiepval • High Wood

Morval

Fricourt • Delville Wood

Albert

Maricourt

Peronne

R. Somme

Chaulnes

0 2 4 6

MILES

The Western Front
Approximate line 1916

0 10 20 30 40 50

miles

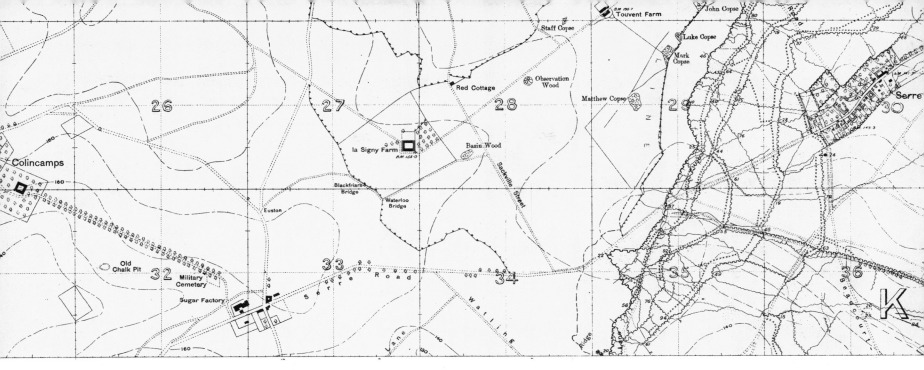

with the impedimenta of war. Hutted encampments, horse lines and gun batteries filled every open space. The marching column constantly made way for staff cars and ambulances. Thousands of troops repaired the pave roads, constructed gun-positions and unloaded stores and ammunition into wayside dumps. The whole area seethed with men, horses and vehicles. Marching through the men of the Battalion could hear above the traffic noise the sound of distant artillery fire. They became infected by the atmosphere, the 'feel', of being behind the lines. The final kilometre into Colincamps ran on high ground, parallel to the front line and alongside the road stretched canvas screens to keep the passage of troops from enemy observation.

Pte. Pollard with his section, and 'W' Company, were directed into an empty barn in the village.

"We were packed inside, in tiers of wooden bunks. We then, in our curiosity and innocence, walked about the streets, gazing round at the wreckage and picking up empty cartridge cases. We thought how wonderful it was to be at the Front."

It was April 4th. Pte. Cowell posted his card to Polly. Written on March 29th — and using postcards bought in Egypt — he said, "You would think you were never going to hear from me again, but we have been moving and they wouldn't take any post until we arrived — I am waiting for my turn for home which I hope comes soon. I haven't received any letters from you for a week now, I suppose they are delayed."[4]

With the 11th East Lancs in Brigade Reserve at Colincamps, 94 Brigade took over the front-line sector running from the Serre — Amiens road to John Copse, the northernmost of four named after the Evangelists, Matthew, Mark, Luke, John. On April 12th, the Battalion moved to Warnimont Wood near Bertrancourt in Divisional Reserve until April 28th. They provided

working parties for the unending, gruelling job of deepening and extending reserve and communication trenches along with moving stores and ammunition to the front line. The trench system before Serre had originally been held by the French, and the bodies of many 'poilus', hastily buried during the battles of 1914, were found and removed.

94 Brigade sector was quiet. Since the autumn of 1914 the French — and later the British — and the Germans held a minimum of infantrymen in the front line and both sides used artillery only to 'warn off' an occasional threatened attack. Both were content so long as each kept to his own side of No Man's Land. The Germans used the time to deepen and reinforce their trench systems, constructing deep, shell-proof, dug-outs and underground tunnels. Cellars in the ruined houses of Serre became imp-

Above: Scene of operations. The British Front Line before the fortified village of Serre. 94 Brigade covered the area from Matthew Copse to John Copse in the north. British trenches were not indicated on this map of the period, for security reasons.

Below: Many of the cottages in Serre were converted into strong-points by the Germans. In this interior view of a similiar German point, an upper platform has been built so as to provide extra fire-power.
B.C.P.L.

SECRET

_____ Denotes Trenches not verified.

Above and below: Typical German trenches on the Somme in 1916. Villages were weaved into the defence system and trench construction was neater and more elaborate than the British and French. **B.C.P.L.**

Far right: Lt/Col. Rickman's own map, printed on cloth, of his sector of the line and the approaches thereto.

regnable machine-gun emplacements. Now, since the arrival of the British Fourth Army and their preparations for the 'Big Push', artillery activity and infantry patrolling had increased on both sides.

Quiet as may be, the sector had territorial disadvantages. The front line ran roughly along the bottom of a broad rolling valley which ran down a watershed south west of Serre past Beaumont Hamel and Thiepval. The ground sloped up, both east and west; east towards the German lines, and west to the British support and reserve trenches. Serre village lay on the summit of a decided rise and was obviously an observation point of great value to the Germans. From 94 Brigade trenches to the edge of the village, a distance of 700 yards, no fewer than four lines of German trenches were visible. The village itself, though battered by shell-fire, still showed some rooftops through a

thick screen of trees and shrubs. Refugee villagers told of house cellars long converted to machine-gun emplacements.

The quietness of the sector clearly deceived the Battalion's unseasoned officers. Captain F. G. MacAlpine described the Battalion's sector — "It is clear any attack on Serre would be an attack uphill and over ground covered by enemy observation. Also, any assembly position for an attack would be on a forward slope. There were few, if any, deep dug-outs — but there were adequate splinter-proof shelters. All parts of the line were accessible by day. Such was the trench system held by the Battalion and it was probably ideal for an inexperienced battalion."[5] Only the quietness was ideal. The ground was an amphi-theatre with one contestant in the arena and the other on the terraces. Private Sayer had entirely different thoughts — "Serre? Sayer! Same name as myself, it can only be lucky for me."

For three weeks prior to their official takeover of their sector of the line on April 28th, advance parties from the 11th East Lancs entered the front line trenches under the supervision of troops of the 1/6th Gloucestershire Regiment of 144 Brigade, 48 Division. N.C.O.'s went first. L/Cpl. Marshall (returned from hospital and newly promoted) had an early taste of things to come.

"We were still behind the reserve trenches, hardly out of Colincamps, when six of us N.C.O.'s, making our way towards the front line, passed in front of a battery of six inch Howitzers as one fired a round. The sudden noise terrified us all. We threw ourselves to the ground, much to the amusement of the gun-crew. The experience broke the nerve of one Sergeant. Although badly shocked, he went with us into the line, but later returned to the rear, never to go into the line again."

Bombers, Signallers, Lewis-gunners went in their turn. Lt. Rawcliffe took in his newly formed Stokes Mortar team.[6]

The men reached the front line through a maze of shallow communication trenches starting inside the ruins of the Sucrerie (a ruined sugar-beet factory) some half mile from the front line. The trenches steadily deepened as they neared the front line. The front line trenches were cut at varying depths in the chalky soil and revetted in places by timber supports. The trenches, about four feet wide at the base, were drained by sumps cut into the floor and covered by duck-boards every few yards. Originally dug by the Germans in 1914, the trench firing-steps (a shelf cut into the trench side for snipers and sentries) and parapets were on the wrong side, consequently front line duties became mainly construction and repair work as shallow parts were deepened, firing-steps re-dug and new parapets strengthened with the spoil.

A number of fifteen man sections went to different parts of the front line for twenty-four hour periods. Pte. Pollard awaited his turn.

"As men came back, they said, 'It's very quiet, there's nowt going on down yon'. The rest of us waiting to go still had mixed feelings — keen to experience it, yet apprehensive. Sam Smith, our section corporal, said 'George, don't say anything to anybody. I'll put your name down for tomorrow to 'go over the top' — as if he were doing me a favour. I went in as reserve with the Lewis-gunners. We marched from Colincamps to Sucrerie, a ruined sugar-beet factory astride the communication trench. Our guide was a Royal Engineer. On our way in we met another section coming out. I saw Harry Kay. Harry said, 'Do you want this steel helmet?' I said, 'What for, if it's so quiet?' At that precise moment, I heard cries of 'Make way! Make way!' We stood aside for stretcher-bearers carrying someone with a blanket over him. Some silly fool said, 'What's to do with him?' My answer was 'Give me that bloody helmet!' "

Above: The Sucrerie (sugar beet factory) See map on page 121. At this point entry was made into the 94 Brigade trench system before Serre. I.W.M.Q1769

For the raw troops the introduction to even a 'quiet' sector could be a nerve-wracking experience. As Pte. Pollard's section arrived in the front line trenches, the Spring sun shone bright and warm.

"It was so peaceful, with hardly a sound or movement. I thought, half seriously, 'the war will last forever at this rate, there's nothing happening.' Each of us received, alternatively, a pick or shovel and were put to work repairing the trench parapet. It was still very quiet. Suddenly there was a metallic ring, we ducked thinking it was a bullet, but someone's pick had struck a shovel. Then I heard a noise. I first thought of a train coming, but it was a train coming through the air and blowing up around me. A shell crashed only yards away. I was never so scared in my life. I tried to get in a small dug-out but it was already full of men (the old hands knew what was coming). I got down on my knees at the bottom of the trench with the other men. I thanked God I had a spade to put over my head. We heard, over the noise, an order to put on our gas-helmets. As we struggled to put them on some men were being carried away and laid out. The shelling eventually ceased and we relaxed. We were given hot tea with bread and cheese. The food attracted huge, bloated rats above us on the parapet. Some men had no more sense than throw pieces of cheese at them. Because of the rats we

Right: Pte. Arthur Riley. The first man from Accrington to die in France. He died of wounds on April 30th, 1916. **Far right:** Pte. Wilfred Ellison. The first Pal from Chorley to die France. He died from an untreated appendicitis on May 25th' 1916.

Above: Pte. Jack Clark. The first Burnley Pal to die in France. He was killed in action on April 29th, 1916.

later slept, as best we could, with our cap comforters over our faces for protection. We were relieved at four o'clock in the afternoon. By seven o'clock, at dusk, we were leaving the communication trench for Colincamps. I thought, 'This is my future and there is no way out of it'."

Nothing in their training prepared the men for this reality. Even seeing the state that the Gallipoli veterans of the 6th East Lancs were in when they had met up with them in Egypt had not done so. The fear of pain and death and the fear of being afraid had to be overcome. The revulsion at body lice and beetle infested bedding, the obscene rats feeding on the bodies of men, the lack of proper sleep and the exhausting fatigues all had to be endured. For most the nervous strain eased, but never entirely went away, and men adapted. On his second turn in the trenches Pte. Pollard watched British artillery fire through a periscope. "The Colonel (Rickman) and Captain Peltzer, the Adjutant, came by. The Colonel said: 'What can you see out there?' I replied, 'I can see we are giving them summat for a change — Sir' ".

Many men, including Cpl. Bradshaw, thought the food much better in the trenches than in the rear area. Despite the conditions, many were glad to be in the trenches 'at last'. Pte. Arthur Riley, of 'W' Company, wrote home, referring to newspaper comments, "We are doing dangerous work here. We have been out in all weathers and all we get in the papers is, 'aren't the Pals in the trenches yet?' Accrington

will be glad to hear that the Pals are in the trenches at last."[7]

The day after the Battalion's official take-over on April 28th of their 350 yard sector of the line, a raid across No Man's Land by the 15th West Yorks Regiment (the Leeds Pals) immediately on the Battalion's right, provoked heavy shelling by the enemy. As a result the Battalion lost its first man in action. As 'Z' Company was on 'Stand To', a shell burst buried four men. One fought his way out and gave the alarm. Pte. Fred Sayer was nearby and he and Sgt. Ben Duckworth ran to help.

"Of two men only the helmets could be seen. With only rifles between us I ran for entrenching tools while Sgt. Duckworth scrabbled with his bare hands to clear the men's faces. When we pulled the men out two were badly injured and Pte. Jack Clark was dead. His brother, who gave the alarm, was unhurt."[8] Pte. Arthur Riley, of Accrington and Pawtucket, USA, wounded by another shell-burst, died four hours later.[9]

Seven others were wounded in this, the Battalion's first serious incident, although in the rear area, as early as April 7th, Pte. Kendall of 'Y' Company had been wounded by stray shrapnel. The Battalion's first eight day front line duty ended with two killed, one dead from wounds and twelve wounded. Until then they had considered themselves as lucky.

Pte. Sayer accompanied the more severely wounded to hospital. Whilst frantically digging out the buried men he injured his leg and sprained his back. He was also weak and fever-ish because of his poisoned hand and his boils. 'My leg, hand and neck were dressed and a belladonna plaster put on my back, which was not helped by the uncomfortable stretcher.'

Only days later, however, his spirits improved so much he wrote in his pocket-book an adver-tisement:

TO BE LET:
Shrapnel View.
Three minutes from the German lines, this attractive and well-built dug-out:
Containing one kitchen-bedroom and up to date funk-hole 4ft by 3ft.
All modern inconveniences including gas and water.
This desirable residence stands one foot above water-level, commanding an excel-lent view of the enemy trenches.
Excellent shooting (Duck and Snipe).
Particulars from the tenant, Room 6, 93rd Field Hospital.

Two days later he was on his way back to 'Shrapnel View'.

During the Battalion's stay, new communi-cation trenches opened up and several saps ex-tended into No Man's Land as advanced listen-ing posts. Working under frequent shell-fire was hard but some found 'standing-to' equally try-ing. Sgt. Martin Folan wrote, "When firing stops everybody 'stands-to' and an awful silence follows. This can last for an hour and a half; it's terrible. You imagine all sorts of things.

You see what is known as 'trench-stare'. Chaps' eyes bulge out of their heads, giving you the impression they are going mad. It's a great relief when the order 'stand-down' is given."[10]

On May 5th the Battalion, relieved by the 13th York and Lancaster Regiment, moved to Warnimont Wood and later Courcelles au Bois in Divisional Reserve. They 'rested' on working parties and fatigues until they occupied the front line again on May 20th. They lost two killed and twenty three wounded as they worked on improving trenches and wiring in No Man's Land.[11]

Sgt. James Rigby, 15587, of 'W' Company, observed three Germans who had been throwing grenades into the Battalion trenches from a disused trench in No Man's Land. Taking four grenades he went out alone and attacked the German position, killing all three. For this ac-tion Sgt. Rigby received the M.M., the Bat-talion's first battle award.

During this period 78 O.R.'s transferred in from 31st Division Cyclist Company (East York-shire Regiment). Lt. Bury (Flash Harry) of the Transport Section left on three months special leave. Captains Milton and Ross, neither of them young men, left to work in more amen-able surroundings at 31 Division H.Q. at Bus les Artois. Captain Watson transferred to the R.A.M.C. as a surgeon with X Corps at 45 CCS, Contay and Lt. Ruttle went to hospital in England with pneumonia.

Above: Sgt. James Rigby

Below: A typical dugout of a British officer. Pte. Sayer's would not have been so elaborate.
B.C.P.L.

Out of the line working parties took up much time. These were 'miserable affairs' and considered worse than being in the line. A party of 72 'W' Company men went to the Trench Mortar Batteries as ammunition carriers. In thirteen days the men brought 3,600 bombs (50 per man) to storage points in two front line saps. Carrying the heavy, bulky bombs taxed the men to the limit. Pte. Kay endured this.

"One night the rain poured incessantly. Our protective gas-capes didn't stop us getting wet through from feet to chest and covered with mud. We were each to carry one Stokes mortar bomb (like a football on a stick) to the forward trenches. As we approached the line, there was a 'bit of a do' on (a night raid) and we came under shell-fire. We tried to continue along the wet and congested communication trench to Matthew Copse. We were soon too exhausted to care about the shell-fire — we had had enough — so we walked along the parapet, in the open and chanced being hit. As it happened, we got away with it."

This unending 'donkey-work' left them only a limited preparation time for the 'Big Push'. In May, G.H.Q. directed Divisional training into two main categories; firstly, the attack against enemy trenches and strong points and consolidation of the positions won; and secondly, the exploitation of a successful break-through of the enemy defence system. With the inexperienced and untried officers and men of many of its new Divisions in mind, G.H.Q. introduced a system of precise, detailed orders to remedy, or at least counteract, any human deficiencies.

In issuing these orders G.H.Q. admitted, "officers and men do not now generally possess that military knowledge arising from a long and high state of training which enables them to act promptly on sound lines in unexpected situations. They have been accustomed to deliberate action based on precise and detailed orders."[11] A training programme based on 'precise and detailed' orders was then promptly issued.

The training to acquire that military knowledge started too late. In the 11th East Lancs. working parties, using every available man, took priority until June 5th. On that day the battalion marched to Gezaincourt, on the outskirts of Doullens, to be inspected and addressed by VIII Corps Commander, Lt. Gen. Sir A. G. Hunter-Weston, or 'Hunter Bunter' as he was more irreverently known. Pte. Snailham was in the front rank.

"He gave us the usual thing about 'doing our bit cheerily' in the Big Push — we knew he said the same to everybody — and he confidently assured us the planned artillery barrage would completely destroy the German wire and forward trenches. He told us there would be no Germans left in the trenches when we got there, 'there would not even be a rat alive', he said."

Many of his audience later remembered this last phrase with bitterness.

Rehearsals for the Battalion and Brigade attack on Serre began immediately.[12] A stretch of land supposedly similar to the Brigade attack area was laid out for the rehearsal. Shallow ditches represented British and German trenches, flags the limits of the British artillery barrage, and tapes the starting and finishing points of each wave. The 11th East Lancs. attacked to the East in three bounds of four waves under a mock moving barrage which lifted from the enemy front trench at zero hour, it then moved forward at the walking pace of the waves of infantry. The Battalion's waves advanced waist high through growing wheat and oats totally unlike the grassy slopes of their own sector. A 'parade-ground like' change of direction to the North, whilst each wave maintained its pace complicated the advance. 94 Brigade was the left flank brigade of the whole attack and after capturing Serre village, its duty was to form a defensive flank facing north with 93 Brigade on its right, facing north east. The 11th East Lancs. and the 12th York and Lancasters were to lead the attack.

Hunter-Weston's confidence reached down to most of his officers, but a few of his men remained sceptical. Pte. Pollard was one.

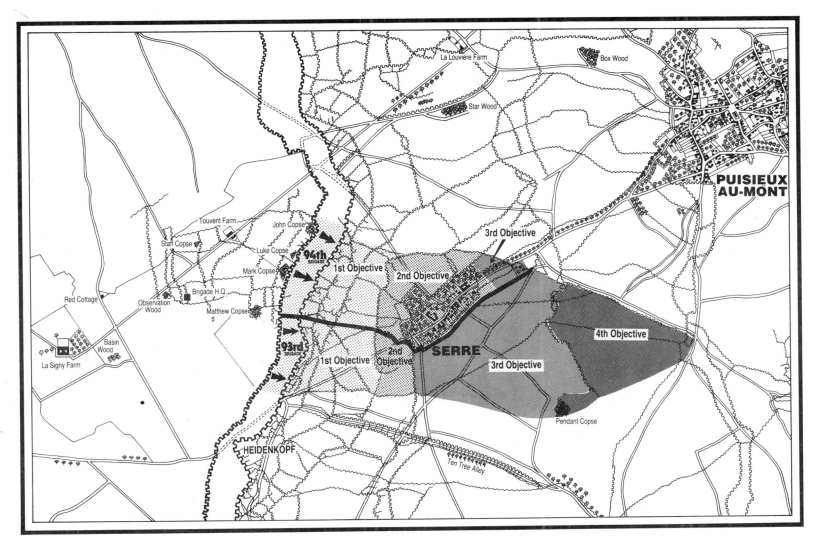

Labels on map: La Louviere Farm · Box Wood · Star Wood · PUISIEUX AU-MONT · Touvent Farm · John Copse · Staff Copse · 3rd Objective · Luke Copse · 94th BRIGADE · Mark Copse · 1st Objective · 2nd Objective · Red Cottage · Brigade H.Q. · Observation Wood · Matthew Copse · 4th Objective · Basin Wood · 93rd BRIGADE · 2nd Objective · SERRE · 3rd Objective · La Signy Farm · 1st Objective · Pendant Copse · HEIDENKOPF · Ten Tree Alley

"We captured Serre three times a day. It was a joke. All the mistakes of the day were later gone over. Each of the four waves was meant to advance at intervals, in daylight, towards the German trenches, occupy them, consolidate, then allow the succeeding waves to pass through. It didn't seem very practical to me. I said to Lt. Ashworth, 'This advance, Sir, it's not just going to be like that. We might be going the other road (retreating) before we are finished'. He said, 'Pollard, don't you know the British Army never retreats?' I said, 'What happened at Mons, then?' 'That', he said, 'was a strategic manoeuvre'. Lt. Ashworth, and the other officers, made it look simple and we were not allowed to think of anything only success. We were treated like imbeciles."

Unknown to Pte. Pollard, his disquiet was shared by at least one experienced senior officer in VIII Corps. A Major Wilson of the 1/8th Royal Warwickshire Regiment, attached to 4th Division later wrote, "I received my Battalion Operation Orders. On reading through the orders I came to the conclusion that we were all going to commit suicide. The General Staff undoubtedly believed enemy machine-guns

would largely be out of action and the orders constrained the attacking force to advance in broad daylight at a steady walk."[13]

There were other criticisms. Brigadier General H. C. Rees took over as G.O.C. 94 Brigade on June 15th, two weeks before the planned attack. "In this terrible document, 'Scheme for the Offensive' — were 76 pages, and 31 Division alone issued 365 supplementary instructions. It took me three days to reduce this to 8 pages and 5 maps. The first principles of war were overwhelmed by a mass of detail which dispensed with individual initiative and any elasticity."[14] Whatever the thoughts of senior officers, however expressed, those of junior officers were obliged to follow G.H.Q.'s dictum to ensure "that all may feel convinced that when we fight, we win."[15]

In Accrington another less weighty conflict brewed. A local newspaper published a letter from Cpl. Bradshaw describing life in the trenches. He concluded, "We have not had anything from the Comforts Fund yet, except cap-badges for which we were charged 2/6d. each. I suppose we will get something in a day or two. There are rumours lots of good things are on the way."[16] Public criticism about the Fund forced a reply from Harwood. "To the Pals have

Above: The plan of attack. 94 Brigade on the extreme left flank of the British front was to capture the fortified village of Serre, then turn north east and shield the northern limit of the entire British attack.

gone 200 cap-badges, canvas covers for machine-guns and rifles, 16 pieces of band music, 500 tins of cocoa, 800 pairs of socks, 144 safety razors and 8 footballs, at a cost of £160. We have not sent any sweets, cakes or cigarettes, but have asked the C.O. to specify any requirements."[17]

Rickman's requirements from the Fund were clearly different from those of his Accrington men.[18] He explained in his reply to Harwood, "The 200 cap-badges have been distributed and in other circumstances the men would have to pay for them — cigarettes can be bought cheaper here than in England." More concerned about future operational needs than sweets or cakes, Rickman appealed to Harwood to send "as soon as possible, several pairs of wire-cutters."[19]

Whilst perhaps seen by some as a 'tempest in a tea-cup,' the incident says much for the value Rickman placed on his relationship with Harwood and the closeness with which the home towns kept in touch with the Battalion. Rickman pursued this correspondence whilst, on the eve of the biggest offensive of the war, he was temporarily O.C. 94 Brigade, in the absence on sick-leave of Brig. Gen. Carter-Campbell.[20]

On June 15th, the day Brig. Gen. H. C. Rees took over command of 94 Brigade from Rickman, the Battalion returned to Warnimont Wood from Gezaincourt, its rehearsals for the 'Big Push' complete. They relieved the 12th York and Lancaster Regiment in the line on June 19th. Twelve were killed and twenty four wounded in their five day 'tour'.

Two were killed instantaneously, in a crowded

trench, by a comrade 'clearing' his rifle (pulling the trigger) after cleaning it. He himself was killed in action on July 1st.

Conditions were worsening but they were learning their trade. Pte. Kay, although a Lewis-gunner, became proficient at sniping, using newly acquired telescopic sights — "we used to put a pencil in a bullet-hole or even a wound, to get the angle and direction of an enemy shot." Pte. Snailham spent many hours in a listening-post in No Man's Land; Pte. Place went on night raids and patrols, with Pte. Pollard, on the Lewis gun giving necessary covering fire. Cpl. Bradshaw's H.Q. signalling section, always under enemy observation, laid miles of telephone cable six feet deep supposedly safe from all but the heaviest shelling.

The Stokes mortar teams moved along the trenches, stopping at intervals to check the range (usually 250-300 yards) then moving on. Lt. Rawcliffe and his men were not popular.

"The place we had just left invariably got 'strafed' with a few 'whizz-bangs' (German 77 millimetre shells) in retaliation. The battalion had several casualities that way. We also held competitions amongst ourselves. By cutting fuses to different lengths we would get up to five bombs in the air exploding at the same time. As the attack drew nearer we were limited to four shots a day."

As the Battalion left the front line heading back to Warnimont Wood on June 24th, Pte. Stanley Clark, of 'W' Company began a most singular experience.[21]

"C.S.M. Hey watched us file towards him. He stopped me, Roger Singleton, Bill Hargreaves and L/Cpl. Sharples, then took us up to a narrow trench to a reserve dump of Mills bombs, boxes of 303 ammunition and sand-bags full of iron rations. He said, 'This is your responsibility. I'll relieve you in a couple of days. Two days later we went to the ration dump at the Sucrerie. Nobody there knew anything about us. An officer in the 'Warwicks' would have nothing to do with us and told us to get back to our posts. It was obvious C.S.M. Hey had forgotten us. Later we came under shell-fire. We got fed up with this so we ran up to the front-line whenever shelling started, sheltered in a sap, then returned to the dump when the shelling stopped. Unfortunately, Royal Engineers, experimenting with gas discharges, used the same sap and occasionally gas drifted back into it, so we needed wet blankets over our heads for protection. Coming into the front line on about the fourth night, I got caught in the open by the shelling, so I dived into a funk-hole in a trench. I landed on top of two dead Royal Engineers killed by their own gas. After that we stayed at the

dump. Our dilemma was we couldn't leave, we had to wait for relief whenever it came."

Pte. Clark and the others took over the dump on June 24th, so probably made the decision to stay there all the time on June 30th.

At Warnimont Wood on June 4th, a final batch of 58 O.R.'s and one officer arrived from the Reserve battalion at Prees Heath. Not one had trained under battle conditions, whilst at the same time 17 experienced men were transferred to the Machine Gun Corps. The rest of the battalion spent their time at Warnimont Wood resting, free from working parties at last and preparing for the offensive due to start on June 29th. The accommodation huts were wretched, with neither doors nor windows, with no beds to sleep on. Pte. Pollard was with Ptes. Walt Greaves and Harry Wilkinson.

"We only had one blanket each, so the three of us put one blanket under and two over and so laid together on the floor to keep warm, with me in the middle. They were both a lot older than I was (I was not yet eighteen and they were married

Above: Pte. Walt Greaves

Above: Pte. Harry Wilkinson

129

Above: Part of the intensive artillery bombardment of German positions before the attack. A British heavy gun in action.
B.C.P.L.

Above: Capt. Phillip Broadley

Opposite page: Commander in Chief of the British Forces in France and Flanders, General Sir Douglas Haig, G.C.B.,K.C.I.E.,K.C.V.O.

with families), and so, in their way, they looked after me."

Poor living conditions, the stress of trench life, bad weather and sheer hard work took its toll. Ptes. Place and Coady went exhausted into hospital for short periods. Leave continued to be allocated, though not for Pte. Cowell. Captain Broadley, O.C. 'X' Company, the last of the original Company Commanders, went home suffering from a foot infection and did not return to France. Lt. Rawclife returned from leave, on June 28th in time for the Big Push.

The intensive artillery bombardment to precede the attack opened up on June 24th, the attack itself was planned to start at 7.30 a.m. on 'Z' day, June 29th. The bombardment was intended to shatter the enemy trench system, destroy his barbed wire and machine-gun posts to prepare the way for the attack of seventeen Divisions on the fifteen mile long British sector of the front. The enemy wire had to be cut, if this should remain intact anywhere, the planned walk over No Man's Land into the enemy front line, would end literally, 'on the wire'.

The eighteen pounders and the 4.5in. howitzers, using shrapnel, pounded the German wire. The heavier 6in., 8in. and 9.2 guns and howitzers concentrated on destroying the communication trenches and other approaches to the enemy front line. The bombardment continued day after day with a lull arranged each night for patrols to examine the effect on the enemy wire. Early reports showed the wire not cut as

much as had been hoped. The 'precise and detailed' orders for the artillery allowed no discretion for last minute changes and the heavier guns and howitzers continued to expend their high explosive shells on to the enemy second line trenches. On June 28th bad weather forced the British and French Commanders to postpone 'Z' day 48 hours to July 1st.

Up to the night of June 30th/July 1st, patrols examined the wire and tested the enemy defences .Nowhere on the front line was the wire completely severed in any quantity. In 31 Division's sector two battalions reported no clear gap anywhere on their front; another reported the remaining wire posed no serious obstacle; a fourth returned that there were gaps every 20 yards but they did not stretch for more than 3 to 10 yards. During this period Sir Douglas Haig, the Commander in Chief deprecated VIII Corp's lack of success in breaking into the enemy positions on its front. "He also expressed himself dissatisfied with Corps staff and with the 29th and 31st Divisions."[22]

As 'Z' day approached, the men of the 11th East Lancs., in their open huts seven miles behind the line, prepared themselves materially and mentally. Those selected for the fighting platoons checked and repaired their weapons and equipment. The Battalion boot repairer and tailor busied themselves. Storemen issued new clothing and equipment where necessary. Officers and N.C.O.'s checked and re-checked their written orders and procedures. Regimental bands prepared for their duties as stretcher-bearers.

Captain Riley, now O.C. 'Z' Company, knew that 48 Division, on 94 Brigade's immediate left, would not take part in the attack, thus leaving the Brigade's flank dangerously exposed. His knowledge, combined with the rigid, complex plan of attack, made Captain Riley apprehensive and unsure of success. On the night of June 29th he visited each hut of 'Z' Company. "In his quiet, homely way, he told the men the task before them would be immense. He as much as said it would be as well for us to prepare to meet our Maker."[23] Riley particularly spent time with 15 Platoon, his Lad's Club members, whom he always tried to keep together and perhaps shield from the influence of some of the hard-drinking toughs of 'Z' Company.

A few days before Pte. Fred Sayer returned from hospital after treatment for a leg injury and strained back resulting from his efforts to recover Pte. Clark's body on April 29th.

"Still sick and excused all duties, I had little to do. Captain Riley asked me, "Not in the attack?" 'No, Sir,' "You're lucky," he replied. 'I don't think so, Sir. I want to be with my friends. I've trained for this and now I'm missing it."

During their conversation, he volunteered to look after 'Z' Company reserve bomb store in the front line trench during the attack. Captain Riley gratefully agreed, because it gave him an extra fit man for the attack.

Altogether a quiet air of serious anticipation spread about the camp. During the day men were busy, but in the evenings when at rest they talked and some shared Captain Riley's forebodings. L/Cpl. Marshall:

"A lot of men talked of death and dying. We knew a lot of us would not come back, but we just had to accept it."

Pte. Pollard:

"Everyone knew they were in a position from which they could not extricate themselves and so had to go along with it. The 'fiery zeal' of going over the top with bayonet fixed just wasn't there. They just had it to do, so they did it. Patriotism was getting back alive. The majority prayed for a 'Blighty one'."

About this time Pte. Pollard went down with pneumonia. His friends were moved out of the hut, and others who were sick took their places.

"My sergeant, Jack Pilkington, came to see me. He asked me who I thought could take my place on the Lewis gun team. I told him, 'Either Harry Kay or George Stuttard." From then on I was too ill to care."

Pte. Cowell wrote to Polly, "I have not had a letter for three days — I shall likely get them in a bunch as you did" — and, in a reference **to the coming Chorley July holidays — "You will see me stepping home just as if there never**

Above: Pte. H. 'Kid' Nutter

had been a war on — and we'll have a wagonette for a day out, just see if we don't." [24]

Pte. Coady, out of hospital, wrote to his friend Isaac Edwards "We had rather a rough time in the trenches, but we gave them more than we got. I have had some near do's, but I thank God I am alright as yet. I hope to come out of it, but if it pleases God to take me, it will be alright, I am in his hands." [25] Pte. 'Kid' Nutter, the boxer, wrote more optimistically to his mother. "I can duck the hooks and side-step the straight lefts, but I know I stand no better chance than any of the other boys. I have only once to die, but should I steer clear I will come down our street singing 'Are we downhearted?' — 'not likely' — while the Kid is floating about." [26]

In the preparations Rickman found time to write to Harwood. "We are on the eve of the biggest battle the world has yet known. We are destined for a very hard trial. Work has been very intense and we have been subjected to very hard bombardments. I think you will be proud of the way the men stick it. There have been difficulties those in England could not credit unless they experienced them. I have only now received sixteen watches for the platoon commanders, which are essential for the present operations. The lads realise the seriousness of what is to come and I feel they will do their part. It is a page of history that will take some writing." [27] It seems Rickman secretly did not share the high optimism of his superiors but felt, as Pte. Pollard and the rest, the job had to be done.

At the Advanced G.H.Q. at Beauquesne, twelve miles N.E. of Albert, as at Warnimont Wood, men's minds were on the morrow. Haig received the final reports from his Corps Commanders. In spite of the conflicting reports on the condition of the enemy wire. Hunter-Weston pronounced himself 'satisfied and confident' that VIII Corps would be successful. Haig, taking his line from this, and similar reports from his other Corps Commanders, became convinced of success. "The men are all in splendid spirits, several have said they have never before been so instructed and informed of the nature of the operations before them. The wire has never been so well cut, nor the artillery preparations so thorough." [28]

On the eve of this greatest of offensives, men reflected on the part they had to play. Some were confident and excited, others apprehensive but unafraid. All ranks, from the youngest conscript hurriedly sent from England to the G.O.C. himself, prepared themselves for the known and the unknown. All units from infantry sections to G.H.Q. itself were materially ready for the known. The unknown each individual faced alone.

NOTES

1. A.G. 4/4/16.
2. The Fourth Army took over the front with XIII and X Corps. On July 1st, 1916, Fourth Army was composed of III, VIII, X, XIII and XIV Corps.
3. Joining 31 Division in VIII Corps were 48 Division (Territorial Force) and 4 Division and 29 Division (Regular Army).
4. Postcard written at Bertrancourt and posted at Colincamps. Pte. Cowells' complaint about delays is not a reflection on the Army Postal Service. The Battalion was on the move continuously for a week. Normal postal service from the United Kingdom to the trenches of France and Belgium was three days. (See Military Operations, France and Belgium 1916 pp 125 to 129).
5. History of the East Lancs Regiment in the Great War 1914 - 1918 pp 523 — 4.
6. From April 12th, 1916, light trench mortar (Stokes) teams were formed on a Brigade basis, two per Brigade. 94 Brigade's were designated 94/1 and 94/2 Trench Mortar Batteries. Each had 24 men and 4 Stokes Mortars. On June 13th, 1916, they became 94 Trench Mortar Battery.
7. A.O. 6/5/16.
8. 16033 Pte. J. Clark, of Burnley, aged 20, a single man and formerly a miner. He is buried at Sucrerie B.W.C., Colincamps.
9. 20972 Pte. A. Riley, a native of Accrington, returned from Pawtucket, Rhode Island, U.S.A. to enlist in the Reserve Company during the recruiting march in July 1915. His letter home (See Note 7) was published a week after his death. He was 25, a single man and is buried at Beauval B.W.C.
10. A.O. 1/7/16.
11. See 'Training of Divisions for Offensive Action'. SS 109 Memorandum to all Divisions from G.H.Q. May 8th, 1916. Military Operations, France and Belgium 1916, Appendices Appendix 17 pp 125 - 130.
12. 31 Division, at the Northern extent of the proposed attack, was to advance 1000 yards, capture Serre, then pivot round facing North to form a defensive flank for the remainingg British troops on the 15 mile front. As the whole front broke through the German lines they were to swing in a huge arc into the open country beyond Bapaume.
13. P.R.O. CAB/190.
14. Ibid.
15. Military Operations, France and Belgium 1916, Appendices. Appendix 17 p 130.
16. A.G. 3/6/16.
17. A.O.T. 3/6/16.
18. In March 1916, twelve pounds of tobacco and 5000 cigarettes had arrived for 'Z' Company from Burnley Comforts Fund. A portion of these were 'lent' to Accrington men.
19. A.O.T. 10/6/16.
    N.B. The employees of Park Mill, a cotton weaving firm donated 33/- to the Comforts Fund 'towards the cost of the wire-cutters'. There is no record of their arrival to the Battalion before July 1st. However, 3500 cigarettes did arrive.
20. Another, albeit slighter, link with the Battalion occurred at the same time. Starting June 8th, 1916, at the Grand Theatre, Accrington, the play 'Pals', played to packed houses. The unenlightened asked, 'Is it about our Pals?', but only the French chateau setting gave the merest connection.
21. 17859 Pte. Stanley Clark, of Oswaldtwistle, at 16½ years, left his job in a cottton factory to enlist in the Reserve Company in December 1914.
22. Military Operations, France and Belgium 1916, p 308.
23. History of 'Z' Company page 31.
24. Postcard, undated almost certainly late June 1916.
25. C.D.H. 28/7/16.
26. A.G. 5/8/16.
27. A.G. 8/7/16.
28. The Private Papers of Douglas Haig 1914 - 1919. ed. R. Blake, p 151 Eyre and Spottiswoode, London.

THIS SUMMARY IS A CONFIDENTIAL DOCUMENT AND IT IS NOT TO GO
BEYOND BATTALION OR BATTERY HEADQUARTERS.

VIII CORPS DAILY SUMMARY NO.86.
(From 6.a.m. 26/6/16 to 6.a.m. 27/6/16)

June 27th 1916.

Map Reference,1/20,000.
except paras,3,4,5,&.6.

OPERATIONS.

1. VIII CORPS FRONT.

(a) **Artillery.** In the AUCHONVILLERS Sector the enemy replied to
our bombardment fairly actively. They were particularly active
between 11.p.m. and 12.midnight and damaged our trenches in several
places in the support and front lines.

Our artillery have damaged the enemy's support line and the
houses in BEAUMONT HAMEL. A house at Q.5.c.5.2. was set
on fire about 2.p.m. and burnt till dark.

Great damage appears to have been done to the buildings
between Q.5.c.5.6. and Q.5.c.5.0.

In the SUCRERIE Sector the enemy heavily shelled our front
line trenches and as far back as BURROW Trench - WOLF Trench
between 11.45.p.m. and 12.15.a.m.

Smoke candle discharge was made along our front at 5.45.a.m.
on 27th inst. whereupon the enemy sent up 3 red rockets and
barraged our front line.

About 5.30.p.m. a few shells fell in MAILLY, and at 5.45.
a.m. 27th twelve shells fell between BERTRANCOURT and BUS.
N.W. of BERTRANCOURT on the outskirts of the village.

In the COLINCAMPS Sector at 5.30.a.m. enemy shelled MONK, LE
CATEAU, OBSERVATION WOOD and the line from JOHN to MARK COPSES. This
was repeated at 10.a.m.

From 5.6.p.m. the enemy shelled out first three lines and at
5.15.p.m. LA SIGNY FARM was shelled.

7.8.p.m. our first and second lines from JOHN to MATHEW
COPSE were heavily shelled with H.E.

In the HEBUTERNE Sector the enemy are replying with 15.c.m.,
10.5.c.m. and 77.m.m. shells.

In reply to our smoke demonstration at 10.15.a.m. the enemy
bombarded our trenches in K.23.a.b.c. and d. causing much damage
and a few casualties. This bombardment lasted from 10.30.a.m. to
12.30.p.m.

Our trenches in K.23.a.b. and d. were heavily bombarded between
5 and 6.a.m. this morning, with 10.5.c.m. and 77.m.m. shrapnel
and H.E.

A battery of 15.c.m. hows appeared to be registering junction
of REVEL and PELISSIER at 7.p.m.

COURCELLES AU BOIS, J.29. was also shelled at midday.

(b) **Machine Guns.** In the AUCHONVILLERS Sector two machine guns
were in action last night near BEAUMONT HAMEL sweeping our parapet.

In the SUCRERIE Sector a certain amount of machine gun fire
came from the enemy's front line trenches during the enemy's
bombardment of our lines.

Hostile machine guns were also active in the HEBUTERNE Sector.

(c) **Patrols.** A patrol was sent out from the AUCHONVILLERS Sector
to cut gaps in the enemy's wire. Five gaps were cut and completed
and two others were worked on and are easily passable.

133

The outer edge of the German wire is a row of heavy iron knife rests fastened to each other by very thick wire, and fixed to the ground by strong iron screw staples. These are very difficult to move and are apparently unaffected by anything but a direct hit.

Other patrols went out during the night to examine the enemy's wire.

(4) Raids. Raids attempted by us all along the Corps front were unsuccessful, in some sectors owing to failure to cut the wire, and in others owing to intense machine gun and rifle fire.

2. FOURTH ARMY FRONT. Several successful raids were carried out last night, resulting in the capture of 1 officer of the 119th R.Regt. 12 men of the 99th R.Regt. (26th R. Division). and 7 men of the 111th R.Regt. (28th R.Division). Strong patrols also entered the enemy trenches at several points between MARICOURT and the ANCRE.

Our artillery was very active again yesterday. Large explosions were caused in MAMETZ WOOD, MARTINPUICH, at L.31.d.44. (S.E. of SERRE and near BEAUCOURT sur ANCRE. FRICOURT Farm and many houses in HAMETZ were also much damaged, and an enemy gun was also reported to have been blown up in the air as the result of a direct hit by one of our big shells. 25 direct hits were also reported on gun emplacements by aeroplane observers.

Fires were observed in BOIS de ST. PIERRE-VAAST, MARTINPUICH. COMESES, OVILLERS, MIRAUMONT, PUISIEUX, in X.29.a. (N. of MAMETZ) and a battery emplacement at R.28.c.95. (W. of COURCELETTE).

The enemy's retaliation was feeble in the morning, but increased in power during the afternoon especially N.E. of SERRE.

3. OTHER BRITISH FRONTS. (26th June). We carried out a number of successful enterprises last night at different parts of the front. The hostile lines were penetrated at ten different places. Our

Our parties inflicted considerable casualties on the enemy and took several prisoners. Our casualties were everywhere very slight. Munster Fusiliers and Anzac troops were particularly successful. In connection with these raids there was a good deal of artillery work on both sides yesterday evening and during the night. Our artillery fired with great effect, the hostile trenches being considerably damaged in many places.

Today, our artillery has again been active at various points and considerable damage has been caused to hostile defensive works, notably near GIVENCHY-en-GOHELLE, N. of the LOOS Salient, opposite WYTSCHAETE, and to the East of WEILTJE. 1 hostile kite balloon in addition to those already reported, was destroyed by our aircraft yesterday, making a total of 6 out of 15 attacked. The whole 6 were seen to fall in flames.

4. FRENCH FRONT. N. of VERDUN no infantry attack. On both banks of the MEUSE, the bombardment was less severe, but in the region of Hill 304, both artilleries were fairly active.

5. ITALIAN THEATRE (25th June). Great artillery activity on both sides is reported from the greater portion of the front. On the ISONZO, The Italians continue to make successful raids.

6. RUSSIAN THEATRE (25th June). In the neighbourhood of CZARTORIJSK (1) the Russians captured a strongly fortified enemy redoubt and captured two heavy guns. S.E. of SWIDNIKI (2) the enemy succeeded in occupying certain portions of the Russian Front line, which has been totally demolished by shell fire. but was ejected with heavy losses leaving some 800 prisoners in the hands of the Russians.

| (1) CZARTORIJSK. | 44 miles N.E. of LUCK. |
| (2) SWIDNIKI. | 35 miles E.S.E. of LUCK. |

* EXTRACTS FROM FOURTH ARMY SUMMARY.

Examination of Prisoners. Prisoners belonging to the 111th Res
Inf. Regt. state that owing to movement seen behind our line they wer
expecting some local attacks. In consequence of this they have
recently brought their formations up from Rest billets to the support
and reserve trenches, and now hold the line with two battalions
in front and one battalion in reserve trenches. Some Labour Battalion
are in rear of these again.

This information corresponds with that given by the prisoners
belonging to the 180th Regt. captured yesterday.

The prisoner thought that the 2nd Guard R. Division went away
sometime in May.

His own Regt. was resting in BAPAUME at Easter about April 23rd.

The prisoners belonging to the 99th Res. Inf. Regt. were not
expecting an attack, but were on the look out for raids.

They knew nothing of any Bavarian troops being in the
neighbourhood nor had they heard of any artillery having been
brought up.

Forecast to midday tomorrow:- Wind W. 5 to 10 m.p.h.
becoming N.W. 10.m.p.h. Showers with fair intervals. probably
thunder storms. 60 to 65 in the day, 50 at night. Note. there are
no indications of settled fair weather and changeable cloudy
weather is probable for two days. Afterwards fair weather and
unsettled weather are almost equally likely.

LATER. The enemy has been shelling HAMEL at intervals since 2.20.
p.m.
. A smoke cloud drifted over enemy's trenches from AUCHONVILLERS
Sector at 2.30.p.m.
A fire broke out in MIRAUMONT at 12.45.p.m. and smoke was
still rising at 1.35 p.m.
We bombarded BEAUCOURT with 15." shells and enemy retaliated
on our front line trenches at THIEPVAL WOOD.

C.G. Leslie.
Capt.

General Staff (I), VIII Corps.

Sun Rises. 3.4.42.a.m. Sets 9.07.p.m. 28th.
Moon Rises. 2.34.a.m. Sets 8.02.p.m. 28th.   (Summer Time).

S P E C I A L   O R D E R   O F   T H E   D A Y

By

BRIGADIER-GENERAL H. C. REES, D.S.O.,

Commanding 94th Infantry Brigade.

You are about to attack the enemy with far greater numbers than he can oppose to you, supported by a **huge** number of guns.

Englishmen have always proved better **than** the Germans were when the odds were heavily against them.   It is now our opportunity.

You are about to fight in one of the greatest battles in the world, and in the most just cause.

Remember that the British Empire will **anxiously watch** your every move, and that the honour of the North Country rests in your hands.

Keep your heads, do your duty, and you will utterly defeat the enemy.

Captain,
Brigade Major,
94th Infantry Bde.

Chapter Seven

God help the sinner

At Warnimont Wood on the morning of June 30th, each company held a final sick parade. A medical orderly visited those unable to attend, Pte. Pollard was still ill in his bed.

"I could hear him coming, calling at the huts before he got to mine — 'medicine and duty,' 'medicine and duty.' Then he appeared. He looked around. 'Everyone in here, medicine and duty, except Pollard — and the ambulance is coming for him.' I was left in my bed, alone in the hut. I hadn't seen a doctor for three days."

The detailed final preparations continued. Each man tied onto his haversack a small triangle cut from a biscuit tin. On his shoulder he tied a three inch wide strip of cloth, appropriately coloured for his particular wave. In theory the metal and colours were to assist observers to identify each wave and so monitor progress over the enemy-held ground. All this part of the minutiae of detail developed by Divisional and Corps staff trying to legislate for every contingency. Even the two men per Company detailed to carry, in addition to their normal load, 'a maul or mallet' wore a separate distinguishing yellow armband. The detailed, complex orders designed so that no one, attacking infantry-men, company commanders, artillery observers et al, should lack anything, proved a burden in more ways than one. The desire of 'staff' to leave nothing to chance, neither in quantity of material nor in men's behaviour, was to have disastrous consequences. Meanwhile men occupied themselves with the more prosaic tasks of bayonet sharpening and rifle cleaning.

In the late afternoon, the Battalion paraded for the last time. Col. Rickman read a message from the ever-optimistic Lt. Gen. Hunter-Weston, "My greetings to every officer, N.C.O. and men of the 31st Division in the coming battle. Stick it out, push on, each to his own objective and you will win a glorious victory and make a name in history. I rejoice to be associated with you as Corps Commander."[1] Col. Rickman added his own assurances. He reminded the men of the Battalion's origins, the towns and villages the people they represented, and what was expected of them on the morrow.

With a final "Good Luck," and, "we will soon be on our way to Berlin," he dismissed them to their last meal and rest before leaving. For Col. Rickman with his own inner doubts, and for many of his men, with their's, it was a telling moment.

Pte. Sayer missed the occasion. In concession to his state of sickness he left, with Captain

Below: Behind the British lines on June 29th, 1916. The scene on the road between Mailly-Maillet and Colincamps as final preparations are made for the Big Push.
I.W.M. Q737

Above: Behind the German lines. 169 Infantry Regiment troops move up to the front line after resting in the village. Note some wear spikeless covered Pickelhauben whilst others wear the steel helmet. Note also the rolled blankets worn crossed over the left shoulder. R. Baumgartner

Riley's permission, at 2 p.m. to make his own way to the front line. He later realised he possessed neither pass nor written authority to show why he was alone. He was never challenged. He was after all walking in the right direction. At 6.15 p.m. the Battalion moved out of Warnimont Wood to begin the seven mile march, via Bus les Artois, Courcelles and Colincamps, to their front line positions before Serre. Pte. Pollard was moved from his bed to the roadside and lay awaiting transport to Gezaincourt (near Doullens) five miles to the rear. As 'W' Company marched by, his friend Pte. Place handed him his cap-badge, asking him to give it to his mother if he didn't come back. Pte. Place, newly returned from hospital, went up to the line for the first time in two months.

Through Bus les Artois then 'overland' through fields on a route marked by white-tape the Battalion marched to Courcelles. Those few villagers who had decided to stay watched silently as they passed. Just outside the village the

Battalion encamped in a lane, where they had hot tea and hard biscuits and rested in the sunshine of a perfect, balmy, evening. After the meal each man received five bars of chocolate, a box of matches — and a sausage. The incongruity of this made men suspicious. Thinking they might have been drugged to ease the fear of going over the top, no one would eat them.

Pte. Sayer got his sausage at 'Z' Company's field kitchen. 'It reeked of garlic or something so I hung it on my haversack out of sight. Most people threw them as far away as possible!'

Each man also received a final addition to the already cumbersome burden of Field Service Order (with haversack only) a bandolier of S.A.A. (Small Arms Ammunition), gas-helmet, groundsheet, water-bottle and iron rations. Also there were four empty sandbags, to be used in trench repair on consolidation; two Mills bombs for the later reserve supply to bombing parties; entrenching tools (two men to carry shovels to every man carrying a pick) and for some unfortunates, a roll of barbed wire.[2]

Specialists had their own burdens. Each bombing party of eight men, for example, collected "100 Mills bombs and 25 rifle grenades with cartridges and detonators in Bucket Bomb Carriers, each party using six buckets for the purpose. Each party will, in addition, carry two empty bomb buckets to collect bombs from the men carrying the reserve supply."[3]

With all issues complete the Battalion with Col. Rickman at its head, left Courcelles at dusk. They marched through Colincamps on to the half-mile straight stretch of poplar-lined pave road leading to the shattered remains of the Sucrerie. They made slow progress through the congestion of troops, horses and vehicles as other units made their way to their own places in the front line.

The men entered the Sucrerie in single file and entered the communication trench. The British artillery bombardment had temporarily eased, but the familiar battery of 'eighteen pounders' fired as they filed past. L/Cpl. Marshall thought of his first time along the same trench. He wondered what happened to the Accrington sergeant who had been thrown into a state of shock when the Battery had fired. "Better off than me, anyway," he mused. A more optimistic Pte. Hindle, of the Concert Party and 'X' Company later wrote, "You can judge how cheerful we were. On our way in the trenches we passed the Royal Field Artillery Battery. One of our chaps said, 'What do you want bringing back — a German helmet or an officer's watch?' Jokes abounded. We all promised each other a drink in the village of Serre."[4]

The journey along the communication trench aptly named 'Excema,' although a tributary was 'Zambuk', became a nightmare. The men fell silent and apprehension took hold. At the junction with Sackville Street, every mans' head

Above: A party of British bombers move up to the front line.
B.C.P.L.

Below: The Sucrerie. Here began the nightmare journey through the trenches up to the front line.
I.W.M. Q1815

turned to look at a large open common grave, dug by the 12th (Service, Miners Pioneers) K.O.-Y.L.I. the Pioneer Battalion of the Division, at the side of the new R.A.M.C. Advanced Dressing Station in Basin Wood. Quantities, only to be guessed at, of wooden crosses were stacked outside a wooden hut.

Loaded as they were, men struggled along the narrow congested trench. "I had round my neck two sandbags filled with Lewis gun drums. They alone must have weighed forty pounds." (Pte. Kay). In places, because of heavy rain, muddy water rose above men's knees. Each traverse brought bunching and confusion as men struggled round corners. Those who fell needed the help of their comrades to regain their footings. "We struggled; Nansen, Peary and Scott

struggled no less." (Pte. W. Clarke). Telephone wires strung along and across trench sides became an added abomination.

Frequently, 'normal' difficulties turned to chaos as other units got lost as direction signs and tapes disappeared. Working parties on trench repair held up progress. Officers became agitated as they fell behind their scheduled time. Fortunately, throughout the night, only a desultory enemy shell-fire intervened. In the minds of the men, at least the German trenches and wire had been 'getting summat' in the past few days, which would eventually make their own job easier.

The last thousand yards or so from Observation Wood to the splintered remains of Matthew and Mark Copses lay on a downward slope and the going eased considerably. At 2.40 a.m. with great relief, the Battalion reached the blown in, waterlogged traffic and front line trenches.

Minutes after Col. Rickman formally took over from the 10th East Yorks Regiment of 92 Brigade, Brigadier Rees decided the blown in trenches were too badly damaged to accommodate the first wave and ordered the whole attacking force back one trench.[5] Moving the lines of

Below: Brig. Gen. Hubert C. Rees D.S.O.
I.W.M. 51889

tired, grumbling men into their new positions created further chaos and exhausted the men. It took until 4 a.m. and daylight before all were in place. The journey from Warnimont Wood to Matthew Copse, seven miles as the crow flies, had taken almost ten hours. The Battalion War Diary recorded the cryptic entry:- "6.15 p.m. marched via Courcelles to positions in assembly trenches, arriving in position 4 a.m. 1/7/16."[6] Pte. Sayer, in 'Z' Company's dug-out/ bomb-store, and now with Ptes. Rountree and Pickering, also 'unfit for duty,' did not know that with the move back one trench left them forward of the first wave until 7.20 a.m.

At this time, 720 men of the Battalion were disposed over a frontage of some 350 yards as follows:-

First Wave:- Two platoons each of 'W' and 'X' Companies under Captain A. B. Tough, occupied numerous bays of the front and traffic trench between Matthew and Mark Copses.

Second Wave:- The two remaining platoons of 'W' and 'X' Companies under Captain H. Livesey in Copse Trench.

Third Wave:- Two platoons of 'Y' and 'Z' Companies under Lt. G. G. Williams in Campion Trench.

Fourth Wave:- The two remaining platoons of 'Y' and 'Z' Companies under Captain H. D. Riley in Monk Trench.[7]

The remainder, i.e. two officers and sixty men in reserve, the transport section and cooks, etc., and those detailed for carrying forward food, water, ammunition, etc., after the advance waited at Courcelles.

The open secret of the 7.30 a.m. zero hour confirmed, the men settled down to await the next three hours. Both British and German shelling, intermittent all night, eased off. Men with nothing to do huddled in any funk-hole or dug-out they could find. With neither blankets nor greatcoats (left behind at Warnimont Wood) they tried to snatch some sleep. Officers and N.C.O.s checked and re-checked their battle orders. From habit or instinct men checked and oiled their rifle bolts again and again. Lt. Rawcliffe with his men struggled to set up the Stokes mortar positions in readiness for his own zero hour of 7.22 a.m. Somewhere behind the lines Pte. Clark and his three colleagues sheltered in their 'dump' still forgotten, still afraid to move.

As the four waves rested, German artillery fire of every calibre intensified. The German observation posts on the rising ground on which stood Serre village, overlooked the whole of 94 Brigade front and assembly trenches. At daylight the Germans knew of the impending attack. The gaps in the Brigade's own wire and the white tapes laid on No Man's Land overnight as guides for the attacking waves could be easily seen from their lines.[8]

The German artillery, which in theory should have been destroyed by the 'counter-battery,' i.e. locating and knocking out enemy artillery, part of the British bombardment, quickly found the range of the front and assembly trenches. More German guns, not used until then to prevent British observers spotting them, joined in.

Machine-guns added to the barrage and sprayed the front line parapets.

As the shells burst in and around the crowded trenches — "they were throwing most of Krupps at us" — the men sprawled on the floor, pushed themselves against the trench sides and took what limited cover they could. Inevitably some were hit and well before zero hour a steady trickle of wounded made its way to the Regimental First aid Post in Excema Trench, then on to the Advanced Dressing Station at Basin Wood.

The interminable wait passed in different ways. Small groups quietly sang favourite music hall songs together, others, ignoring Brigade orders, sat and smoked.[9] Each N.C.O.'s small bottle of thick black rum passed between those who wanted it. Many men prayed silently and thought of home and loved ones. Some even tried to sleep. Yet others, remembering it was Saturday with weather perfect for cricket, bantered each other about their respective home team chances in the Lancashire League matches in the afternoon. Accrington, the League leaders were to play Rishton, Burnley to play Church, and rivalry between supporters often got intense.[10] During the wait, Pte. Tom Coady the devout, comical doyen of the Concert Party, died instantly when a machine-gun bullet hit him in the head.[11]

At 6.25 a.m. complying with their week-long time-table, the British artillery started to bombard the German trenches intensively. Until the barrage lifted at 7.20 a.m. the men endured a colossal, tumultuous cannonade of shells rushing and whining overhead to crash onto the enemy lines three hundred yards away. In time the noise became almost unbearable. It seemed to those waiting, that there could not indeed 'be a rat alive' in those trenches.

As 7.20 a.m. approached the Battalion first wave received the order to 'fix bayonets', then with nerves tense the men watched and listened for Captain Tough's signal to move out of the trench. C.S.M. Hey suddenly walked along the trench, revolver in hand, and pulled aside the makeshift covers over dug-outs looking for 'skivers.' "He had no need to do that — all the lads were ready to go." (Pte. Bewsher).

At 7.20 a.m. precisely the British bombardment stopped. Captain Tough blew his whistle and after hastily shaking hands and wishing each other good luck the men went over. Handicapped by the weight and bulk of their loads (supposedly 66lbs but often much more) they struggled up ladders and steps and made for the narrow gaps cut in their own wire. As quickly as they could, under a hail of German shellfire they advanced into No Man's Land. Captain Tough was wounded immediately, but urging the men on, he led them to their positions one hundred yards forward of the trenches. They laid down and waited — in the 'shilling seats,' as they had been christened during training at Gezaincourt.

It was not going to be like Gezaincourt, however, and it was desperately clear the British bombardment had failed. In the face of unexpected heavy fire there was no plan, nor indeed desire, to do anything other than carry out the rehearsed battle orders. For the time being, those in the shilling seats, forward of the German shells raining on the trenches, were comparatively safe. "I felt more at ease when we got over than I ever had in the trench." (Pte. Hindle) They were past the critical first test of courage in climbing over the parapet in the face of shell fire aimed directly upon them.

Men reacted differently to this supreme test. Pte. Bewsher, 'number one' in his Lewis gun team on the extreme right of the Battalion (the next man to him was in the 15th West Yorks, Leeds Pals) treated it as another training exercise and felt inwardly calm. C.S.M. Hey appeared to be unable to move until encouraged by Captain Tough, but then was immediately wounded in the arm and leg. Most men were as Pte. W. Clarke; later in a letter home he wrote: "At 7.20 a.m. with a prayer commending my soul to my Heavenly Father's keeping, we sprang up and climbed out of the rapidly disappearing trench (we weren't getting it all our own way) and doubled forward to be greeted by a murderous fire. How gently my comrades fell to earth! What was left of us got down in position. I looked round and to my utter surprise

Far left: Lightly camouflaged German artillery.
B.C.P.L.

Above: Capt. A. B. Tough

Above: Capt. H. Livesey

Above: Lt. G. G. Williams

Above: Capt. H. D. Riley

Right: A Stokes mortar as used by Lt. Rawcliffe and his men.
I.W.M. Q79486

Below: A German shell burst close to the British trenches.
B.C.P.L.

I saw moving human beings."[12]

It was the second wave Pte. Clarke saw as they left Copse Trench at 7.22 a.m. and entered the front trench. At 7.25 a.m. led by Captain Livesey, with walking stick in one hand and revolver in the other, they advanced under heavy fire and lay in position fifty yards behind the first wave. Also at 7.22 the Stokes mortars of the Brigade Trench Mortar Battery started their barrage. For ten minutes, each of the four mortars fired over twenty five bombs per minute. At the same time Col. Rickman, Major Reiss and Captains Peltzer and MacAlpine moved into the Battalion H.Q. in 'C' Sap.[13]

In spite of the British Stokes mortar and artillery barrage, German shells and bullets continued onto the Battalion front line and assembly trenches as the third and fourth waves awaited the signal to go at 7.30 a.m. Amongst the awful noise at least one man slept, overcome by exhaustion. Pte. Roberts, of 'Z' Company, in Mark trench, later wrote home: "As the bombardment went on and we were waiting, men were smoking and joking. I squatted down, as miners do, and fell asleep. I woke to see Captain Riley leaning against the trench side. He said, 'Sleepy, Roberts?' and as I said 'Yes, Sir,' he was called away as a shell had burst a few yards away. I never saw Captain Riley again."

It is highly probable this was the shell which killed Pte. Arthur Tyson and wounded his brother-in-law L/Cpl. Nixon. The men were in a group of bombers. Sgt. Ernie Kay got to the scene first. "Arthur was lying there in the trench — his face had a lot of loose dirt on it and I noticed he had difficulty in opening his eyes. I asked him how he felt. He told me he was 'easy' but thirsty. I borrowed a water-bottle from a man nearby and wiped Arthur's face. He was quite cheerful and not in any pain, though I could see he was badly hit. It was then 7.26 and I had to lead my platoon at 7.29. Before I left him I told him it would be some time before he could be moved. He said it didn't matter, it would be alright. He thanked me as I was leaving, though he was quite helpless."[15] Pte. Tyson died a few minutes later.

"As 'Z' Company moved out of Monk trench into the front line, L/Cpl. Marshall saw his constant friend from Burnley Lads Club days, Sgt. Ben Ingham being carried from the trench. "I knew he had been killed."

At 7.20 a.m. before Serre, as on the whole of the British front the Stokes mortars and artillery lifted their fire. For a few minutes there was silence as the artillery gunners elevated their gun-sights to locate the German second line. In those vital few minutes the German infantry, alerted by the sudden cease-fire, came from their safe, deep dug-outs and bunkers and with machine-guns and rifles manned their front line. [16]

Left: A German sentry in a wet and muddy trench looks out towards the British lines.
B.C.P.L.

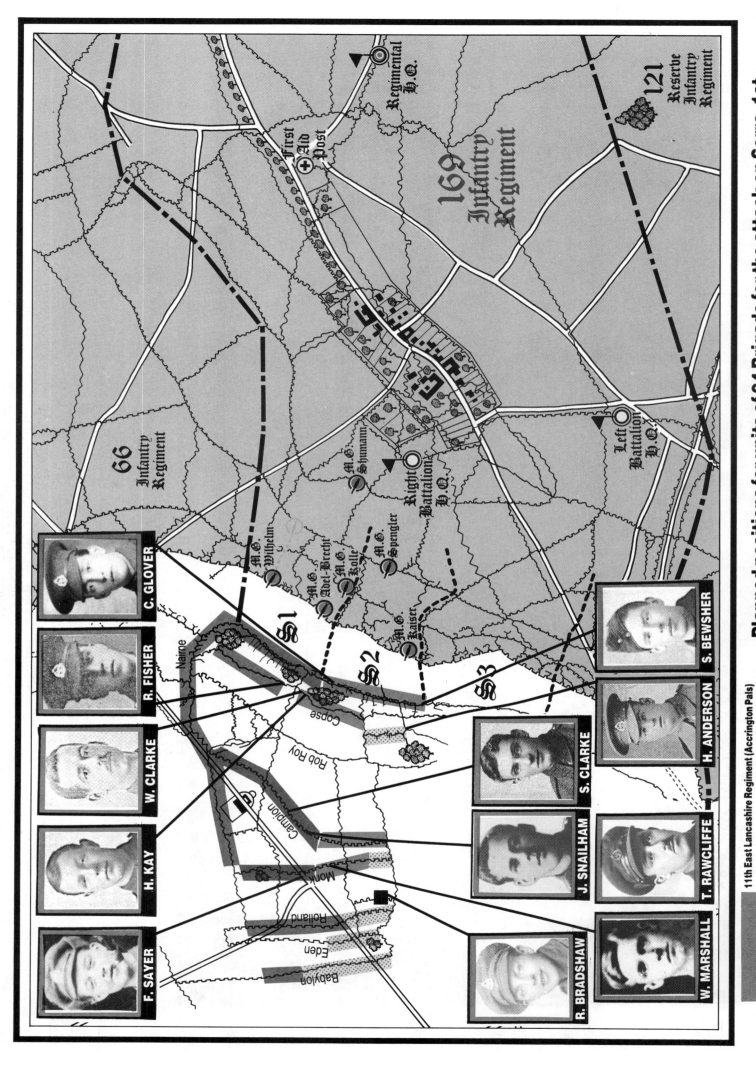

Planned positions for units of 94 Brigade for the attack on Serre, 1st July, 1916. The locations of the machine-guns of 1st Machine Gun Kompanie, 169 Infantry Regiment are shown thus

11th East Lancashire Regiment (Accrington Pals)
12th York & Lancashire Regiment (Sheffield City)
13th York & Lancashire Regiment (1st Barnsley Pals)
14th York & Lancashire Regiment (2nd Barnsley Pals)

C. GLOVER
R. FISHER
W. CLARKE
H. KAY
F. SAYER
S. BEWSHER
H. ANDERSON
S. CLARKE
J. SNAILHAM
T. RAWCLIFFE
W. MARSHALL
R. BRADSHAW

121 Reserve Infantry Regiment

169 Infantry Regiment

66 Infantry Regiment

Regimental H.Q.

First Aid Post

M.G. Schumann
M.G. Wilhelm
M.G. Abel-Brecht
M.G. Kolle
M.G. Spengler
M.G. Kaiser

Right Battalion H.Q.

Left Battalion H.Q.

Nairne
Copse
Rob Roy
Campion
Monk
Rolland
Eden
Babylon

S1
S2
S3

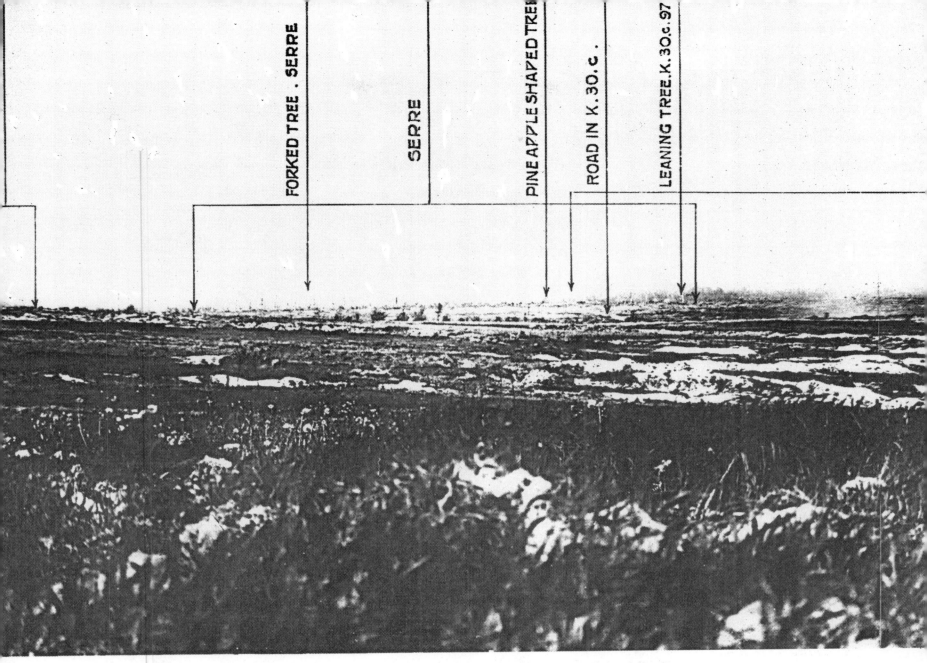

FORKED TREE . SERRE

SERRE

PINE APPLE SHAPED TREE

ROAD IN K.30.c.

LEANING TREE.K.30.c.97

At the precise moment of 7.30 a.m. signalled by whistles and shouts of encouragement by their platoon commanders, all four waves rose up and moved forward. They walked, 'dressing to the right', up the grassy slope towards the enemy positions, leaving their dead and wounded scattered in No Man's Land and huddled in the trenches. Lt. Rawcliffe and his Stokes mortar teams took what rest they could after firing 1100 rounds in less than ten minutes.

In the face of continuing German artillery fire and now heavy machine-gun and rifle fire, the waves continued their advance.

"I saw many men fall back into the trench as they attempted to climb out. those of us who managed had to walk two yards apart, very slowly, then stop, then walk again and so on. We all had to keep in line. Machine-gun bullets were sweeping backwards and forwards and hitting the ground around our feet. Shells were bursting everywhere. I had no special feeling of fear except I knew we must all go forward until wounded or killed. There was no going back. Captain Riley fell after thirty yards. I didn't see him killed, but I knew immediately. When we stopped once, the message passed down the line, from man to man — 'Captain Riley has been killed'." (L/Cpl. Marshall).

As the waves moved forward they were quickly torn apart by enfilading machine-gun fire from the direction of Gommecourt Park on the Battalion's left. The guns were in much greater strength than realised but there was a simple answer — when the Germans saw 143 Brigade of 48 Division on 94 Brigade's left were not attacking, they quickly turned their artillery and machine-guns to enfilade the attack of 94 Brigade.

Moments after the first wave moved forward Captain Tough was wounded a second time. A few minutes later he was killed outright, shot in the head. At 7.39 a.m. Lt. Col. Rickman reported to 94 Brigade H.Q. by runner (the telephone lines were already destroyed) that his first two waves had crossed 'according to time-table' and that there was still intense

Above: The terrain before Serre 1916. The view from the British lines south of the 94 Brigade sector.
I.W.M. Q48152

145

Above: A German Maxim machine-gun of the type used at Serre.

German fire of all description. By 7.50 he reported all waves gone forward and heavy machine-gun fire was still coming from the north (Gommercourt Park).

At least two Maxim machine guns 'M.G. Kaiser' and 'M.G. Schloss' faced the Battalion. Unteroffizier (Sergeant) Fritz Kaiser and his team fired at the advancing Pals up to twenty metres range in spite of four men wounded and one killed. The machine gun later jammed and had to be replaced. On Kaiser's right, Unteroffizier Schloss and his team fired until the firing-pin broke. No sooner were repairs

completed than shrapnel hit the gun casing, putting it out of action. 'In order not to let the machine-gun fall into enemy hands the service team of the M.G. took it to Leutnant (Second Lieutenant) Bayer in the third trench, where a makeshift repair was carried out. Lt. Bayer, together with the service team, returned it to the first trench. There the M.G. continued firing.'[17]

By now the survivors of the first wave with those of the leaderless second wave were mixed together and yet split into small groups each struggling to go forward to the German front line. Capt. Livesey, with his orderly, Pte. Glover and several others, got through the German wire and into the front line trench.

"Five Germans came from nowhere, the first of whom hurled a bomb which grazed Captain Livesey's face but didn't explode. Captain Livesey shot at the group with his revolver. More Germans came so Captain Livesey and I made for a shell-hole just as a shell landed nearby. I must have been knocked out. When I came round I looked for Captain Livesey but couldn't find him. At length I gave him up as lost. I was wounded but felt myself lucky to be alive. My cigarette case had turned a bullet which made a slight wound in my side and my gas-helmet had stopped another from doing much damage. I was also wounded in the thumb."[18]

Below: A ration party brings food and water to German troops in the trenches. B.C.P.L.

The German infantrymen facing the Battalion fought courageously. Oberleutnant (Lieutenant) Emil Schweikert, commanding 6 Company, although almost immediately wounded in the head by a shell splinter, kept command until the first wave of Pals was broken. Later, as the small parties of Pals continued their attack, he stood high on the side of the trench 'half-bandaged, with a naked upper body and heavily bloodied bandages' leading the firing and encouraging his Company. Only after an hour, after much persuasion, did he go to the rear for medical treatment. Forty year old Landsturmer (Private) Freidrich Essig was wounded in the right arm shortly before 7.30 a.m. Unable to use his rifle, and in severe pain, he supplied his comrades with ammunition and hand-grenades during the attack. He also reluctantly went to the rear for medical treatment. [19]

Above: Serre Village after the artillery bombardment. A photograph taken in February 1917 after British troops finally entered the village.
I.W.M. Q1909

Left: Hans Amann — a soldier of 169 Infantry Regiment. He enlisted in August 1914 at the age of seventeen. By 1916 he was the longest surviving member of his company. All others were either dead or prisoners. He was four years on the Western Front and came through without a scratch. His mother believed he had special luck because he was born on Christmas Day. Hans Amann finished the war with the rank of Vizefeldwebel.
R. Baumgartner

Far left: Most German trenches were deep and wide. Here a timber built observation post is incorporated.   B.C.P.L.

Above: Lt. Col. Rickman

When Col. Rickman made his report at 7.50 a.m. he knew the attack had failed. From that moment he could only watch in despair the slaughter of his Battalion. The past fifteen months of his life, since his celebrated entry into Castle Square, Caernarvon on St. David's Day 1915, had been devoted, not simply to train a New Army Battalion for its role in battle, but to the well-being and care of men whom he knew represented the best in camaraderie and fellow-feeling. Those friendships formed in pre-war days in factories, mines, offices, Sunday Schools and sporting-clubs were matured and shaped through his military discipline and training into a battalion equal to any in the New Army. Col. Rickman now impotently watched its destruction.

As Col. Rickman anxiously awaited reports from 'his waves', hundreds of dead and wounded men lay in No Man's Land — the wounded left behind by comrades pushing forward. Now the elaborate battle plans had been literally blown apart, it was up to individuals to survive.

"While we were walking in line, my section came to a shell-hole. We had to decide which way to go round. Some went to the left. I went to the right. A shell came over and I was thrown to the ground by the blast of the explosion. I picked myself up and realised I had a flesh wound in the leg. I looked around and to the left of me was nothing — not a man. For fifty yards on either side, no other man was going forward, only dead and wounded on the ground. I went forward about twenty yards and again was wounded, this time in the arm. The wound was quite bad. My hand dropped and was useless. I remember it felt cold. I thought 'I'm not going forward with this hand, I'd better get back and get a dressing on it'. Then another shell burst and knocked me over.

"I was still lying prone on the ground when a piece of shrapnel hit me behind the ear. I slipped into a shell-hole about 25 yards from the German front trench, wiped away the blood and pulled the shrapnel out. Creeping forward I spotted some Germans. I fired just one shot. Then, thud! I thought my head was blown in two. I was blinded with blood". (Pte. Clarke).

"I was blown off my feet twice but got up unhurt each time and carried on. Suddenly, I don't know how, where or when, such was the clamour and confusion, a piece of shrapnel went into my hand. It must have struck my rifle at the same time. I just stood there, in complete surprise and watched my rifle go up into the air, spinning over and over. My hand felt dead, and quite calmly — I wasn't a bit afraid) I thought 'It's no good I can't do anything now, I'd better go back. I looked around me and I was by myself, there was nobody there." (Pte. Fisher).

"We advanced about eighty yard or so in a small group separated from the rest. We got so near to the German wire that they were throwing grenades at us. I got hit in the leg and I made for a shell-hole and dived in it. They must have known I was there because they kept throwing grenades in. I was on my own. I could see no signs of anyone else. I looked again and saw some Germans coming towards me. A shell exploded right on them. I got another flesh wound in the leg. It was cruel for them but lucky for me. It gave me a chance." (Pte. Anderson).

Pte. Kay had a similar experience.

"My job in the attack was to follow my No. 1 on the Lewis gun team and supply him with the drums I carried round my neck. The Germans had their machine-guns on us as soon as we were over the parapet. We waited for our artillery to lift their fire from the German front to the second line. We got as far as their wire and I

Below and on succeeding pages are shown 46 (20% or 1 in 5) of the 235 killed in action on July 1st, 1916. 135 (57%) of the total have no known grave.

PTE. G. STUTTARD

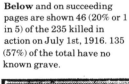

L/CPL. N. LIGHTFOOT

PTE. J. YOUNG

CPL. S. SMITH

was wounded in the leg. My Corporal, Sam Smith, was killed outright. A piece of shrapnel went right through his entrenching tool. I dropped into a shell-hole with Pte Bill Bowers. We were no sooner in there than the Germans threw stick-grenades in at us. I caught a wound in the arm."

"Six men were killed in our section of the trench before the whistle blew to go. My best friend, Pte. James Leaver, was killed by my side as we struggled out of the firing-step towards the gap in our wire. We found our wire had not been cut for us to get through. [20] *We couldn't run because of the weight of our packs and men were going down like ninepins. By some miracle, I got to the German wire about ten yards in front of their trenches completely untouched. I then dropped to the ground. I looked round and saw not a soul moving, just dead and wounded. The Germans must have thought I was dead. Moments later a shell burst above me. I felt a pain and a piece of shrapnel was sticking out of my leg. It started bleeding. There was a German on top of the trench playing a machine-gun over my head. There was still nobody to be seen. Another shell burst and a piece of shrapnel went in my other leg. I couldn't move and I could feel blood running from me. I must have gone unconscious because the next thing I remember was the sun sinking down over the horizon."* (L/Cpl. J. Snailham).

During the attack the Battalion signalling section had two main functions. Firstly, three signallers each were attached to the second and fourth waves. During the advance they were to 'take out a wire' from the signal office in Mark Copse to the respective objectives of the 'bounds' and prepare a forward report centre to maintain telephone communication with Battalion and Brigade H.Q. as, in theory, the advance progressed. A second group of signallers, 'H.Q. group', were to maintain the lines between Company H.Q's in the forward trenches and Battalion H.Q. in 'C' Sap and the Brigade H.Q. in Observation Wood, on the rising ground some five hundred yards behind Matthew Copse. Unfortunately these lines were destroyed by shell-fire as early as 7.50 a.m. so consequently communication was by runner.

Cpl. Bradshaw and his friend L/Cpl. Harry Bury were in H.Q. group. They stood outside their shelter, next to Brigade H.Q. 500 yards behind the lines and looked down the slope into the 'arena' of the attack. *"We were able to see our comrades (the Pals) move forward in an attempt to cross No Man's Land only to be mown down like meadow grass. I felt sick at the sight of this carnage and remember weeping."*[21]

During the morning Cpl. Bradshaw and L/Cpl. Bury saw men moving from shell hole to shell hole in their attempts to return to the British front line. One who returned was a fellow signaller, Cpl. Harry Hale. Cpl. Hale, with Pt. Orrell Duerden and Pte. Bill Stuart was attached to the fourth wave.

"At zero hour we advanced a hundred yards when a shell burst a dozen or so yards from us. The force knocked me down. Orrell and Bill said 'Are you hit?' I said, 'No, I'm O.K.' so we carried on. We could see the lads dropping all around, and we remarked it was marvellous we were being missed. We got to the German front line and I was hit in the hand by a bullet. Orrell and I got into the trench and he bandaged my hand. He then said, 'Will you remove this piece of shrapnel from my head?' This surprised me because it was the first he'd said about it. He must have got it from the shell which knocked me down. I took it out — it was only a small piece, and although near the temple he said it didn't hurt. Anyway, he didn't look any the worse for it. A shell came over and knocked the parapet in, burying two

PTE. T. MULHALL   **L/CPL. W. BRIGGS**   **PTE. T. ATKINSON**   **CAPT. A. B. TOUGH**

chaps and almost smothering us. Orrell and I decided it was rather unhealthy there so we had to part — he to go onward to keep communication going and me back to the dressing station, for my left arm was now useless. We shook hands and wished each other 'good luck'."

Cpl. Hale never saw Orrell Duerden again. [22]

It was a frustrating ninety minutes for Col. Rickman who could see no sign of his four waves, except for small groups of wounded. Then Sgt. Rigby, of 'W' Company returned to report seven of his platoon with Captain Livesey (and presumably Pte. Glover) had got into the German front line and held it for twenty minutes before running out of bombs. Later at 11.15 a.m., Pte. Glover returned to say the remains of the first, second and third waves had combined, under the command of Captain Livesey to attack the Germans in their own front line. Such reports from wounded men were to be the sole source of direct information for Col. Rickman. Months of meticulous planning to ensure good communication during the attack ended in a dreadful irony.

By a miracle, Pte. Bewsher returned to 'C' Sap unwounded. Carrying his Lewis gun, Pte. Bewsher had reached a German communication trench with the first wave.

"I was right in front of a machine-gun post. I emptied a drum at a few Germans who were on the trench parapet. They were throwing 'potato-mashers' (stick bombs) over my head — I'd got a bit too near. Some of them went back down the trench — I was surprised to see how wide it was — and I went after them. I got nearly to their second line. I looked around and there was only me there so I decided to go back. Still holding the Lewis gun I went back to a shell-hole about twenty yards into No Man's Land. I waited there thinking the lads (the rest of the wave) would be coming. I suddenly saw some Germans coming back up their communication trench. I didn't know whether they were picking up wounded or not, I didn't wait to see. I fired at them and they vanished. I was sure they were going to counter-attack so I ran back to our own lines. I had some near squeaks. One bullet hit my water bottle. I felt the water on my leg and I thought it was blood. Another went through my haversack. It broke all my biscuits and hit a tin of bull-beef. A piece of shrapnel hit my Lewis gun. It bent the barrel and knocked the foresight clean off. I saw a dead Sheffield Pal with his Lewis gun alongside him. I threw mine down, picked his up and dropped into a shell-hole. Then Gerry came back and I had another go at them. I picked up my gun, then made for our front line. By a stroke of luck I'd got to 'C' Sap. Lt. Col. Rickman was there with Captain MacAlpine, the Signals officer. The Colonel said, 'Was that you firing that gun out there?' I said, 'Yes, Sir, I thought they were going to attack, I didn't know whether they were stretcher-bearers or infantry men, but I had a do at them.' 'That's my lad' — he said. Then he turned to Captain MacAlpine and said, 'Take his name and number.' I thought, 'What the hell for?' Having your name and number taken was always for a crime."[23]

The original front line trench, now almost levelled to the ground by shell-fire, became untenable so the 'line' moved back to part of Excema and Rob Roy trenches. These were held by those remaining of two companies of the 13th York and Lancaster Regiment under Captain Gurney. They were originally brought forward to reinforce the 11th East Lancs but stopped on the orders of Brigadier Rees when it became obvious the attack had failed. With Lt. Rawcliffe's Stokes mortars and some slightly wounded East Lancs, plus four East Lancs officers and forty other ranks hurriedly sent from Colincamps, they were, under intense

PTE. O. DUERDEN   **PTE. R. INGHAM**   **PTE. J. GRIMSHAW**   **PTE. W. CLEGG**

150

German shell-fire, awaiting a possible counter-attack.

At least one German M.G., that commanded by Unteroffizier Spengler, fired from the German second trench over the heads of those embattled in the German first trench. This concentrated on the two companies of the 13th York and Lancaster Regiment held in the new British front line. "They paused only to fire, with great success, at small groups of English who were to be seen over the first (German) trench parapet. Their steel helmets were clearly recognisable."[24]

Col. Rickman, after ensuring Pte. Bewsher was alright, sent him to join the defenders.

"I was just setting my stall up (preparing his Lewis gun position) when I was hit on the head. I didn't know what hit me. Next I knew I woke up in the Advanced Dressing Station at Colincamps."

Pte. Clark had a meeting with Col. Rickman of a remarkably different kind. With his three colleagues he had been guarding the advanced store of ammunition and iron-rations for six days — since June 24th. During the morning of July 1st, he left the store and met a sergeant who took him to Col. Rickman.

"I was very worried about what he would do to us. I didn't know the half of it. He greeted me in a rage. 'Where the hell have you been?' 'Do you know you've been posted as deserters?' He then added, for good measure, 'You could all be shot for cowardice!' I soon learned C.S.M. Hey had got a 'Blighty One', and I realised the only person who could help us was gone. The Colonel's final words were, 'I'll deal with you when this business is over!' He then ordered us into the front line with the others. We reported to L/Cpl. Frank Bath. He stared at us in amazement. His first words were also, 'Where the hell have you been?' 'You're in real trouble!' We knew that alright. With this in mind we stayed in the front line until we were relieved."[25]

2LT. W. KOHN

L/CPL. THORNLEY

L/CPL. R. ORMEROD

CPL. E. HAYDOCK

PTE. S. ROLLINS

PTE. J. MOLLOY

PTE. J. O'CONNOR

SGT. A. LANG

Throughout the assault and bombardment, Ptes. Sayer, Rountree and Pickering waited to issue the bomb reserves but nobody came.

"Suddenly a piece of shrapnel hit Joe Rountree on the leg. His clothing set alight, I knocked the shrapnel away and smothered the flames. I asked Pte. Pickering to go for the stretcher-bearers. I made Joe as comfortable as I could with splints made from box lids. He was in agonising pain, his leg smashed. A runner on his way to Brigade came into the dug-out. He obviously knew me but I didn't know him. 'Hallo Fred, how's things?' he said. I told him, 'It's a wasted effort to come here to issue bombs, nobody wants them.' He replied, 'Bugger t'bombs, everybody's gone — it's been a wash out.' He told me as much as he knew. As he left I gave him a postcard for my sister. She later got the postcard so I knew he had made it to Brigade. Sometime later the stretcher-bearers came for Joe." (Pte. Sayer)

By now it was almost mid-day. Although the British trenches — and their own front and second line — were under fire from German artillery, the machine-gun fire eased off. "There was nothing left for them to shoot at." (L/Cpl. Snailham).

An area, once meadowland, approximately 700 yards by 300 yards was filled with some 2,000 dead and wounded of the 11th East Lancs, 12th York and Lancasters and the supporting companies of the 13th and 14th York and Lancasters. Hundreds of dead stretched from British parapets across to German parapets and beyond. In shell-holes with the dead, lay the 'lucky' wounded, who had managed to scramble in. Others, less 'lucky', lay in the open in the searing sun of a glorious sunny day. By some insane contrast, unknown to those who earlier had dreamed of cricket, it was pouring with rain throughout East Lancashire. 'Accrington versus Rishton' was rained off. Burnley scored one run in one over against Church before they too, were rained off.

PTE. W. COWELL

PTE. A.H. LORD

L/CPL. H. DIXON

PTE. H. PROCTOR

PTE. J. PENDLEBURY

PTE. J. SPEAKMAN

PTE. T. ROBINSON

PTE. A. MULHALL

As wounded men crawled and inched themselves painfully back to their own lines, some of their comrades, amazingly, continued their advance. Staff officers, acting as observers, and positioned on the rising ground behind the lines, at first sent optimistic — and completely erroneous — reports to VIII Corps H.Q. At one stage during the morning the whole of 31 Division was reported on the western edge of Serre and consolidating. By 2.45 in the afternoon this had been amended to — "It is believed there are still some men in Serre but the remainder are back in our front line."[26]

In spite of months of intricate planning it was now obvious events were out of Division, Brigade, even Battalion control. There were no means of knowing what was happening, let alone exercising any measure of command. Information came only from returning wounded and, less reliably, from individual observers. The G.S.O. (Operations) later wrote "The striking thing was the gradual change in the outlook and in the information received. Very elaborate arrangements had been made to get information back. Reports at first were very rosy and it was not for some time that we realised something was amiss".[27]

By then it was too late. The attack had failed. Brigadier Rees realised this and so decided not to bring forward any reinforcements into the horrific enemy fire. Col. Rickman's preoccupation was solely to get information from his wounded, to prepare as best as he could to defend his own front line and desperately get information to and from Division and Brigade H.Q.s.

Several observers saw isolated parties of 11th East Lancs men beyond the German front line, still following the rehearsed plan of attack. Brigadier Rees — "We could see these men from Brigade H.Q. when the smoke cleared. They were in a definite line and were probably all shot in the back from trenches they had crossed. An aeroplane later reported our troops in Serre, which I couldn't believe."[28] Observers from the 18th Durham Light Infantry and the 15th West Yorks (93 Brigade) also saw men from

Below: The killing ground. An aerial view of the German trenches attacked by the Accrington Pals. The first, second and third lines of trenches are clearly seen. B.C.P.L.

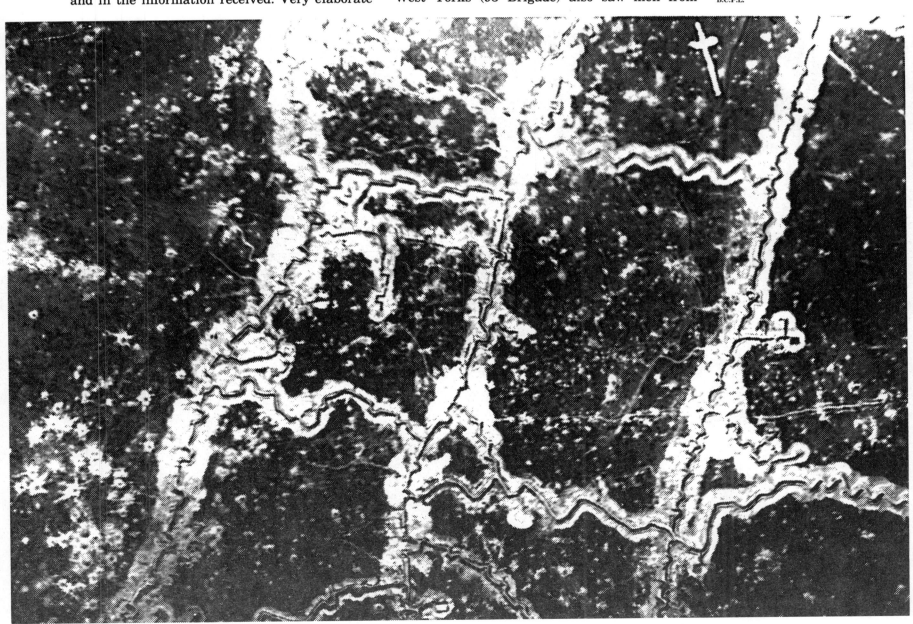

94 Brigade in the German trenches and in Serre village.[29] 92 Brigade reported about one hundred East Lancs just west of Serre.

As the gallant, encircled, men behind the German lines fought for their lives, every wounded man in No Man's Land knew that all that was left of the plan of attack was for him to get back alive. So began a nightmare journey which would push some to the edge of their reason. The fatalism of the advance was now gone, in its place a desperation to survive. For those slightly wounded, who got back within hours, it was nightmare enough. For others who spent up to three days and nights in No Man's Land it was a harrowing experience, the memory of which haunted them always.

"The shell blast must have knocked me unconscious. I don't know how long I was out. I had to get back although there was as much danger going back as forward. I could hear machine-gun fire all around. I was knocked over again by a shell burst. Another few yards and I got into one of our dug-outs. Someone put a piece of rag over my arm so I went forward into our trenches for it to be properly attended to. The trench was crowded with wounded so I crawled, best as I could, to another trench. That was as bad. It was unbelievable. Someone at the Regimental Aid Post innoculated me against lock-jaw but ignored my wounds. I couldn't get near to get bandaged. I met Sgt. Ernie Kay. He was also wounded. He suggested we went back to Colincamps on our own. We walked and rested, walked and rested. Some Royal Artillery men gave us water, I remember, that was all we had. Somehow we got to the Advanced Dressing Station at Colincamps and I collapsed through loss of blood. I came round, outside, in a field. There were hundreds and hundreds out in the open. I asked a man where we slept. He said, 'Here, with one blanket to five men, if you're lucky'." (L/Cpl. Marshall)

"I was blinded with blood. I started to roll

CPL. W. CLARKSON

PTE. E. PLACE

PTE. C. WIDDUP

PTE. J. DICKINSON

CPL. W.C. BILLINGTON

PTE. W. BRETHERTON

PTE. W. CARR

PTE. J. LAFFY

154

back to our lines but my equipment prevented me. In spite of the machine-gun fire, I knelt up, and God knows how, I threw off my equipment. Crawling, stumbling and rolling over our own barbed wire I reached our lines. I was dazed with loss of blood and someone, unknown to me, saved my life and bound my head up. What followed was a dream, I knew nothing until I was in hospital." (Pte. Clarke).

"Suddenly, a shell burst near me and I was on the ground, with of all things, a plank of wood (probably from a dug-out) on top of me. That plank saved my life, I'm sure. Next I knew I was falling into our trenches. Things were so bad there I was left on my own to go to the Advanced Dressing Station for treatment." (Pte. Fisher).

After getting a second chance, Pte. Anderson didn't hesitate.

"I quickly made my way to another shell-hole. A wounded sergeant was in there. We daren't move. Sniper fire was so accurate they could put a bullet through your hand with ease. The sergeant kept asking for a drink, but I had none to give him. I must have fainted, because the next I knew it was dark. The sergeant was dead. I was gasping for a drink and my leg was paining me. I knew I would have to make a move, so I started to creep back. The sky was lit up by shell bursts and Very lights. As I passed a shell-hole I heard a voice. Someone called my name and asked me to help him. I couldn't, I was so weak I could barely crawl and I had no water. I never did know who it was, or whether he got back alive. I eventually got back to our trenches. A voice said, 'Are you East Lancs? Your lot's been wiped out.' An officer gave me a drink of water. Only then I realised my pack had been blown away, my rifle gone and every button on my tunic blown off. I was put in a dug-out and I laid on what I thought was a heap

PTE. W. GREEN

PTE. W. BOLTON

PTE. J. ENDERBY

SGT. T. GRIMSHAW

PTE. C. LEE

L/CPL. L. SAUNDERS

CPL. I. EDGE

PTE. C. COX

Above: Lt. C. Stonehouse

Below: Rigid in death. The body of a British soldier. B.C.P.L.

of sacks. They were dead men, piles of them. An order was given for anyyone who would walk to go down to the A.D.S. at Colincamps. I couldn't stay where I was so went there best as I could. After treatment, open lorries took us down to the Casualty Clearing Station in the 'Citadel' in Doullens. This was crowded with thousands of wounded." (Pte. Anderson).

"We laid in the shell-hole all night and the following day. Bill Bowers could see Lt. Stonehouse lying wounded a few yards away and went to see how he was. He got hit before he reached him. Later I thought, 'Well, I'm going back'. I crawled out and passed Bill Bowers and Lt. Stonehouse. They were both dead. I took Lt. Stonehouse's revolver and put it in my pocket — I later lost it. I then managed to get to an old listening post and tried to get in. I couldn't, it was so full of dead and wounded I couldn't crawl over the top of them. As I got out I caught my tunic on

our own barbed wire. I could hear bullets flying past as I struggled. Somehow I got loose and crawled to our line. I was just going to drop in when Frank Curran said, 'Come on lad, I'll give you a lift down'. It was quite a drop. I fell in, right on top of Harry Bloor, and onto the trench bottom where I could crawl into a dug-out. Tom Carey was laid out dead in there. It was full of dead and wounded mixed together. I tied my first aid pack round my leg. Later someone at Colincamps looked at my leg and shoulder. I was the luckiest man alive." (Pte. Kay)[30]

Lying two yards in front of the German wire, L/Cpl. Snailham knew he would have to move or die where he was.

"I unbuckled my equipment and pushed myself along, on my back, with my hands. I could hear their machine-guns all the time. I was getting near our line when I passed a shell-hole with three or four of

the lads in. One shouted, 'Watch out, there's a sniper getting everybody who goes past there.' I said, 'I'm bleeding and I need treatment so I'll have to get somewhere.' So I chanced it and carried on. I was just getting through when he shot me through the top of my arm. I was lucky. I dropped into our trench and wandered about in a daze. The trench was empty. I was lucky again, 'old' Mather, 'a general duty man' now one of the Regimental Police, came towards me. (He was old to me, he was a family man, about forty, I was just turned eighteen). He said, 'What's up, Jimmy?' I told him, and he half dragged, half carried me to the road leading to the Advanced Dressing Station at Colincamps. He left me there, with all the other wounded. An ambulance took me to the Citadel at Doullens (35 Casualty Clearing Station). When my turn came I was placed on a pig-trestle. One man held my arms, another my legs, while they took the shrapnel out of my leg. The bullet had gone right through my arm. Two days later I was on my way to Southampton."

Some were not so lucky. Pte. Harry Fielding, of 'Y' Company and formerly the Blackburn Detachment, was wounded in the head and leg. Whilst crawling back, he was confronted by four Germans, who took him back to their lines as a prisoner of war. Pte. Fielding was one of only seven men of 94 Brigade taken prisoner that day. He spent the rest of the war in a P.O.W. camp in Nuremberg, Bavaria.

As L/Cpl. Snailham and the others lay at Doullens, Col. Rickman was en-route to hospital in London. At 9.40 p.m. on July 1st, after living through the anguish of seeing his Battalion all but destroyed, he was badly concussed and shell-shocked when a shell exploded nearby. Major Reiss became C.O. of what was left of the Battalion.

There were others not in the attacking companies who shared the horrors of July 1st and after. During the morning Cpl. Bradshaw and L/Cpl. Bury were ordered with others — transport drivers, sanitary men, general duty men, etc. — to help carry away the wounded and dead from what remained of the front-line trenches. The numbers of wounded had completely overwhelmed the Battalion medical services, in spite of an increase from 16 to 32 stretcher-bearers as part of the preparation. Many of the Regimental Band, traditionally stretcher-bearers in battle, were dead or wounded. Conditions in the front and assembly trenches were vile. Hundreds of wounded, mixed with the dead, were packed into half demolished trenches and dug-outs. Enemy shells were screaming everywhere at any signs of movement. The whole area was under constant German observation. Stretchers were almost useless because of the congestion.

"I vividly remember seeing two comrades carrying out on a stretcher a sergeant with his leg badly shattered. As I flattened myself to the trench side to allow them to pass, the sergeant said to the bearers, 'If you keep jolting me I'll bloody get off and walk.'" (L/Cpl. Bury)

The German shelling lessened during the night of July 1st/2nd and Corporal Bradshaw and L/Cpl. Bury were able to snatch some sleep.

"We dug a hole in the trench side and

Below: A wounded British soldier on the way to the rear and Blighty.
I.W.M. 721

157

Right: A wounded German soldier being placed in an ambulance en-route for hospital.
B.C.P.L.

hung a ground-sheet over the front. We slept little and were out of the trench at dawn. On looking at Bradshaw, I recall saying, 'Your eyes are sticking out of your head,' to which he retorted, 'And so are yours.' We started immediately carrying out wounded and handing them over to the R.A.M.C."[31] (L/Cpl. Bury).

On July 2nd, Pte. Sayer lay alone in the bomb-store, with neither food nor water.

"A Cyclist Company man dropped into the dug out. He had been wounded in the attack and was now lost. As he crouched with his back to me looking out towards the German lines I felt a blow on my helmet. I choked with fumes and was blinded with blood and gore, I thought I was dead. A shell had exploded and shrapnel had pierced my helmet. The 'Cyclist' hadn't moved — he was still looking forward. I crawled to him, then saw the lower part of his body was gone. It was his blood and gore, not mine."

For four days and nights men laboured to bring wounded to the overburdened Regimental Aid Posts and the Advanced Dressing Station at Colincamps. From there men were taken onward by ambulance and lorry to the Main Dressing Stations at Bertrancourt and Louvencourt and the Casualty Clearing Stations (Nos. 11 and 35) at Doullens. For many it was then hospital in 'Blighty.' In the line, in Matthew and Mark Copses, rain on July 2nd, and a violent thunderstorm at mid-day on July 4th which

flooded some trenches up to four feet deep, added to the wretchedness.

On the morning of July 1st, there began the worst 48 hours of Lt. Rawcliffe's life. After the advance Lt. Rawcliffe and his Stokes mortar teams retired to Rob Roy Trench. They found it impossible to advance, as planned, when the infantry attack had failed. Only one Stokes mortar was able to fire, — and without much effect — at the enemy machine-guns enfilading on the Battalion's left.

"We watched from behind the lines. We could see the men being simply slaughtered, then there seemed to be nobody there. The trench mortars never got a chance to help, our range was too limited. During the morning I decided to go down to the front line. I met a Staff Captain who said, 'You can't go down there, there's been a wash-out.' I was so upset I said, 'I'm not taking orders from you, sir,' brushed past him, and carried on down. Things down there were unbelievable. Shells were continuously exploding all over the place. I came to a sergeant screaming and crying like a child, obviously shell-shocked. I was talking to him, trying to calm him, when a whizz-bang burst at our side. The blast caught my steel helmet under the rim, blew it back and the strap nearly choked me. I almost blacked out. When I got up the sergeant was nowhere to be seen. He had been blown to pieces. At nightfall I went into No Man's Land, with my orderly

and two volunteers, looking for wounded. We crept along and listened but didn't hear a soul. Later, however, we helped about thirty into the trenches who had somehow dragged themselves back. That night I will never forget. We continued without rest into the following day."

In a period of black horror there was just one incident which gave Lt. Rawcliffe some relief.

"I was making my way along a communication trench when I saw some feet sticking out from under a ground-sheet. I turned it over and thought 'Poor old Gurney' (Captain Gurney, 13th York and Lancasters) and prepared myself to move the 'body.' At this he woke up and ticked me off for disturbing the first rest he'd had in days. I was overjoyed to get that ticking off! I later came out of the line and went to Louvencourt. There, as one of the few officers unwounded, I got the job of going through the belongings of officers and men killed, in order to return personal belongings to their families. It was heart-breaking. I'd lost so many of my friends. My own brother-in-law Sgt. Harry Chapman was amongst them."[32]

Major Ross came over from 31 Division H.Q. to help, presumably with the belongings of men from 'Z' Company, of which he had so long been the Company Commander. A fortnight later, Major Ross was in hospital in London, suffering a 'break-down in health.'

Sometime in the afternoon of July 4th, Lt. Heys of 'Z' Company entered Pte. Sayer's dug-out. "Lt. Heys said, 'Come on, we're getting relieved shortly.' I said, 'I can't walk because of my leg and back.' He said, "You'll have to, we can't carry you. Go any time and any way you like, but get out of here." 'I still had no pass or written authority to travel alone but I didn't need one this time.' Long after darkness had fallen, and dead on his feet with pain and exhaustion, Pte. Sayer arrived at Colincamps.

"I fell in a heap and slept for ten hours. I awoke to find someone had removed my boots and equipment, bandaged my head and put me in a bunk."

"I did get a laugh however when I saw the sausage was still on my haversack, quite undeterred by its adventures. I must say though, that was the worst birthday I ever had."

On July 4th, 1916 Pte. Sayer was nineteen.

On the evening of July 4th, 144 Brigade of 48 Division took over the 94 Brigade section of the line. One company of the 1/6th Gloucestershire Regiment relieved the 11th East Lancs. at 12.30 a.m. on July 5th. As the weary East Lancs., with spirits at their lowest ebb, came out of the line, the incoming Gloucesters watched in respectful silence. They were seeing men pushed to the limits of their endurance. After

Above: British prisoners of war are marched to the German rear.
B.C.P.L.

four days the East Lancs. were leaving many of their dead in No Man's Land and in the forward trenches. The men made their way as best they could, asleep on their feet, to Colincamps for assembly and roll-call. Even there the agony continued. As 'Z' Company assembled for roll-call a shell burst nearby and killed 18496 Pte. Wilkinson outright. This left 42 to answer the roll-call. From Colincamps they continued, through Courcelles, Bertrancourt and Bus les Artois, the five mile march to Louvencourt and Warnimont Wood.

"When I heard they were back, I got out of bed and went down to the end of the lane and found them. I spoke to Charlie Birtwell and two or three others but I never asked them about the attack, there were so few of them. Frank Bath was coming down the road. He managed to say, 'George, Ernie's gone."[30] (Pte. Pollard).

Of Pte. Pollard's close friends and comrades only L/Cpl. Bath was unscathed. Ptes. Bowers, Carey, Stuttard and Place, and Cpl. Smith were dead. Apart from Pte. Birtwell (wounded on the left cheek), Ptes. Greaves, Kay and Wilkinson, and Sgt. Pilkington, were lying wounded in hospitals scattered throughout the United Kingdom.

The end came for Pte. Pollard.

"I was stretchered, taken by lorry to the hospital train and then to Etaples. Later via Boulogne I sailed to Folkestone. Four hospital trains awaited us. Orderlies came round. 'Where you from, chum?' I said, 'North of England.' I finished up at Keighley. The hospital was in the old workhouse. We were the first troops in."[31]

In a letter intended for his mother's peace of mind, L/Cpl. Marshall later wrote from hospital in Liverpool. '— my wounds are only of a slight nature. Arthur (Brunskill) was still going on when I got hit. I can only hope he is alright

Above: Pte. Pollard

and has got through. Ben (Ingham) was badly hit before we went over and I do not know how he is going on as yet. I have been a very lucky chap. I hope Arthur will be as lucky. As you know we were the best of chums. I need hardly say what it was like — but if hell is like a battle-field, then God help the sinner.'[35]

Despite the desperate valour of those who fought and bombed their way along the first, second and even third German trenches, the German troops at all times kept their nerve. They fought with great courage with their leaders always in control. The battle-report of their No. 1 Machine Gun Company summed up their feelings, 'With great sacrifices but with great bravery a complete victory was achieved.' To achieve victory, 169 Infantry Regiment used 74,000 rounds of M. G. and rifle ammunition, and over a thousand hand grenades. The Regiment lost 81 officers and men killed, 151 wounded and 10 missing.

Not only did Pte. Sayer see a verbal play on the name 'Serre.' The writer of the battle-report of No. 7 Company, 169 Regiment (opposite 93 Brigade) could not resist ending his entry for 1st July 1916 with the pun, 'SEHR HABEN SIE GEKRIEGT ABER NICHT SERRE!' — 'They had much but they did not have Serre!'

234 of the 11th East Lancs died before Serre. 131 of these have no known grave. At least 360 men were wounded. Fourteen died in hospital within a month. Numbers unknown died directly and in-directly of their wounds in future months and years. With Captain Riley died ten of his Lads Club members. Another died of wounds on July 9th. With their comrades, died 15259 Sgt. Walter Todd, who tried so hard at Malta to rejoin his Battalion, and 17882 Cpl. Joe Bell, who served with Rickman in South Africa; 15644 Pte. Will Cowell, also died, he who had so longed for leave to see Polly. Their bodies were never identified.[36]

Below: German positions in Serre obliterated by shell-fire. A picture taken by a British photographer in February 1917.
I.W.M. Q1812

Left: Shell-torn iron girders, part of the German defences on the road leading into Serre. Taken in February 1917.
I.W.M. 1786
Below: Some of the officers wounded on July 1st, 1916.

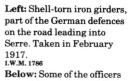

Far left: Capt. B. Endean
Left: Capt. A. Peltzer
For many wounded the ordeal ended in a hospital in England. After treatment some returned to the Battalion. Others were transferred to other Battalions of the East Lancashire Regiment or to other regiments to serve again in the trenches on the Western Front.

Lt. J. V. Kershaw

Lt. H. Ashworth

Lt. L. Rydern

Below and on succeeding pages are shown 70 (20% or 1 in 5) of the 350 wounded on 1st July, 1916.

Sgt.-Major Hey

Sgt. Instructor Barnes

Sgt. Southworth

Sgt. Duffy

Sgt. Lyon

Sgt. W. Swallow

L/Cpl. T. Ingham

L/Cpl. W. Holding

L/Cpl. B. W. Cotter

L/Cpl. C. Birtwell

Pte. J. R. Pickup

Pte. J. Haining

Pte. J. Rawcliffe

Pte. F. Holgate

Pte. John Hindle
Great Harwood

Pte. John Hindle
Accrington

Pte. A. Laycock

Pte. C. Hulme

Pte. Martin

Pte. T. Broadley

Pte. Fred Haworth

Pte. A. Akred

Pte. A. Brindle

Pte. F. Mellelieu

Pte. H. Bloor

Pte. Lunt

Pte. Wright

Pte. W. Chapman

Pte. T. Davies

Pte. B. F. Laycock

Pte. H. Bridge

Pte. W. Greaves

Pte. T. Passmore

Sgt. J. H. Woods

Pte. S. Woods

Pte. A. Woods

Pte. J. Baron

Pte. L. Colclough

Pte. R. W. Jackson

Pte. F. Foote

Pte. T. Alston

Pte. A. Robinson

Pte. J. W. Robinson

Pte. T. Pemberton

Pte. W. Johnson

Pte. Henry Rigby

Pte. W. Fifield

Pte. J. Walton

Pte. A. Magrath

Pte. O. Fairweather

Cpl. A. Naylor

Pte. P. Martin

Pte. E. Cutler

Pte. E. Culley

Pte. W. Varley

L/Cpl. E. Whittaker

Pte. R. Barrow

Pte. S. Holgate

Pte. A. S. Edwards

Pte. J. Lowe

Pte. W. Peart

Pte. W. Breaks

Pte. V. Wardleworth

Pte. C. Glover

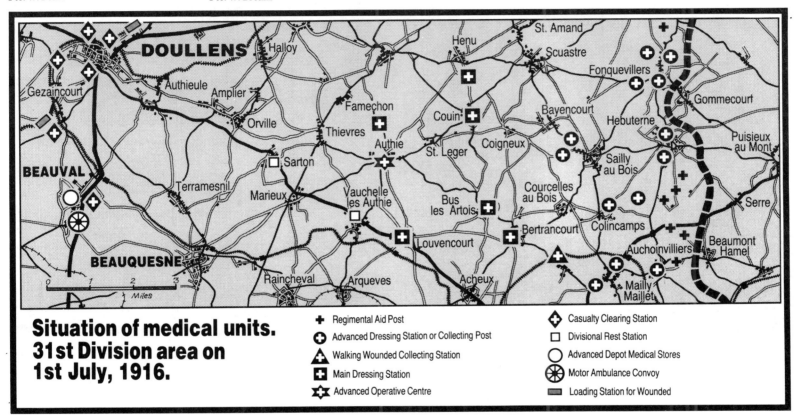

Situation of medical units. 31st Division area on 1st July, 1916.

✚ Regimental Aid Post

✚ Advanced Dressing Station or Collecting Post

▲ Walking Wounded Collecting Station

✚ Main Dressing Station

✡ Advanced Operative Centre

◆ Casualty Clearing Station

☐ Divisional Rest Station

◯ Advanced Depot Medical Stores

⊛ Motor Ambulance Convoy

▨ Loading Station for Wounded

Left: Their wounds now dressed, British troops await transport to the rear.
B.C.P.L.

NOTES

1. See 'The York and Lancaster Regiment', Volume 2, p 235. Col. H. C. Wylly, 1930.
2. In the haversack were small things, mess tin, towel, shaving kit, extra socks, message book, the unconsumed portion of the days ration, extra cheese, one preserved ration and one iron ration'. See Military Operations, France and Belgium 1916, p 313.
3. Operational Orders 94 Brigade 26/6/16 para 5, 'Bombs'.
4. A.O.T. 22/7/16.
5. See Brigadier H. C. Rees Papers (77/179/1) Imperial War Museum.
6. 11th East Lancs War Diary WO 95/2366 Public Record Office.
7. See 'History of the East Lancashire Regiment in the Great War 1914-1918' p 526.
   N.B. Subsequent material, and eye-witness descriptions, show Captain Tough, not Captain Livesey led the first wave.
8. Some tapes were seen before daylight. 'A' Company of the 12th York and Lancaster Regiment, on the 11th East Lancs immediate left, reported at 4 a.m. that there was no sign of the white tape which was laid during the night. "It had apparently been removed. It served no purpose at all except to give the enemy warning. The wire in front of our own lines had been cut away too much and as the gaps were not staggered our intention to attack must have been quite obvious". (Battle Report, 12th York and Lancaster Regiment).
9. 'Troops will take up positions in the trenches during the night prior to the attack. Absolute silence will be maintained. No smoking will be permitted and great care will be taken that bayonets are not shown above the parapet prior to the advance'. Operational Orders 94 Brigade 26/6/16 para 8, 'Assembly'.
10. The Lancashire League formed in 1890 had clubs representing Accrington, Bacup, Burnley, Church, Colne, Enfield (Clayton-le-Moors), East Lancs (Blackburn), Haslingden, Lowerhouse, Nelson, Ramsbottom, Rawtenstall, Rishton and Todmorden. Of these only two, Ramsbottom and Todmorden, were outside the Battalion recruiting area. Many supporters and ex-players served in the Battalion, e.g. Lt. Rawcliffe's brother-in-law Lt. Ramsbottom had been captain of Accrington in 1914. Lt. Rawcliffe's orderly was ex-wicket keeper for Enfield.
11. Often the first intimation to the family was not the War Office telegram but a letter from a comrade. Pte. Shorrock wrote to Mrs. Coady in Oswaldtwistle. "I am sorry to tell you your son Tom is killed. All the boys are down about losing him. He was a good soldier, always in for a bit of life and cheering the others up. He was my best pal. We went everywhere like brothers. We all send our deepest sympathy". (A.O.T. 18/7/16).
12. A.O.T. 15/7/16 15193 Pte. William Clarke was wounded on July 1st and was in hospital in Sheffield.
13. 'C' Sap, one of four 'Russian Saps' i.e. shallow tunnels, like small mine galleries. Previously excavated by the ex-miners of the 14th York and Lancaster Regiment, 'C' Sap ran at a right-angle from the front line trench into No Man's Land. It had been intended for the leading waves to enter No Man's Land but it had been badly blown in by enemy shell-fire. (This caused the last minute change of plan which meant Lt. Col. Rickman's delay on arrival).
14. B.E 19/8/16 15184 Pte. J. Roberts was wounded on July 1st and was in hospital in Kent.
15. B.E 29/7/16 Letter to Pte. Tyson's father. Sgt. E. D. Kay was wounded in the arm, back and shoulder on July 1st.
16. Opposite 94 Brigade were the troops of 169 (8th Baden) Regiment from the province of Wurttemberg/Baden. To their right, in an enfilading position, were troops of 66 (3rd Magdeburg) Regiment from the province of Saxony. Both regiments were in 52 Division.
17. Baden Generallandarchiv Karlsruhe 456 EV 42 Bd 115 (hereafter B.G.K.).
18. A.G. 15/7/16 15013 Pte. Glover, with three wounds on July 1st, entered hospital in Radcliffe, Manchester, on July 8th.
19. Quoted in 'Heroic deeds of members of 6 Company, Infantry Regiment 169, in the Battles of the Somme 1916'. B.G.K. 456 EV 42 Bd 127.
20. At 6.20 a.m. 94 Brigade H.Q. assured G.H.Q. the wire had been 'perfectly' cut.
21. See 'The First Day on the Somme', Martin Middlebrook pp 150/151.
22. A.G. 8/8/16 Letter to Mrs. Duerden in response to her newspaper advert asking for news of her son. 15463 Cpl. Hale was in hospital in Cheshire. Pte. Stuart wrote from France saying he would enquire about Pte. Duerden's whereabouts. He was unsuccessful. 17870 Pte. Orrell Taylor Duerden's body was never found. His name (incorrectly as C. T. Duerden) was placed on a supplementary panel on Thiepval Memorial in 1933. For the rest of her life his mother refused to believe he was dead.
23. 18048 Pte. S. Bewsher was awarded the M.M. for his coolness and bravery.
24. B.G.K. 456 EV 42 Bd 115.
25. 17859 Pte. S. Clarke, served with the Battalion, with Lt. Col. Rickman as O.C. until March 1919. The matter of his absence was never 'dealt with' and Pte. Clarke was content for it to remain so.
26. See VIII Corps Reports to General Staff H.Q. 1/7/16 - 3/7/16 P.R.O.
27. C.A.B. 45/188 P.R.O.
28. C.A.B. 45/190 P.R.O.
29. C.A.B. 45/188 (D.L.I.) and C.A.B. 45/190 (W. Yorks) P.R.O.
30. For reference to Pte. Bloor's experiences, see 'The First Day on the Somme' p 248.
31. Quoted by kind permission of Mr. Martin Middlebrook.
32. Lt. T. W. Rawcliffe was awarded the M.C. for his conspicuous gallantry and devotion to duty.
33. 15261 Pte. W. Greaves in hospital in Cosham, Hampshire with ankle, head and leg injuries wrote to Pte. Place's mother. "The last time I saw him was in the front line, just before I got hit. I enquired about him as I got my wounds dressed and a stretcher-bearer told me he was dead. I am more than sorry. He was a good lad and a good soldier". (A.O.T. 29/7/16).
34. 15139 Pte. G. Pollard was claimed out of the Army, as under age, by his father. He continued his engineering apprenticeship in munitions work in Accrington and Woolwich Arsenal, then joined the R.F.C. He served in France as armourer to Major Bill McCudden V.C. He left the R.F.C. in 1919.
35. B.E. 25/8/16. A later letter to L/Cpl. Marshall from Captain Heys of 'Z' Company, told him Pte. Brunskill's body had been found.
36. By an oversight, discovered during research for this book, the names of 15644 Pte. W. Cowell, 15476 Pte. T. E. Francis and 15964 Pte. S. Rollins were not placed on the Thiepval Memorial. The author is grateful to the C.W.G.C. for their amendments to the Memorial and the Register.

'ACCRINGTON "PAL'S" FUNERAL.

The funeral took place on Thursday at the Accrington Cemetery of a member of the "Pals" Battalion who was fatally wounded

PTE. CHAS. HARLING (Died of Wounds).

in the great attack on July 1st and died at Aldershot on July 14th. The remains were those of Pte. Charles Harling, of 48, Dowry-street, aged 28 years, whose death took place at the Cambridge Hospital, Aldershot. The injuries he sustained were of a frightful character, the deceased being severely wounded in the body and having his right foot blown off. Efforts had been made to give him full military honours but this was found to be inexpedient. As one tribute to his having fallen in battle, however, the coffin was covered with a Union Jack, kindly supplied by Capt. Harwood. The deceased, who was formerly employed as a traveller by Mr. Sutcliffe, tea merchant, leaves a widow and three young children. Of a genial disposition his sad end evoked the deepest sympathy of all who knew him. The funeral service was conducted by the Rev. J. W. Wilkinson, Vicar of St. John's Church. The funeral arrangements were carried out by Mr. I. Wainman, Whalley-road.

The Women's Peace Negotiations Crusade organised a demonstration held in Glasgow, and when the public showed a willingness to listen to the speeches the weather took a hand and a thunderstorm forced the demonstrators to sheek shelter.

Chapter Eight

The aftermath

At Louvencourt laudatory messages from Hunter-Weston and Rees awaited the survivors. The compliments provoked a cynical reaction from the exhausted men. Hunter-Weston's pre-battle assurances, 'there would not be a rat alive in the German trenches,' now had a hollow ring. Just over 400 men of the 11th East Lancs gathered at Louvencourt after the battle. Of these about 135 were survivors of the fighting platoons, the remaining 265 or so were men of Battalion and Company H.Q. administration and clerical sections (e.g. transport, stores, sanitary, etc.), stretcher-bearers and reserves who had succoured wounded and buried dead in the days after the attack (all but one of the medical staff and stretcher-bearers were casualties). At Louvencourt the burnt-out survivors rested for the first time in six days, the nightmare over.

Whatever the reasons for the failure of the attack — poor planning, bad tactics, staff incompetence, over-confidence of the British High Command, quality of the German defence — those remaining of the 11th East Lancs slept knowing none could have bettered their efforts in the attack.

Several interlinked reasons caused the tragedy on the slopes before Serre. In common with the rest of the British front the seven day bombardment by British artillery proved for the most part ineffective against the German trench system. Contrary to High Command belief, shrapnel shells failed to completely cut the wire. Many H.E. shells failed to explode. In the relative comfort of twelve-feet deep dug-outs the Germans endured the shelling of the heavy guns. After five days the decrease in intensity of the bombardment convinced them the worst was over. When the bombardment suddenly ceased on the seventh day, an imminent attack was obvious. Within minutes, as the British troops were leaving their front-line positions, the Germans with great skill and gallantry brought their machine-guns up from the deep dug-outs and opened fire on the advancing waves.

The pace and spacing of the four waves provided perfect targets. Succeeding waves continued their slow, remorseless advance to be cut down with the machine gunners having ample time to fire at each wave before the next took

Left: After the battle, temporary wooden crosses for men buried where they fell. B.C.P.L.

MESSAGE.

From
Lieut.-General SIR AYLMER HUNTER-WESTON, K.C.B., D.S.O.

To
All OFFICERS, N.C.O.'s and MEN of the VIII. Army Corps

In so big a command as an Army Corps of four Divisions (about eighty thousand men) it is impossible for me to come round all front line trenches and all billets to see every man as I wish to do. You must take the will for the deed, and accept this printed message in place of the spoken word.

It is difficult for me to express my admiration for the splendid courage, determination and discipline displayed by every Officer, N.C.O. and Man of the Battalions that took part in the great attack on the BEAUMONT-HAMEL-SERRE position on the 1st July. All observers agree in stating that the various waves of men issued from their trenches and moved forward at the appointed time in perfect order, undismayed by the heavy artillery fire and deadly machine gun fire. There were no cowards nor waverers, and not a man fell out. It was a magnificent display of disciplined courage worthy of the best traditions of the British race.

Very few are left of my old comrades, the original "Contemptibles," but their successors in the 4th Division have shewn that they are worthy to bear the honours gained by the 4th Division at their first great fight at Fontaine-au-Pire and Ligny, during the great Retreat and greater Advance across the Marne and Aisne, and in all the hard fighting at Ploegsteert and at Ypres.

Though but few of my old comrades, the heroes of the historic landing at Cape Helles, are still with us, the 29th Division of to-day has shown itself capable of maintaining its high traditions, and has proved itself worthy of its hard earned title of "The Incomparable 29th."

The 31st New Army Division, and the 48th Territorial Division, by the heroism and discipline of the units engaged in this their first big battle, have proved themselves worthy to fight by the side of such magnificent regular Divisions as the 4th and 29th. There can be no higher praise.

We had the most difficult part of the line to attack. The Germans had fortified it with skill and immense labour for many months, they had kept their best troops here, and had assembled North, East, and South-East of it a formidable collection of artillery and many machine guns.

By your splendid attack you held these enemy forces here in the North and so enabled our friends in the South, both British and French, to achieve the brilliant success that they have. Therefore, though we did not do all we hoped to do you have more than pulled your weight, and you and our even more glorious comrades who have preceded us across the Great Divide have nobly done your Duty.

We have got to stick it out and go on hammering. Next time we attack, if it please God, we will not only pull our weight but will pull off a big thing. With such troops as you, who are determined to stick it out and do your duty, we are certain of winning through to a glorious victory.

I salute each Officer, N.C.O. and Man of the 4th, 29th, 31st, and 48th Divisions as a comrade-in-arms and I rejoice to have the privilege of commanding such a band of heroes as the VIII. Corps have proved themselves to be.

H.Q., VIII. CORPS,
4th July, 1916.

AYLMER HUNTER-WESTON,
Lieut.-General.

ARMY PRINTING AND STATIONERY SERVICES A. 7/16 60,000.

---

its place.[1] The troops who got as far as the German lines were stopped (as L/Cpl. Snailham was) by unbroken wire up to five feet high. Had this been cut, those who survived the initial advance might possibly have dealt with the machine gunners.

This was not to be as the survivors were too few, mostly wounded and perforce sheltering in shell-holes (one of the 'blessings' of the artillery bombardment). Of the wounded survivors only Pte. Clarke and Pte. Bewsher record firing a shot. The Battalion bombers and Lewis gunners were too few and too short of ammunition, the trench-mortars, unable to advance, were out of range. Those who were left could neither see nor reach the enemy machine-gun emplacements. However Cpl. Earl Whittaker of 'Z' Company, on his return, swore he saw a German machine-gunner in his shirt-sleeves.

Although much can be said in hindsight, the importance of Stokes mortars in the attack was over-rated. The stocks of bulky shells took up an enormous amount of room in trench and sap. Putting them there consumed precious time and energy. The general belief in their effectiveness was probably based on a demonstration behind the lines, on June 8th, for the Brigadier and his staff. 94/1 and 94/2 Trench Mortar Batteries fired a hundred shells at a line of trench and barbed wire. The wire 'was well-cut' and 'much damage' done to the trench.[2] This 'success' undoubtedly gave Brigade staff confidence in Stokes mortars as support for the unopposed advance they anticipated. Those staff officers who proposed more machine-guns instead were brushed aside. These men believed machine-guns firing over the advancing waves would keep German heads down the moment the artillery bombardment ceased, so enabling the waves to overcome the front line trenches. In the event, the Stokes mortars, after their hurricane bombardment at 7.20 a.m. could not later help the attacking infantry because of the hold-ups in No Man's Land and at the German wire. Also — ironically — the heavy German machine gun fire raining on the British front and support trenches.

The battle plan itself, however, became a major cause of failure. The over elaborate plans drawn up so carefully to cover every contingency were rendered useless by the over-looked contingency of the enemy contesting the 'walk' across No Man's Land. The elaborate plans, much too cut and dried and inflexible, meant the 11th East Lancs. along with their comrades in the York and Lancaster Regiment lost the battle before it started. From zero hour Rickman remained powerless and impotent with no communications to Brigade, Division or Corps. With his signals wire destroyed and his signallers in the waves dead or wounded, he lost control over the attack. The momentum and conduct of the attack remained in the hands of small, isolated, groups led in many cases by N.C.O.s or men. (C.S.M. Leeming, with all his officers killed or wounded, continued to lead a 'Z' Company wave into the attack. He received the D.C.M.).

Brigade also lost control. Brigade H.Q., a steel shelter ten feet underground in Observation Wood, lay 500 yards behind the line. On July 4th, Rees could only say — "From bits of information and from what the intelligence officer saw, it appears some of the East Lancs. got

Below: Few of 94 Brigade were taken prisoner on July 1st, 1916. those who were would spend the rest of the war in the desolate confines of a German prisoner of war camp, such as this at Zwickau, Saxony.

11TH (SERVICE) BATTALION, EAST LANCASHIRE REGIMENT (ACCRINGTON)

IN THE FIELD.
7th. July.1916.

APPRECIATIONS
----

1. The following message to the Division from the Corps Commander
begins:-
WELL DONE ! MY COMRADES OF THE 31 DIVISION.
YOUR DISCIPLINE AND DETERMINATION WERE MAGNIFICENT AND IT
WAS BAD LUCK ALONE THAT HAS TEMPORARILY ROBBED YOU OF SUCCESS.
10-15 a.m.
2.7.16.   (sgd) AYLMER HUNTER-WESTON.

2. The subjoined copy of letter received from G.O.C. VIII Corps
to the Division begins :-
G.O.C. 31st DIVISION. SIR AYLMER HUNTER-WESTON DESIRES ALL
RANKS TO KNOW THAT GENERAL JOFFRE HAS EXPRESSED HIS APPRECIATION
OF THE HARD FIGHTING CARRIED OUT BY THE TROOPS ON THE ENGLISH
LEFT.   IT IS GREATLY DUE TO THE FACT THAT THE GERMANS WERE
SO STRONG AND SO WELL PROVIDED WITH GUNS IN FRONT OF THE VII
AND VIII CORPS, THAT THE FRENCH AND THE BRITISH TROOPS IN TOUCH
WITH THEM ON THE RIGHT OF THE FOURTH ARMY WERE ABLE TO MAKE THEIR
BRILLIANT AND SUCCESSFUL ADVANCE.
SIR AYLMER HUNTER-WESTON CONGRATULATES ALL OFFICERS, NON-
COMMISSIONED OFFICERS AND MEN OF THE VIII CORPS ON THE
MAGNIFICENT COURAGE, DISCIPLINE AND DETERMINATION DISPLAYED
BY THE TROOPS WHO CARRIED OUT THE ATTACK.
NO WORD OF PRAISE CAN BE TOO HIGH, AND SIR AYLMER HUNTER-WESTON
CONSIDERS IT AN HONOUR TO BE THE COMRADE OF SUCH HEROES.

3.7.16   (signed) AYLMER HUNTER-WESTON.

3. SPECIAL ORDER OF THE DAY BY BRIGADIER GENERAL B.C.REES. D.S.O.
          -: COMMANDING 94TH INFANTRY BRIGADE :-

ON GIVING UP COMMAND OF THE 94TH INFANTRY BRIGADE TO BRIGADIER
GENERAL CARTER CAMPBELL, WHOSE PLACE I HAVE TEMPORARILY TAKEN
DURING THIS GREAT BATTLE,I DESIRE TO EXPRESS TO ALL RANKS
MY ADMIRATION OF THEIR BEHAVIOUR.   I HAVE BEEN THROUGH MANY BATTLES
IN THIS WAR AND NOTHING MORE MAGNIFICENT HAS COME TO MY NOTICE.
THE WAVES WENT FORWARD AS IF ON A DRILL PARADE AND I SAW NO MAN
TURN BACK OR FALTER.   I BID GOOD-BYE TO THE REMNANTS OF AS
FINE A BRIGADE AS AS EVER GONE INTO ACTION

3.7.16.   (signed) B.C. REES   Brigadier General.

into Serre. He is very positive about this — also that after they entered the village the Germans shelled half way up the village, lifting off our front line. Two men of the 11th who saw this also bear it out, one was in the third line —."[3]

The courageous attempts of the 11th East Lancs. and the 12th York and Lancasters of 94 Brigade to continue the attack — which may have taken some into Serre village — were not brave 'forlorn hopes', but the actions of men who believed the success of others depended on them. The rigid instructions which left nothing to individual discretion were followed to the death. Only men wounded and alone turned back, their obligation to go on at an end, thus saving their lives. Those wounded and unable to return lingered for up to three days, isolated and in agony from wounds and thirst, until they died.[4]

Many varied reasons for the failure, all inter-linked, can be put forward. The absence of an effective counter-battery attack by the British Artillery enabled the German guns to fire an intense and accurate counter-bombardment until 2 a.m. on July 2nd, causing many casual-ties.[5] The 11th East Lancs orders meant a pre-battle seven mile, ten hour journey, each man carrying a load half his own weight. Men collapsed exhausted in their attack positions only three hours before zero hour. In spite of the training sessions, inexperienced men were used. Some of the 11th East Lancs men — replacements for the May and June casualties — were raw conscripts, who only nine weeks before were clerks and shop assistants in Blackburn or Burnley. Nineteen such men died in action on July 1st.

Similarly the untrained 31 Division Cyclists transferred to fighting companies in May. Of these, eight men from the East Yorkshire Regiment and Hull died. Also, whatever tactical and logistical difficulties the Battalion overcame, the complex wheeling manoeuvre to be carried out as they advanced would not be an easy exercise for a battalion in training, let alone in the battleground conditions before Serre.[6]

In Rees' opinion the time for the manoeuvre was also too short. Rees had a severe argument with Hunter-Weston before he induced him to allow an extra ten minutes for the capture of an orchard 300 yards beyond Serre. "In twenty minutes I had to capture the first four lines of trenches in front of Serre. After a check of twenty minutes I was allowed forty minutes to capture Serre and twenty minutes later to capture an orchard on a knoll 300 yards beyond." He added, "My criticisms on these points are not a case of being wise after the event. I did not like them at the time but I do not profess to have foreseen the result should a failure occur. A great spirit of optimism prevailed in all quarters."[7]

An officer much closer to the men than Hunter-Weston and Rees also praised the men in their defeat. 94 Brigade's Brigade Major F. S. G. Piggott, later wrote, "The New Army 31st Division was no whit behind the Regular 4th

Left: Lt. General Sir Aylmer G. Hunter-Weston, D.S.O. Commander of VIII Corps. I.W.M.

and 29th Divisions in gallantry, determination and efficiency." Speaking of 94 Brigade on July 1st he went on, "In spite of its failure, it was a very remarkable feat of arms by the temporary soldiers of Accrington, Barnsley and Sheffield."[8]

At G.H.Q. Haig knew nothing of individual battalions and saw matters differently. His earlier judgements about the effectiveness of VIII Corps were unchanged. VIII Corps, on July 1st,

Left: British wounded sent to 'Blighty' sometimes went to small hospitals run by the British Red Cross Society or the St. John's Ambulance Brigade. The photograph shows a group in a St. John's Ambulance hospital in Elmfield Hall, Accrington. Many of the nurses and staff were related to Pals' officers and men. As far as is known, however, none of the Pals wounded on July 1st, 1916 were lucky enough to arrive here.
L.L.H.D.

Right: On July 16th, 1916 General von Below passed this, the Kaiser's message, on to his troops:

ARMY ORDER

His Majesty the Emperor and King has expressed at his visit today to the Army High Command his warm appreciation of the heroic resistance of the 2nd Army of an opponent by far superior in number. His Majesty is fully confident that his glorious troops will continue to hold out and resist successfully against the enemy's persistent attacking, remaining steadfast in defence. The commanders and troops can be proud of the unshakeable confidence of their Supreme Commander. This Army Order is to be issued immediately to all members of the Army.

Armee-Oberkommando 2.

A. H. Qu., 16. Juli 1916

Armeebefehl.

Seine Majestaet der Kaiser und Koenig haben bei Seinem heutigen Besuch beim Armee-Oberkommando Allerhoechst Seine warme Anerkennung für den heldenmütigen Widerstand der 2. Armee gegen einen an Zahl weit überlegenen Gegner ausgesprochen. Seine Majestaet sind voll überzeugt, dass Seine ruhmreichen Truppen weiter durchhalten und den anstürmenden Feind niederringen durch unbedingtes Draufgehen beim Angriff und festes Ausharren in der Verteidigung. Die Führer und die Truppen koennen stolz sein auf dieses felsenfeste Vertrauen ihres Obersten Kriegsherrn. Jeder rechtfertige es weiter an seiner Stelle.

Dieser Armeebefehl ist allen Angehoerigen der Armee sofort bekannt zu geben.

v. Below.

lost 662 officers and 13,363 men, but Haig still noted in his Diary — "few of VIII Corps left their trenches."[9] Such a view surely could only rest on the fragmentary reports of the observers. In fairness to Haig he later, in a despatch written on December 23rd, 1916, spoke of "striking progress made at many points" north of the River Ancre (VIII Corps sector) and of parties of troops penetrating enemy positions at, amongst other places, Pendant Copse (4 Division) and Serre (31 Division).[10] He referred also, in his diary for July 1st, 1916, to "two battalions which occupied Serre village and were, it is said, cut off."[11]

As early as 7 p.m. on July 1st, Rawlinson, Commander of the 4th Army, agreed with Haig to transfer VIII Corps, with X Corps, to Lt. Gen. Sir Hubert Gough's Reserve Army on the morrow. Haig's comment being, "The VIII Corps seem to need looking after."[12] This criticism, directed more against Hunter-Weston, whom Haig disliked personally and wanted out of the way, again reflected on the officers and men of VIII Corps. Gough, though disappointed at

the turn of events, reacted more favourably towards VIII Corps. "In one day my thoughts and ideas had to move from consideration of a victorious pursuit to those of the rehabilitation of the shattered wing of an army."[13]

In East Lancashire, with the rest of the country, the long anxious wait for the 'Great Offensive' with its 'victorious pursuit' was ended. At first the news was optimistic. 'The Times' on Monday, July 3rd, gave unofficial news (from a German source) of the capture of Serre and La Boiselle with heavy losses. In Burnley on July 5th, the day of Pte. Wilkinson's death in Colincamps, the Burnley News, not knowing the offensive had already ground to a halt, spoke of the magnificent start made and of British troops steadily making headway.[14] However, by Saturday, July 9th, the story radically changed. Although the East Lancashire newspapers published the official, censored reports which gave an optimistic view of events, their editors could not contain a growing anxiety. They knew a stream of letters from the East Lancashire Records Office at Preston had been arriving in local homes since Wednesday. Earlier in the week a train full of wounded stopped outside Accrington station. A voice shouted to a group of women,

"Where are we?"

"Accrington!"

"Accrington? The Accrington Pals! They've been wiped out!" The news quickly spread, adding to the tension.[15] Rumour now abounded and scores of people called at the newspaper offices every day asking for news. Something was 'up'.

By the end of the week, wives and mothers whose regular flow of letters from France had dried up, visited friends and neighbours for news of others in the Battalion. Letters of assurance from wounded men in hospital in England were already arriving for some families. The numbers of these alone were enough to feed the rumours that the unthinkable had happened. Pte. Glover, placed in No. 2 Western Hospital, Manchester, by Wednesday July 5th, received a visit from his father on July 7th. He brought back Pte. Glover's story for publication in the Accrington Observer and Times.

The difference between official news stories and the reality in their home towns at first forced newspaper comment to be equivocal. The Accrington Observer declared, "What is certain is the Pals Battalion has won for itself a glorious page in the record of dauntless courage and imperishable valour — the dead and wounded are more numerous than we would fain have hoped." In an attempt to allay fears, it continued, "In the case of the wounded it is consoling to know the injuries are comparatively slight."[16]

Other editions tried to say one thing and mean another. "The Chorley Pals have suffered considerable losses in the offensive. So far none have been officially reported killed. In the majority of cases the men are wounded, many only slightly." It added, with more candour, "We fear next week the casualty list will be augmented, for the attack was of such a nature one cannot possibly think otherwise."[17]

Left: Pte. Clarry Glover, wounded on July 1st, 1916 spent two months in hospitals at Manchester and nearby Radcliffe. Clarry, here seen on the right, along with a friend escort a St. John's Ambulance Voluntary Aid Detachment nurse on a walk in Radcliffe.

175

The Burnley comment though more direct — had a sting. "The Burnley Pals have earned themselves a glorious mention in the records for dauntless courage in the face of the heaviest odds. They were some time getting to the Front, but that was not their fault. Though many have fallen the Pals have earned the laurels of fame."[18] All editorials, shared a pride in the achievements of their respective Pals Companies, with sorrow for the losses and sympathy for the bereaved. Over a week passed, however, before any real conception of the Battalion's disaster spread through the community.

Firm news — and more letters and telegrams — began to arrive on the eve of the annual Summer holiday. In Burnley they began on July 8th, in Accrington and Chorley on July 15th.[19] Families hurried from sea-side resorts to get what news they could, or to letters already delivered. In Accrington, Harwood naturally became the focus of many enquiries at the Town Hall and his home. He wrote to the War Office to request an advance list of casualties. He soon discovered no privileges accrued to the raisers of battalions. On July 13th, the War Office replied that a list of 'other rank' casualties had not been compiled and that only next of kin would receive news direct from Army Records Office. No advance copies could be supplied to individuals. Harwood, therefore was in the dark as much as anyone else. A week later Rickman, from his London hospital sent Harwood a list of officer casualties — 7 killed, 12 wounded, one missing.

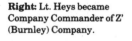

Right: Lt. Heys became Company Commander of 'Z' (Burnley) Company.

Burnley was luckier. Contact with 'Z' Company in France had not broken down. Lt. Heys, now Company Commander, wrote to the Mayor offering help with individual enquiries.[20] Rickman could do little more than send his own condolences to the Mayors of Accrington, Burnley and Chorley. To Harwood he expressed his pride in the Battalion he had cared for for the past sixteen months and his own despair. "No words can express what I feel for the losses, but it may be consolation to those who have lost their all to know the Battalion contributed its share of the offensive."[21]

The War Office list of 'other rank' casualties arrived in the newspaper offices on August 5th, it listed just 31 wounded. Three days later, 40 killed in action were officially named and thereafter weekly lists of dead, wounded and missing appeared. For most the lists were out of date. As soon as the news of the offensive came through and the truth suspected, local newspapers appealed to readers to supply them with news and photos of the killed and wounded. In this way 17 casualties were reported in Accrington on July 8th. Then, with obituary after obituary, photo after photo, the tragedy unfolded to the readers, there were 32 featured in the paper on July 11th, 40 on July 15th, 32 on July 18th — until they decreased in number in mid-August. The official casualty lists, when finally published, were almost superfluous. The row after row of biographies and photographs had already made its dramatic effect on public morale.

The last of the next of kin of the dead were officially informed in mid-September. Anxieties about those missing increased as time passed. Wives and mothers, desperate for news, advertised in the newspapers — "Mrs. Florence Mercer of Rishton, would be grateful for any news of her son, 15085 L.Cpl. Albert Mercer. 'Pte. Herbert Aspin of Church. Mother would be pleased if any soldier can give information on his fate.' Pte. George Stuttard, machine gunner, 'W' Company Accrington, any information gratefully received by his parents."[22]

Pte. J. Birch of 'W' Company, a survivor of July 1st, helped by arranging with his mother in Accrington to receive enquiries from relatives of missing men. Within two or three weeks she forwarded thirty seven names. Pte. Birch devoted all his spare time out of the line in search of information.

Some families were lucky. Their 'missing' men turned up wounded in hospital. Others would never know. Pte. John Laffy, who enlisted in the July 1915 recruiting march, disappeared from the face of the earth. On January 25th, 1919, he was still officially listed as 'missing'. Some information came from comrades in France or in hospital, but often the only information to be gleaned came as 'he simply disappeared;'

'I saw him wounded, then never saw him again.' Scores of wives and parents, up to their own deaths, clung to the slight hope this gave them that 'he' was not dead but might somehow, some day return. Sometimes a letter, sometimes a tattered photograph, the sole object of grief throughout their lifetimes.

Some men died in circumstances so horrific their comrades could not describe them, even many years later. Pte. Ormond Fairweather of 'Y' Company saw his friend Pte. Carswell Entwhistle die on July 1st, 1916. "After the war Mrs. Entwhistle begged Ormond many times to tell her how Carswell died, but he always refused. She desperately wanted to know and he couldn't tell her, both of them were heart-broken.[23] Lt. Williams, the only Company Commander to survive July 1st, 1916, was too shocked to be interviewed by anxious relatives, when home on sick leave in August 1916.

Equally with East Lancashire the news of July 1st, 1916 shocked Caernarvon. The close ties formed in the early Spring of 1915 had been maintained by correspondence and court-ship and the town closely followed the Battalion's progress. On July 11th, 1916, copies of East Lancashire newspapers, showing photographs of dead and wounded were posted in Caernarvon shop-windows. The news spread quickly and scores of friends and ex-landladies came to learn the fate of their billetees. On July 21st, the Caernarvon and Denbigh Herald published its own list of 26 officers and men dead and 114 wounded. Most were Accrington men, the names probably supplied by Accrington newspapers. Captain Livesey and Pte. Tom Coady were especially mourned as men popular with the townspeople. For Caernarvon in July 1916 the sorrow from the loss of friends in the 11th East Lancs became intensified by the loss of many local men of the Royal Welsh Fusiliers and the Welsh Brigade at Mametz Wood on July 10th, in the continuing fighting on the Somme.

In East Lancashire, as elsewhere, the impact of July 1st, 1916, lessened in time as other battles, in France and Flanders, in Mesopotamia and Salonika, brought more casualties and losses to local families. The sacrifices of the men of the 11th East Lancs faded and their families adjusted to their grief as best they could.

For the survivors at Louvencourt, Gough's 'rehabilitation' did not last long. With Carter-Campbell returned from sick leave and back in command, the remnants of 94 Brigade, including the 11th East Lancs, moved, on July 8th, north to Calonne-sur-Lys as 31 Division transferred into XI Corps, First Army. A composite company of two officers and 160 men, formed from two depleted companies, again held front line positions in the Neuve Chapelle sector, near Bethune, on July 24th. The line lay in swampy, mosquito-infested country. Trench conditions

Tho' Far Apart To-Day We Be, This Dainty Card I Send To Thee.

Left: This postcard was returned to the family of L/Cpl W. Briggs with his effects after his death on July 1st, 1916 (see page 149.) Sent by his fiancee Amelia, it bears a verse on the reverse side which said:
'I'll never love another boy but you
I'll never love another boy with eyes so blue
Night and day while you are away my love
For I'll never love another boy but you."

Below: After July 1st, 1916 specialist groups were reformed. Here are 'Z' (Burnley) Company bombers 'Somewhere in France,' in 1917.

Above: Regimental Band of the 11th East Lancashire Regiment after it was re-formed in February 1917. The former band had been wiped out on the morning of July 1st. All but one were either killed or wounded as they carried out their battle role of stretcher bearers.

Below: Transport Section of the Pals outside their billet in France in November 1916. A.O.&T.

were particularly foul. Here the Battalion inherited 'Tupper', "a huge piebald rat with three legs and one bloodshot eye. He was handed over with trench stores to every incoming Battalion.[24] 94 Brigade was now so weakened that the combined strengths of the 11th East Lancs, the 12th York and Lancasters and one company of the 13th York and Lancasters equalled only a Battalion.

After alternating between the front line and the reserve area for almost six weeks, 94 Brigade moved to the area of Festubert of Chorley Territorials ill-fame. Here, in mid-September 1916, a draft of 182 officers and men arrived from Prees Heath.

With these and later additions the subsequent story is of a new battalion. The events of July 1st had radically changed the survivors outlook. Their original enthusiasm had gone — blown away before Serre. With the High Command not so infallible as they once imagined, the war could go on for years. In spite of their misgivings the survivors of the 'old' battalion passed something of their 'Pals' spirit of comradeship on to the new, although the loss of so many local officers, N.C.O.s and men weakened the old East Lancashire associations. The 'old' 11th East Lancs had lost its singular character formed by the close nature of its origins. It had also lost its innocent enthusiasm to become an exclusive group of veterans within a 'new' battalion. In this form, in October 1916, and now in XIII Corps, Fifth Army, (formerly the Reserve Army), they came again to Warnimont Wood and to John Copse, in the old shattered front line of even worse ill-fame.

In January 1917, 320 reinforcements joined. In the draft were some of those wounded on July 1st, newly discharged from hospital, Pte. Glover and Cpl. Whittaker amongst them, they considered themselves fortunate to return. Other wounded never returned but transferred to other East Lancs. battalions in France, Mesopotamia, Salonika and even Blighty. Still others served with a variety of infantry regiments from all parts of the United Kingdom. Many of the more badly wounded were still in hospital, some to be discharged as unfit for military service. A few, Sgt. Kay, L/Cpl. Challon and Pte. Platt of 'Z' Company amongst them, left for officer training and a commission.

Pte. Sayer returned from hospital to the job of training 32 volunteer bandsmen as stretcher-bearers.

"Major Kershaw, then on Brigade staff, told me he wanted me to train the replacement stretcher-bearers. 'I can't do it Sir, I'm a bomber.' 'Nonsense, I know you were a doctor's pupil before you enlisted. You used to treat my wife's mother in Burnley. If you can do that you can teach first-aid.' From then on I taught first-aid on

actual casualties, often under fire from snipers. It was tougher than being a bomber."

In February 1917, six officers and 200 other ranks joined the Battalion making a total of 700 replacements and returned wounded since July 1916. Thus, the Battalion was brought up to full establishment. In the later groups were many recovered wounded from other regiments, partly a military expediency to flesh out depleted battalions with experienced men and partly War Office policy to break up the community based New Army Battalions whose losses had so affected public morale.

In February 1917, the Germans made a tactical withdrawal of approximately 18,000 yards from their front lines on the Somme to prepared positions known as the Hindenburg Line. The British forces, including the 11th East Lancs, moved up to fill the gap. The route of the 11th East Lancs, through Colincamps and Beaumont Hamel, took them some two miles south of Serre. The Germans evacuated Serre on February 24th and the incoming 22nd Manchester Regiment found the bodies of some of those who had fought their way through the German lines in July 1916. Some men, buried by their enemy, had their names and regimental numbers inscribed on wooden crosses. The remains of others lay where they had fallen or hung, still entangled, on the German wire.[25] Two weeks later, in mid March, whilst in reserve at Courcelles and working near Serre on road repairs, it fell to some of the 11th East Lancs to discover the bodies of several of their comrades reported missing since July 1st, 1916.[26]

Above: Signalling Section of the Pals taken at Merville, April 1917.
A.O.&.T.

casualties. Only three 'nil' monthly casualty returns were made by the Battalion in thirty three months service in France and Flanders. Endless 'donkey work' and training occupied their time out of the line.

In February 1918, as part of a large scale Army re-organisation Infantry Divisions were reduced from twelve to nine Battalions, with Brigades reduced from four to three Battalions. 94 Brigade, 31 Division ceased to exist and on February 11th, the 11th East Lancs transferred to 92 Brigade, 31 Division to join the 10th and 11th East Yorkshire Regiments. The partnership of almost three years with the 12th, 13th

Left: Bodies of many of the British dead of July 1st, 1916 lay in No Man's Land or entangled in the German wire until February 1917 when the Germans withdrew to new positions and British troops moved into Serre. The ravages of rats, weather and time upon human remains are here depicted.
B.C.P.L.

During the early months of 1917 the Battalion had a 'quiet war', a mixture of holding and patrolling a relatively inactive sector of the front and training and re-organising behind the line. With newly returned Rickman in command, on June 28th, 1917, almost a year to the day, the Battalion attacked successfully, though at a cost of twelve dead, the German positions in Cadorna trench in Oppy Wood, near Arras. The remainder of 1917 continued 'quiet', although patrolling and German shell-fire caused

and 14th York and Lancaster Regiments broke up. On the same day these Battalions were amalgamated and re-designated the 13th York and Lancaster Regiment. The 11th East Lancs thus escaped the fate of their comrades from Sheffield and Barnsley — and also the fates of the 2/4th , 2/5th, 7th and 8th East Lancs Regiments, similarly disbanded. Twenty officers and 400 men from the 8th East Lancs joined the Battalion.[27] However diverse in make-up, the 11th East Lancs in the re-organisation were

Below: German troops look on as a hitherto undamaged village is shelled before they move in to take possession, during their advance in the Spring of 1918.

paid the compliment of keeping their name and Commanding Officer.

The first major trial of the Battalion in 1918 started on the morning of March 21st. After an artillery barrage of almost 6,000 guns, 62 German infantry divisions attacked the British Third and Fifth Armies along a line from the Somme to Cambrai. The 11th East Lancs with the rest of 31 Division rushed to meet the enemy at Hamelincourt, near Arras. For eight long days, until relieved, 31 Division resisted the forces of five German divisions. Between March 27th and April 4th, the 11th East Lancs lost 240 men killed, wounded or missing. Cpl. Earl Whittaker was one killed in the attack.[28] In the same period no less than twenty eight awards including the V.C. were won by the Battalion.[29]

On April 9th, the Germans broke through the line held by Portuguese troops on the River Lys. The 11th East Lancs, with 31 Division, again raced to fill the gap and again suffered heavy losses. By June, however, the Allied Armies steadily regained the initiative. On June 28th the Battalion took part in a successful counter-attack on a German salient in the Nieppe Forest and gained 2,000 yards of ground. Pte. Cheetham, an ex-member of the 8th Battalion, took part in the attack.

"I was in 'X' Company as a Lewis Gunner. We saw the Germans running away. I fired just two shots, then the Lewis gun jammed (they were very prone to do so). We thought we were going to miss getting the Germans, but my No. 2 on the gun cleared it and we fired seventeen magazines without a stoppage. We thought of claiming it as a world record!"

On July 1st the Battalion handed over the captured ground to relieving forces.[30] By a coincidence the three major attacks of the Battalion were at almost yearly intervals.

The Battalion's final main action — to clear Ploegsteert Wood — started on September 28th. They achieved it at a high price of 370 killed, wounded and missing. Although October and November brought several more casualties, on this day, September 28th, Pte. Fred Leeming died, the last of the original 'Pals' to be killed in action.[31]

The weeks leading up to the Armistice on November 11th, were free of major incidents. The Battalion, now in II Corps, Second Army, was busy pursuing the retreating Germans. On October 25th cheering crowds welcomed them into the textile towns of Wattrelos and Roubaix. On the evening of November 10th, the Battalion halted east of Renaix (Ronse) in Belgium, and settled for the night in barns, outhouses and stables. At 4 a.m. on November 11th, a sentry, Pte. John Pollitt of 'Z' Company, challenged an approaching motor-cyclist.

"He dismounted, and to my surprise, threw his arms round my neck and asked where the C.O. was billetted. Then he read me his despatch in code — 'Armistice signed 3 a.m. this morning; all firing to cease at 11 a.m.'. I immediately ran to my comrades to break the good news."[32]

In this way all 'Z' Company knew of the Armistice before the C.O. It was specially fitting that the bearer of the news was an 'original' Pal.

At 9 a.m. as the Battalion assembled to continue their march, Rickman went through the

Above: Re-formed stretcher bearers of the Pals at Merville 1917. Pte. Fred Sayer is seated in the middle row to the officer's left, Captain De Courcy Keogh.

Left: Pte. Fred Leeming of Great Harwood, the last original Pal to be killed in action, September 28th, 1918.

181

Handwritten annotations on photograph:
See overleaf
Yours truly
an "Ex-Regular" Officer
Capt Conway. My last Company Commander a very fine officer — see letters.
Canadian

Above: CQMS Jack Hindle poses with officers of 'W' (Accrington) Company. Written overleaf: Turcoing, France. Almost Armistice Day prior to the last push. The lady was the photographer's wife.

Above: Pte. A. Magrath, a survivor of July 1st, 1916 caught a chill and died as the war ended thus becoming the last of the original Pals to die on active service.

formality of reading them the despatch. At 11 a.m. the Battalion halted and every man listened. For the first time in their Western Front service no sound could be heard — no guns firing, no transport rumbling on the pave, no marching feet. Unbelievably the war was over. At dusk the Battalion entered Grammont (Geraadsbergen), twenty miles east of Brussels. Here, at Grammont, Pte. Andrew Magrath, a bandsman/stretcher-bearer and survivor of July 1st, 1916, in a terrible irony, caught a chill whilst out celebrating Peace and became ill with pneumonia. He died on November 21st, 1918, the last of the original Pals to die on active service.[33]

As the remainder of II Corps advanced into Germany to become part of the Army of Occupation, on November 13th, the 11th Battalion started its return march, through Courtrai, Menin and Ypres, to St. Omer, northern France. In spite of an appeal by Rickman to the War Office to allow him to bring the Battalion to Accrington for a farewell parade before demobilisation, the break-up of the Battalion started in December as men in certain occupations, particularly coal-mining, were released.

On February 7th, 1919, at St. Omer, a cold wintry day, the Regimental Colours were presented to a fast dwindling Battalion by Brig. Gen. T. de L. Williams. Four weeks later, just four years and one week after his memorable take-over at Caernarvon, Rickman relinquished his command. In his Farewell Order, he spoke of his regrets at leaving the Battalion he had hoped to take home to its birth-place. He thanked all ranks for their unswerving loyalty, their high sense of esprit-de-corps and comradeship and wished them all God Speed.

It took until October 1919 for the Battalion to finally fade away and for the men to return unheralded, unnoticed, to their home towns. For the original Pals the return to East Lancashire saw no cheering crowds, no mayoral speeches — five years had seen too many changes. The Pals themselves, who in their innocent enthusiasm bade their farewells so cheerily in February 1915, were also changed. Too many of their comrades were lying in France, the Middle East and Blighty. Too many had perished on the slopes before Serre. For those left, warweariness had long replaced the high spirits of Rugeley, Ripon and Salisbury Plain and the impatience of 'getting to the Front.' The High Command errors of judgement and organisation of July 1st, 1916 were still seen by many Pals as deliberate decisions made by men indifferent to their fate.[33] 'Not a rat alive' was still a sardonic joke.

Left: 'Somewhere in France' 1918. Members of 'W' (Accrington) Company. Fifth from the left front row is AQMS J. Hindle. Fourth from right front row is Sgt. J. Rigby, M.M.

Below: 'X' (District) Company in the public gardens St. Omer in December 1918. By this time men were being demobilised in small groups.

Far right: The Farewell Order by Lt. Col. Rickman. Every officer and man in the Battalion received his personal copy.

FAREWELL ORDER.

BY Lt. Col. RICKMAN D.S.O. ON RELINQUISHING COMMAND OF THE 11 TH BATTALION EAST LANCASHIRE REGIMENT MARCH 6/1919

On relinquishing command of the Battalion, I wish to express my deep appreciation to the Officers, Warrant Officers. N.C.Os & Men of the Battalion for their great loyalty and splendid example of devotion to duty throughout the whole period of my Command.

The Higher Command have been good enough to express their appreciation of the fine work done by the Battalion, and without the splendid co-operation of all ranks it would have been impossible to accomplish all that the Battalion has been given to do.

It is with the greatest regret that I leave the Battalion which I had hoped to bring home to its birth-place, and I wish to thank all ranks for their unswerving loyalty, and for their high sense of Esprit de Corps and comradeship, which has maintained in the Battalion the Highest traditions of the British Army.

I wish all ranks God speed, and I hope to renew in the near future the friendships I have made and which I hope I shall never lose.

(Signed) A. W. RICKMAN.

March 6/1919.   Lt. Colonel.

NOTES

1. Survivors of the 12th York and Lancaster Regiment who reached the German wire said they looked towards their own lines and could see every movement. "This being so, any attack by day was hardly likely to succeed". (Battle report 1/7/16, 12th York and Lancaster Regiment.)
2. P.R.O. WO95/2366.
3. Note to Maj. Gen. R. Wanless O'Gowan, O.C. 31 Division, July 4th, 1916. (File 77/179/T, Brig. Gen. H. C. Rees, A Personal Record of the War I.W.M.).
   N.B. Unfortunately, there is no confirmation or otherwise from German sources. The war diaries of 2, 3 and 6 Companies, 169 Infantry Regiment (opposing 94 Brigade) are unavailable 'presumed lost through enemy action in W.W.1.' (B.G.K., letter to author dated 3.7.87.)
4. It is estimated as many as one third of those 'killed in action' died as a result of wounds, and left to die on the battlefield. (See 'Face of Battle', John Keegan, Penguin 1978, P 274.)
5. See 'The Somme', A. Farrar-Hockley, Batsford 1964, for a detailed analysis of the artillery bombardment and the counter-barrage.
6. Captain MacAlpine, later asked for his comments for the Official History of the Great War, specifically requested the 'wheels' (manoeuvres) to be carried out by the 11th East Lancs during their attack to be explained in detail. The request was ignored. (P.R.O. CAB/190).
7. See 'Brig. Gen. H. C. Rees, A Personal Record of the War', I.W.M.
8. P.R.O. CAB/190.
9. The Private Papers of Douglas Haig 1914 - 1919, ed. R. Blake, Eyre and Spottiswoode, 1952 pp 153 - 154.
10. Sir Douglas Haig's Despatches 1915 - 1919, ed. J. H. Boraston, Vol. 1, Dent 1919, p 26.
11. The Private Papers of Douglas Haig 1914 - 1919, p 153.
12. Ibid.
13. 'The Fifth Army', Gen. Sir H. Gough, Hodder & Stoughton, London 1931, p 139.
14. July 1st, 1916, was the worst day in the history of the British Army. 57,470 officers and men were killed, wounded or missing. By November 18th, 1916, the official end of the battle, casualties totalled 415,000.
15. Recalled by Edith Roughsedge who vividly remembered the women coming directly into her parents' shop with the news. She later related the story to her daughter Mrs. Enid Briggs.
16. A.O.T. 8/7/16.
17. C.G. 8/7/16.
18. B.E. 15/7/16.
19. By coincidence the dependents of those of the Chorley Company who enlisted before December 26th, 1914, attended a meeting at Chorley Town Hall on July 10th. Each received on behalf of the men, from the Mayor a Christmas 1914 present of a tin-box containing tobacco and a pencil, etc. from H.R.H. Princess Mary's Comforts fund.
   N.B. (The Accrington Companies, or the survivors, were not to get theirs until August 1919.)
20. Advert B.E. 5/8/16.
   'The Mayor wishes to announce that Lt. F. A. Heys, O.C. 'Z' Company, has given him facilities for obtaining particulars as to the killed, wounded and missing of his Company. If any friends of men in the Company have been unable to obtain news, the Mayor will take up the matter with Lt. Heys'.
21. A.O.T. 11/7/16.
22. A.O.T. 2/9/16.
   All were 'killed in action' July 1st, 1916.
   Pte. Stuttard's parents received official confirmation in April 1917.
23. Conversation with Mr. H. Entwhistle, Chorley 1983.
24. History of 'Z' Company Page 39.
25. Those recovered were buried, with men from other regiments, in the Serre Road (1, 2 and 3) group of cemeteries, by troops of V Corps in the Spring of 1917.
26. Very probably amongst these was Pte. Stuttard's body. (See Note 22).
27. The 8th East Lancs Regiment, formed at Preston, September 1914 (K3), had been in France since July 1915.
28. 15735 Cpl. Earl Whittaker, of Burnley, was reported as wounded, then missing. His body was never found. In November 1918, his wife, firmly believing him alive and a prisoner of war, visited Arras in an effort to find him. For the rest of her life she never believed he was dead. Cpl. Whittaker's name is on the Arras Memorial.
29. The awards were: V.C. — (2/Lt. B. A. Horsfall of the 1st East Lancs attached to the 11th East Lancs); Bar to the D.S.O. (Lt. Col. Rickman's D.S.O. awarded after July 1st, 1916); 2 D.S.O.s; 7 M.C.s; 3 D.C.M.'s and 14 M.M.s.
30. 31 Division, then in XV Corps, Second Army, transferred to XI Corps, First Army for this operation. Brig. Gen. T. de L. Williams of 92 Brigade later told Rickman he had chosen the 11th East Lancs to attack the strongest part of the German line because they were his most capable troops. This compliment cost the 11th East Lancs 51 men killed in action.
31. 15774 Pte. Fred Leeming, of Great Harwood, is buried, with fourteen other men of the Battalion, at Underhill Farm War Cemetery, Ploegsteert.
32. Letter to 'Twenty years after' feature, B.E. 12/11/38.
33. 15860 Pte. Andrew Magrath, of Chorley, died in a Base Hospital in France and is buried in Terlincthon British Cemetery.
34. This belief persisted after the war. Ex-Cpl. R. Bradshaw, addressing Burnley Rotary Club, spoke of '94 Brigade purposely massacred and activities shown to the enemy to deceive them and mask preparations further south'. B.E. 11/11/31.

Epilogue

John Harwood's name did not appear in the 1919 New Year Honours List. During the war no man in Accrington worked harder in his patriotic duty. He put the name of the town in the title of a British Infantry Battalion and an Artillery Brigade (158 (Accrington and Burnley) Howitzers, R.F.A.) His appointment by the War Office as their military representative on the Accrington Military Tribunal took place in January 1916.[1] In this lay his downfall.

The Accrington Military Tribunal quickly gained a reputation for harshness and bias. Objections to military service on the grounds of conscience were subjected to humiliating interrogations, with questions often deliberately phrased to produce laughter from an audience there 'to see the fun.' Shop-keepers and the self-employed were often exempted without hesitation. This rarely happened to employed persons, regardless of circumstance. As early as March 1916, a current of ill-feeling in Accrington led Philip Snowden, M.P. for neighbouring Blackburn, to criticise Harwood in a debate in the House of Commons, as "a prominent Conservative, instrumental in deciding whether political opponents should or should not, be granted exemption."[2]

The good regard held for him in his home town had become diminished by his zeal and lack of objectiveness. Perhaps because of this he got neither recognition nor reward from his country. In 1919, aged 70, tired and worn-out, he retired from public life.

Harwood, nevertheless attended three functions concerning the Battalion. He helped organise a combined 'welcome home and reunion'-party for the Battalion and 158 Howitzer Brigade in July 1919. On October 18th, 1919, as guest of honour he attended the ceremonial handing over of the Battalion Colours to the town of Accrington by Lt. Col. Rickman's successor, Lt. Col. Ingpen, D.S.O.[3] In his final public act Harwood laid the first wreath in memory of the fallen of the Battalion at the ceremonial unveiling of Accrington War memorial in Oak Hill Park on July 1st, 1922.

When published, the order of procession to the ceremony became a source of controversy. The Accrington Company of the 5th East Lancs.

Left: John Harwood, J.P. Mayor of Accrington

Left: John Harwood attended this welcome home' and grand reunion for the Pals and Howitzers in the Town Hall, Accrington in July 1919. A high tea in the Wesleyan School, Union Street preceded the Smoking Concert and Social which commenced at 7 pm.

1914 - 1919.

E.L.R. Re-union R.F.A.

PALS & HOWITZERS,

At the Town Hall, Accrington,
on Wednesday, July 23rd, 1919.

ENTERTAINMENT.

Artistes from the Hippodrome Company,

"A TRIP TO PARIS"
(BY KIND PERMISSION).

ERNEST LORD'S

"EXCELSIORS"

Company of Ladies and Gentlemen.

MR. WHIPP, Elocutionist.

MISS EMMIE HYDE, Contralto.

Stage Manager: JOHN HOLGATE.

FOULDS. TYP.

Above: Laying wreaths on the steps of Accrington War Memorial after the unveiling ceremony on July 1st, 1922.

Right: A general view of Accrington War Memorial after the unveiling ceremony.

Territorials — some but youths too young to have served in the War — were to lead. Following were simply 'Ex-Servicemen', i.e. any who were eligible and willing to march. A group of ex-Pals protested. They considered that they, as an 'Accrington' Battalion, held the right to lead the procession. The protests revived wartime resentments by the Territorials and their families who often felt the Pals received an undue share of publicity and 'glory'. The controversy ended and the Town Council's original intention fulfilled, when ex-Pals and ex-Territorials marched side by side. John Harwood laid the first wreath as the sole concession to 'his' 'Accrington' Battalion.

The reluctance of Accrington Town Council to have any special post-war relationship with the Battalion is evident in the town's absence from any association with the villages on the Somme. Burnley, home of many 1st Battalion men as well as 'Z' Company, in 1920 adopted Miramont, Colincamps and Courcelles and helped finance the rebuilding of those villages.[4] Official links ceased in 1930 with a visit by the mayor of Burnley to lay wreaths on the graves of Burnley men in Euston Road, Queens and Railway Hollow cemeteries. Nevertheless, no public memorial to the Burnley Company was proposed or considered by the Town Council.

In contrast, Chorley Town Council, although at first reluctant, did pay tribute to its Chorley Company. As early as November 1916, a group of women led by Miss Knight proposed at a public meeting, the erection of a home for twenty five maimed soldiers to be known as "The Pals' Memorial Home for Crippled Soldiers." This led immediately to bitter controversy. Most men prominent in Chorley public life, including Dr. Rigby in his role as a Town Councillor, wanted instead the memorial to be for all the fallen of Chorley and forced a postponement of the idea. The idea, in time, died. Six years passed before Miss Knight could commemorate 'her' Pals in her three Golden Books of Remembrance in Chorley's Memorial Room in Astley Hall. Chorley Town Council finally played their part with a Chorley Company Roll of Honour listing 55 dead and 158 survivors, and three large framed photographs of 'C' Company taken in 1914.[5]

Unlike East Lancashire, Sheffield kept contact with Serre and formed a post-war friendship with the village. Within the village is a Memorial in memory of the men of the 12th York and Lancaster Regiment who died in the attack. On July 5th, 1936 a hundred strong civic delegation from Sheffield attended a memorial service in the newly opened Sheffield Memorial Park. The event solely concerned Sheffield and Serre. Of Accrington, and the 11th East Lancs Regiment — no mention. The reason can lie only with Accrington Town Council's lack of interest. The Sheffield Memorial Park, by a

strange irony, stands partly on ground held by the 11th East Lancs Regiment on July 1st, 1916.

The 1920s and early 1930s passed with most of East Lancashire preoccupied in surviving the inter-war industrial depression. (As early as 1919, Accrington had some 11,000 unemployed). The heartbreak of the war continued. Each November 11th, looms and lathes stopped at 11 a.m. and schoolchildren gathered at War memorials, for silent remembrance.

July 1st, became a date filled with poignancy. Each year scores of family 'In Memoriam' notices appeared, each year editorials condemned the war and the tragic losses on the Somme. In 1926 the 'Accrington Observer' compared July 1st, 1916 with the economic chaos of industrial life of the General Strike — "As we revere the memory of those who fell at Serre, we reflect if some of those whose mission it was to give us a brighter and better England would have played their parts as resolutely as those who sacrificed their lives to win the war, the years that followed would have been a good deal less troubled and uncertain."[6]

The survivors of the war — and the widows and children of the dead — continued to endure the indignities of the 'Means Test' and the semi-starvation of unemployment. Some escaped by emigration. Pte. Bloor, Pte. Clark and Pte.

Above: Sheffield Memorial Park, by the copses in France.

Below: Serre village in 1932, the houses have been rebuilt and the villages have returned to normal life.
IWM

Above: Major G. N. Slinger.

Above: Col. R. Sharples.

Davy went to Canada, Cpl. Bath to Australia. But the shadow of war remained. The Battalion still had its casualties. Amongst many, Pte. Varley died, aged 36 in 1924, directly of pneumonia, indirectly from gassing. A parsimonious government denied his widow a war pension because the medical authorities diagnosed his death as 'natural causes'. Sgt. Rigby M.M., wounded July 1st, 1916, wounded in April, in August and again in September 1918 died, aged 41, in 1928 of Tuberculosis contracted as a result of war service.

By a sad coincidence four men closely concerned with the Battalion's early days died in the 1920's; Captain Slinger, aged 43, in October, 1923; John Harwood, aged 74, in December of that year; Lt. Col. Rickman, aged 51, in October 1925 and Col. Sharples, aged 79, in August 1929.

Lt. Col. Rickman's accidental death (his clothing caught in the flywheel of an electricity generator) shocked his many admirers, but Col. Sharples' death broke the final link with the memorable, often semi-comic, days of the autumn and winter of 1914. Each man had his favourite memory of the Colonel's amiable discipline — his sending home, with mild reproof, those who paraded with a 'pint or two' inside them; his taking a parade, in full military uniform except for a workman's flat cap, 'to keep the wind out;' the occasional late parade because of pressing business matters in his solicitor's office; and his admonishment to a private (age 40) who swore at a Second Lieutenant (age 18) — 'don't use that naughty word to a lad again.'

Col. Sharples' paternalistic eccentricity and his men's good-natured respectful, response helped, no doubt, form the good character of the Battalion. No greater contrast with Lt. Col. Rickman's command from 1915 to 1919 and

those early formative years can be imagined, but the Battalion's active service performance and reputation had its origins in the early leadership of Col. Sharples.

The spirit of comradeship which produced the protests of 1922 did not last. No organised group of 'ex-Pals' formed in any of the three main towns, although individuals did charitable work within the newly-formed British Legion branches.[7]

Many personal friendships, strengthened by the shared experiences of the Somme, continued to endure. Old comrades, often unknown to the bereaved family, but warned by the 'bush telegraph', would turn up to pay their last respects at the funeral of an ex-Pal. In Burnley, when Major Ross, a bachelor with no family died alone, ex-Ptes. Edwards and Walton, ex-Sgts. Kay and Barrow and ex-Capt. Kershaw were his chief mourners. From this accord in 1935 emerged a revival of interest in the Battalion. A small group led by A.Q.M.S. Hindle organised the 'First Annual Reunion' of the 11th and 12th (Reserve) Battalions in Accrington in April 1935.

The event was an immediate success, three ex-Officers and 318 ex-N.C.O.s and men attended. Although most came from Accrington and Burnley (only two from Chorley) men travelled from other parts of the country to be there. With the exception of the ex-officers who, from 1919 until Lt. Col. Rickman's death in 1925, held their own reunion dinner every July 1st, some met old comrades for the first time since July 1st, 1916. For many the reunion became a deeply moving experience, as men thought long dead met again.

The 'Hindle' group organised other events. On July 1st, 1936, they placed a large wreath 'in remembrance of the Pals who gave all' on

Right: First Annual Reunion of the Pals, held in the Drill Hall, Accrington in April 1932.

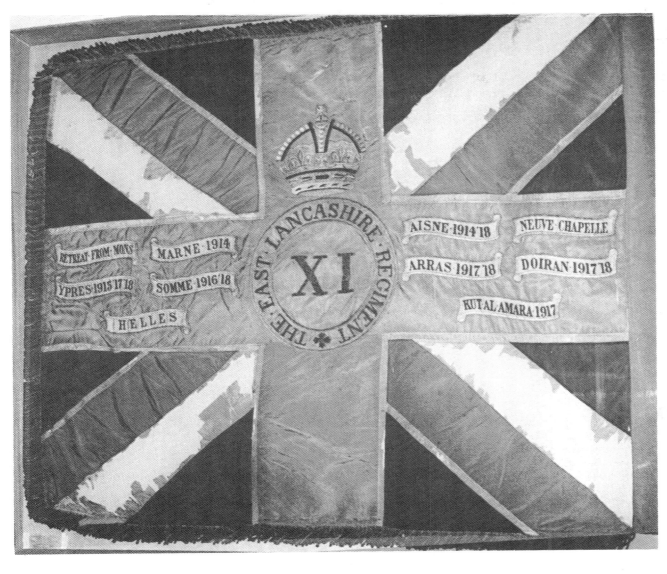

Left: Regimental Colours of the 11th East Lancashire Regiment in St. James' Parish Church Accrington. Because of the deterioration of the white fabric the Colours were mounted in a glass case in 1968.

the Accrington War Memorial. A similarly worded 'In Memoriam' notice appeared in the local newspaper. At the group's suggestion the Battalion Colours were removed from the Accrington Town Hall Council Chamber where they had hung since 1919. On November 6th, 1938, over a hundred Pals led by 80 year old ex-C.S.M. Muir, escorted the four man Colour Party into St. James' Parish Church for the Colours to be formally blessed and laid up. Three months later, on February 20th, 1939, again in St. James' Church, the lamp of the Accrington branch of TocH was dedicated to the officers and men of the Battalion.[8] Regrettably, the 1939-45 war ended the revival. Two hundred attended the fifth and last reunion dinner in April 1939.

Public interest faded for almost thirty years, the only reminder being the annual 'Somme Sunday' service held in Blackburn Cathedral on the Sunday nearest July 1st, to commemorate all the East Lancs Regiment war dead. In 1966 the Accrington Observer, ever since 1914, a supporter and friend of the Battalion, suggested a special service in their memory be held in St. James' Church on the 50th anniversary of the first day of the Somme. Public interest

quickened and many hundreds attended.[9] Unfortunately a public squabble also began. This revived the old differences with local Territorials. Pte. Bloor, who since his return from Canada in 1934, made an annual pilgrimage to the Somme, suggested the town organise commemorative events every July 1st. This provoked a reply in the Accrington Observer by the local British Legion secretary (an ex-Territorial) saying not only the Pals were worthy of special remembrance. Other correspondents joined in and some acrimony arose. Bloor's idea faded away, again leaving remembrance to individuals.

The controversy nevertheless rekindled interest in the Battalion. In February 1969, an article appeared in the Accrington Observer. Full of inaccuracies (e.g. "On July 2nd, 1915, the Battalion suffered terrific casualties." "At the roll-call only forty men responded") the article tendered the improbable view of the Battalion not being commemorated in Accrington because there were so few survivors. It concluded "Accrington never made a great deal of the memory of the Pals — the sheer size of the disaster rather numbed the imagination."[10] The

"Pals'" Fifth Annual Reunion

The happiest cameraderie was once again in evidence at the Argyle-street Drill Hall on Saturday, when the fifth annual reunion of the "Pals" Battalion (11th Service Battalion, East Lancashire Regiment) drew an attendance of over two hundred. A full report of the proceedings appeared in Tuesday's "Observer."

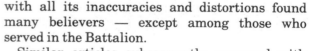

"Observer" Photo.

Above: Fifth and last Annual Reunion held in March 1939.
A.O.& T.

Below: A group of ex-Pals march to St. James' Church on Rememberance Sunday 1952. Harry Bloor front right, Fred Illingworth front centre.

article neglected to say only one Company of four came from Accrington so implying the forty respondents to the roll-call to be solely from the town. The article ignored the wounded who served again and ignored the numbers who attended the reunions of 1919 and 1935 to 1939. From such stuff myths are made. The story, with all its inaccuracies and distortions found many believers — except among those who served in the Battalion.

Similar articles subsequently appeared with some frequency in East Lancashire newspapers. All continued — and added to — the myths and exaggerations. July 1st became, not a time for simple remembrance, but a focal point for an emotive imagery of the wholesale massacre of Pals. This overrode the normality of the experiences, horrific as they were, the Battalion shared with many other British and Empire Battalions on July 1st, 1916, of whom several suffered more killed and wounded than the 'Accrington Pals'.[11]

The myths, together with a romantic view of 'little' Accrington raising its 'own' battalion in competition with the major cities of industrial Britain, placed the 'Accrington Pals' as the epitome of the Kitchener New Army Battalions of 1914. In the minds of many the 'Accrington Pals' represent those, who in the innocence of youthful ideals of patriotism and service, 'started early in the fight.' They represent those whose abstract ideals were destroyed — with their youth — in the terrifying realities of the slaughterhouse of the Somme. Myths notwithstanding, by their loyalty, endurance and sacrifices, the 11th East Lancs earned the right to be so honoured.

Below: Railway Hollow Cemetery situated directly behind the old British Front Line in the fields in front of the village of Serre. Luke copse is on the left and Mark Copse is on the right, with Sheffield Memorial Park between.

Above: The battlefield today looking from the old German Line towards the line of trees which were once the three copses Mark, Luke and John (Matthew Copse is no longer there.)
Queens Cemetery, in the foreground, stands in the old No Man's Land.
Below: Memorial to the Missing, Thiepval commemorates the officers and men who fought and died on the Somme from July 1915 to February 1918, and have no known grave. The names of 135 officers and men of the Accrington Pals are inscribed on the memorial.

NOTES

1. Under the Military Service Act of January 1916, objections to military service on family, moral or religious grounds had the right to apply for exemption before a Military Tribunal held in public. The Tribunals consisted of a small group of local civilians, representing different interests in the town, plus a Military Representative.

2. Hansard, Parliamentary Debates, House of Commons, No. 191, Volume LXXXI, March 1916.

3. The last man of the Battalion was demobilized on October 11th, 1919. The four N.C.O. Colour Party volunteered to stay on until October 18th. The Battalion officially ceased to exist on October 20th, 1919, when its records were delivered to the East Lancashire Regiment Record Office, Preston.

4. The movement for the adoption by British towns of devastated towns and villages in France, opened at a meeting at the Mansion House on June 30th, 1920. Lord Derby wrote to the Mayors of Lancashire towns expressing the hope they would participate. In East Lancashire, Blackburn adopted Perronne and Maricourt; Burnley adopted Miramont, Colincamps and Courcelles. There is no record of any response by Accrington to the appeal.

5. The 'Memorial Room', in Astley Hall, Chorley, dedicated to the men from Chorley who died in the war, was formally opened in 1922 as the town's war memorial.

6. A.O.T. 3/7/26.

7. Apart from the Regimental Colours in the Town Hall, the only visible token in Accrington was a privately owned Pals Cafe, which served the mills and workshops in the Bull Bridge area during the 1920's. Blackburn Corporation Museum and Art Gallery displayed a Maxim heavy machine-gun captured by the Battalion in the German retreat in 1918 and presented to the museum in 1919.

8. Toc H (Army signalling code for T.H.) started in December 1915 in Talbot House, Poperinghe, Flanders, as a chapel and club for servicemen. Toc H became a world-wide, inter-denominational, Christian fellowship for the continuance of comradeship and social service. The Accrington branch opened in February 1928.

9. On the same day Burnley Lads Club held their own commemorative service for Captain Riley and the Club members who gave their lives in the attack.

10. A.O.T. 15/2/69.

11. See 'The First Day on the Somme', App. 5, p 320.
These casualties should be regarded as minimum figures from a variety of sources.

Appendices

APPENDIX 1 *Personae — 1916 and after*

ANDERSON, H. 15980 of Accrington was just over 18 on July 1st. After hospital treatment in England he returned to France to the 7th East Lancs. He was wounded at Passchendaele and again came to Hospital in England. He returned to France to the 1st East Lancs, and came back to Accrington in 1919. After a year on the 'dole' he worked in the cotton and dyeing industries until he retired at 73, in 1971.

BAKER, H. T. M.P. Born 1877, Educated Winchester and New College, Oxford. Barrister. Liberal M.P. for Accrington Division 1910-1918. Warden of Winchester College 1933 to 1946. Fellow of Winchester from 1933. Unmarried. He died July 12th, 1960.

BATH, FRANK 15108. A plumber, he returned from France to Accrington and set up in business. Shortly after emigrating to Australia in 1924, he lost a leg in a railway accident. He worked as a caretaker until his death in the 1930's.

BELFIELD, SIR H. E. Lt. General. K.C.B., K.C.M.G., K.B.E., C.B., D.S.O. Born 1857, he served in West Africa and South Africa. He was O.C. 4 Division 1907-11 and Colonel of the Duke of Wellington Regiment in 1909. From late 1914 to 1920 he was Director of Prisoners of War. He died April 19th, 1934.

BEWSHER, STANLEY M.M. 18048. After hospital treatment he spent the remainder of the war as a transport driver/chauffeur at Army depots in Manchester and the North East. He left the Army in 1919 and worked as a driver until 1921. He returned to his home in Yorkshire and was a farmer until his retirement in 1968.

BIRTWELL, CHARLES 15412 of Accrington was 22 and single in 1916. He had worked at Howard & Bulloughs. He was one of four brothers in the Army. Wounded on July 1st he eventually went to hospital in Hampshire. From September 1917 he served in France with the 1st East Lancs. He returned to Accrington, and Howard & Bulloughs, in 1919. He died in 1975.

BOWLES, HENRY Brigadier General. C.B. Born 1854. He served as a private soldier in the 1st Berkshire Rifle Volunteers 1872-76. After his commission he served in England, the Sudan and South Africa, where he was severely wounded. Recalled as a Brigadier General in 1914, he was O.C. 94 Brigade, January to September 1915. He then retired. He died May 1932.

BRADSHAW, RUSSELL M.M. 15400 of Accrington, remained with the Battalion throughout the war. He was awarded the Military Medal for 'great gallantry' on June 28th, 1918. He returned to Accrington in February 1919 to the family business of gents outfitters and clothiers, and later opened his own sportswear business.

BRIDGE, JAMES of Rishton was 21 and unmarried when he enlisted in 1914. He married in 1925. He was employed at a local domestic appliance manufacturer for most of his working life before retiring as Senior Sales Director at 67 in 1960. He was active in local politics and became Chairman of Rishton Urban District Council in 1946. He died, aged 89, in 1982.

BROADLEY, PHILIP J. O.B.E. of Clayton-le-Moors. After hospital treatment in England he spent the remainder of the war with the 3rd East Lancs in Yorkshire. He was awarded the O.B.E. in 1919. He returned to direct the family printing business for 45 years until his death in 1962.

BURY, HARRY M.M. 15402 of Accrington, remained with the Battalion throughout the war. He was awarded the Military Medal for his actions on September 28th, 1918. He returned to Accrington in February 1919 to resume his apprenticeship as a motor engineer. He died in 1976, aged 80.

CARTER-CAMPBELL, G. T. C. C.B., D.S.O. Born 1869, he entered the Army in 1889. He served in the South African War and was mentioned in despatches. A Brigadier General in 1915, he was a Major General in 1918. He died December 19th, 1921.

CHEETHAM, ARTHUR 29504 of Oldham. A cotton spinner, he joined the Manchester Regiment in January 1916, wounded in April 1916, then transferred firstly to the 8th East Lancs, then in June 1917, to the 11th East Lancs. He was wounded on June 28th, 1918. He rejoined the Battalion in September 1918 and was demobilised in April 1919.

CLARK, STANLEY 17859. Came home from France to East Lancashire in 1919. Unable to settle down in civilian life he joined the East Lancs as a Regular and served in Ireland during the 1921-22 Civil War. He later emigrated to Canada and 'rode the rails' to get work as a lumberjack and salmon fisherman. He returned to England in 1933 and worked for local cotton firms until his retirement in 1965.

CLARKE, WILL 15193 of Rishton, was unmarried and had been a grocers' assistant. He recovered from his wounds and later served in another infantry regiment in India. He returned in 1919 to his job in Rishton, married and opened his own shop. He died in a road accident, in 1974, aged 77.

CLAYTON, HERBERT 15711 of Burnley, was killed in action July 1st, 1916. He was 22, married with a daughter he had not seen. He had been a weaver. From 1917 to 1977, on the anniversary of his death, an 'In Memoriam' notice from his widow and daughter was placed in the local newspaper.

COWELL, WILL 15644 of Chorley was 25, married with no children. He was a miner at Chorley Colliery. 'Polly' remained a widow until her death in 1966. His name was inscribed in the Thiepual Memorial in 1983.

DICKSON, E. T. Major General. Born 1850, educated King William College I.O.M. and Cheltenham. Joined 49th Foot in 1869. After service in India, the Sudan and West Africa he retired in 1912. Recalled in 1914 as Inspector of Infantry. He retired in 1916. He was Colonel of the Royal Berkshire Regiment 1913 to 1930. He died in 1938.

DUERDEN, ORRELL 17870 of Accrington was 21, unmarried, the eldest of three brothers. He was a weaver. His parents were notified on August 5th, 1916, only that he was wounded. His name was inscribed in the Thiepual Memorial in 1933.

FAIRWEATHER, ORMOND 20971 of Chorley was 24 and unmarried in 1916. A stretcher-bearer/bandsman, he was wounded in the left hand on July 1st. He returned to the 11th East Lancs after hospital treatment and came home to Chorley in 1919. He was a bus-driver until his retirement. He died in 1966.

FISHER, ROBERT 20517 of Accrington was 21 and unmarried in 1916. He had been a cotton spinner. After hospital treatment he transferred to the Machine Gun Corps and fought at Ypres and Passchendaele. He was discharged from the Army in September 1918, suffering from shell-shock and a foot wound. Unable to follow his old occupation, he worked as a railway porter for many years until his retirement.

FRANCIS, THOMAS E. 15476 of Church was 21, unmarried and had worked at Howard and Bulloughs. He was a Roman Catholic. He was first reported on September 2nd, 1916 as missing, then later listed as killed in action on July 1st, 1916. His name was inscribed in the Thiepval Memorial in 1983.

GLOVER, CLARENCE 15013 returned to his job as a billiard table fitter in 1919. He worked as the firm's representative in S.W. England until 1942, when he became Company Manager in Accrington. He retired in 1962. He died in 1966 aged 74.

GREAVES, WALT 15261 of Accrington was married with two children in 1916. He had worked at a brickworks. He was wounded in the head, ankle and leg on July 1st. He survived the war and returned to the brickworks in 1919. He later had two more children, and died in 1942 aged 54.

GOUGH, SIR HUBERT DE LA POER G.C.B., K.C.B., G.C.M.G., K.C.V.O., D.S.O. Born 1870. Joined 16th Hussars 1889. Served in Indian and South Africa where he was severely wounded. Commanded the Fifth Army on the Somme in 1916 and at Passchendaele in 1917. In March 1918 the Fifth Army was broken by the German advance and he was recalled to London. He was Colonel of the Home Guard in 1942. He died in 1963.

HAIG, DOUGLAS Born 1861. Joined 7th Hussars in 1885. Served in the Sudan, India and South Africa. Knighted in 1909. Appointed C. in C. B.E.F. in December 1915. Created Earl in 1919 and voted £100,000 by Parliament. In 1920 he was given Bemersyde Mansion by public subscription. He was C. in C. Home Forces from 1919 to 1921. He was President of the British Legion for seven years until his death in 1928.

HARWOOD, JOHN J.P. Born 1847, he was in the cotton industry in the United States and India until his return to Accrington in 1898. He was an honorary Captain in the Cawnpore Rifles. A director of several local engineering firms, he was Conservative Mayor of Accrington 1914 to 1916. From 1916 to 1918 he was the Military Representative on the Accrington Military Tribunal. He died, unhonoured for his war efforts, on December 12th, 1923 aged 74.

HIBBERT, SIR HENRY F. M.P. J.P. Knighted 1903. Unionist M.P. for Chorley Division 1913-1918. Chairman of Lancashire County Council 1921-1927. He died on November 15th, 1927.

HINDLE, JAMES of Accrington. He formed the Battalion Orderly Room in September 1914 and was responsible for its operation until his demobilisation in March 1919. He was slightly wounded in 1917. He was honorary secretary to all five (1935 to 1939) Battalion reunions. In 1927 he was appointed as Accrington's Chief Sanitary Inspector. He retired in 1955 after 51 years service. He died on March 17th, 1976 aged 85.

HINDLE, RALPH J.P. Born 1846. He was Conservative Mayor of Chorley 1913 to 1915. His son, Lt. Col. Hindle, C.O. of the 4th Loyal North Lancs (Territorial Force) was killed in action at Festubert in 1915. Ralph Hindle was a self-employed leather-merchant in Chorley. He died on March 14th, 1936.

HORSFALL, BASIL A. 2nd Lieutenant V.C. Born 1891 in Columbo, Ceylon (Sri Lanka). He enlisted in December 1916 in the 3rd Battalion East Lancs Regiment and attached to the 11th Battalion in the spring of 1917. He was posthumously awarded the V.C. 'for most conspicuous bravery and devotion to duty' in March 1918. After years in a private collection, in July 1982 the V.C. was purchased and placed on display in the East Lancs Regimental Museum, Blackburn.

HUNTER-WESTON, SIR AYLMER G. Born 1864. Joined the Royal Engineers in 1884. Served in India and South Africa, where he won the D.S.O. He was Director of Military Training 1911 to 1914. He was O.C., 8 Corps in Dardenelles and France, 1915 to 1918 and was mentioned in despatches ten times. He was M.P. for North Ayrshire, then Buteshire and North Ayrshire from 1916 to 1935. He retired from the Army in 1920 and died on March 18th, 1940.

INGHAM, RICHARD 17901 of Church, was killed in action July 1st, 1916. He was 24, married with one child. He was listed as presumed dead in March 1917. From 1919 to 1954, on the anniversary of his death an 'In Memoriam' notice from his Mother was placed in the local newspaper.

JONES, WILLIAM HAMILTON 39369 from Caernarvon, joined the 11th East Lancs in France in November 1917. He was badly wounded in the German advance in March 1918. He returned to Caernarvon in 1919 and was an auctioneer and valuer in Caernarvon and district for fifty years before his retirement in 1969.

KAY, ERNEST D. 16041, M.C. After hospital treatment he was commissioned as a 2nd/Lt. He returned to the 11th East Lancs in 1917. The only 'Pal' to return to the Battalion as an officer, he won the M.C. in April 1918. He returned to Burnley in 1919 and became a leading businessman in the town as an importer of china, glassware and cutlery. He died on 6th June, 1956.

KAY, HARRY 15510 of Accrington. After hospital treatment, returned to France, worked firstly as a messenger at 4th Army H.Q., then helped run the canteen at Talbot House, Poperinghe. He returned to his old job at Howard and Bulloughs in 1919.

KNIGHT, MISS S. M. of Chorley. After July 1st, 1916, she tried, through public debate, but unsuccessfully, to have a memorial to the dead Chorley Pals erected. In September 1916 she was presented with a copper cross, made from material picked up on the battlefield, by the Chorley Company. After the war she made up three Golden Books of Remembrance (i.e. photographs and Biographies) of Chorley men who died in the war. After her death in December 1948, the Chorley Soroptimist presented the books to the town as a permanent memorial.

LEEMING, FRED 15774 of Great Harwood was 22, unmarried and had been a 'reacher' in a cotton mill. He was an only son.

LIVESEY, HARRY of Blackburn, was 35 and unmarried, was educated at Rossall School. He was, with John Harwood, a director of the family firm of textile machinery makers in Blackburn and had travelled extensively for them abroad. He was a leading member of St. Silas's C. of E. church in Blackburn.

MAGRATH, ANDREW 15860 of Chorley was 24, unmarried and had been a cotton worker. He was a Roman Catholic. Slightly wounded on July 1st, 1916, he served from March 1916 to November 1918 as a bandsman and stretcher-bearer.

MARSHALL, WILL 15369 of Burnley was 23 and unmarried in 1916. He had been a cotton weaver. After eight months in various hospitals he was discharged, as unfit for War Service, from the Army. He worked as an inspector of munitions work for the remainder of the war. He worked as a weaver and then as an engineer until his retirement at 68, in 1960.

McKINNON, SIR W. H. Major General. G.C.B., K.C.B., K.C.V.O., C.V.O., C.B. Born 1852 and joined Genadier Guards in 1870. Served in Malta, India and South Africa. Director-General Territorial Force 1908 to 1910. C. in C. Western Command 1915. Director of Recruiting War Office 1916. He died 17th March, 1929.

MILTON, J. C. O.B.E., M.B.E. Born 1869. In practice as a solicitor in Chorley from 1897 to 1915. Transferred on medical grounds in June 1916 to a War Office post in U.K. later serving in Ireland as a Provost Marshall. He returned to his Chorley practice in 1921, then moved to Droitwich where he was very active in British Legion affairs. One of seven brothers in the forces. He died 14th April, 1931.

MORRELL, PHILIP M.P., J.P., M.A. Born 1870, educated Eton and Balliol College, Oxford. in 1902 married Lady Ottoline, Cavendish-Bentinck (later member of the 'Bloomsbury Set', an influential group of writers and artists). Liberal M.P. for Burnely 1910 to 1918. He and his wife were strong pacifists and campaigned in Burnely and in Parliament against persecution of conscientious objectors. He died February 5th, 1943.

MURRAY, SIR A. J. General. K.C.B., G.C.B. Born 1860, gazetted to 27th Regiment (Royal Inniskilling Fusiliers) in 1879. Served in South African War 1899-1902. Inspector of Infantry 1912 to 1914 and Sir John French's Chief of General Staff August 1914 to January 1915. Deputy Chief of Imperial General Staff with responsibility for training the New Army from February 1915 to September 1915. Chief I.G.S. September 1915, then Commander of the forces in Egypt January 1916 to June 1917. G.O.C. Aldershot 1917 to 1919. He died in 1945.

PELTZER, ANTON of Accrington, was the son of the Company Secretary of Howard and Bulloughs. Wounded in the right hand on July 1st, 1916, he later served with the 9th East Lancs in Salonika. He was wounded, and awarded the D.S.O. in 1918 whilst Lt. Col. O.C. the 9th Battalion. From 1919 he was a director of Howard and Bulloughs until his retirement in 1942. He died in 1973.

PILKINGTON, JACK 15035 of Accrington was wounded in the back and right arm on July 1st, 1916. In 1919 he returned to Howard and Bulloughs and worked in the same department as G. Pollard, until his retirement in 1955.

POLLARD, GEORGE 15139 of Accrington. Left hospital, discharged from the Army because he was under-age. He worked on munitions locally and at Woolwich Arsenal. In 1917 he joined the R.F.C. and returned to France, near Amiens, as an armourer in the squadron of Major McCudden V.C. He returned to Howard and Bulloughs in 1919 and worked there until his retirment in 1965.

RAWCLIFFE, THOMAS W. M.C. Served with the Battalion until 1917, then, as Major, went to the United States as an instructor/advisor with the U.S. Army. In 1919 he returned to the family cotton manufacturing firm in Great Harwood.

REES, HUBERT C. D.S.O., C.M.G. BORN 1882. Joined the Army in 1900 and served in South Africa (mentioned in despatches five times) and the West Indies. He retired from the Army in 1922 and died March 1st, 1948.

RICKMAN, ARTHUR W. Lt. Col. D.S.O. and Bar. After hospital treatment, returned as O.C. Battalion, remaining in command, except for short periods as acting O.C. 94 Brigade and when wounded until March 1919. From 1916 to 1918 he was twice wounded, gassed, four times mentioned in despatches and received the D.S.O. and Bar. He died on October 16th, 1925 from injuries received in an accident at his home in Wiltshire.

RILEY, HENRY D. Captain — J.P. of Burnley. Born 1881, educated at Shrewsbury School, he was a member of a local family of cotton manufacturers. He was appointed a Magistrate in 1912. In 1906 he founded the Burnley Lads Club, of which 600 members served in the armed forces from 1914-1918. In April 1917, £3,000 was raised by public subscription in six weeks to buy the Lads Club premises, for use by them for all time, as a memorial to Captain Riley.

ROLLINS, SETH 15964 of Coppull was 21, unmarried and had been a weaver. He played the organ at St. Johns C. of E. Church, Coppull. On August 26th, 1916 he was reported as missing, then later listed as killed in action on July 1st, 1916. His name was inscribed on the Thiepval Memorial in 1984.

ROSS, RAYMOND On discharge from Hospital and convalescence he remained in England on staff work. He returned to his job as Burnley Borough Analyst and Chemist in 1920 and retired at 65, in March 1930. He was unmarried. he died in 1935.

RUTTLE, JACK He recovered from his illness and returned to France at the end of 1916. For the remainder of the war he was attached to the Chinese Labour Corps (a force recruited in North China to work as stevedores and labourers). After the war he worked for a London engineering firm, then returned to Clayton-le-Moors where he died in December 1946 aged 65.

SAYER, FRED 15971 of Burnley. On leave in England in 1917 he required further hospital treatment for his leg. After a period with a Reserve Battalion he volunteered to return to France for service with the 84th Company, Chinese Labour Corps. After the war he worked as an Insurance Surveyor. In 1940 he helped to form the 4th County of Lancaster (South Lonsdale) Home Guard. He retired in 1945 as Lt. Colonel. He later became well-known in North Lancashire as an hotelier and authority on fishing. He retired in 1962.

SELLERS-KAY, J. Mayor of Burnely 1914-1916. Although a member of a Burnley cotton manufacturing family, he was a practicing solicitor. He was a Conservative member of the Town Council from 1905 until his death in 1933 aged 65.

SHARPLES, R. Lt. Col. J.P. V.D., T.D. Born 1849. For 51 years a member of an Accrington family firm of solicitors. He joined the East Lancs Volunteers in 1869. In 1914 he was C.O. National Reserve Battalion of the 5th East Lancs Territorial Force. He retired in 1915. A J.P. for 43 years, he was a Conservative member of the Town Council for 12 years. He died on August 13th, 1929 aged 79.

SLINGER, G. N. Born 1880. A member of an Accrington family firm of solicitors. In 1914 he was O.C. the Accrington Company of the 5th East Lancs Territorial Force. He was a Conservative member of the Town Council for many years until his death on October 16th, 1923 aged 43.

SNAILHAM, JAMES 15349 of Whittle-le-Woods. After hospital treatment and convalescence he was posted to the 6th East Lancs in Mesopotamia. Taken ill, he spent two years in hospital in India. He returned to his old job at the local printworks in 1920 and later worked in insurance and owned a grocers shop until his retirement.

STUTTARD, GEORGE 15427 was 20, unmarried and was a butcher in the Argenta Meat Company shop in Accrington. On August 12th, 1916, he was reported missing, he was later confirmed as killed in action on July 1st, 1916.

TAYLOR, THOMAS 24787 of Barrowford, near Burnley was 29, unmarried and had been a weaver. He was one of the final batch of reinforcements to arrive on June 24th, 1916. He entered the trenches for the first time in his life on June 30th. His parents were not notified of his death until October 23rd, 1916.

TOUGH, ARNOLD B. of Accrington, was 26 and unmarried. He had been a dentist in Accrington. His brother, John, a Captain in the R.A.M.C. was killed in France in October 1918.

WANLESS-O'GOWAN, R. Major General. C.B., C.M.G. Born 1864 and entered the army in 1886. Served in South Africa as a Major and was severely wounded and twice mentioned in despatches. C.O. 31 Division 1915 to 1918, and six times mentioned in despatches. He was awarded the C.B. in 1915 and C.M.G. in 1919. He died on December 12th, 1947.

WATSON, A. G. M.D., M.B., Ch.B. Born in Scotland. Qualified as a surgeon in 1900 and served in South African War. M.D. in Clayton-le-Moors and Honorary Surgeon Accrington Victoria Hospital in 1914. Transferred to R.A.M.C. as Honorary Captain in June 1916 and worked as surgeon in C.C.S's. until 1919. On his return to England he became Consultant Physician in Physiotherapy at Bath. He was the author of several articles on rheumatism and gout. He died on October 15th, 1949.

WILKINSON, HARRY 17982, wounded in the thigh on July 1st, 1916, after hospital treatment he was transferred to the 5th East Lancs in Salonika. In 1919 he returned to Accrington and Broad Oak Printworks, where he worked for 50 years. In 1937, he had a piece of shrapnel, previously unsuspected, removed from his stomach. He died in 1968 aged 84.

WILLIAMS, GEORGE After qualifying as a municipal engineer he joined the family firm of drapers in Accrington as Company Secretary. He enlisted in the Battalion in September 1914 as a Private and was gazetted 2/Lieutenant in January 1915. Wounded on July 1st, he later transferred to an anti-gas unit of the Royal Engineers. He died at Etaples of pneumonia on February 24th, 1919 aged 25.

WHITTAKER, EARL 15735 of Burnley was 32, married with three children. He had worked in a cotton mill. After he was reported missing in April 1918, his pay-book was returned by the Battalion to his wife. This, and also that his body was never found, caused his wife to believe for many years that he was not dead, but someday would return home.

CAMP CORRESPONDENT'S
REPORTS — JULY AND OCTOBER 1915

The following is a compilation of 'Camp Correspondent's', (Pte. R. Bradshaw) reports of the 'doings' of the Battalion, published in the Accrington Gazette, 10th July, 1915 and 17th July, 1915:

Monday 5th July Evening: Concert organised by A.Q.M.S. Hindle. Regimental Band played selections.

Tuesday 6th July Afternoon: Brigade marched in sections for sham fight. 12th Y. & L. to defend trenches attacked by 11th E. L. and 13th Y. & L. 14th Y & L. acted as reserves to attacking forces.
Evening: Cricket. 11th E. L. versus 12th Y. & L. 11th E. L. 147 all out.

Wednesday 7th July Sixteen mile route march, the whole Brigade taking part. Each man had a substantial meat sandwich for lunch.

Thursday 8th July Morning: Repeat of Tuesday with 11th E. L. defending. Perhaps it would be wise not to state how many were killed in just one action.
Afternoon: Formal opening of Y.M.C.A. Recreation Hut, with new Billiard Room and Concert Room. Chair taken by Brig. Gen. Bowles, C.B.

Friday 9th July Tuesday's cricket match continued. 'Accrington' (11th E. L.) won by an innings and 16 runs.

Saturday 10th July Sports Day at Hagley Park. No prizes came Battalions' way. Up against crack athletes of 12th Y. & L. Running and jumping lost arts in Accrington.

Monday 12th July Morning: Sixteen mile route march to Cannock. Some only arrived back from leave at 3.30 a.m having walked from Rugeley Station.

Tuesday 13th July Football. 12th Y. & L. beaten 2 - 1. Concert in Y.M.C.A.

Wednesday 14th July Report on Battalion orders re: sham fight last Thursday. — 'Defence — the 11th E. L. is to be commended for the manner in which its discipline, when sorely tested, was fully maintained'.

Thursday 15th July Evening: Concert in Y.M.C.A.
Night: Lining and re-lining trenches. Each company alternating at this work.

Compiled from 'Camp Correspondent's' reports, (Pte. R. Bradshaw) Accrington Gazette, 23rd October, 1915 and 30th October, 1915:

Tuesday 12th October Parade a.m. for Battalion attack four miles away through Fovant. Back at 5 p.m. Nothing to eat since 7 a.m. Ready for late dinner.

Wednesday 13th October Brigade field day — route march with full pack through Dinton and Tuffant Manor. We arrived at selected position which we had to defend against all-comers. Aeroplanes flew overhead as part of manoeuvres. Very acceptable hot dinner served by field-kitchens. Returned through Fovant. Back at 5.30 p.m.

Thursday 14th October Another full pack morning. This time on outpost duty and at night went on night patrol work.

Friday 15th October Night patrol duty with 12th, 13th and 14th Y. & L. The 13th, 14th Y. & L. and 11th E. L. were attacked by 12th Y. & L. We left camp at 3.45 p.m. and at nightfall, 12th Y. & L. attacked with much vigour. We were able to repel the attack with heavy losses. Returned to camp midnight.

Saturday 16th October Morning spent cleaning up and preparing for hut and kit inspection. Visit from Quartermaster-General (Lt. Col. J. H. A. Annesley) who enquired if we had enough to eat and would we like supper. Needless to say, we 'liked'. Caught special leave train to London, arrived 3.40 p.m. and returned Sunday evening. Needless to say, saw 'trail of the Zepps'. (Zeppelin bomb damage in the Strand, Aldwych and Holborn).

Monday 18th October Brigade close order drill on the Downs.

Tuesday 19th October Field work under Company arrangements, practising for Battalion and Brigade work. Strenuous day.

Wednesday 20th October Brigade tactical exercises. We had to assail positions held by 12th, 13th and 14th Y. & L. Each Battalion represented a Brigade, each Company a Battalion, so in theory were engaged in Divisional operations. Reveille was 5 a.m. Paraded at 7 a.m. Took up positions eight miles from camp. The battle ended, a two mile march brought us a hot meal. Dinner never more relished. Hot and tiring day. Camp reached at 5 p.m.

Thursday 21st October Half day holiday. Cross-country run of three or four miles. All Battalions in Division entered teams.
N.B. The 11th E. L. do not shine as long-distance runners. The first three places were from 15th W. Y. (West Yorkshire Regiment).

Friday 22nd October Another Brigade day. We defended position. Day warm and fine. Again dinner from field-kitchens and returned home.

REPORT ON OPERATIONS JUNE 30 TO 9.40 p.m. JULY 1, 1916 — LT. COL. A. W. RICKMAN

(Public Record Office WO95/2366)

7.00 p.m.	The 11th E. Lancashire Regt. marched off according to timetable along the prescribed route at 7 p.m. 30.VI.16 and reached Courcelles at 8.30 p.m.
8.30 p.m.	where tea was served to the men.
9.40 p.m.	After synchronising watches at 9.30 p.m. the head of the column left Courcelles at 9.45 p.m. and marched as directed to Central Avenue. The trench
12.20 a.m.	was in a very bad state and over the knee deep in mud which had become glutinous — As the fork in Central Avenue had not been reached by 12.20
1/7/16	a.m. — I proceeded to the head of the 2nd wave and ordered them to go overland — I reported this to 94th Brigade at entrance to Central Avenue — After coming to the batteries the regiment had to proceed in the trenches owing to the batteries firing — I reached with the head of the column the front line system of trenches at 2.40 a.m. — Where I found that orders had been issued by Higher Command that Sap D and Sap C were not to be occupied by any troops — Accordingly I had to make fresh preparations for the accommodation of my first wave — I accommodated No. 1 and 11 Platoon W Company between Warley Avenue and 29A93. No. 5 and 6 platoons X Company between this point and Mark Copse inclusive — in the positions from which the 1st wave would start — They were accommodated in partially blown in fire boys and Traffic Trench. The wave being under command of Capt. Tough. The 2nd wave was under command of Capt. Livesey and was accommodated in Copse Trench — The 3rd wave under 2/Lt. Williams in Campion. 4th wave in Monk under Capt. Riley. Head Quarters at mouth of Sap C — During the night and early morning there was a constant bombardment. Attention was paid to Rob Roy and the Front Line.
7.20 a.m.	At 7.20 a.m. the hurricane bombardment opened and the first wave crossed into No Mans Land. The Germans opened almost immediately with MG and rifle fire putting on a few minutes later an intense barrage.
7.22 a.m.	The 2nd wave proceeded to follow the 1st wave into No Mans Land.
7.23 a.m.	Two platoons 13 Y & L (1st Barnsley Pals) crossed following my 2nd wave.
7.29 a.m.	I saw my 3rd and 4th waves advancing from Campion and Monk respectively. By this time there was intense rifle, MG fire and a very heavy barrage of artillery fire. They crossed into No Mans Land crossing the front line about 7.32 a.m.
7.39 a.m.	I reported by runner via Mark Copse 1st two waves crossed according to timetable. Heavy MG and rifle fire still coming from German 1st line. Intense fire of all description.
7.42 a.m.	I reported by runner intense fire of all description.
7.50 a.m.	I reported by runner all four waves have gone forward — MG fire still coming from the north. Report from Lt. Gay. Left platoon through 1st line. Lt. Gay wounded. MG much less intense. I sent Lt. Macalpine to establish telephone communication between Mark Copse and my HQ — Lt. Macalpine returned and informed me all communication was cut and it was not re-established all day.
8.10 a.m.	I reported MG fire still coming from the north traversing from beyond Mark Copse over Sap C. Capt. Gurney 13 Y & L arrived with only 9 men in his two platoons. I further reported I could see odd groups in my front believed to be wounded. Also that I could not see any of my waves. No further report from waves. Heavy artillery barrage on front line.
8.22 a.m.	Machine gun fire still crossing from direction of Mark Copse. Heavy artillery barrage front line. No information from my waves. Line not entered about 8.55. Very little rifle fire to my front. Heavy MG fire still coming from my left over Mark Copse. And now and then a burst from right. No information from my waves.

9.00 a.m. **Report from Corpl. Rigby wounded, belonging to 1st wave states that 7 of his platoon got into 1st line.**
They held it for about 20 minutes and bombing Germans back till bombs were exhausted. Capt. Livesey was with Corp. Rigby and was wounded.
Corpl. Rigby saw remains of 2nd wave in front of Ger. barbed wire.
Germans still holding out.
Saw no sign of 3rd or 4th wave.
Heavy barrage on front line.
Capt. Currin 13 Y & L reported arrived.
Capt. Smith 13 Y & L was informed was going forward to 2nd line German trenches.

10—1 a.m. **No report from my waves — Excema heavily shelled — Capt. Roberts RAMC wounded.** Message from O.C. 13 Y & L that C Company 13 Y & L/Capt. Currin was going forward to occupy German 1st line trenches.
Heavy barrage (   ) front line trenches. MG fire from right.
Capt. Currin is putting his company into front line from Matthew Copse to Sap C.
10 wounded men 11ⁿ E.L. have returned and they state front line still in German hands.

11.25 a.m. **No information from my waves.**
Pte. Glover 1st wave (   ) Capt. Livesey states 1st wave encountered heavy MG, rifle and grenades and bombs and artillery fire in crossing No Mans Land.
Capt. Livesey 1st wave with remnants of 2nd wave together with 3rd wave charged German trenches led by Capt. Livesey.
Lt. Thompson also entered German trenches.
Capt. Livesey sent back a message for reinforcement — this never reached me — Capt. Currin is holding from Matthew Copse to Sap C. 18th W. Yorks (2nd Bradford Pals) (   ) his line to the south.
A number of wounded in Sap C and in Excema. Field Dressings urgently required.

11.50 a.m. **Capt. & Adt. Peltzer d & Lt. Ryden wounded. Lt. Ryden remained on duty.**
No reports from my waves except statements of wounded men.
I asked for reinforcement of one Company as only a few of Capt. Currin's party arrived. Was promised Company HXQ — they never arrived.

12 noon I proceeded to put Front Line in state of defence as far as possible against counter-attack — Sap C which had been opened up was blocked by bomb stops. I asked Staff Capt. for supply of bombs which arrived later.

3.10 p.m. The trench mortars 92nd Brigade occupying Sap C were withdrawn and put in emplacements on right and left of Sap C. I went by my whole front line and reported there were very few bays defensible — Men mostly driven out of them and are located in Excema. 93rd Brigade have withdrawn their men and I have only left 1 off & 25 O.R. of my own Regiment available. 2 Stokes guns in position and details of KOYLI & Capt. Currin & Capt. Gurney and about 30 men 13 Y & L. 12 Y & L (Sheffield City Battalion) HQ are in Mark Copse and have no one except their HQ and that they are not in touch with any of their waves. I am holding (   ) by means of bomb stops.

3.50 p.m. Very intense bombardment of my front line — All posts driven in by artillery fire — Men accommodated in Excema.
Urgently require more men.
Bombardment still intense especially from Rossignol.
Lt. Ryden severely wounded.
I have 55 men in all some of whom are wounded. 2 Lewis guns only two men to work them one of them wounded — pans filled by officers servants.

9.20 p.m. I beg to report that at 9.20 p.m. I saw 2 Germans removing our wounded back to their lines from No Mands Land. As regards numbers I have at present 56 (may be 50) men including Stokes mortars & HQ HLR. I have also 1 officer 25 men, 18th West Yorks — holding 3 posts in 93 area. 1 & 2 posts opposite Warley Ave. Then there is a gap — until you come to Capt. Gurney who holds 4 posts (   ) s. of Sap C. I have one post between Sap C and Mark Copse.
There are no Lewis or MG in line.
I am getting the wounded evacuated as soon as possible but there are a good number yet to be attended to.
I have 5 red rockets at Sap C & 12 Y & L have their rockets but I have no rockets at Warley or any Very lights or pistols.
The men are a good deal rattled.
And have very few NCOs.
Just completed inspection SOS rockets in position.

9.40 p.m. Here I was knocked out by shell.

Battle Report (Extract) 12th York and Lancaster Regiment July 15/1916

The extract below is from a battle report made by the Adjutant of the 12th York and Lancaster Regiment after the events of July 1st, 1916. The description of the German trenches and the suggestions/criticisms apply equally to those encountered by the 11th East Lancs. Regiment.

NOTES ON THE GERMAN TRENCHES, ETC. 1.7.16

1) The German front line trench was 12 ft. deep and 3 ft. wide at the bottom sloping upward. There was no parapet at all, but a very high parados 3 or 4 ft. in height, immediately behind the fire trench. There were no fire steps at all. The wire in front of the German trench is very thick, from 2 to 5 ft. high, thinner at the bottom than at the top, and comes to within three feet of the edge of the trench.
Trenches revetted with basket work and floor boarded. The traverses very wide. No information is available regarding the second line, reserve and communication trenches.

2) **DUG-OUTS.** One Dug-out was noted. This was deep and of a type similar to the one in MONK trench. It had about 18 steps and would accommodate eight men. The dug-out was run out under the parapet and was just at the corner and close to the traverse. The man who saw this states that there was a notice up with the following in English characters:

M. G. No. 1 POST

He was quite positive about this. The Dug-Out was not damaged by our fire.

3) **MACHINE GUNS.** Machine guns were fired both from emplacements and from behind parados. One emplacement in particular was noted to be situated in a parados. The parados was hollowed out and a mound raised behind it, so as to conceal the emplacement. This gun caused a great number of casualties and was situated in the German front line just to the south of MARK COPSE.

4) **UNDERGROUND TRENCHES.** Although no underground trenches were found by men reaching to the front line, it is suggested that these exist, owing to large numbers of the enemy apparently appearing from nowhere, in the front line.

SUGGESTIONS AND CRITICISMS

a) The wait in the Assembly trenches was too long.
b) The first wave should not have occupied the front line. Owing to the Trench Mortars being in position in the front line, it became a death trap when the enemy retaliated against them.
c) More bombardment slits should have been dug. It was found that men occupying these suffered very slightly compared with those in Assembly trenches, those that were dug should have been deeper.
d) More men should have been trained in the use of the Bangalore torpedo. It was found that all trained men had become casualties by the time the torpedoes were actually required.
e) Smoke bombs would have been useful to conceal our efforts to cut the enemy's wire. As it was, anyone attempting to cut the wire was immediately sniped.

TACTICS

i) The assault should have been made at dawn or soon after. As it was the enemy had 4½ hours to prepare for an attack, as our intention was undoubtedly given away by the gaps cut in our wire and the tapes laid out in front. Men who reached the German wire state that on looking towards our own lines, they could see almost every movement. This being so any attack by day was scarcely likely to succeed.
ii) The attack should have been in double time.
iii) The waves were too far apart, the distance between them allowing the enemy to pay attention to each wave before the next came up.

MISCELLANEOUS

Assaulting bombers state that they think they could have carried their bombs better in jackets than in the buckets.
The general opinion was that Officers, N.C.O.'s and machine gunners were marked men.

APPENDIX 5

LETTER (EXTRACT) FROM MR. C. A. PELTZER, JULY 1916.

The following is an extract from a letter dated July 9th, 1916 written by Mr. C. A. Peltzer (father of Captain A. Peltzer) to his sister in California, in which he gives some account of Captain Peltzer's description of July 1st and his subsequent experiences.

N.B.S.H.H. — Spring Hill House, the family home in Accrington.
Ethel — Capt. Peltzer's wife.
Tony — Capt. Peltzer.
* Line 24 — Lt. G. G. Williams of Accrington, (O.C. the third wave).
C.B. — Colwyn Bay, where the family had a second home.
Paddock
House — A mansion in Oswaldtwistle, converted to a 75 bed Red Cross Hospital. Mr. and Mrs. C. A. Peltzer were members of the organising committee with a daughter, Miss Peltzer, as a 'Lady Probationer'. John Harwood was President of the Committee.

S.H.H. Accrington,
Sunday July 9th, 1916.

Dearest Hilda,

Knowing of the advance on the Western front, you will be anxious to know how Tony has fared. Thank goodness he has come out of the turmoil alive, although wounded in the right hand.

He wrote us a line on 30th June to say they would commence next day and occupy an important point on the line. On Wednesday Ethel had a message at C.B. from the War Office saying he was wounded in right hand by gun shot. Mother and Ethel went on Thursday to Oxford, where he now is (3rd Southern General Hospital, Somerville, Oxford) and Mother returned yesterday. He is quite well in health — the lower joint of his first finger (right hand) is shattered, the middle finger was also damaged, but not badly; also the back of the hand a little. The hand will be X rayed in a day or so, and it will then be decided whether the first finger can be saved. Ethel does not mind if he has to lose it, provided it will save him from being sent to the fighting line again. Tony helped another man shot in the leg, by name G. G. Williams to cover the 7 miles they had to walk before they got to a dressing station where they could be attended to. He was one night in Rouen Hospital, where he saw Gertie Hoyle, who has acted there as nurse for some time. He arrived in this country hatless and minus other things, but stuck to my field glasses. He meant to have come to Manchester, to which place his haversack was sent, but by some confusion was put in the Oxford train. We are all very thankful he is back in this country. It was a big strain during the uncertainty of events whilst the first move was on. The 11th East Lancs. have suffered heavily. Capt. Tough and Capt. Riley are both killed — Livesey was reported killed at first, but afterwards as wounded. His father goes to the War Office in London today to ascertain. Tony feels certain he was killed, being wounded twice, the second time right on the German trenches, when he was seen to fall as if dead. Perhaps he fell unconscious and managed to crawl away later.

I have mailed you an 'Observer', giving some particulars. Regarding Col. Rickman, Tony says he was at his post all day, and towards the end was blown out of his dug out, which knocked him shell sick. They all behaved splendidly and with great coolness. Man for man they feel themselves superior to the enemy if it came to a hand to hand fight. It is these hidden machine guns that do so much damage during an assault.

Ethel has remained in Oxford, and baby Joan is here — quite well — in charge of Mrs. Cooper.

Mother gos up on Tuesday — probably with father — to St. Andrews to the annual prize giving. Paddock House is filling up, but Lydia will not need to return till Mother is back from Scotland.

MESSAGES/APPRECIATIONS —
EAST LANCASHIRE JULY 1916

(A) On July 15th, 1916 each local newspaper of Accrington, Blackburn, Burnley and Chorley published its own appropriately worded copy of the following letter, e.g.:-

In the Field,
July 10th, 1916

His Worship the Mayor of Accrington

Dear Sir,

I forward you herewith some appreciations from the higher command of the gallantry shown by the 94th Infantry Brigade in the action of July 1st, 1916.

As Accrington plays such a large part in the composition of the 11th (S), Accrington, East Lancashire Regiment, I feel sure you and the citizens of Accrington will feel a just pride in the communications.

Personally, I feel that I have been greatly honoured by being allowed to serve with such gallant comrades.

I wish to express to you sir, and to all such citizens of Accrington as have lost their relatives, the sincere sympathy of myself and all officers, N.C.O.'s and men who are now serving with the 11th (S) Battalion, East Lancashire Regiment.

I remain Sir,
Yours faithfully,
E. L. REISS,
Major For Lieut. Colonel Commanding 11th East Lancashire Regiment
(Accrington Observer, July 15th, 1916)
N.B. Only one Mayor publicly acknowledged the letter from Major Reiss.

Town Hall, Blackburn
July 14th, 1916

Dear Sir,

I beg to acknowledge receipt of your letter enclosing the appreciation of the services of the 11th Battalion, East Lancashire Regiment (Accrington Pals) in the recent operations. Although it is with the greatest regret that one mourns the loss of so many gallant lads from this town and neighbourhood, it is some solace to hear they have conducted themselves in the field as splendid specimens of Lancashire lads. Believe me.

Yours faithfully,
ALFRED NUTTALL, Mayor
(Blackburn Times, July 15th, 1916).

(B) Letter received by Mayor of Accrington from General Commanding 31 Division:-

July 7th, 1916

Dear Sir,

I am certain you will be interested to know how well the York and Lancaster Brigade (sic) fought on Saturday last. All the battalions, the 12th, 13th and 14th York and Lancasters and the 11th East Lancashires (Accrington and Chorley Pals) (sic), distinguished themselves by their coolness, dash and extraordinary bravery. Their advance in face of a terrific bombardment was beyond all praise and one of the finest performances ever accomplished by British soldiers.

I am sure Yorkshire and Lancashire will appreciate the way the whole Division behaved.

Yours,
R. WANLESS-O'GOWAN
Major General Commanding 31 Division.
(Accrington Gazette, July 15th, 1916)

Men of the 11th East Lancs Regiment died, killed in action or died of wounds, November 1914 to July 1916 (including those, died of wounds sustained July 1st, 1916).

N.B. 170 of the 'other ranks', with Regimental numbers commencing '15' or '16' (62% of total listed), enlisted in September 1914.

(A) Men Who Died In The United Kingdom And Middle East 1914 - 1916

Name	Rank	Number	Date	Cause	Hometown	Age	M/S*	Rel.	Occupation	Burial Place
McGregor, Robert	Pte	N.K.	9/11/14	Drowning	Rishton	27	S	R.C.	Paper Mill Lab.	Family grave
Milton, George	Pte	15538	1/2/15	Pneumonia	Chorley	21	S	C. of E.	—	Chorley M.B. A 1295
Brierley, John	Pte	N.K.	2/2/15	Pneumonia	Blackburn	27	S	C. of E.	—	Family grave
Ollett, Samuel S.	Pte	22097	7/9/15	Pneumonia	Accrington	20	S	—	Engineer	Accrington M.B. DR 55
Hacking, Fred	Pte	15584	18/9/15	Pneumonia	Oswaldtwistle	22	S	N.C.	Engineer	Family grave
Wixted, James C.	Pte	15835	29/12/15	Siriasis	Accrington	24	S	R.C.	—	At Sea (Helles Mem.)
Mitchell, Henry H.	Lt.	—	23.2.16	Accident	Hoghton	29	S	N.C.	Insurance Clerk	Port Said W.M.C. J 21
Baron, William	Pte	15478	25/3/16	'sickness'	Rishton	23	M	—	Engineer	Port Said W.M.C. J 7
[1]Connor, John	Pte	18103	10/4/16	Drowning	Oswaldtwistle	40	S	R.C.	Print Worker	Amara W.C. XII L5

* M = Married   S = Single
  C. of E. = Church of England
  N.C. = Nonconformist
  R.C. = Roman Catholic
1 Attached to 6th East Lancs Regiment

(B) Men Killed In Action, Died of Wounds Or Died In France Before July 1st, 1916

Name	Rank	Number	Date	Cause	Hometown	Age	M/S*	Rel.	Occupation	Burial Place
Clark, Jack	Pte	16033	29/4	K. in A.	Burnley	20	S	N.C.	Miner	Sucrerie 1 H 60
Hartley, Joseph G.	L/Cpl	15718	29/4	K. In A.	Nelson	21	S	C. of E.	—	Sucrerie 1 H 61
Riley, Arthur	Pte	20972	30/4	D. of W.	Accrington	24	S	C. of E.	Billiard Hall Caretaker	Beauval E 7
Ellison, Wilfred	Pte	15267	26/5	Sickness[1]	Chorley	21	S	—	Weaver	Beauval E 28
Jackson, Thomas H.	Pte	15935	27/5	K. in A.	Clayton L.M. +	19	S	N.C.	Miner	Sucrerie 1 H 53
Pickering, Robert	Pte	15942	27/5	K. in A.	Darwen	30	M1C	C. of E.	Overlooker	Sucrerie 1 H 54
Nutter, Arthur	Pte	16043	17/6	Accident[2]	Burnley	23	S	C. of E.	Weaver	Bertrancourt 1 C 12
Duckworth, William	Sgt	15984	20/6	K. in A.	Oswaldtwistle	20	S	C. of E.	Shop Assistant	Bertrancourt 1 C 13
Hoyle, John	Pte	15807	21/6	K. in A.	Accrington	28	M	C. of E.	Laundry Worker	Bertrancourt 1 A 15
Whittaker, Thomas	Pte	15949	21/6	K. in A.	Clayton L.M. +	22	S	C. of E.	Carter	Bertrancourt 1 B 14
Young, David	Pte	15952	21/6	K. in A.	Rawtenstall	20	S	—	—	Bertrancourt 1 B 13
Burrows, James R.	Pte	15561	22/6	D. of W.	Burnley	25	M1C	C. of E.	Weaver	Couin 1 A 10
Cliffe, Bernard	Pte	27268	22/6	K. in A.	Hull	20	S	—	—	Bertrancourt 1 B 5
Downes, Alfred	Pte	15231	22/6	K. in A.	Accrington	26	M2C	—	Engineer	Bertrancourt 1 D 5
Roberts, Fred	Pte	24175	22/6	K. in A.	Blackburn	22	S	—	Clerk	Bertrancourt 1 B 6
Yates, Thomas	Pte	15432	22/6	K. in A.	Accrington	21	S	N.C.	Blacksmith	Bertrancourt 1 B 7
Fawcett, Frank	Pte	15932	23/6	K. in A.	Accrington	20	S	C. of E.	Engineer	Bertrancourt 1 A 14
Haworth, Albert	Pte	22183	23/6	K. in A.	Oswaldtwistle	23	S	—	Weaver	Bertrancourt 1 D 6
Kenyon, Ernest	Pte	18037	23.6	K. in A.	Accrington	37	M4C	—	Calico Printer	Bertrancourt 1 A 13
Hargreaves, Percy	Pte	15505	26/6	D. of W.	Accrington	19	S	C. of E.	Engineering	Gezaincourt 1 F 7
Heys, James L.	Pte	15760	26/6	K. in A.	Burnley	35	M1C	—	Weaver	Bertrancourt 1 D 18
Pettie, Philip J.	Sgt	15138	26/6	D. of W.	Accrington	—	M	N.C.	Engineer	Doullens X1 II B 16

* M = Married   S = Single   C = Children
1 **Died of Untreated Appendicitis**
2 **Killed by Grenade Explosion in Training**
+ **Clayton-le-Moors**
  Whittle-le-Woods
  Clayton-le-Woods

MEN WHO DIED JULY 1st to 5th, 1916

235 Officers and men of the 11th East Lancs. Regiment are recorded as losing their lives July 1st to 5th, 1916. With the exception of one man interred at Tilloy, near Arras, their remains are buried in six War Cemeteries near Colincamps and Serre. 135 Officers and men have no known grave and their names are on the Thiepval Memorial.

1. EUSTON ROAD CEMETERY — COLINCAMPS

Name	Rank	Number	Hometown	Age	M/S	Religion	Occupation	Grave No.
Atkinson, Thomas	Pte.	15399	Accrington	20	S	N.C.	Engineer	A 1
Beacall, Arthur	2/Lt.	—	Gloucester	21	M	C.of E.	Bank Clerk	1 D 1
Blackstone, John	L/Cpl.	16057	Croston	23	S	C.of E.	Labourer	1 A 41
Briggs, Robert	Pte.	24417	Brierfield	25	S	C.of E.	Pupil Architect	1 D 8
Brunskill, Arthur	Pte.	15738	Burnley	22	S	C.of E.	Weaver	1 D 5
Clarkson, William	Cpl.	15956	Chorley	22	S	C.of E.	Overlooker	1 A 14
Clayton, Herbert	Pte.	15711	Burnley	22	M1C	N.C.	Weaver	1 A 42
Edwards, Alfred	Pte.	18969	Accrington	—	—	C.of E.	—	1 A 17
Halstead, Albert	Pte.	15567	Burnley	22	S	C.of E.	Weaver	1 D 12
Hardman, Harry	Pte.	15855	Chorley	39	M	—	Mill Worker	1 A 39
Ingham, Ben	Sgt.	15368	Burnley	24	S	—	Weaver	1 D 9
Irvine, Andrew	Pte.	17963	Accrington	22	S	C.of E.	French Polisher	1 A 38
Kohn, Wilfred A.	2/Lt.	—	London	22	S	Jewish	—	1 D 13
Lockett, John	L/Cpl.	15574	Burnley	28	M	—	Weaver	1 B 34
Mundy, Richard H.	Pte.	17868	Accrington	21	S	—	Railway Porter	1 B 32
Myerscough, William	Pte.	17926	Accrington	33	M4C	R.C.	Engineer	1 A 32
Omerod, Richard	Cpl.	15173	Blackburn	22	S	—	Clerk	1 A 24
Sharpe, William	Pte.	15908	Burnley	20	S	N.C.	Weaver	1 D 15
Smith, Sam	Cpl.	15254	Accrington	25	M1C	—	Engineer	1 D 7
Thornley, Ralph H.	L/Cpl.	15429	Oswaldtwistle	28	M	—	Chemical Worker	1 A 20
Tuhey, James	Pte.	15734	Burnley	—	—	—	—	1 B 44
Wade, Fred	Pte.	27302	Bradford	—	S	R.C.	Overlooker	1 B 33
Walsh, James	Pte.	15151	Accrington	29	S	—	Moulder	1 A 43
Watson, James A.	Pte.	24797	Colne	28	S	—	—	1 G 22

2. QUEENS CEMETERY — PUISIEUX

Name	Rank	Number	Hometown	Age	M/S	Religion	Occupation	Grave No.
Ashworth, Fred	Pte.	15179	Burnley	21	S	—	Mill Manager	C 8
Astley, Robert	L/Cpl.	15433	Chorley	31	M3C	C.of E.	Mill Worker	C 29
Baxter, Richard	Pte.	15560	Nelson	23	M1C	N.C.	Weaver	D 4
Blakey, Fred	Pte.	21811	Burnley	21	S	—	Mill Worker	B 12
Bolton, William	Pte.	15641	Chorley	25	M	C.of E.	Bleach Worker	E 20
Coady, Tom	Pte.	18011	Oswaldtwistle	33	S	R.C.	Dental Mechanic	A 20
Conway, Arthur P.	Pte.	15194	Rishton	20	S	C.of E.	Weaver	C 55
Cook, Thomas	Pte.	15915	Gt. Harwood	—	S	C.of E.	—	C 61
Cox, Charles	Pte.	15927	Accrington	23	S	R.C.	Engineer	A 29
Cunliffe, John	L/Cpl.	15007	Accrington	26	M	—	Engineer	C 33
Davis, John T.	Pte.	17987	Oswaldtwistle	—	—	C.of E.	Engineer	A 24
Dix, Alfred B.	Pte.	18017	Blackburn	39	M2C	C.of E.	Tailor's Presser	D 29
Dixon, Harry	L/Cpl.	15689	Blackburn	24	M	N.C.	Cashier	B 11
Edge, Israel	Sgt.	15082	Rishton	23	S	—	Weaver	A 46
Emmett, James H.	Pte.	21987	Burnley	21	S	N.C.	Weaver	B 10
Gibbens, Sydney	Cpl.	27295	London	—	—	—	—	D 48
Grimshaw, Thomas	Sgt.	16011	Chorley	36	M5C	R.C.	Miner	E 2
Hardman, Samuel D.	Pte.	15504	Accrington	26	S	—	Engineer	C 67

2. QUEENS CEMETERY — PUISIEUX

Name	Rank	Number	Hometown	Age	M/S	Religion	Occupation	Grave No.
Hargreaves, Albert	Pte.	15412	Church	21	S	N.C.	Clerk	A 31
Hitchon, James F.	Lt.	—	Hoghton	22	S	—	Pupil Architect	A 16
Hodson, William A.	Pte.	15809	Accrington	28	M1C	R.C.	Engineer	B 30
Holden, Ernest	Cpl.	15989	Accrington	35	M	C.of E.	Mill Manager	A 22
Holden, Fred	Pte.	24485	Rishton	19	S	N.C.	—	A 50
Holden, Richard	Pte.	17830	Clayton L.M.	—	—	N.C.	Weaver	B 52
Houlker, Albert	Pte.	17943	Accrington	21	S	C.of E.	Mill Worker	B 46
Howley, Herbert	Sgt.	15303	Gt. Harwood	35	M1C	R.C.	Fireman	E 41
Jackson, Robert	Pte.	17972	Clayton L.M.	26	M2C	C.of E.	—	B 4
Kennedy, Thomas	Pte.	15199	Gt. Harwood	21	S	N.C.	—	C 21
Lambert, Thomas	Pte.	17998	Accrington	22	S	—	—	C 50
Lee, Clifford	Pte.	27315	Hull	28	S	C.of E.	Tannery Worker	D 47
Lightfoot, Norman	L/Cpl.	15026	Accrington	21	S	N.C.	Trainee Manager	C 9
Lord, Willie	Pte.	20989	Colne	19	S	C.of E.	Quarryman	D 46
Lund, Giles	L/Cpl.	15025	Accrington	29	S	—	Carter	A 27
Molloy, John	Pte.	15941	Rishton	26	M1C	R.C.	Moulder	C23
Mulhall, James	Pte.	17838	Accrington	42	M2C	R.C.	Labourer	A43
Mulhall, Tom	Pte.	15817	Accrington	21	S	R.C.	Engineer	A40
Parkinson, William H.	Pte.	15925	Clayton L.M.	30	M3C	—	Engineer	B40
Peel, Herbert S.	Pte.	20990	Accrington	32	M1C	—	Painter	C32
Pendlebury, Richard	Pte.	15448	Chorley	21	S	R.C.	Bleach Worker	C27
Proctor, Harry	Pte.	15469	Burnley	26	M1C	C.of E.	Mill Worker	C72
Rodwell, Harry	Cpl.	27294	Bradford	24	S	—	—	B14
Russell, John	Pte.	15088	Rishton	24	S	—	Paper Worker	A 48
Singleton, William	Pte.	22108	Burnley	18	S	R.C.	Paper Worker	C 64
Smith, John	Pte.	15425	Accrington	26	M3C	—	Miner	D 36
Talbot, Joseph T.	Pte.	24076	Nelson	24	S	N.C.C.of E.	Weaver	D 35
Thompson, John	Pte.	24570	Gt. Harwood	21	S	C.of E.	Clerk	D 18
Tootell, William	Pte.	15676	Coppull	20	S	C.of E.	Miner	A 38
Tough, Arnold B.	Capt.	—	Accrington	26	S	C.of E.	Dentist	D 62
Uttley, Richard	Pte.	15832	Crawshawbooth	22	S	C.of E.	Weaver	C 40
Wray, William	Pte.	24903	Darwen	31	M		Cotten Manuf.	D 13

3. RAILWAY HOLLOW CEMETERY — HEBUTERNE

Name	Rank	Number	Hometown	Age	M/S	Religion	Occupation	Grave No.
Billington, Walter C.	Cpl.	27274	Hull	22	S	—	Shipping Clerk	A 2
Chadwick, Edward	Pte.	15794	Accrington	—	—	R.C.	Print Worker	A 27
Dust, Thomas F.	L/Cpl.	15556	Crawshawbooth	24	M2C	C.of E.	Print Worker	A 5
Haigh, Reginald	Pte.	18041	Darlington	—	S	—	Driver	A 28
Hart, Alfred	Cpl.	21878	Whalley	19	S	C.of E.	Clerk	A 6
Holmes, Frederick	Pte.	24844	Darwen	20	S	N.C.	Clerk	A 12
Ingham, Harry	Pte.	15465	Burnley	28	S	R.C.	Weaver	B 12
Ingham, Richard	Pte.	17901	Church	24	M1C	C.of E.	Mill Worker	C 20
MacKenna, William	L/Cpl.	15028	Church	26	S	R.C.	Engineer	A 18
Mawdsley, James H.	Pte.	17949	Clayton L.M.	34	M3C	N.C.	Print Worker	A 15
Ormerod, William A.	L/Cpl.	15388	Rishton	24	S	C.of E.	—	A 29
Pickering, William J.	Pte.	16027	Blackburn	24	S	N.C.	Grocer	B 17
Pickup, Frederick	L/Cpl.	15594	Rishton	25	M	—	Weaver	B 10
Simpson, Harry	Pte.	24141	Brierfield	20	S	—	Weaver	B 11
Stott, Frederick	Pte.	15582	Burnley	25	M1C	N.C.	Foundry Worker	B 3

4. SERRE ROAD CEMETERY NO.1 BEAUMONT HAMEL, HEBUTERNE

Name	Rank	Number	Hometown	Age	M/S	Religion	Occupation	Grave No.
Winter, John	Pte.	24514	Bacup	21	S	C. of E.	Debt Collector	VC 9

5. SERRE ROAD CEMETERY NO. 2 — BEAUMONT HAMEL, HEBUTERNE

Name	Rank	Number	Hometown	Age	M/S	Religion	Occupation	Grave No.
Hindle, John	Cpl.	15124	Haslingden	25	S	N.C.	Clerk	XXVII,F11
Moore, Arthur	L/Cpl.	27277	Hull	21	S	C.of E.	Clerk	XL,E9
Webster, Harry	Pte.	18062	Oswaldtwistle	28	M	N.C.	Print Worker	XII, B11

6. SERRE ROAD CEMETERY NO. 3 — PUISIEUX

Name	Rank	Number	Hometown	Age	M/S	Religion	Occupation	Grave No.
Allen, William	L/Cpl.	18003	Accrington	32	M2C	N.C.	Spinner	B 23
Denney, John	Cpl.	15872	Blackburn	28	M	R.C.	Paper Worker	B 18
Hull, Jack	Pte.	15857	Whittle L.W.	20	S	C.of E.	Weaver	B 20
Taylor, William A.	Pte.	15878	Blackburn	28	M	N.C.	Clerk	C 8
Topping, John J.	Pte.	15946	Blackburn	18	S	R.C.	Shop Assistant	C 1
Widdop, Clarence	Pte.	15453	Chorley	—	—	N.C.	—	B 13

7. TILLOY BRITISH CEMETERY

Name	Rank	Number	Hometown	Age	M/S	Religion	Occupation	Grave No.
Dent, Arthur	Pte.	15362	Burnley	19	S	C.of E.	Weaver	PC 7,B 10

THE THIEPVAL MEMORIAL — PIER 6, FACE C

Name	Rank	Number	Hometown	Age	M/S	Religion	Occupation
Aspin, Herbert	Pte.	22178	Church	19	S	C.of E.	Engineer
Banks, Roland	Pte.	15216	Accrington	22	S	C.of E.	Engineer
Barnes, George	L/Cpl.	15479	Rishton	23	S	—	Weaver
Barnes, George W.	Pte.	15217	Accrington	26	M2C	N.C.	—
Barnes, James	Pte.	15788	Accrington	23	S	C.of E.	Moulder
Barnes, Joseph	Pte.	15769	Rishton	30	M	—	Joiner
Beaghan, David	Pte.	15316	Rishton	22	S	C.of E.	Engineer
Bell, Joseph	Pte.	17882	Accrington	34	M1C	—	—
Berry, Thomas	Pte.	15526	Heath Charnock	27	M1C	C.of E.	Bleach Worker
Bowers, Walter	Pte.	24430	Blackburn	25	M	C.of E.	Clerk
Bowers, William	Pte.	15790	Accrington	19	S	N.C.	Engineer
Breckell, George E.	Sgt.	15361	Burnley	27	M1C	—	Weaver
Bretherton, William	Pte.	16070	Chorley	31	M	C.of E.	Miner
Briggs, Walter	L/Cpl.	15223	Accrington	20	S	C.of E.	App. Engineer
Brindle, Francis	Pte.	15159	Chorley	20	S	—	Mill Worker
Broadley, Fred	Pte.	17839	Accrington	18	S	—	—
Brooks, John	Pte.	27264	Barnsley	—	M	—	Miner
Bury, Albert	Pte.	15493	Accrington	—	—	N.C.	Print Worker
Bury, Percy	L/Cpl.	15224	Accrington	22	M1C	N.C.	Print Worker
Calvert, Jack	Pte.	15886	Burnley	20	S	C.of E.	Weaver
Camm, Fred	Pte.	15739	Burnley	19	S	—	App. Tailor
Carey, Thomas	Pte.	15494	Accrington	32	S	R.C.	Railway Fitter
Carr, William	Pte.	16006	Chorley	20	S	N.C.	Miner
Chapman, Harry	Sgt.	15005	Accrington	35	M	C.of E.	Print Worker
Chapman, William	L/Cpl.	27255	Hull	—	—	—	—
Charnley, Robert	L/Cpl.	17862	Accrington	30	M3C	—	Electrican
Clark, Charles	Pte.	18031	Church	—	—	—	—
Clayton, George	Pte.	15077	Gt. Harwood	21	S	N.C.	—
Clegg, William	Pte.	17983	Clayton L.M.	19	S	C.of E.	Shop Assistant
Clinton, Harry	Pte.	24176	Blackburn	23	S	—	Shop Assistant

Name	Rank	Number	Hometown	Age	M/S	Religion	Occupation
Coates, James	Pte.	24152	Burnley	23	S	N.C.	Weaver
Cook, William	Pte.	24924	Bacup	21	S	C.of E.	—
Cowell, Will	Pte.	15644	Chorley	25	M	R.C.	Miner
Cross, Arthur	Pte.	18973	Accrington	28	M	—	Miner
Cullen, Michael	Pte.	18966	Accrington	22	S	R.C.	Miner
Davies, Harry N.	2/Lt.	—	Southend	21	S	—	—
Davies, John H.	Cpl.	15715	Burnley	44	M7C	—	Watch Maker
Delaney, Thomas	Pte.	13744	Manchester	24	M	R.C.	Engineer
Dickenson, James	Pte.	15957	Chorley	18	S	R.C.	Print Worker
Dougherty, William	Pte.	16035	Burnley	26	S	R.C.	Upholsterer
Duerden, Orrell T.	Pte.	17870	Accrington	21	S	C.of E.	Weaver
Enderby, Joseph	Pte.	15646	Chorley	23	S	R.C.	Mill Worker
Entwistle, Carswell	L/Cpl.	15437	Chorley	25	S	N.C.	Piecer
Finney, William	Pte.	17989	Accrington	30	M1C	—	Brick Worker
Francis, Thomas E.	Pte.	15476	Church	21	S	R.C.	Engineer
Gibson, Albert	Pte.	15501	Accrington	—	—	—	—
Green, William	Pte.	15164	Chorley	25	M1C	R.C.	Miner
Greenwood, Fred	Pte.	24523	Blackburn	25	M	C.of E.	Weaver
Grimshaw, Joseph	Pte.	17920	Accrington	29	M2C	R.C.	Canal Worker
Grimshaw, William	Pte.	17834	Oswaldtwistle	33	M	—	—
Halewood, George L.	Pte.	15690	Blackburn	21	S	C.of E.	Painter
Harrison, Henry B.	Pte.	27286	Hull	—	—	—	—
Haydock, Edgar B.	Cpl.	15283	Pleasington	24	S	—	—
Hersey, Harold	Sgt.	15486	Clayton L.M.	26	M	C.of E.	—
Heys, Walter B.	Pte.	24154	Burnley	22	S	—	—
Hogan, Peter	Pte.	18072	Accrington	24	S	—	Print Worker
Holden, Joseph	Pte.	24209	Blackburn	23	S	—	Pawnbroker
Holden, Joseph T.	L/Cpl.	15593	Rishton	26	M	—	Weaver
Holland, Harold	Pte.	15328	Accrington	21	S	C.of E.	Clerk
Iddon, Richard	Pte.	16059	Chorley	28	M2C	N.C.	Mill Worker
Iley, James	Pte.	15811	Accrington	25	S	R.C.	Moulder
Jackson, Arthur	Pte.	22126	Burnley	30	M3C	N.C.	Miner
Jackson, James	Pte.	15304	Rishton	21	S	—	Weaver
Jones, Norman	Pte.	20931	Accrington	20	S	N.C.	Barber
Kenworthy, Albert W.	Pte.	27314	Barnsley	28	S	—	Miner
Laffy, John	Pte.	22088	Haslingden	32	S	R.C.	Painter
Lang, Austin	Sgt.	15657	Chorley	31	M2C	R.C.	Miner
Leaver, James M.	Pte.	22138	Accrington	19	S	—	—
Livesey, Harry	Capt.	—	Blackburn	35	S	C.of E.	Man. Director
Lord, Alfred H.	Pte.	16015	Chorley	21	S	N.C.	Barber
Lord, Alfred	Cpl.	22191	Accrington	22	S	N.C.	—
Lord, Samuel	Pte.	17860	Clayton L.M.	22	M2C	—	Mill Worker
Marsden, Frank	Sgt.	15938	Blackburn	33	M	R.C.	Plumber
Marsland, Edmund	Pte.	15597	Clayton L.M.	32	M	N.C.	Fireman
Mercer, Albert	L/Cpl.	15085	Rishton	20	S	—	Weaver
Metcalf, John	Pte.	17851	Oswaldtwistle	17	S	—	Student
Milton, William	Pte.	20943	Oswaldtwistle	39	M3C	—	—
Mulhall, Albert	Pte.	15818	Accrington	23	S	R.C.	Engineer
Murphy, John	Pte.	15902	Burnley	24	S	R.C.	Weaver

Name	Rank	Number	Hometown	Age	M/S	Religion	Occupation
Nickson, Edward	L/Cpl.	15334	Accrington	—	—	—	—
Noble, John W.	Pte.	15371	Burnley	23	S	R.C.	Weaver
Nutter, Harry	Pte.	15920	Rishton	19	S	—	Miner
O'Connor, John	Pte.	18035	Church	26	M1C	R.C.	Print Worker
O'Hare, William	Pte.	15134	Accrington	24	S	R.C.	Engineer
Parkington, Fred	Pte.	15822	Accrington	26	M1C	C.of E.	Engineer
Parkinson, Edward	Pte.	15421	Accrington	21	S	N.C.	Engineer
Parry, Thomas O.	L/Cpl.	15539	Coppull	24	S	C.of E.	—
Pendlebury, James	Pte.	15861	Chorley	28	M4C	C.of E.	Mill Worker
Pickup, George	Pte.	15552	Darwen	26	S	N.C.	Cotton Manuf.
Place, Ernest	Pte.	15036	Accrington	20	S	N.C.	Engineer
Pollard, John	Pte.	15824	Accrington	22	S	C.of E.	Print Worker
Ratcliffe, William	Pte.	15540	Chorley	22	S	R.C.	Bleach Worker
Rawcliffe, Herbert C.	Pte.	17936	Church	23	S	C.of E.	Bleach Worker
Rayton, Henry	Pte.	17966	Gt. Harwood	26	M	—	Weaver
Rigg, Albert	Pte.	15038	Accrington	20	S	—	Moulder
Riley, Ernest	Pte.	15586	Church	24	S	N.C.	Clothing Club Agt.
Riley, Henry D.	Capt.	—	Brierfield	35	S	C.of E.	Co. Director
Riley, Willie	Pte.	15731	Burnley	21	S	C.of E.	Weaver
Rimmer, Oliver	Cpl.	15397	Clayton L.M.	36	M2C	—	Miner
Robinson, Thomas	Pte.	15449	Eccleston	28	S	C.of E.	Mill Worker
Robinson, Willie	Pte.	15103	Clayton L.M.	21	S	C.of E.	—
Rogers, Albert E.	Cpl.	17980	Clayton L.M.	34	M	N.C.	T.U. Secretary
Rollins, Seth	Pte.	15964	Coppull	21	S	C.of E.	Weaver
Sanders, George	L/Cpl.	27254	Hull	28	S	—	—
Saunders, Leonard	L/Cpl.	15966	Euxton	27	S	C.of E.	Paper Worker
Shaw, Crowther	Pte.	15559	Crawshawbooth	30	M	N.C.	Spinner
Shuttleworth, Edward	Pte.	15632	Gt. Harwood	23	S	—	—
Smithies, Robert	Pte.	15311	Accrington	23	S	N.C.	Shop Assistant
Speakman, James	Pte.	15673	Chorley	29	M1C	R.C.	Bleach Worker
Spedding, Thomas	Pte.	15757	Burnley	20	S	—	Weaver
Squires, James	Pte.	18060	Accrington	23	S	C.of E.	Moulder
Stonehouse, Charles	Lt.	—	Blackburn	34	—	N.C.	Architect
Stuttard, George	Pte.	15427	Accrington	20	S	C.of E.	Shop Assistant
Sunley, Walter	Pte.	27298	Hull	20	S	—	—
Sutcliffe, Walter	Pte.	24074	Nelson	23	S	—	Weaver
Taylor, Thomas	Pte.	24787	Barrowford	29	S	—	Weaver
Thompson, Herbert W.	2/Lt.	—	London	21	S	—	—
Thompson, James F.	Pte.	22146	Gt. Harwood	—	S	C.of E.	—
Thompson, Jerry	Cpl.	15755	Burnley	22	S	—	Weaver
Todd, Walter C.	Sgt.	15259	Accrington	21	S	C.of E.	Indu. Chemist
Tomlinson, William	Cpl.	15635	Accrington	35	M	C.of E.	Ship's Steward
Tuton, John Henry	Pte.	27300	Hull	—	—	—	—
Tyson, Arthur	Pte.	16055	Burnley	22	M	C.of E.	Spinner
Unsworth, Herbert	Pte.	15866	Chorley	34	M3C	N.C.	Miner
Ward, John E.	Pte.	15351	Clayton L.W.	22	S	C.of E.	Weaver
Watson, Harry	Pte.	24887	Darwen	19	S	C.of E.	Weaver
Webb, Frederick	Pte.	24153	Burnley	23	S	N.C.	Weaver
Whalley, Joseph	Pte.	15488	Oswaldtwistle	18	S	N.C.	Weaver

Name	Rank	Number	Hometown	Age	M/S	Religion	Occupation
Whewell, Herbert	Pte.	15834	Accrington	21	S	—	Weaver
Wilkinson, Albert	Pte.	18496	Rawtenstall	19	S	C.of E.	Mill Worker
Wilkinson, Fred	Pte.	20946	Oswaldtwistle	—	S	C.of E.	Doctor's Coll.
Wixted, John	Pte.	15778	Church	19	S	R.C.	Print Worker
Wood, Herbert	Pte.	17917	Accrington	—	—	—	—
Yates, Thomas H.	Pte.	17863	Accrington	—	—	N.C.	—
Young, John	Pte.	17884	Oswaldtwistle	25	M3C	N.C.	Boiler Lagger

MEN DIED OF WOUNDS SUSTAINED JULY 1st to 5th, 1916

Name	Rank	Number	Date	Hometown	Age	M/S	Religion	Occupation	Burial Place
Lawrenson, John	Pte.	15658	4/7/16	Chorley	30	M2C	C.of E.	Miner	Beauval B 37
Heys, James	L/Cpl.	24225	6/7/16	Crawshawbooth	23	M	N.C.	Weaver	Doullens EX1 IV C 13
Radcliffe, Fred W.	Pte.	15730	6/7/16	Loerhouse	32	M6C	C.of E.	Piecer	Doullens EX1 IV C 18
Baines, John W.	Pte.	15107	7/7/16	Accrington	22	S	C.of E.	Painter	Beauval Comm. F 12
Holding, James	Pte.	17957	7/7/16	Accrington	34	M	R.C.	Stonemason	Accrington M.B. CF 416
Jolly, David	Pte.	15747	9/7/16	Burnley	22	S	C.of E.	Weaver	Doullens IV D 2
Makinson, James	Pte.	15960	9/7/16	Chorley	19	S	R.C.	Miner	Etretat, LeHavre, 2 D14A
Hewitt, Edwin R.	Sgt.	27311	11/7/16	Hull	36	M	—	—	Doullens EX1 IV D 10
Bullen, Robert	Pte.	15708	13/7/16	Padiham	24	S	N.C.	Painter	Padiham M.B. B 1120
Hirst, Adam	Pte.	21809	13/7/16	Brierfield	19	S	N.C.	Weaver	St. Sever A 298
Harling, Charles	Pte.	15238	14/7/16	Oswaldtwistle	28	M3C	C.of E.	Com. Traveller	Accrington M.B. EK 161
Gaskell, Thomas	Pte.	15438	18/7/16	Chorley	26	S	—	Mill Worker	St. Pol Comm. EXB 13
Fletcher, Peter	Sgt.	15071	21/7/16	Church	—	S	—	Engineer	St. Pol Comm. EXB 10
Ward, James	Pte.	16001	24/7/16	Accrington	24	M1C	—	Mill Worker	Accrington M.B. EJ 79
Pollitt, James H.	Pte.	15067	1/11/16	Burnley	40	M5C	C.of E.	Miner	Family grave
Laycock, Benjamin F.	Pte.	17898	22/6/17	Accrington	24	S	N.C.	—	Accrington M.B. DQ 138
Lyon, James A.	Sgt.	15027	18/2/19	Accrington	36	M	C.of E.	—	Accrington M.B. DH 387

APPENDIX 8

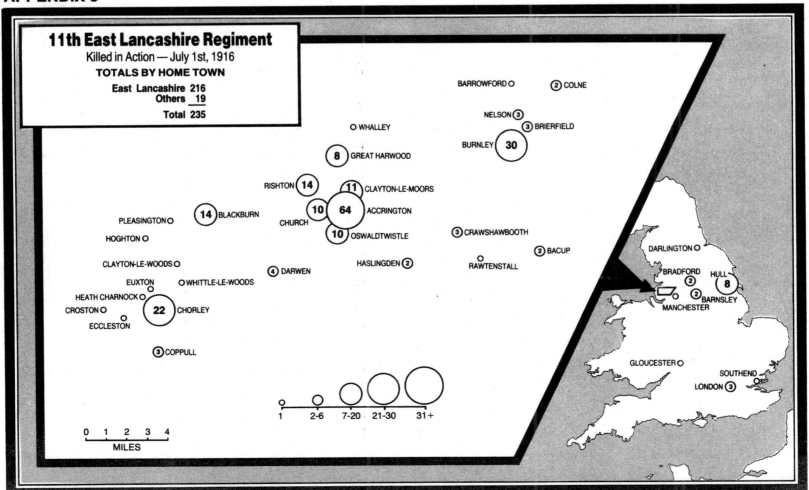

11th East Lancashire Regiment
Killed in Action — July 1st, 1916
TOTALS BY HOME TOWN
East Lancashire 216
Others 19
Total 235

11th BATTALION EAST LANCASHIRE REGIMENT.

CASUALTIES (approx.)

Period. 30/4/16 - 11/11/18.	Killed in action. Off.	O.R.	Missing. Off.	O.R.	Wounded. Off.	O.R.
30/4/16 - 30/6/16.	-	17	-	-	1	88
1/7/16 -	7	139	2	88	12	336
2/7/16 - 31/12/16.	1	31	-	2	8	225
1/1/17 - 31/12/17.	3	43	2	5	13	450
1/1/18 - 24/3/18.	-	8	-	-	-	24
25/3/18 - 29/3/18.	4	30	-	93	7	205
11/4/18 - 14/4/18.	2	25	-	33	5	144
15/4/18 - 27/6/18.	2	16	-	1	5	50
28/6/18 - 30/6/18.	2	49	-	-	9	200
1/7/18 - 31/8/18.	-	20	-	2	12	126
1/9/18 - 30/9/18.	3	43	4	44	6	255
1/10/18 - 11/11/18	-	8	-	-	2	108

GRAND TOTAL 112 Officers; 2808 o.r.

(By kind permission of Major G. Rickman)

Nominal Roll

N.C.O's and OTHER RANKS' who served in the 11th (Accrington) Battalion, EAST LANCASHIRE REGIMENT, 1914 - 1919 and incorporating a Roll of Honour.

Complied by Fergus Read (Member O.M.R.S. 1910)

Sources: Official Medal Roll Returns, East Lancashire Regiment, British War Medal/Victory Medal.
Absent Voters Lists.
Soldiers Died in the Great War.
Registers of the Commonwealth War Graves Commission.
Local Newspapers.

NOTES

The nominal rolls has been compiled primarily from the medal returns. Where possible details have been checked against the other sources.

It is believed that this is the first occasion on which a near-complete roll has been attempted for a wartime infantry battalion. The total number of individuals is over 3,600. The battalion therefore had to duplicate itself more than 3 times during the course of the war, to replace casualties — a classic illustration of the carnage of the First World War.

The 'original' pals, whom we might define as those who left for North Wales in February 1915 and who were listed by the **Accrington Observer and Times** of 23rd February 1915, were numbered in sequence 15,000 - 16,070, and approximately 17,830 to 18,080. Special emphasis was placed on tracing the eventual fates of these individuals. Several were found to have died later serving with other units; details of others will be gratefully received.

N.B.

The Medal Rolls are not always easy to interpret, especially with regard to ranks held in a particular battalion. For this reason, and given the wartime necessity for 'acting' and 'temporary' ranks, all ranks in this roll should be treated with flexibility. Many Privates had periods of being Acting Corporals, even Sergeants, but remained, in the official records, as Privates.

The compiler would like to thank Julia Marsh, Simon Baines and Maureen Wignall for their assistance with extracting and collating the information, and Colonel J.A.C. Bird, O.B.E. for granting access to the medal rolls.

All revisions, please, to Fergus Read,
c/o Lancashire County and Regimental Museum,
Stanley Street,
PRESTON,
PR1 4YP.

Please note that the medal rolls are not available for public access at present, but will be available shortly at the Public Records Office, Kew, and, for approved researchers, at Regimental Headquarters, Queen's Lancashire Regiment, Fulwood Barracks, Preston.

Surname	Forename(s)	Number	Rank
ABBOTT	ROBERT	242226	PTE
ABBOTT	THOMAS	15473	PTE
ABBOTTS	JOSEPH	28291	PTE
ABRAM	ROBERT	17201	PTE
ACASTER	WILLIAM	27312	A/CPL
ACKRILL	F.	17928	PTE
ACKROYD	ERNEST	21800	PTE
ADAMS	ALBERT HENRY	31112	PTE
ADAMS	ERNEST	40777	PTE
ADAMS	FREDERICK	29913	PTE
ADAMS	WILLIAM CHARLES	15883	CPL
ADDERLEY	THOMAS	30577	PTE
ADDISON	THOMAS	17612	PTE
ADSHEAD	HERBERT	33821	PTE
AINSCOUGH	T. W.	15839	PTE
AINSWORTH	ARTHUR	17846	PTE
AINSWORTH	ELI	15156	CPL
AINSWORTH	TOM	37336	PTE
AIREY	GEORGE	32002	PTE
AKRED	ALBERT	20960	PTE
ALDERSON	JOHN WILLIAM	24773	PTE
ALEXANDER	DAVID WILLIAM LEWIS	49249	PTE
ALGER	ARTHUR	29432	PTE
ALLEN	ALBERT	32001	PTE
ALLEN	FRANK	30701	PTE
ALLEN	HARRY	39589	PTE
ALLEN	HERBERT	235157	PTE
ALLEN	THOMAS ALFRED	32330	PTE
ALLEN	THOMAS PENDLEBURY	29763	PTE
ALLEN	WILLIAM	18003	PTE
ALLEN	WILLIAM	29762	PTE
ALLOTT	ERNEST	33505	PTE
ALLSOP	FRANCIS	49282	PTE
ALLSUP	JAMES	15525	CPL
ALLSUP	PERCY	15524	SGT
ALMOND	ERNEST	24712	CPL
ALMOND	JOHN	20838	PTE
ALMOND	JOHN WILLIAM	40833	PTE
ALMOND	ROBERT	15383	PTE
ALSTON	JOHN JAMES	15599	CPL
ALSTON	T.	15600	PTE
AMES	JOHN THOMAS	29203	PTE
AMES	WALTER	18077	PTE
AMOS	J.	18012	PTE
ANDERS	WALTER JOHN	235222	PTE
ANDERSON	ARTHUR	5838	PTE
ANDERSON	HARRY	15980	PTE
ANDERSON	HARRY	35463	PTE
ANDERTON	WILFRED	23141	PTE
ANDREW	EDWARD	15178	A/CPL
ANDREWS	WILLIAM	28624	PTE
ANDREWS	WILLIAM	49333	PTE
APLIN	CLARENCE ALFRED	33854	PTE
APPLETON	JAMES	14562	PTE
APPLEYARD	JAMES	16703	PTE
ARCHER	CHARLES	35614	PTE
ARCHER	WILLIAM JOHN	15213	PTE
ARCHIBALD	LEO	32000	PTE
ARKWRIGHT	ROBERT VINCENT	25150	PTE
ARLICK	RUEBEN	236007	PTE
ARMSTRONG	CHARLES HENRY	27258	PTE
ARMSTRONG	JOHN	49250	PTE
ARMSTRONG	WILFRED ASPINALL	31393	PTE
ARNOLD	GEORGE	40810	PTE
ARNOLD	JOSEPH	29433	PTE
ARROWSMITH	ALBERT	235983	PTE
ARTHUR	JOHN HALSTED	35124	PTE
ASHCROFT	JOHN	39260	PTE
ASHCROFT	PETER	40690	PTE
ASHTON	GEORGE	15589	PTE
ASHTON	JAMES ALBERT	26493	CPL
ASHTON	JOSEPH	28458	PTE
ASHURST	THOMAS	33963	PTE
ASHWORTH		15398	PTE
ASHWORTH	FRED	15179	PTE
ASHWORTH	FRED	25493	PTE
ASHWORTH	HAROLD	241324	PTE
ASHWORTH	HENDERSON	29077	PTE
ASHWORTH	JAMES	31482	PTE
ASHWORTH	JOHN	24540	CPL
ASHWORTH	ROBERT	33867	PTE
ASHWORTH	ROBERT	37639	PTE
ASHWORTH	THOMAS	26742	PTE
ASHWORTH	THOMAS	30578	PTE
ASHWORTH	WILLIAM	15981	PTE
ASHWORTH	WILLIAM	26816	PTE
ASPDEN	ALBERT	29434	PTE
ASPDEN	AUSTIN SEGAR	25220	PTE
ASPDEN	ELIAS	40323	PTE
ASPDEN	JOSEPH	35615	PTE
ASPIN	GEORGE ALFRED	28824	PTE
ASPIN	HERBERT	22178	PTE
ASPIN	NICHOLAS	202022	CPL
ASPIN	THOMAS	35611	PTE
ASPIN	TOM	20386	PTE
ASPINALL	HARRY	15384	CPL
ASPINALL	JOHN	235695	A/CPL
ASPINALL	THOMAS YATES	30579	PTE
ASPINALL	WILLIAM	15780	PTE
ASPINALL	WILLIAM	201531	PTE
ASPLET	REGINALD	31481	PTE
ASTIN	HARRY	37238	PTE
ASTLEY	ANTHONY	24237	PTE
ASTLEY	ROBERT	15433	PTE
ASTON	EDWARD ALBERT	41001	PTE
ATHERTON	EDWARD	21211	PTE
ATHERTON	EDWARD	29360	PTE
ATHERTON	JAMES	23143	PTE
ATHERTON	REGINALD	31418	PTE
ATHERTON	STANLEY	27108	PTE
ATHERTON	THOMPSON	35612	PTE
ATHERTON	TOM	31560	PTE
ATKINSON	ARTHUR	27947	PTE
ATKINSON	GEORGE	33842	PTE
ATKINSON	HERBERT	18069	PTE
ATKINSON	JAMES	15913	SGT
ATKINSON	RICHARD	19702	PTE
ATKINSON	STRANGER	23835	PTE
ATKINSON	THOMAS	15399	PTE
ATKINSON	THOMAS KITCHING	30580	PTE
ATKINSON	WRIGHT	36890	PTE
ATTWOOD	ALFRED	49311	PTE
AUCHTERLONIE	JAMES	29418	PTE
AUSTIN	RICHARD HAROLD	36447	PTE
AUSTIN	THOMAS HENRY	19185	PTE
AYRES	HARRY	235550	PTE
AYRTON	ALBERT EDWARD	27027	PTE
BACHE	E. E.	15214	PTE
BAILEY	ALAN	22270	PTE
BAILEY	ALBERT	35688	PTE
BAILEY	ALBERT EDWARD	17861	CPL
BAILEY	CECIL	40951	PTE
BAILEY	CHARLES WILLIAM	49334	PTE
BAILEY	JAMES THOMPSON	18046	PTE
BAILEY	JOHN	32124	PTE
BAILEY	ROBERT	29439	PTE
BAILEY	WILLIAM	15215	L/CPL
BAINES	GEORGE HENRY	27259	PTE
BAINES	JOHN WILLIAM	15107	PTE
BAKER	THOMAS WILLIAM	17399	PTE
BAKER	WALTER	240302	PTE
BALDWIN	A.	19694	PTE

BALDWIN	EDWARD	22142	PTE
BALDWIN	GEORGE	13365	PTE
BALDWIN	JOHN RICHARD	15781	PTE
BALDWIN	JOSEPH	15602	PTE
BALL	JOHN ALBERT	37482	PTE
BALL	WILLIAM	30447	CPL
BAMFORD	HAROLD	17593	PTE
BAMFORD	WILLIAM	31435	PTE
BANKS	ROLAND	15216	PTE
BANKS	THOMAS	20975	PTE
BANNISTER	ALBERT	15768	PTE
BANNISTER	ARTHUR	15603	PTE
BANNISTER	HAROLD	202597	PTE
BARKER	ERNEST LEONARD	33948	PTE
BARKER	JAMES	15157	PTE
BARKER	JOHN	35617	PTE
BARKER	THOMAS	11474	PTE
BARKER	WALTER	33927	PTE
BARLOW	EDMUND	15300	PTE
BARLOW	RANDLE	29695	PTE
BARNES	BERTRAM	24899	PTE
BARNES	E.	17942	PTE
BARNES	EDGAR	15314	A/CPL
BARNES	FRED	31419	PTE
BARNES	GEORGE	15479	PTE
BARNES	GEORGE WORSWICK	15217	PTE
BARNES	HARRY	24266	PTE
BARNES	J.	15798	PTE
BARNES	JAMES	15301	PTE
BARNES	JAMES	15788	PTE
BARNES	JAMES	22288	PTE
BARNES	JAMES WILLIAM	26909	PTE
BARNES	JOSEPH	15769	PTE
BARNES	THALBERG	15262	PTE
BARNES	WAINWRIGHT	24777	CPL
BARNES	WILLIAM	32004	PTE
BARNES	WILLIAM	202132	PTE
BARON	ALBERT	15914	PTE
BARON	ALONZA	17967	PTE
BARON	J.	15315	PTE
BARON	JOSEPH	20935	PTE
BARON	PERCY	25310	PTE
BARON	WILLIAM	15478	PTE
BARON	WILLIAM	32114	PTE
BARRACLOUGH	FRANK	27275	CPL
BARRACLOUGH	FRED	27260	SGT
BARRAS	THOMAS	21856	PTE
BARRETT	ARTHUR	15687	PTE
BARRETT	RALPH	27276	PTE
BARRETT	THOMAS	10793	PTE
BARRETT	WILLIAM	33894	PTE
BARRON	RICHARD	16056	PTE
BARROW	ERNEST	16050	SGT
BARROW	JOHN	29428	PTE
BARROW	RICHARD	34365	PTE
BARROW	RICHARD MYERS	15841	PTE
BARTLETT	ERNEST	242726	PTE
BARTON	JAMES	29364	PTE
BARTROP	WILLIAM	15001	PTE
BATE	REGINALD	29411	PTE
BATE	WILLIAM	32080	PTE
BATEMAN	WALTER	27261	PTE
BATES	THOMAS	20904	A/CPL
BATESON	T.	16030	PTE
BATESON	THOMAS	35408	PTE
BATH	RANK	15108	CPL
BATHURST	GEORGE	25273	PTE
BATLEY	GEORGE ALEXANDER	19733	PTE
BATTS	MAURICE	31113	PTE
BAXENDALE	JAMES	33881	PTE
BAXTER	JAMES	33976	PTE

BAXTER	JOSEPH	15604	PTE
BAXTER	RICHARD	15560	PTE
BAXTER	ROBERT	31486	PTE
BAYLISS	JAMES	30567	PTE
BAYNES	FRED	39725	PTE
BEAGHAN	DAVID	15316	PTE
BEAGHAN	R.	15770	PTE
BEARD	ERNEST	15218	PTE
BEARLEY	JAMES	24711	PTE
BEAUMONT	WILFRED	33844	PTE
BECK	DOUGLAS	49246	PTE
BECKETT	WALTER	27029	SGT
BEDDARD	HORACE JAMES	29429	PTE
BEECH	JOSHUA	31474	WOII
BEESLEY	HARRY	33845	PTE
BEESTON	GEORGE	33896	PTE
BEETHAM	T. E.	17360	PTE
BEGBIE	ERNEST JONES	203235	PTE
BELL	EDMUND	33895	PTE
BELL	HAROLD	15737	PTE
BELL	JAMES	49263	PTE
BELL	JOSEPH	17882	PTE
BELL	WILLIAM	32078	PTE
BELL	WILLIAM	32079	PTE
BENBOW	ARTHUR	20984	PTE
BENBOW	ARTHUR JAMES	49480	PTE
BENNETT	CHARLES SYDNEY	31492	PTE
BENNETT	E.	15057	PTE
BENNETT	JAMES	31415	PTE
BENNETT	JAMES OSBORNE	49227	PTE
BENNETT	JONATHAN	21717	PTE
BENNETT	MATTHEW	16228	PTE
BENNETT	THOMAS	15953	CPL
BENNETT	WILLIAM	29436	PTE
BENSON		15455	PTE
BENSON	JOHN	49239	PTE
BENSON	WILLIAM	242397	PTE
BENTLEY	J.	15491	PTE
BENTLEY	JOHN	17971	PTE
BENTLEY	JOHN JAMES	40567	PTE
BENTLEY	OSWALD	15002	SGT
BENTLEY	W. H.	17925	PTE
BENTLEY	WILLIAM HENRY	35445	PTE
BERESFORD	STARKEY	15605	PTE
BERRY	ERNEST	26962	PTE
BERRY	GEORGE	202060	PTE
BERRY	JOHN	15842	COL.SGT
BERRY	ROBERT	241568	PTE
BERRY	THOMAS	15098	PTE
BERRY	THOMAS	15526	PTE
BERRYMAN	JAMES HENRY	23352	PTE
BEST	JOSEPH WATSON	32196	PTE
BEST	WILLIAM	15219	PTE
BESWICK	BERTRAM ROBERT	242490	A/CPL
BESWICK	CHARLES	242680	A/CPL
BETHELL	WILLIAM HERBERT	235076	PTE
BEWSHER	STANLEY M	18048	PTE
BEWSHER	WILLIAM DEMAIN	200558	PTE
BIBBY	ARTHUR	29015	PTE
BIBBY	CHARLEY	240475	PTE
BIBBY	CLEMENT ANDERTON	25283	PTE
BIBBY	HENRY	25007	PTE
BIBBY	JAMES	19013	PTE
BIBBY	WILLIAM HENRY	32123	PTE
BIBBY	WILLIAM THOMAS	201601	PTE
BICKLEY	ARTHUR	203151	PTE
BILLINGTON	ALFRED	24813	PTE
BILLINGTON	JOSHUS	28837	PTE
BILLINGTON	LESLIE	37019	PTE
BILLINGTON	WALTER CYRIL	27274	CPL
BIMPSON	JOHN	29419	PTE

BINGHAM	MATTHEW	19557	PTE
BINLESS	JOHN	16229	PTE
BIRCH	H.	17843	PTE
BIRCH	JAMES EDWARD	17996	PTE
BIRCH	RICHARD	40920	PTE
BIRCH	ROBERT	29437	PTE
BIRCHENOUGH	FREDERICK	6683	SGT
BIRD	F.	15220	PTE
BIRD	W. O.	15606	PTE
BIRNEY	JOSEPH	31489	PTE
BIRTWELL	A.	15838	PTE
BIRTWELL	CHARLES THOMAS	15317	PTE
BIRTWISTLE	JOHN WILLIAM	17864	A/SGT
BIRTWISTLE	LEONARD	35689	PTE
BIRTWISTLE	RICHARD	15109	PTE
BIRTWISTLE	RICHARD	16924	PTE
BLACK	FRED	40432	PTE
BLACKBURN	ALBERT	31394	PTE
BLACKBURN	FREDERICK WOOD	34392	PTE
BLACKBURN	WALTER	26672	PTE
BLACKHURST	ALBERT EDWARD	16960	PTE
BLACKLEDGE	THOMAS	15221	SGT
BLACKLER	JOHN	37904	PTE
BLACKLEY	THOMAS	16353	SGT
BLACKSHAW	JOHN GASCOYNE	37016	**PTE**
BLACKSTONE	JOHN	16057	PTE
BLACKWELL	HERBERT VICTOR	33873	PTE
BLACKWELL	REGINALD	31562	PTE
BLAKEY	FRED	21811	PTE
BLAMEY	WILLIAM HENRY	25241	PTE
BLAMIRE	ISAAC	40940	PTE
BLEARS	HERBERT	33921	PTE
BLEASDALE	R. E.	15003	PTE
BLEASDALE	RICHARD	27107	PTE
BLENKINSOP	JAMES WALTER	27262	SGT
BLEWITT	JOHN	31269	PTE
BLEZARD	JOHN	241545	PTE
BLOCK	MICHAEL	49346	PTE
BLOOR	HARRY	18047	PTE
BOARDMAN	EDWARD	17892	PTE
BOARDMAN	THOMAS	18024	PTE
BODEN	WILLIAM	15177	A/SGT
BOGLE	JAMES HENRY	37941	PTE
BOLTON	ALBERT JOHN	22378	PTE
BOLTON	JAMES ISHERWOOD	31561	PTE
BOLTON	WILLIAM	15641	PTE
BOND	FREDERICK	32003	PTE
BONNER	THOMAS WAMSLEY	30720	PTE
BOOCOCK	GEORGE ERNEST	25469	PTE
BOON	THOMAS EDWARD	20693	PTE
BOOTH	A.	15926	PTE
BOOTH	BERTRAM	15791	PTE
BOOTH	FREDERICK	23313	PTE
BOOTH	GEORGE	18044	PTE
BOOTH	GEORGE WILLIAM	49292	PTE
BOOTH	HAROLD THOMAS	242707	PTE
BOOTH	JOHN	12826	CPL
BOOTH	JOHN	26853	PTE
BOOTH	JOHN SPIERS	23304	PTE
BOOTHMAN	JOSEPH	20744	PTE
BORDESSA	ALPHONSO GEORGE	17488	PTE
BORMAN	THOMAS	37153	PTE
BOSWORTH	HAROLD ARTHUR	32313	PTE
BOTTOMLEY	HARRY	15885	PTE
BOTTOMLEY	JAMES WILLIAM	235563	PTE
BOTTOMLEY	LESLIE VINCENT	31488	PTE
BOTTOMLEY	WILLIAM	34947	PTE
BOUGHEY	WALTER ETHELBERT	38851	PTE
BOULTON	ALBERT	33922	PTE
BOUND	ERNEST	31421	PTE
BOWDEN	HENRY	202435	PTE

BOWDEN	JAMES EDWARD	33950	PTE
BOWERS	J. E.	15076	PTE
BOWERS	WALTER	24430	PTE
BOWERS	WILLIAM	15790	PTE
BOWKER	JOHN	18223	PTE
BOWLER	HAROLD	39057	PTE
BOWLING	JAMES	28570	PTE
BOWLING	JOHN	27087	PTE
BOWMAN	FRED	22252	PTE
BOX	JAMES	40099	PTE
BOX	SAMUEL	21255	PTE
BOYD	JOHN FREDERICK	18879	PTE
BOYLE	JAMES	8792	PTE
BOYNTON	GEORGE WILLIAM	32113	PTE
BRACEWELL	FREDERICK WILLIE	26316	A/CPL
BRACEWELL	WILLIAM	24999	PTE
BRADDOCK	FRED	201963	PTE
BRADDOCK	WILFRED	31566	PTE
BRADFORD	CLARENCE	30047	PTE
BRADFORD	FRED	36747	PTE
BRADLEY	ALBERT	28539	PTE
BRADLEY	ARTHUR	20961	PTE
BRADLEY	JOHN	16031	PTE
BRADLEY	WILLIAM HENRY	24412	PTE
BRADSHAW	JONATHAN	21875	PTE
BRADSHAW	RENNIE	25338	PTE
BRADSHAW	RUSSELL	15400	CPL
BRADSHAW	TOM	22865	PTE
BRADY	DANIEL	17950	A/SGT
BRADY	H.	15158	SGT
BRAITHWAITE	JOHN WILLIAM	49229	PTE
BRAMALD	WILFRED GEORGE	29440	PTE
BRAMALL	THOMAS	31564	PTE
BRAND	ISSAC	30279	PTE
BRANNIGAN	PATRICK	26130	PTE
BRAYLEY	ERNEST	17405	PTE
BRAYSHAW	JAMES WILLIAM	31565	PTE
BREAKS	**WILLIAM**	17837	PTE
BRECKELL	GEORGE EDWIN	15361	CPL
BREEN	WILLIAM	9708	PTE
BREEN	WILLIAM	29431	PTE
BRENNAN	ALBERT	36179	PTE
BRENNAN	EDMUND	35687	PTE
BRENNAN	JAMES	36324	PTE
BRENNAND	ARTHUR	38360	PTE
BRENNAND	TOM ASH	15222	PTE
BRETHERTON	WILLIAM	16070	PTE
BRICE	R.	15407	PTE
BRIDDON	BENJAMIN STANLEY	31563	PTE
BRIDGE	FRED HUDSON	40964	PTE
BRIDGE	JAMES	15385	COL.SGT
BRIDGE	ROBERT HENRY	24845	PTE
BRIGGS	EBENEZER	35618	PTE
BRIGGS	ROBERT	24417	PTE
BRIGGS	SAMUEL	7196	SGT
BRIGGS	WALTER	15223	PTE
BRINDLE	ARTHUR	19110	PTE
BRINDLE	FRANCIS	15159	PTE
BRINDLE	MATTHEW	38348	PTE
BRINDLE	ROBERT EDWARD	22304	PTE
BRISCOE	HENRY	29644	PTE
BRISTOW	SAMUEL	17647	PTE
BRITCLIFFE	JOSEPH	40893	PTE
BRITTLEBANK	ARTHUR	15293	CPL
BROADBENT	FRANK	22349	PTE
BROADBENT	JOHN	31396	PTE
BROADBENT	THOMAS HINDLE	32121	PTE
BROADHURST	JAMES	39642	PTE
BROADLEY	FRED	17839	PTE
BROADLEY	THOMAS	15111	L/CPL
BROMILEY	WILLIAM ARTHUR	35678	PTE

BROMLEY	JAMES	16004	PTE
BROMLEY	WILLIAM HENRY	37000	PTE
BROOKE	HERBERT	27265	PTE
BROOKFIELD	LEONARD	32125	PTE
BROOKS	ARTHUR	31395	PTE
BROOKS	JOHN	23142	PTE
BROOKS	JOHN	27264	PTE
BROOME	DAVID HENRY	32112	PTE
BROOME	JAMES	33832	PTE
BROTHERTON	JOHN FREDERICK	31423	PTE
BROUGHTON	EDWARD	17858	PTE
BROUGHTON	WALTER	20675	PTE
BROWN	ALBERT	30926	PTE
BROWN	ARTHUR	22977	PTE
BROWN	ARTHUR	31491	PTE
BROWN	BIRKETT	5553	PTE
BROWN	CHARLES HENRY	27001	PTE
BROWN	ERNEST	19693	PTE
BROWN	FRED	26200	PTE
BROWN	HARRY	16005	PTE
BROWN	HENRY	15527	PTE
BROWN	JAMES	31485	PTE
BROWN	JOHN WILLIAM	33830	SGT
BROWN	JOSEPH	15456	PTE
BROWN	JOSEPH	49251	PTE
BROWN	RUFUS	24452	PTE
BROWN	WALTER	54156	PTE
BROWN	WILLIAM	15707	PTE
BROWN	WILLIAM	21993	PTE
BROWN	WILLIAM	33959	PTE
BRUMWELL	ALBERT CHARLES	30582	PTE
BRUNSKILL	ARTHUR	15738	PTE
BRYAN	PERCY	32460	PTE
BRYCE	ROBERT	15401	PTE
BRYERS	DANIEL	15955	PTE
BUCKEL	ALBERT	20979	PTE
BUCKLEY	ARTHUR	16483	CPL
BUCKLEY	FRANK	15528	PTE
BUCKLEY	FRED	15982	SGT
BULCOCK	HENRY	31484	PTE
BULLEN	ROBERT	15708	PTE
BULLEN	THOMAS	16058	PTE
BULLEN	WALTER	29374	CPL
BULLOCK	ALFRED	23767	PTE
BULLOCK	DAVID	18049	PTE
BULLOCK	HERBERT	15608	PTE
BURBRIDGE	RICHARD	9184	SGT
BURGESS	ALFRED	32005	PTE
BURGESS	HENRY	31569	PTE
BURGESS	WILFRED	20280	PTE
BURGOYNE	RICHARD	33962	PTE
BURKE	WALTER FREDERICK	40980	PTE
BURLAND	JOHN WILLIE	24077	PTE
BURNS	WILLIAM	49254	PTE
BURR	LESLIE JAMES	31114	PTE
BURROW	RICHARD	40674	PTE
BURROWS	CHARLES	29492	PTE
BURROWS	JAMES RICHARD	15561	PTE
BURROWS	ROBERT	242852	PTE
BURROWS	STANLEY	20087	A/CPL
BURT	CHARLES EDWARD	31487	PTE
BURT	HAROLD REGINALD	26110	PTE
BURTENSHAW	ERNEST GEORGE	22194	T/WOI
BURTON	GEORGE FREDERICK	28864	PTE
BURY	ALBERT	15493	PTE
BURY	HARRY	15402	CPL
BURY	PERCY	15224	PTE
BURY	R. H.	15225	PTE
BURY	W.	17995	PTE
BURY	WILLIAM	18014	SGT
BUSH	WILLIAM	33326	PTE

BUTLER	A.	17341	PTE
BUTLER	HORACE	33869	PTE
BUTLER	JOHN	29408	PTE
BUTLER	JOHN WILLIAM	5302	CPL
BUTLER	THOMAS	29365	PTE
BUTTERFIELD	RICHARD	16285	CPL
BUTTERS	HARRY	31490	PTE
BUTTERWORTH	FRED	34460	PTE
BUTTERWORTH	GEORGE	202015	PTE
BUTTERWORTH	JORDAN	24272	PTE
BUTTERWORTH	RICHARD	34315	PTE
BUXTON	THOMAS	38420	PTE
BYRNE	DENIS	202344	PTE
BYRNE	JOHN LAWRENCE	36330	PTE
BYRNE	WALTER	15709	SGT
CAIGER	BENJAMIN	31436	CPL
CAIN	JAMES	32009	PTE
CALDERBANK	ARGYLL	25126	PTE
CALDERBANK	H.	15843	PTE
CALDERBANK	HENRY	15845	PTE
CALDWELL	HENRY	37839	PTE
CALVERLEY	ROBERT	15782	PTE
CALVERT	JACK	15886	PTE
CAMM	FRED	15739	PTE
CAMM	ROBERT	17553	PTE
CAMPBELL	DONALD	29069	PTE
CAMPBELL	HAROLD	6317	PTE
CAMPBELL	WILLIAM	200031	CPL
CANN	ARTHUR	33970	PTE
CANNON	WILLIAM	15160	PTE
CAREY	THOMAS	15494	PTE
CARNCROSS	ARTHUR EDWARD	30593	PTE
CARR	ARTHUR	30590	PTE
CARR	HARRY	31496	PTE
CARR	JOHN FRANCIS	49262	PTE
CARR	JOSEPH	36803	PTE
CARR	REUBEN	33946	PTE
CARR	WILLIAM	16006	PTE
CARRICK	MICHAEL THOMAS	30540	PTE
CARRICK	THOMAS EDWARD	49224	PTE
CARTER	ALFRED GERALD	30574	PTE
CARTER	GEORGE	27846	PTE
CARTER	HARRY	25190	PTE
CARTER	J.	18931	PTE
CARTER	THOMAS	25484	PTE
CARTIN	JOHN	39912	PTE
CARTMELL	WILLIAM	25460	PTE
CASELEY	WILLIAM JOHN GEORGE	31115	PTE
CASEY	JOSEPH	200768	PTE
CASS	EDWARD	31572	PTE
CASSIDY	FRANCIS	15929	PTE
CASSIDY	TOM	39214	PTE
CASSON	THOMAS	49256	PTE
CASSON	WALTER VICTOR	36971	PTE
CASTLE	GEORGE	30478	PTE
CATES	EDWARD	25317	PTE
CATLOW	ALFRED	21812	PTE
CATLOW	HARTLEY	35679	PTE
CATLOW	JAMES	13851	PTE
CATLOW	THOMAS	17475	PTE
CATTERALL	JAMES	9633	PTE
CATTERALL	RALPH	15264	PTE
CAUNCE	WALTER	32480	SGT
CAWLEY	FRANK LEE	16416	PTE
CAWTHRA	GEORGE HENRY	39428	PTE
CHADDERTON	STANLEY	33925	PTE
CHADWICK	EDWARD	15794	PTE
CHADWICK	GEORGE	29507	PTE
CHADWICK	HENRY	17997	PTE
CHADWICK	HERBERT	15227	PTE
CHADWICK	HERBERT	22265	PTE

215

Surname	Forename(s)	Number	Rank
CHADWICK	JOSEPH	15226	PTE
CHADWICK	THOMAS	240199	PTE
CHADWICK	TOM	35685	A/C/SGT
CHADWICK	WALTER	15112	PTE
CHADWICK	WALTER	33880	PTE
CHALLEN	STEPHEN BENJAMIN	15054	PTE
CHALLENDER	THOMAS	17106	PTE
CHAMBERLAIN	ROBERT	23900	PTE
CHAMBERLAIN	WALTER	39551	PTE
CHAMBERS	JOHN	17850	PTE
CHAMBERS	JOHN	20430	PTE
CHAPMAN	HARRY	15005	SGT
CHAPMAN	RICHARD	9211	A/CPL
CHAPMAN	WILLIAM	17876	PTE
CHAPMAN	WILLIAM EDWARD	27255	L/CPL
CHARLES	JOHN	27870	PTE
CHARNLEY	JAMES	40890	PTE
CHARNLEY	ROBERT	17862	PTE
CHATTLE	ALFRED	23307	PTE
CHEETHAM	ALFRED	240662	PTE
CHEETHAM	ARTHUR	29504	PTE
CHEQUER	JOHN	241690	PTE
CHERREY	JOSEPH	21718	SGT
CHESTER	ISAAC	33897	PTE
CHESTER	JAMES	26973	PTE
CHESWORTH	FRANK	235986	PTE
CHEW	JOSEPH RICHARD	24571	PTE
CHRIMES	THOMAS	29410	PTE
CHRISTIAN }	ABRAHAM	15562	PTE
CHRISTIAN }	ABRAHAM	35418	PTE
CHRISTOPHER	JOHN HENRY	31497	PTE
CLAGUE	WALTER SHIMMIN	32008	PTE
CLAPHAM	HENRY	24213	PTE
CLAPHAM	JOHN STUART	54322	PTE
CLAPHAM	JOHN WILLIAM	22363	PTE
CLARK	CHARLES	18031	PTE
CLARK	HARRY	240093	COL.SGT
CLARK	JACK	16033	PTE
CLARK	PERCY EDWARD	31118	PTE
CLARK	SAMUEL WALTER	31116	PTE
CLARK	W.	15461	PTE
CLARKE	F.	17946	PTE
CLARKE	WILLIAM	15193	PTE
CLARKE	JAMES PATRICK	37025	PTE
CLARKE	LESLIE WILLIAM	31107	PTE
CLARKE	PETER STANLEY	17859	PTE
CLARKE	SIDNEY	33834	PTE
CLARKE	THOMAS	32201	PTE
CLARKE	THOMAS	203549	PTE
CLARKSON	EDWARD	35620	PTE
CLARKSON	WILLIAM	15956	A/CPL
CLAWSON	HERBERT HOLLIS	32126	PTE
CLAYPOLE	CHARLES LESLIE	31495	PTE
CLAYTON	FRANK	30592	PTE
CLAYTON	GEORGE	15077	PTE
CLAYTON	HERBERT	15711	PTE
CLAYTON	JOHN REGINALD	16068	SGT
CLAYTON	T.	15642	PTE
CLAYTON	WILFRED	35425	PTE
CLEGG	HORACE	31498	PTE
CLEGG	JAMES	40212	PTE
CLEGG	PERCY	32131	PTE
CLEGG	SAMUEL	15206	SGT
CLEGG	WILLIAM	17983	PTE
CLEMENTS	ARTHUR JOHN	29381	PTE
CLEMMEY	WALTER	27143	PTE
CLIFFE	ALBERT EDWIN	24435	PTE
CLIFFE	ARTHUR	15889	PTE
CLIFFE	BERNARD	27268	PTE
CLIFFORD	THOMAS JEFFREY	32081	PTE
CLIFTON	RICHARD	242193	SGT
CLINCH	WILLIAM	26755	PTE
CLINTON	HARRY	24176	PTE
CLITHEROE	T.	15265	PTE
CLOUGH	HAROLD	32006	PTE
CLOUGH	JOHN CLARENCE	31571	CPL
CLOUGH	THOMAS	15869	PTE
CLOUGH	THOMAS	17916	PTE
CLOUGH	THOMAS EDWARD	39375	PTE
COADY	J.	15403	PTE
COADY	THOMAS	18011	PTE
COATES	JAMES	24152	PTE
COCHRANE	JOHN WILLIAM	32127	PTE
COCK	CHARLES	29443	PTE
COCK	JOHN ROPER	22261	CPL
COCKER	JAMES	28078	PTE
COCKER	JOSEPH	17932	PTE
COCKER	SAMUEL	37021	PTE
COCKLE	CHARLES	22540	PTE
CODD	A.	18982	PTE
COFFEY	JAMES	35619	PTE
COFFEY	JOHN	49316	PTE
COLCLOUGH	LUKE	15497	PTE
COLE	HAROLD WILLIAM	32132	PTE
COLE	NORBERT	242301	PTE
COLECLOUGH	J. W.	15610	PTE
COLEMAN	BERNARD	36977	PTE
COLEMAN	RICHARD ALEXANDER	31426	PTE
COLGAN	JOHN	15078	PTE
COLL	ROLAND	17984	PTE
COLLIER	GEORGE	15161	A/SGT
COLLIER	HENRY AUSTIN	31570	PTE
COLLIER	JAMES	41043	PTE
COLLINGE	HARRY	26918	PTE
COLLINGE	SQUIRE	37887	PTE
COLLINGE	WILLIAM ROBERT	15294	WOII
COLLINSON	JAMES	38805	PTE
COLLINSON	R.	15793	PTE
COLLIS	CHRISTOPHER	33850	CPL
COLLIS	LAWRENCE	20929	PTE
COLLISON	HARRY	23147	PTE
COLLUM	JAMES	200261	PTE
COMSTIVE	WILLIAM HENRY	28857	PTE
CONNOR	HARRY	32012	PTE
CONNOR	JOHN	18103	PTE
CONROY	THOMAS	5599	WOII
CONSTABLE	WILLIAM HENRY	32011	PTE
CONWAY	ARTHUR	15194	PTE
CONWAY	AUGUSTUS	22883	PTE
CONWAY	PATRICK	16489	PTE
COOK	GEORGE	15555	PTE
COOK	JAMES HEDLEY	40950	PTE
COOK	JOHN	15712	PTE
COOK	RICHARD	27629	PTE
COOK	THOMAS	15915	PTE
COOK	VICTOR	200787	PTE
COOK	VINCENT	15888	PTE
COOK	WALTER	22374	PTE
COOK	WELLINGTON	36538	PTE
COOK	WILLIAM	24924	PTE
COOKE	ALBERT EDWARD	29387	PTE
COOKSON	EDWARD	35427	PTE
COOKSON	GEORGE	15713	CPL
COOKSON	SAMUEL	13675	PTE
COOPER	A.	18057	PTE
COOPER	EDWIN JOHN	30389	PTE
COOPER	HARRY	39426	PTE
COOPER	JAMES	36385	PTE
COOPER	LEONARD DAUNT	37857	PTE
COOPER	ROBERT	28805	PTE
COOPER	ROBERT	40339	PTE
COOPER	ROBERT CUMMING	200930	PTE

Surname	Forename(s)	Number	Rank
COOTE	FRANCIS	201126	PTE
CORBRIDGE	LEONARD	36266	PTE
CORBRIDGE	WALTER	35143	PTE
CORDERY	MORTIMER GEORGE	31437	PTE
CORK	WILLIAM RENNIE	37634	PTE
CORNES	FREDERICK	32007	PTE
CORNWALL	J.	17848	PTE
CORNWELL	JOHN	39077	PTE
CORNWELL	T.	15643	L/CPL
COSGROVE	MICHAEL	31438	SGT
COSGROVE	PATRICK	15485	PTE
COSTELLO	JOHN	22188	PTE
COTTAM	ISAAC	240375	PTE
COTTER	BENJAMIN	17831	PTE
COTTER	HENRY	18636	PTE
COTTOM	J.	17844	PTE
COULTHARD	ROBERT	37921	PTE
COULTHIRST	WILLIAM	30589	PTE
COULTON	JOHN	241058	PTE
COULTRIP	HENRY JAMES	9964	SGT
COUNSELL	JAMES	29442	PTE
COUPE	EDWARD	15870	PTE
COURTNEY	GEORGE	14979	PTE
COURTNEY	JOHN	16664	PTE
COUSINS	WILLIAM HENRY	236005	PTE
COWBURN	HARRY	15079	SGT
COWELL	JOHN WILLIAM	15644	PTE
COWGILL	ALBERT	22343	PTE
COWGILL	N.	15006	L/CPL
COWIE	ARTHUR	30533	PTE
COWLEY	WILLIAM	38233	A/CPL
COWLING	FRED	204166	PTE
COWPE	HARRY	36817	PTE
COWPE	WILLIAM	16034	PTE
COWSILL	JOHN	13502	PTE
COWX	THOMAS	32128	PTE
COX	CHARLES	15927	PTE
COX	JOHN	15404	PTE
COX	JOHN	240301	PTE
COYNE	MICHAEL	6615	PTE
CRABTREE	CHRISTOPHER	23314	PTE
CRABTREE	GEORGE WILLIAM	15714	PTE
CRABTREE	JAMES ARTHUR	37024	PTE
CRABTREE	JOHN	6240	PTE
CRABTREE	PERCY	24799	PTE
CRABTREE	SAM	15928	L/CPL
CRAGG	ALAN	16405	PTE
CRAGGS	ANTHONY	20016	PTE
CRANE	WILLIAM	16371	PTE
CRANKSHAW	ERNEST	37285	PTE
CRANKSHAW	SYDNEY	240765	PTE
CRANSHAW	RALPH	39291	PTE
CRAVEN	JAMES	33928	PTE
CRAWFORD	WILLIAM WILSON	15405	PTE
CRAWSHAW	EDMUND	26169	PTE
CRAWSHAW	FRED	240204	PTE
CRAWSHAW	GEORGE	5593	PTE
CREASEY	WILLIAM JAMES	28244	PTE
CREER	EDWARD	32172	PTE
CRITCHLEY	J. H.	15848	PTE
CRITCHLEY	MARK	38639	PTE
CRITCHLOW	ARTHUR	39749	CPL
CROMARTY	MAGNUS JAMES	32487	SGT
CROMPTON	ARTHUR	27269	PTE
CROMPTON	EDWARD	29352	PTE
CROMPTON	WILLIAM	32130	PTE
CRONKSHAW	HOWARTH	22335	PTE
CRONSHAW	RICHARD	10990	PTE
CROOK	FRED	31494	PTE
CROOK	GEORGE	21845	SGT
CROPPER	JOSEPH	235290	PTE
CROSBY	JOHN	33516	PTE
CROSBY	WILLIAM	29918	PTE
CROSS	ARTHUR	18973	PTE
CROSS	FRED	39594	PTE
CROSS	HAROLD	31424	PTE
CROSS	RICHARD	22313	PTE
CROSS	WILLIAM	22828	CPL
CROSSLEY	DANIEL	35430	PTE
CROSSLEY	HAROLD	31422	PTE
CROSSLEY	HERBERT	15740	PTE
CROSSLEY	HERBERT	35621	PTE
CROSSLEY	JOHN LESLIE	21990	PTE
CROSSLEY	WILLIE	40698	PTE
CROUCHER	WILLIAM HENRY	36455	SGT
CROWE	ARTHUR	31108	PTE
CROWTHER	PHILIP	37020	PTE
CRYER	HERBERT	15890	PTE
CUERDEN	AUSTIN	15850	PTE
CULLEN	MICHAEL	18966	PTE
CULLEN	P.	18078	PTE
CULLEN	PETER	25468	PTE
CULLEY	ERNEST	15795	CPL
CULSHAW	GEORGE	15849	PTE
CUNLIFFE	BENJAMIN	21978	CPL
CUNLIFFE	FRANK	15306	PTE
CUNLIFFE	GEORGE VICTOR	203725	PTE
CUNLIFFE	JOHN	15007	L/CPL
CUNLIFFE	ROBERT	22348	PTE
CUNLIFFE	WILLIAM JAMES	26989	PTE
CUNLIFFE	WRIGHT	22285	PTE
CUNNINGHAM	PETER	17852	PTE
CUNNINGHAM	SAMUEL	33936	PTE
CURLEY	FRANK	32107	PTE
CURNOCK	BERNARD	31117	PTE
CURTIS	EDWARD	24815	PTE
CUTLER	ERNEST	15645	CPL
DAKIN	FRANK	15871	PTE
DAKIN	WILLIAM	15277	PTE
DALE	ALFRED	39877	PTE
DALE	WILLIAM	33828	PTE
DALEY	JOHN	240025	CPL
DALGLEISH	JAMES SCOT	22104	PTE
DALTON	HUGH	16060	PTE
DARBYSHIRE	JAMES	203660	PTE
DARLINGTON	JOHN	15408	PTE
DARWIN	LEONARD	29445	PTE
DAVEY	JOHN DENNIS	15741	PTE
DAVIES	DAVID JAMES	40798	PTE
DAVIES	FREDERICK	15376	PTE
DAVIES	HENRY	15595	PTE
DAVIES	HENRY	26177	PTE
DAVIES	JOHN HENRY	15715	CPL
DAVIES	JOSEPH	29401	PTE
DAVIES	LEONARD	32017	PTE
DAVIES	ROBERT EDWARD	33982	PTE
DAVIES	ROBERT JAMES	32016	PTE
DAVIES	SIDNEY PHILLIP	14613	PTE
DAVIES	TALIESIN	41048	PTE
DAVIES	WILLIAM	35428	PTE
DAVIES	WILLIAM HENRY	32085	PTE
DAVIS	ERIC	202470	PTE
DAVIS	HENRY	15762	PTE
DAVIS	JOHN THOMAS	17987	PTE
DAVIS	THOMAS	17986	PTE
DAVISON	JAMES	35623	PTE
DAWSON	ALBERT	31503	PTE
DAWSON	J. E.	18792	PTE
DAWSON	JOHN	20080	PTE
DAWSON	JOSEPH ARTHUR	40361	PTE
DAWSON	OSCAR	29444	PTE
DAWSON	RICHARD	17977	PTE

DAY	ALFRED	32082	PTE		DOWD	JOSEPH WILLIAM	24085	CPL
DAY	H.	16844	PTE		DOWELL	STANLEY JAMES	32110	CPL
DEACOCK	JOHN BRINSMEAD	31119	PTE		DOWLING	SAMUEL	40295	PTE
DEAN	BOB	35454	A/CPL		DOWNES	ALFRED	15231	PTE
DEAN	GEORGE	15930	PTE		DOWNEY	J.	15059	PTE
DEAN	HAROLD	34907	PTE		DOWNING	WILLIAM	29678	PTE
DEAN	HAROLD FRANK	31499	PTE		DOYLE	JAMES	241088	PTE
DEAN	HERBERT	26266	PTE		DOYLE	LAWRENCE	32115	PTE
DEAN	JOHN	22312	PTE		DRAINE	ROBERT	30715	PTE
DEAN	JOHN	31425	PTE		DRAPER	HARRY	31501	PTE
DEAN	R.	15391	PTE		DRAY	FREDERICK	10013	PTE
DEARNALEY	AMOS	31473	WOII		DRINKWATER	THOMAS WILLIAM HENRY	16009	PTE
DEGENHARDT	HORACE GEORGE	40014	PTE		DRIVER	JOHN	26792	PTE
DELANEY	JOSEPH	33944	PTE		DRIVER	ROBERT	17941	SGT
DELANEY	THOMAS	13744	PTE		DRIVER	ROBERT	200579	SGT
DELLOW	LEVI	30290	PTE		DUCKETT	JOHN	36319	PTE
DEMBRY	RALPH	33898	PTE		DUCKWORTH	BENJAMIN TREASURE	15278	SGT
DEMPSEY	PATRICK	15499	PTE		DUCKWORTH	HERBERT	37880	PTE
DENNEY	JOHN	15872	CPL		DUCKWORTH	JAMES	28469	PTE
DENT	ARTHUR	15362	CPL		DUCKWORTH	JAMES	35682	PTE
DENT	HARRY	39227	PTE		DUCKWORTH	ROBERT	27089	PTE
DENTON	EDWARD	32134	PTE		DUCKWORTH	THOMAS HENRY	15771	PTE
DERBYSHIRE	JOSEPH	15851	PTE		DUCKWORTH	W.	15797	PTE
DERBYSHIRE	WILLIAM	15436	PTE		DUCKWORTH	WILLIAM	15984	SGT
DEWHURST	ALFRED	17890	PTE		DUDDLE	ALBERT	242167	PTE
DEWHURST	HENRY	15230	PTE		DUDDLE	HENRY	235987	PTE
DEWHURST	JOHN HENRY	23760	PTE		DUDLEY	THOMAS	24274	CPL
DEWHURST	RICHARD HENRY	26952	PTE		DUERDEN	DAVID	23146	PTE
DEWHURST	THOMAS	27092	PTE		DUERDEN	EDWIN	34823	PTE
DEWHURST	THOMAS	40965	PTE		DUERDEN	FRED	41031	PTE
DEWHURST	WILLIAM	31417	PTE		DUERDEN	ORRELL TAYLOR	17870	PTE
DICKENS	JOHN	39526	PTE		DUERDEN	ROBERT EDWARD	15322	PTE
DICKENSON	JAMES	15957	PTE		DUFFELL	ALFRED ERNEST	241893	PTE
DICKINSON	A.	15742	PTE		DUFFY	CHARLES STUART	15116	SGT
DICKINSON	GEORGE ALFRED	241890	PTE		DUFFY	JOHN THOMAS	51233	PTE
DICKINSON	JOHN	242713	PTE		DUGDALE	JOHN	19369	A/SGT
DICKINSON	JOSEPH CLARENCE	31500	PTE		DUGDALE	WILLIAM	11727	PTE
DICKINSON	ROBIN	34905	PTE		DUGGAN	PETER JOHN	38363	PTE
DICKINSON	THOMAS	15563	PTE		DULLENTY	MARTIN	22165	PTE
DIGGLE	HORACE EDMUND	31502	PTE		DUNCAN	FREDERICK ALEXANDER	10801	PTE
DILLON	FRANCIS RAYMOND	26168	PTE		DUNKLEY	WILLIAM	15207	PTE
DILWORTH	EDGAR	27141	PTE		DUNN	CHARLES REGINALD	32105	PTE
DITCHBURN	LLOYD	49235	PTE		DUNN	GEORGE	25488	PTE
DIX	ALFRED BOON	18017	PTE		DUNN	WALTER STUART	27251	PTE
DIXON	ALBERT	40433	PTE		DURRANT	HAROLD WARREN	32133	PTE
DIXON	EDMUND	49234	PTE		DURRANT	WILLIAM HENRY	31120	PTE
DIXON	ERNEST	22364	PTE		DUST	THOMAS FRANK	15556	PTE
DIXON	FRANK BRADLEY	37849	PTE		DUTSON	T.	15296	PTE
DIXON	HARRY	15689	PTE		DUTTON	HAROLD	241898	PTE
DIXON	R.	15979	PTE		DUTTON	JOHN THOMAS	31427	PTE
DOBSON	ALFRED	15080	SGT		DUTTON	RICHARD	38706	PTE
DOBSON	FRANK	26677	PTE		DUXBURY	ALBERT	17773	PTE
DOBSON	GEORGE	37118	PTE		DUXBURY	JAMES	5604	CPL
DODD	HERBERT	23296	PTE		DUXBURY	WILLIAM	24202	PTE
DODD	J. W.	15378	PTE		DWYER	FRANK	10993	CPL
DODDS	LANCELOT	49226	PTE		DYKE	FRANK	33862	A/CPL
DOE	JOHN CHARLES JAMES	201746	PTE		DYSON	JAMES	17945	PTE
DOHERTY }	THOMAS	15008	PTE		DYSON	WILLIAM	33893	PTE
DOHERTY }	THOMAS	203609	PTE		EAGLES	ARTHUR	15307	CPL
DOIDGE	THOMAS HENRY	25154	PTE		EALES	CHRISTOPHER PALMER	33900	PTE
DONALD	WILLIAM RAY	49257	PTE		EARDLEY	EDWARD	30602	PTE
DONNELLY	HARRY	32015	PTE		EARNSHAW	JOSEPH ADAMSON	34381	PTE
DONNELLY	JOHN	201495	PTE		EARNSHAW	THOMAS	21849	PTE
DOOLEY	J.	17885	SGT		EASTHAM	ALBERT	37823	PTE
DOOLEY	JAMES	30595	PTE		EASTHAM	JOHN	40697	PTE
DORNING	HARRY	30572	L/CPL		EASTWOOD	JOSEPH	31504	PTE
DORRINGTON	HARRY	17237	CPL		EASTWOOD	WILLIAM	30600	PTE
DORWARD	GEORGE	33899	PTE		EBORN	J. H.	18039	PTE
DOUGHERTY	WILLIAM	16035	PTE		ECCLES	JAMES	24951	PTE
DOUTHWAITE	WALTER	24723	PTE		ECCLES	JAMES	26514	L/CPL
DOVEY	HENRY WILFRED	32151	PTE		ECKERSLEY	HARRY	242459	SGT

218

Surname	Forename(s)	Number	Rank
EDDLESTON	ARNOLD	37115	PTE
EDDLESTON	E.	15233	PTE
EDDY	CHARLES RITCHIE	39726	PTE
EDGE	ISRAEL	15082	SGT
EDGE	WILLIAM	201791	PTE
EDMONDSON	FRANK	27012	PTE
EDMUNDSON	ARTHUR	235045	PTE
EDMUNDSON	JOHN	37274	PTE
EDWARDS	ALFRED	18969	PTE
EDWARDS	ALFRED SIDNEY	15891	PTE
EDWARDS	CHARLES	25157	PTE
EDWARDS	JOHN	21391	PTE
EDWARDS	ROBERT	202514	PTE
EDWARDS	WILLIAM	29389	PTE
EDWARDS	WILLIAM	32019	PTE
EDWARDS	WILLIAM	32156	PTE
ELLIOTT	FRED	35684	SGT
ELLIOTT	JOHN	33425	PTE
ELLIOTT	OTHO RICHARD	31559	SGT
ELLIS	CHARLES	29649	PTE
ELLIS	J.	17075	PTE
ELLIS	STANLEY	36555	PTE
ELLIS	W.	16061	PTE
ELLISON	BENJAMIN	26104	PTE
ELLISON	JOHN	34761	PTE
ELLISON	THOMAS	40722	PTE
ELLISON	WILFRED	15267	PTE
ELLWOOD	EDWARD	31505	CPL
ELMS	ARTHUR	18163	PTE
EMMETT	JAMES HARGREAVES	21987	PTE
EMMOTT	WALTER	36978	PTE
EMMOTT	WALTER	36978	PTE
ENDERBY	JOSEPH	15646	PTE
ENGLISH	ROBERT	21816	PTE
ENGLISH	THOMAS FRANCIS MALONE	32018	PTE
ENGLISH	W.	15119	PTE
ENTWISTLE	CARSWELL	15437	PTE
ENTWISTLE	GEORGE	201715	PTE
ENTWISTLE	HERBERT	21985	PTE
ENTWISTLE	JOHN	26281	PTE
ENTWISTLE	JOSEPH	24770	PTE
ENTWISTLE	JOSEPH	36331	PTE
ENTWISTLE	T.	15409	PTE
ENWRIGHT	A.	15716	PTE
ETHERIDGE	THOMAS STANLEY	51230	PTE
ETHERINGTON	WALTER	35626	PTE
EVANS	BRIAN	10524	SGT
EVANS	JOHN ELWIN	30603	PTE
EVANS	JOHN HOWARD	15986	PTE
EVANS	WILLIAM	31506	PTE
EVANS	WILLIAM CLEMENT	15500	CPL
EWING	CYRIL GEORGE	31507	PTE
FADDEN	MICHAEL	15958	CPL
FAGG	ARTHUR JAMES	33964	PTE
FAIREY	STANLEY	16036	PTE
FAIRWEATHER	ORMOND	20971	PTE
FARGEN	MICHAEL	26153	PTE
FARLEY	HERBERT	26878	PTE
FARMER	ALBERT JOHN	31121	PTE
FARNWORTH	JOHN	24688	PTE
FARRAR	HARRY	38342	PTE
FARRELL	JAMES	15323	PTE
FAULKNER	PERCY	35709	PTE
FAWCETT	EDWARD REAY	30606	PTE
FAWCETT	FRANK	15932	PTE
FEASEY	CHARLES FREDERICK	31111	PTE
FEATHERS	HARRY	32021	PTE
FELDWICK	THOMAS	200769	CPL
FELL	EDGAR	35140	PTE
FELL	FRANK	15010	PTE
FELL	HARRY	15235	PTE
FENDER	JOHN SAMUEL	30473	CPL
FENN	ALFRED	27280	PTE
FENNELL	WILLIAM BROMFIELD	32022	PTE
FENTON	GEORGE	29351	CPL
FERGUSON	DAVID	29446	PTE
FIELD	CHARLES HORACE	11039	PTE
FIELDING	AARON	200533	PTE
FIELDING	HENRY	17640	PTE
FIELDING	HENRY	24137	PTE
FIELDING	J.	17827	PTE
FIELDING	JAMES WILLIAM	37826	PTE
FIELDING	JOHN	38350	PTE
FIELDING	ROBERT	22152	PTE
FIELDING	THOMAS GOODWIN	31428	PTE
FIELDING	WILLIAM THOMAS	15801	PTE
FIFIELD	WALTER	15011	PTE
FINAN	THOMAS	15269	PTE
FINNEY	WILLIAM	17889	PTE
FINNIGAN	JOSEPH	35627	PTE
FIRTH	ARTHUR	31195	PTE
FIRTH	JOHN	10061	SGT
FIRTH	WILFRED	34911	PTE
FISH	GEORGE	36287	PTE
FISH	JAMES	23134	PTE
FISHER	ARCHIBALD	29412	PTE
FISHER	FRED	36351	PTE
FISHER	ROBERT	20517	PTE
FISHWICK	ARTHUR INCE	40661	PTE
FISHWICK	WILLIAM ALFRED	29028	PTE
FISHWICK	WILLIAM ALFRED	29082	PTE
FISK	ERNEST	32137	PTE
FITZGERALD	ALBERT EDWARD	31429	PTE
FIXTER	GILBERT	54469	PTE
FLANAGAN	JAMES	240669	PTE
FLEGG	JOHN	18208	PTE
FLEMING	JAMES	16316	WOII
FLEMING	THOMAS	204019	PTE
FLETCHER	ALFRED	26993	PTE
FLETCHER	ALFRED SALISBURY	33969	PTE
FLETCHER	ARTHUR KAY	15566	PTE
FLETCHER	HERBERT	31430	PTE
FLETCHER	PETER	15071	CPL
FLETCHER	WALTER	15717	PTE
FLYNN	C.	17855	PTE
FLYNN	FRANK	23592	CPL
FODEN	JOHN	27007	SGT
FODEN	JOHN WILLIAM	16037	PTE
FOGG	ROBERT	15615	PTE
FOLAN	MARTIN	15987	SGT
FOREMAN	ARTHUR	16419	PTE
FORREST	ARTHUR	29447	PTE
FORREST	HENRY DACRE	15279	PTE
FORT	HENRY	28034	PTE
FOSTER	GEORGE	23866	PTE
FOSTER	J. H.	17096	PTE
FOSTER	PHILIP	18013	SGT
FOSTER	THOMAS	54426	PTE
FOULDS	ARTHUR	39396	PTE
FOULDS	WILLIAM	26718	PTE
FOWLER	FRANK ROBINSON	32023	PTE
FOX	FRANCIS	16381	CPL
FOX	WILLIAM	26865	PTE
FRANCE	ALBERT	15647	PTE
FRANCE	JOHN RICHARD	33878	PTE
FRANCIS	THOMAS EDWARD	15476	PTE
FRANCIS	WILLIAM HORACE	29802	PTE
FRANKLAND	ARTHUR	34821	PTE
FRANKLAND	JOHN EDMUND	201058	PTE
FREE	JOSEPH	32020	PTE
FREEMAN	WILLIAM	38703	PTE
FRYER	JOHN	40975	PTE

Surname	Forename(s)	Number	Rank
FULLALOVE	ALFRED	24316	PTE
FULLELOVE	WILLIAM	32136	PTE
FULLER	JOHN WILLIAM	51228	PTE
FULLER	THOMAS DYSON	30292	PTE
FULLER	WILLIAM	14763	PTE
FULTON	WALTER	28295	PTE
GADD	FRANK	37163	PTE
GALE	WILLIAM EDWARD	49248	PTE
GALLAGHER	BRIAN	40169	PTE
GALLAGHER	JOHN	5455	A/WOI
GALLAGHER	JOHN	30479	PTE
GALLAGHER	JOHN	40792	PTE
GALLAGHER	THOMAS	30620	PTE
GALLAGHER	WILLIAM	15280	PTE
GALLON	JOSEPH WILLIAM	32503	PTE
GAMMON	RICHARD	30018	PTE
GARBERT	GEORGE STANLEY	31508	PTE
GARBUTT	JACK	30497	PTE
GARDNER	HARRY	31511	PTE
GARDNER	JAMES	27101	PTE
GARDNER	JOHN JAMES	33902	PTE
GARNER	THOMAS	40966	PTE
GARNHAM	GEORGE WILLIAM	39131	PTE
GARRATT	HILTON	31398	PTE
GARSFIELD	J.	16900	PTE
GASKELL	ARTHUR	20895	PTE
GASKELL	JAMES	15162	CPL
GASKELL	JOHN	8722	SGT
GASKELL	T.	16424	PTE
GASKELL	THOMAS	15438	PTE
GATWARD	ALBERT LESLIE	29390	PTE
GEE	WILLIAM	39352	PTE
GELDARD	JOSEPH	18433	PTE
GELLING	JAMES	18411	PTE
GENT	JOHN	15529	PTE
GEORGE	JOHN IEUAN	34526	SGT
GERAGHTY	THOMAS LOUIS	22109	PTE
GERRARD	GEORGE STANLEY	39445	PTE
GERRARD	WILLIAM JAMES	20496	PTE
GIBBENS	SIDNEY HOLLOWAY	27295	A/CPL
GIBBONS	EDWIN	40732	PTE
GIBBS	EDWIN	34406	PTE
GIBSON	ALBERT	15501	PTE
GIBSON	EDWARD	17370	PTE
GIBSON	T. S.	15502	PTE
GIBSON	THOMAS EDWARD	201461	PTE
GIBSON	THOMAS SPENCER	15012	PTE
GILBANK	FREDERICK	236006	PTE
GILBERT	RICHARD MORGAN	236249	PTE
GILCHRIST	HENRY	49284	PTE
GILES	ROBERT	36502	CPL
GILL	CHRISTOPHER	33823	PTE
GILL	JAMES	242222	PTE
GILL	ROBERT	19592	PTE
GILLESPIE	ARCHIBALD	33884	PTE
GILLESPIE	WILLIAM	5662	PTE
GILLINGS	HERBERT	16352	PTE
GILMARTIN	WILLIAM	15208	PTE
GIRLING	SIDNEY VICTOR STANLEY	23922	SGT
GLEAVE	JOSEPH HENRY	30615	PTE
GLEDHILL	NEWTON	25189	PTE
GLEDHILL	THOMAS LAWRENCE	32552	COL.SGT
GLEWS	JOHN THOMAS	14797	SGT
GLOVER	CLARENCE	15013	PTE
GLOVER	FRANK	202301	PTE
GODFREY	ALBERT	23960	PTE
GODFREY	CHARLES STRATFORD	40819	PTE
GOLIGHTLY	JOHN ARNOLD	49231	PTE
GOOD	WILLIAM CHARLES	34829	PTE
GOODFELLOW	SYDNEY	39649	A/CPL
GOODIER	ERNEST	22314	PTE
GOODWIN	HAROLD	30611	PTE
GOODWIN	SIDNEY HARRY	33931	PTE
GORDON	BERNARD	27163	PTE
GORDON	HARRY	17386	PTE
GORSE	JAMES	37126	PTE
GORST	HARRY	37704	PTE
GORST	WILKINSON	15462	PTE
GOTTS	CLARENCE AUGUSTUS	31122	PTE
GOULDSBROUGH	THOMAS	27079	PTE
GOULSTONE	ARCHIBALD	29391	PTE
GOWER	JAMES	33947	PTE
GRADY	WILLIAM	40850	PTE
GRAHAM	ARCHIBALD	32024	PTE
GRAHAM	GEOFFREY	18036	PTE
GRAHAM	GEORGE	17836	PTE
GRAHAM	GEORGE	36915	PTE
GRAHAM	GEORGE ALBERT	40827	PTE
GRAHAM	JAMES EDWARD	30495	PTE
GRAHAM	REGINALD	238002	SGT
GRAHAM	THOMAS	30618	PTE
GRAHAM	WILLIAM ARTHUR	30614	PTE
GRAVELL	FREDERICK	49478	PTE
GRAY	JOHN	49258	PTE
GRAYSMARK	WILLIAM	31123	PTE
GRAYSON	JAMES	17939	PTE
GREAVES	GEORGE	15302	PTE
GREAVES }	WALTER	15261	PTE
GREAVES }	WALTER	35421	PTE
GREEN	ALFRED	29421	PTE
GREEN	JAMES	35628	PTE
GREEN	JAMES HENRY	33865	PTE
GREEN	JAMES RICHARD	17149	PTE
GREEN	JESSE	15387	PTE
GREEN	JOHN	30610	PTE
GREEN	JOHN	30612	PTE
GREEN	JOHN THOMAS	30619	PTE
GREEN	JOSEPH	19959	PTE
GREEN	LEWIS WALTER	37038	PTE
GREEN	ROBERT	38859	PTE
GREEN	W.	15417	PTE
GREEN	WILLIAM	15164	PTE
GREEN	WILLIAM	29404	CPL
GREENHALGH	FRED	15591	PTE
GREENHALGH	WILLIAM	31510	PTE
GREENING	BERTRAM	40801	PTE
GREENLAW	WILLIAM HENRY	30617	PTE
GREENWELL	MARK	33901	PTE
GREENWOOD	ANDREW RAYMOND	5062	CPL
GREENWOOD	BARTHOLOMEW	28483	PTE
GREENWOOD	BRIDGE	15616	PTE
GREENWOOD	FRANK	32138	PTE
GREENWOOD	FRED	24523	PTE
GREENWOOD	GEORGE WILLIAM	35690	PTE
GREENWOOD	HARRY	36383	PTE
GREENWOOD	JOHN	40512	PTE
GREENWOOD	JOHN	40717	PTE
GREENWOOD	JOHN ROBERT	40296	PTE
GREENWOOD	JOHN WILLIAM	16972	PTE
GREENWOOD	JOSEPH HENRY	17914	PTE
GREENWOOD	PETER	26842	PTE
GREENWOOD	ROBERT	29392	PTE
GREENWOOD	WILLIAM	15854	PTE
GREGORY	HARRY	40141	PTE
GREGORY	JAMES	28023	PTE
GREGORY	JOSEPH HENRY	33903	PTE
GREGSON	DAVID	25387	PTE
GREGSON	FRED	36558	PTE
GREGSON	HAROLD GEORGE	32025	PTE
GREGSON	JOHN BROADLEY	29448	PTE
GRESTY	JAMES	39385	PTE
GRIBBIN	CHARLES EDWARD	38279	PTE

Surname	Name	Number	Rank
GRICE	J. W.	25482	PTE
GRICE	WILLIAM	17849	PTE
GRIERSON	THOMAS	16715	CPL
GRIFFIN	THOMAS JOSEPH	34690	PTE
GRIFFIN	WALTER	25247	PTE
GRIFFITHS	EDWARD	20410	PTE
GRIFFITHS	HUGH HAROLD	32026	PTE
GRIFFITHS	ROBERT	29402	PTE
GRIFFITHS	THOMAS	15237	PTE
GRIFFITHS	THOMAS	202233	PTE
GRIFFITHS	THOMAS CLIFFORD	33932	PTE
GRILLS	GEORGE MOSS	36372	PTE
GRIME	JOHN	37646	PTE
GRIME	JOSEPH	40087	PTE
GRIMSHAW	FREDERICK	201521	PTE
GRIMSHAW	GEORGE	35629	PTE
GRIMSHAW	GEORGE	41049	PTE
GRIMSHAW	HENRY	15121	PTE
GRIMSHAW	JOSEPH	8152	PTE
GRIMSHAW	JOSEPH	17920	PTE
GRIMSHAW	SYDNEY ROBLEY	32027	PTE
GRIMSHAW	THOMAS	16011	SGT
GRIMSHAW	WALTER	40080	PTE
GRIMSHAW	WILLIAM	15211	CPL
GRIMSHAW	WILLIAM	17834	PTE
GRIMSTONE	RALPH	49288	PTE
GRINDALL	STANLEY	27253	PTE
GRINDLEY	HARRY	32086	PTE
GRINDROD	JAMES HENRY	26102	PTE
GROGAN	LEO	49253	PTE
GROOME	ARTHUR	12054	PTE
GROVES	ARTHUR	22027	PTE
GRUE	HENRY	21214	SGT
GRUNDRILL	ARTHUR	27283	PTE
GRUNDY	T.	18029	PTE
GUNNING	THOMAS	10614	PTE
GURNHILL	GEORGE WILLIAM	29513	PTE
GUY	ERNEST	34615	PTE
HACKING	ALBERT	40713	PTE
HACKING	FRED	15584	PTE
HACKING	PERCY	24758	PTE
HADDEN	FRED	23308	PTE
HADDOCK	CHARLES	38673	PTE
HADFIELD	JAMES	15898	PTE
HAGGART	WILLIAM	38685	PTE
HAGGERTY	GEORGE	15503	PTE
HAGUE	JAMES	16252	PTE
HAGUE	WILLIAM	240231	PTE
HAIGH	REGINALD	18041	PTE
HAIL	THOMAS GORDON	49247	PTE
HAILWOOD	WILLIAM	15959	PTE
HAINES	HAROLD ADOLPHUS	31453	A/CPL
HAINING	J.	15614	PTE
HALE	CHARLES	37113	PTE
HALE	HENRY	15463	CPL
HALEWOOD	LEWIS	15690	PTE
HALL	HARCOURT	241966	PTE
HALL	HERBERT	49260	PTE
HALL	JAMES EDMUND	32139	PTE
HALL	JOHN	241015	PTE
HALL	WILLIAM	15439	SGT
HALL	WILLIAM	33926	PTE
HALL	WILLIAM HENRY	40093	PTE
HALLIWELL	ARTHUR	15550	C/SGT
HALLIWELL	JAMES	39468	PTE
HALLIWELL	WILLIAM HENRY	38179	PTE
HALSTEAD	ALBERT	15567	PTE
HALSTEAD	CHARLES	240018	PTE
HALSTEAD	EDWARD	26832	PTE
HALSTEAD	FREDERICK	19215	PTE
HALSTEAD	HERBERT	37264	PTE
HALSTEAD	WILLIAM HENRY	23697	SGT
HALTON	GEORGE FRANCIS	15569	SGT
HALTON	SAMUEL	15531	PTE
HAM	JOSEPH	7622	PTE
HAMER	GEORGE	40947	PTE
HAMER	HARRY	235070	PTE
HAMER	JAMES	242757	PTE
HAMER	WILLIAM	31514	PTE
HAMILTON	HENRY	9730	CPL
HAMMERTON	JOHN WILLIAM	27049	PTE
HAMMOND	THOMAS EDWARD	17545	PTE
HAMPSON	THOMAS	32140	PTE
HANCOCK	GEORGE LOFTUS ELLIOTT	32141	PTE
HANCOCK	ISAAC	12948	PTE
HANLEY	JOHN	29417	PTE
HANLEY	JOHN	35681	PTE
HANSFORD	THOMAS EASTHAM	29383	PTE
HANSLIP	EDWARD	15744	CPL
HANSON	GEORGE	241260	PTE
HANSON	JOSEPH EDWIN	36346	PTE
HANVEY	ROBERT JACKSON	49261	PTE
HARBOUR	HAROLD	30013	PTE
HARDIKER	HENRY HERBER	23101	PTE
HARDMAN	HARRY	15855	PTE
HARDMAN	SAMUEL DAVIES	15504	PTE
HARDY	ERNEST	32030	PTE
HARGREAVES	ALBERT	15083	PTE
HARGREAVES	ALBERT	15412	PTE
HARGREAVES	ANGUS EDMUND	15327	PTE
HARGREAVES	BENJAMIN	240494	PTE
HARGREAVES	C.	15570	PTE
HARGREAVES	DANIEL	31518	PTE
HARGREAVES	ERNEST	25472	PTE
HARGREAVES	ERNEST	37513	PTE
HARGREAVES	FRED	37822	PTE
HARGREAVES	FREDERICK	38370	PTE
HARGREAVES	HENRY	35065	PTE
HARGREAVES	HERBERT	22329	PTE
HARGREAVES	ISRAEL	35633	PTE
HARGREAVES	J. A.	16032	PTE
HARGREAVES	J. H.	16957	PTE
HARGREAVES	JAMES	26626	PTE
HARGREAVES	JAMES ALLAN	16052	PTE
HARGREAVES	JAMES HENRY	27098	PTE
HARGREAVES	JOHN	26312	PTE
HARGREAVES	JOHN	36367	PTE
HARGREAVES	JOSEPH	5657	PTE
HARGREAVES	JOSEPH	201751	PTE
HARGREAVES	PERCY	15505	PTE
HARGREAVES	THOMAS	21999	PTE
HARGREAVES	WILFRED	24215	PTE
HARKIN	JAMES	15933	PTE
HARLING	CHARLES	15238	PTE
HARMAN	WILLIAM	20944	PTE
HARPER	HARRY	23	PTE
HARRADINE	BERTRAM	29393	PTE
HARRIES	ROSSER	40789	PTE
HARRINGTON	JOHN	15015	PTE
HARRIS	JAMES WILLIAM	21977	PTE
HARRIS	JOSEPH	17355	PTE
HARRIS	PERCIVAL SAMUEL	30485	PTE
HARRIS	WILLIAM SIDNEY	33975	WOII
HARRISON	ALFRED	33951	PTE
HARRISON	EDGAR	15189	PTE
HARRISON	HARRY	15530	PTE
HARRISON	HEDLEY	33786	PTE
HARRISON	HENRY BERNARD	27286	PTE
HARRISON	JOHN GOULD	29370	PTE
HARRISON	LOUIS	201085	PTE
HARRISON	STEPHEN	15873	PTE
HARRISON	STEPHEN	30483	PTE

Surname	Forename(s)	Number	Rank
HARRISON	W.	16038	PTE
HARSTON	JOHN CHARLES	27287	CPL
HART	ALFRED	21878	A/CPL
HART	ARCHIBALD	18042	PTE
HART	JAMES	15440	PTE
HART	PATRICK	41295	PTE
HARTLEY	ALAN	36376	PTE
HARTLEY	ALBERT	26979	PTE
HARTLEY	ARTHUR	29453	PTE
HARTLEY	BENJAMIN	29026	PTE
HARTLEY	EDWARD	40666	PTE
HARTLEY	FRED	37041	PTE
HARTLEY	HAROLD	29452	PTE
HARTLEY	HARRY	40675	PTE
HARTLEY	HERBERT	24865	PTE
HARTLEY	JOHN THOMAS	36843	PTE
HARTLEY	JOSEPH GEORGE	15718	L/CPL
HARTLEY	S.	18514	PTE
HARTLEY	WALTER	36362	PTE
HARTLEY	WILLIAM	240974	PTE
HARVEY	CONRAD	39384	PTE
HARVEY	FRANK	33965	PTE
HARWOOD	ALEXANDER WILLIAM ROYDEN	31517	PTE
HARWOOD	ERNEST	36387	PTE
HARWOOD	FRANCIS	23427	PTE
HASLAM	ERNEST ALBERT	40826	PTE
HASLAM	NEDDY HOLDEN	24960	PTE
HASLEM	FRANK	15783	CPL
HASTINGS	EDMUND	15653	PTE
HASWELL	JOHN WILLIAM GLADSTONE	33904	PTE
HATTON	GEORGE	34634	PTE
HATTON	GEORGE FRANCIS	15764	PTE
HAUGHTON	JOSEPH	37231	PTE
HAUGHTON	THOMAS	30233	CPL
HAWKES	HAROLD JOHN	30966	PTE
HAWKINS	FREDERICK	39415	PTE
HAWKSWORTH	STANLEY	39896	PTE
HAWORTH	ALBERT	18004	PTE
HAWORTH	ALBERT	22183	PTE
HAWORTH	ALBERT	25483	PTE
HAWORTH	ALFRED	37698	PTE
HAWORTH	DAVID	17896	PTE
HAWORTH	EPHRAIM	26840	PTE
HAWORTH	FRED	17879	PTE
HAWORTH	H.	17869	PTE
HAWORTH	HAROLD PARRIN	36500	CPL
HAWORTH	HARRY	26197	PTE
HAWORTH	HERBERT BRISCOE	25133	PTE
HAWORTH	JAMES ARTHUR	40494	PTE
HAWORTH	JOHN	200397	PTE
HAWORTH	JOHN GEORGE	15897	PTE
HAWORTH	JOHN WILLIAM	28453	PTE
HAWORTH	WALTER	17897	PTE
HAYDEN	HAROLD	30621	PTE
HAYDOCK	EDGAR	15283	CPL
HAYDOCK	JAMES	201304	PTE
HAYES	HARRY	31455	PTE
HAYES	RICHARD	6398	PTE
HAYES	T.	15441	PTE
HAYES	THOMAS	15442	PTE
HAYES	THOMAS EDWARD	13153	PTE
HAYES	WALTER	40813	PTE
HAYHURST	HERBERT	37151	PTE
HAYNES	GEORGE EDWARD	15993	SGT
HAYWARD	WALTER THOMAS	21791	PTE
HAZEL	LEONARD	40787	PTE
HEALEY	JOHN	240822	PTE
HEALY	DENNIS	31431	PTE
HEANEY	EDWARD	30501	PTE
HEAP	ALBERT	25169	PTE
HEAP	CROASDALE	15413	PTE
HEAP	H.	15363	L/CPL
HEAP	JOHN	20977	PTE
HEAP	JOHN WILLIAM	24602	PTE
HEAP	ROBERT HENRY	15571	PTE
HEAP	ROGER	242322	PTE
HEAP	THOMAS	28390	PTE
HEAPS	JOHN	51293	PTE
HEAPS	THOMAS PERRY	28626	PTE
HEARNE	JOHN	4743	PTE
HEATH	ARTHUR	33861	PTE
HEATHCOTE	ERNEST	49264	PTE
HEATON	JOHN	15414	CPL
HEATON	TOM THACKRAY	15060	WOII
HEATON	WILLIAM	15532	SGT
HEBSON	ALBERT	35695	PTE
HEGGS	WILLIAM	31432	PTE
HENDERSON	FRANK	31520	PTE
HENSHALL	JOHN HOLDEN	33939	PTE
HEPBURN	HENRY	16224	PTE
HERSEY	HAROLD	15486	SGT
HESELTINE	ALBERT	15970	PTE
HESLOP	ROBERT	30626	PTE
HETHERINGTON	PHILIP	33952	PTE
HETHERINGTON	THOMAS	36389	PTE
HEWITT	EDWIN ROSS	27311	A/WOII
HEWSON	JAMES	28306	PTE
HEY	FREDERICK	15123	WOII
HEY	STANLEY	34939	PTE
HEYES	J. H.	18025	PTE
HEYES	ROBERT	22263	PTE
HEYS	ERNEST	26734	PTE
HEYS	GEORGE EDMUND	37938	PTE
HEYS	JAMES	24225	PTE
HEYS	JAMES EDWARD	15760	PTE
HEYS	WALTER BARNETT	24154	PTE
HEYWOOD	P.	15197	PTE
HEYWOOD	WILLIAM	35634	PTE
HEYWOOD	WILLIAM JOSEPH	24239	PTE
HEYWORTH	ALBERT HAROLD	16039	CPL
HEYWORTH	ALFRED	203812	PTE
HEYWORTH	ARNOLD RICHARD	37707	PTE
HEYWORTH	JAMES ROBERT	32031	PTE
HICK	JAMES ARTHUR	30379	PTE
HICKS	GEORGE WILLIAM	235572	PTE
HICKSON	JOSEPH	35632	PTE
HIGGIN	JIM	15181	PTE
HIGGINS	HARRY	14321	PTE
HIGGINS	JOHN ROBERT	30950	PTE
HIGGINS	OWEN	16704	PTE
HIGGINS	PATRICK	16859	CPL
HIGGINSON	HENRY	20965	PTE
HIGGINSON	SYLVESTER	18330	PTE
HIGGON	GEORGE MORGAN	32088	PTE
HIGHAM	ALFRED	15443	PTE
HIGHAM	SAMUEL	22346	PTE
HILL	CALVIN	240591	PTE
HILL	HARRY	25249	PTE
HILL	JAMES	35694	PTE
HILL	JAMES	40845	PTE
HILL	JAMES	41052	PTE
HILL	JAMES CHARLES	30625	PTE
HILL	JONATHAN	240169	PTE
HILL	RICHARD	27288	PTE
HILL	ROBERT	242864	PTE
HILL	SIDNEY	32143	PTE
HILL	THOMAS ARTHUR	29297	PTE
HILL	WILLIAM	38099	CPL
HILL	WILLIAM	40160	PTE
HILTON	CHARLES	15444	PTE
HILTON	CHARLES	33943	PTE
HILTON	FRED	33889	PTE

Surname	Forename	Number	Rank
HILTON	HENRY	33863	PTE
HILTON	WILLIAM	36738	PTE
HINDLE	CLARENCE	15772	PTE
HINDLE	HARRY	17927	PTE
HINDLE	HENRY JAMES	33791	PTE
HINDLE	HERBERT	28868	PTE
HINDLE	JAMES	15074	COL.SGT
HINDLE	JAMES	15619	PTE
HINDLE	JOHN	15124	CPL
HINDLE	JOHN	15240	SGT
HINDLE	JOHN	15916	PTE
HINDLE	JOHN	17887	PTE
HINDLE	JOHN	18007	PTE
HINDLE	JOHN ARTHUR	15017	COL.SGT
HINDLE	LUKE	241556	PTE
HINDLE	PRESS	40113	PTE
HINDLE	THOMAS	15379	PTE
HINGLEY	LEONARD	27289	PTE
HINKS	SAMUEL	32087	PTE
HIRD	JOHN	23434	PTE
HIRD	THOMAS	36997	PTE
HIRST	ADAM	21809	PTE
HIRST	HUGH	37228	PTE
HIRST	JAMES	38712	PTE
HIRST	JOHN WILLIAM	35122	PTE
HIRST	NORMAN	39251	PTE
HIRST	ROBERT	235084	PTE
HIRST	WILLIAM	240609	PTE
HIRST	WILLIAM	241477	PTE
HITCH	ERNEST	36334	PTE
HITCHEN	ABRAHAM THOMAS	32457	CPL
HITCHEN	HAROLD	32142	PTE
HOBSON	FRED	41034	PTE
HODGSON	GEORGE	33511	PTE
HODGSON	HARRY	15241	SGT
HODGSON	JOHN THOMAS	30372	PTE
HODGSON	SETH	15874	PTE
HODKINSON	GEORGE HENRY	201734	PTE
HODKINSON	JOHN	34441	PTE
HODSON	ENOCH	37538	PTE
HODSON	HERBERT SMITH	33856	PTE
HODSON	JOHN	15649	PTE
HODSON	THOMAS	15893	CPL
HODSON	WILLIAM	29355	PTE
HODSON	WILLIAM ARTHUR	15809	PTE
HOGAN	JOHN	40122	PTE
HOGAN	PETER	18072	PTE
HOLDEN	ALBERT	24973	PTE
HOLDEN	ALBERT	40127	PTE
HOLDEN	ARTHUR	40110	PTE
HOLDEN	ERNEST	15989	CPL
HOLDEN	FRED	24485	PTE
HOLDEN	GREENWOOD	15100	PTE
HOLDEN	HENRY	15019	PTE
HOLDEN	JAMES	26910	PTE
HOLDEN	JAMES BRIGGS	200069	PTE
HOLDEN	JOHN	15125	CPL
HOLDEN	JOHN	40886	PTE
HOLDEN	JOHN JAMES	27088	PTE
HOLDEN	JOSEPH	24209	PTE
HOLDEN	JOSEPH THOMAS	15593	PTE
HOLDEN	MARTIN WILLIAM	25086	PTE
HOLDEN	RICHARD	17830	PTE
HOLDEN	THOMAS	25114	PTE
HOLDEN	WILLIAM	36883	PTE
HOLDING	ARNOLD JAMES	15856	PTE
HOLDING	JAMES	17957	PTE
HOLDING	WILLIAM CLARKE	17953	PTE
HOLDSWORTH	HUBERT	16066	PTE
HOLER	HARRY	20105	PTE
HOLGATE	ERNEST	24534	PTE
HOLGATE	FREDERICK	17833	PTE
HOLGATE	STANLEY	15650	PTE
HOLGATE	YATES	35631	PTE
HOLLAND	ALBERT EDWARD	31454	PTE
HOLLAND	HAROLD	15328	PTE
HOLLAND	J. W.	15475	PTE
HOLLAND	JOHN	29078	PTE
HOLLIDAY	HARRY BERTRAM	27284	PTE
HOLLIDAY	JAMES	34454	PTE
HOLLINRAKE	GEORGE HENRY	37791	PTE
HOLLINS	CHARLES	31056	PTE
HOLLOWS	GEORGE WILLIAM	26360	PTE
HOLMES	FRANK	28764	PTE
HOLMES	FRED	24844	PTE
HOLMES	HENRY SELDIN	27290	PTE
HOLMES	JAMES HENRY	33937	PTE
HOLMES	JOHN	15892	CPL
HOLMES	JOHN	23302	PTE
HOLMES	W.	15507	PTE
HOLMES	WILFRID	32032	PTE
HOLMES	WILLIAM	29358	PTE
HOLROYD	ARTHUR	34957	PTE
HOLROYD	BENJAMIN	15506	PTE
HOLT	CHARLES	15365	PTE
HOLT	ERNEST	15364	PTE
HOLT	FREDERIC	241013	PTE
HOLT	JOSEPH	20054	PTE
HOOLE	JAMES WILLIAM	34618	PTE
HOOLEY	FRED	29285	PTE
HOPE	GEORGE	29450	PTE
HOPE	GEORGE LAWRENCE	38369	PTE
HOPE	H.	15242	PTE
HOPE	HARRY	16435	A/CPL
HOPE	PERCY	24164	PTE
HOPKINSON	ALFRED	35691	PTE
HOPKINSON	JAMES EDWARD	36564	SGT
HOPKINSON	JONATHAN	34316	PTE
HOPKINSON	WILLIAM	17286	SGT
HORNE	RICHARD	27133	PTE
HORNE	RICHARD	36347	PTE
HORNER	TOM	22262	A/CPL
HORROCKS	THOMAS	40755	PTE
HORROCKS	WILLIAM	16012	PTE
HORSEFIELD	PERCY	15808	PTE
HORSFALL	FRANK	203257	PTE
HOUGH	ARCHIE	240415	PTE
HOUGH	LEONARD	32029	PTE
HOUGH	WILLIAM	25008	PTE
HOUGHTON	EDWARD	37854	PTE
HOUGHTON	GEORGE	21801	PTE
HOUGHTON	JAMES	32028	PTE
HOUGHTON	WILLIAM	242415	PTE
HOULKER	ALBERT	17943	PTE
HOWARD	ERNEST JAMES	30566	CPL
HOWARD	G.	15719	PTE
HOWARD	GEORGE	35451	PTE
HOWARD	GEORGE	235888	PTE
HOWARD	THOMAS	20909	PTE
HOWARD	VICTOR BERNARD	30782	PTE
HOWARTH	ABRAHAM	38353	PTE
HOWARTH	ERNEST	13274	PTE
HOWARTH	ERNEST	15592	PTE
HOWARTH	FRANK	19763	PTE
HOWARTH	GEORGE WATSON	34174	PTE
HOWARTH	HAROLD	15061	PTE
HOWARTH	JOHN	19634	PTE
HOWARTH	ROBERT	21451	PTE
HOWARTH	ROBERT EDWARD	15062	A/SGT
HOWARTH	W. E.	29585	CPL
HOWARTH	WILLIAM THOMAS	15366	PTE
HOWE	THOMAS WILLIAM	49252	PTE

HOWELL	CHRISTOPHER	31516	PTE		ISHERWOOD	CLARENCE	27034	PTE
HOWLEY	HERBERT	15303	A/SGT		ISHERWOOD	JOSEPH	15021	PTE
HOWORTH	JOSHUA	201670	PTE		ISHERWOOD	PERUDA	22112	CPL
HOYLE	JOHN	15807	PTE		ISHERWOOD	ROBERT	18034	PTE
HOYLE	JOHN JONES	23154	PTE		ISHERWOOD	VINCENT	11069	PTE
HOYLE	JOHN NELSON	25326	PTE		ITHELL	JOHN WILLIAM	39368	PTE
HUDSON	JOHN RICHARD	17944	PTE		IVESON	MATTHEW	34176	PTE
HUDSON	T.	15810	PTE		JACK	ARTHUR JAMES	30528	PTE
HUGHES		15773	SGT		JACKSON	ARTHUR	22126	PTE
HUGHES	ALAN	31513	PTE		JACKSON	ARTHUR	32116	PTE
HUGHES	ERNEST	15620	PTE		JACKSON	HERBERT	40115	PTE
HUGHES	FRED	240313	PTE		JACKSON	HERBERT JOHN	32319	PTE
HUGHES	HUGH GRICE	38965	PTE		JACKSON	HERMAN	30631	PTE
HUGHES	JOHN	32089	PTE		JACKSON	JAMES	15304	PTE
HUGHES	PATRICK	33503	PTE		JACKSON	JOHN	31456	PTE
HUGHES	THOMAS	12938	PTE		JACKSON	ROBERT	17972	PTE
HUGHES	THOMAS	39542	PTE		JACKSON	ROBERT SAMUEL	38047	PTE
HUGHES	WILLIAM	14796	PTE		JACKSON	SAMUEL	40074	PTE
HULL	CHARLES	15165	CPL		JACKSON	THOMAS	15722	PTE
HULL	JACK	15857	PTE		JACKSON	THOMAS HENRY	37222	PTE
HULL	JAMES	24267	PTE		JACKSON	THOMAS HOWARTH	15935	PTE
HULL	JOHN	18948	PTE		JACKSON	WILFRED	15285	A/SGT
HULL	RICHARD	24246	PTE		JACKSON	WILLIAM	38339	PTE
HULME	CLARENCE	15621	PTE		JACKSON	WILLIAM HENRY	32117	PTE
HULME	EDWARD	12089	A/SGT		JACOBSON	HERBERT	36322	COL/SGT
HUMPHREY	C. E.	15637	PTE		JAGGER	ARCHIE	24505	PTE
HUMPHREYS	CHARLES EDWARD	15367	A/SGT		JAGGER	FRANK	12819	PTE
HUMPHREYS	TALIESIN	30502	PTE		JAMES	WILLIAM	38365	PTE
HUNNISETT	EDWARD JAMES	38511	PTE		JAQUES	F.	18009	PTE
HUNT	HARRY	29765	PTE		JEFFERSON	ROBERT	15329	A/CPL
HUNT	JAMES	54415	PTE		JENKINSON	ERNEST	33891	PTE
HUNT	P.	15348	PTE		JENKINSON	RICHARD	40656	PTE
HUNTER	HENRY	15651	PTE		JEPSON	ARMENA	201535	CPL
HUNTINGDON	EDWARD	40888	PTE		JOHNS	FREDERICK GEORGE	15746	PTE
HUNTON	THOMAS	15273	PTE		JOHNS	THOMAS BUTLER	24249	PTE
HURST	JOHN	15652	PTE		JOHNS	THOMAS GEORGE	30466	PTE
HUSBAND	GEORGE	21477	PTE		JOHNSON	C.	17902	PTE
HUTCHINGS	WILLIAM ARTHUR	23860	PTE		JOHNSON	HENRY	16351	PTE
HUTCHINSON	GEORGE	202303	PTE		JOHNSON	HENRY	32033	PTE
HUZZARD	GEORGE WILLIAM	33905	PTE		JOHNSON	JOHN	41009	PTE
HYDE	FRANK	201225	PTE		JOHNSON	JOSEPH	26699	PTE
HYDE	WILLIAM	39039	PTE		JOHNSON	ROBERT	202743	PTE
IBBETSON	JAMES	26314	PTE		JOHNSON	ROBERT WILLIAM	32145	PTE
IBBOTSON	ARTHUR	37199	PTE		JOHNSON	WILLIAM	15509	PTE
IDDON	MILES FREDERICK	32106	PTE		JOHNSTON	PETER JAMES	49267	PTE
IDDON	RICHARD	15445	PTE		JOHNSTONE	HUGH MCGOLDRICK	49345	PTE
IDDON	RICHARD	16059	PTE		JOHNSTONE	ROBERT	49225	PTE
ILES	JOHN HENRY	31521	PTE		JOHNSTONE	THOMAS DONALD	31524	PTE
ILEY	JAMES	15811	PTE		JOLLEY	WILLIAM ROBERT	31457	PTE
ILLINGWORTH	F.	15508	L/CPL		JOLLY	DAVID	15747	PTE
ILLINGWORTH	FRED	28479	PTE		JOLLY	JOSEPH	29652	CPL
IMESON	GEORGE THOMAS S.	31067	PTE		JONES	ALFRED HENRY	51232	PTE
INETT	THOMAS	40856	PTE		JONES	BERTRAM THOMAS	39886	PTE
INGERSON	GEORGE	32090	PTE		JONES	CHARLES	30504	PTE
INGHAM	BEN	15368	SGT		JONES	DAVID HOPKINS	38944	PTE
INGHAM	CHARLES HORACE	27310	A/CPL		JONES	FREDERICK ALFRED	27069	PTE
INGHAM	HARRY	15465	PTE		JONES	GEORGE	12802	CPL
INGHAM	HERBERT	28564	PTE		JONES	GEORGE	38459	PTE
INGHAM	J.	15894	PTE		JONES	GEORGE BROOKFIELD	30570	PTE
INGHAM	JAMES	14371	PTE		JONES	GEORGE EDWARD	41037	PTE
INGHAM	LAWRENCE	31522	PTE		JONES	HAMILTON	39369	PTE
INGHAM	RICHARD	17901	PTE		JONES	HARRY	33940	PTE
INGHAM	THOMAS	15020	PTE		JONES	HERBERT	16650	PTE
INGHAM	WILLIAM	15572	PTE		JONES	JOHN	49222	PTE
INGLEFIELD	THOMAS	29566	PTE		JONES	JOHN JOSEPH	37911	PTE
IRELAND	RICHARD	15765	PTE		JONES	JOSEPH	200548	PTE
IRELAND	ROGER	240852	SGT		JONES	MILBURN ALFRED	49280	PTE
IRVINE	ANDREW	17963	PTE		JONES	NORMAN	20931	PTE
IRVING	EDWARD	34619	L/CPL		JONES	RICHARD	29403	PTE
IRVING	GEORGE	27050	PTE		JONES	RICHARD WILLIAM	49479	PTE
IRVING	LAWRENCE	236244	PTE		JONES	ROBERT	33872	PTE

Surname	Name	Number	Rank
JONES	THOMAS EDWARD	38722	PTE
JONES	WALTER	27291	PTE
JONES	WILLIAM HENRY	6579	PTE
JONES	WILLIAM JOHN	32091	PTE
JORDAN	HARRY	32034	PTE
JORDAN	JAMES DOUGLAS	28555	PTE
JORDAN	WALTER	33923	PTE
JORDAN	WILLIAM JOHN	242003	PTE
JOYCE	JAMES	38346	PTE
JOYS	JAMES WILLIAM	27292	PTE
JUSTICE	HORACE	30376	PTE
KANE	THOMAS	32036	PTE
KAVANAGH	WILLIAM	32037	PTE
KAY	ERNEST DAVID	16041	SGT
KAY	HARRY	15510	PTE
KAY	HAROLD	9774	WOII
KAY	JAMES	30871	PTE
KAY	ROBERT	26582	PTE
KAY	THOMAS HENRY	200094	PTE
KEARNEY	WALTER	24693	PTE
KEARNS	FRED	37674	PTE
KEARSLEY	JOHN	200690	PTE
KEEBLE	ROYSTON WOOD	29376	CPL
KEEFFE	JOHN THOMAS	32035	PTE
KEEGAN	EDWARD	41047	PTE
KEIDEL	STEPHEN ALBERT	33983	PTE
KELLETT	PETER	5033	L/SGT
KELLY	FRED	24081	PTE
KELLY	HARRY	30815	PTE
KELLY	ROBERT HENRY	39282	PTE
KENDAL	J.	15899	PTE
KENDAL	ROBERT	15814	PTE
KENDALL	FRANCIS	15723	PTE
KENDALL	JOHN SMITH	30096	PTE
KENDALL	WALTER	28973	PTE
KENDRICK	WILLIAM	29899	PTE
KENNEDY	GEORGE	15655	PTE
KENNEDY	GEORGE ALFRED	20999	PTE
KENNEDY	J. E.	18071	PTE
KENNEDY	THOMAS	15199	PTE
KENNEDY	THOMAS	20516	PTE
KENNETT	HARRY PATRICK	33785	PTE
KENNY	J.	18020	PTE
KENT	EDWIN CEDRIC	15623	SGT
KENWORTHY	ALBERT WILLIE	27314	PTE
KENYON	ARTHUR WALLACE	200503	PTE
KENYON	ERNEST	18037	PTE
KENYON	GEORGE	28740	PTE
KENYON	J.	15749	PTE
KENYON	JAMES	18043	PTE
KENYON	JOHN CHARLES	35285	PTE
KENYON	JOSEPH	22325	PTE
KENYON	LUTHER	17886	PTE
KENYON	NATHAN HENRY	40097	PTE
KENYON	RICHARD	200328	PTE
KENYON	THOMAS	15487	CPL
KENYON	WALTER	24126	PTE
KENYON	WILLIAM	23346	PTE
KERFOOT	STANLEY	203168	PTE
KERMEEN	JOHN WILLIAM	15126	PTE
KERSHAW	DAVID	31075	PTE
KERSHAW	FRED	19960	PTE
KERSHAW	MARCUS LEON	33924	PTE
KERSHAW	WILLIAM	26287	PTE
KEWLEY	HERBERT	19084	PTE
KIDD	WILLIAM	32219	PTE
KIELECHER	JOSEPH	38713	PTE
KILBURN	JOHN EDWARD	33859	PTE
KILLILEA	JOHN	200346	PTE
KILNER	WILLIAM	15976	PTE
KING	WILLIAM	32108	PTE
KIRBY	GEORGE	31399	PTE
KIRK	EDWIN ERNEST	29304	PTE
KIRKHAM	CHARLES ARTHUR	29532	PTE
KIRKHAM	HARRY AUSTIN	15511	PTE
KIRKHAM	JOHN	35635	PTE
KIRKHAM	JOSEPH	15023	PTE
KIRKPATRICK	JACK	31525	PTE
KIRKUP	JOSEPH	30635	PTE
KIRWAN	CHRISTOPHER THOMAS	33907	PTE
KITCHEN	JAMES	18348	PTE
KITCHEN	WILFRED	31526	PTE
KITCHENER	EDWIN	15024	WOCLII
KITCHIN	JOHN THOMAS	30716	PTE
KIVELL	STEPHEN	17234	PTE
KNAPPER	ARTHUR	29227	CPL
KNEEN	WILLIAM EDWARD	39624	PTE
KNIGHT	THOMAS ALFRED	37053	PTE
KNIGHTON	JOHN	235554	PTE
KNOWLES	HARRY	35636	PTE
KNOWLES	HUGH	40917	PTE
KNOWLES	JAMES	22187	PTE
KNOWLES	ROBERT WILLIAM	15573	PTE
KNOWLES	THOMAS	29456	PTE
KNOWLES	WILLIAM	19539	PTE
KNOWLES	WILLIAM	200942	PTE
KNOWLES	WILLIAM SHORROCK	25455	A/CPL
KUPRESKIN	STEPHEN	51309	PTE
LACEY	CORNELIUS	23893	WOII
LAFFY	JOHN	22088	PTE
LAMBERT	HARTLEY	35698	PTE
LAMBERT	JAMES NAYLOR	15624	PTE
LAMBERT	THOMAS	17998	PTE
LAMBERT	WILLIAM	30641	SGT
LAMBERT	WILLIAM MCMILLAN	32041	PTE
LAMONT	ALEXANDER	200734	PTE
LANCASTER	GEORGE	40778	PTE
LANCASTER	JAMES	15656	PTE
LANDON	WALTER	15200	PTE
LANE	CECIL ARNOLD PERCY	31109	PTE
LANE	CORNELIUS	17383	PTE
LANE	WILLIAM EDWARD	15418	PTE
LANG	AUSTIN	15657	SGT
LANG	THOMAS	238003	SGT
LANGAN	EDWARD	17094	PTE
LANGLEY	EDWARD	17094	PTE
LANGLEY	GEORGE VICTOR	40897	PTE
LANGTON	JOHN	28719	PTE
LARABY	ALBERT	40139	PTE
LAST	HAROLD EDGAR	21102	PTE
LATHAM	JAMES	240665	PTE
LATHAM	JAMES HENRY	40425	PTE
LAVERTY	PERCY	36464	PTE
LAW	CHARLES	40834	PTE
LAWLESS	GEORGE AUSTIN	16137	PTE
LAWRENCE	STEPHEN	32405	PTE
LAWRENSON	JOHN	15658	PTE
LAWSON	ALBERT	32039	PTE
LAWSON	WILLIAM	28843	PTE
LAWTON	EBENEZER	39697	PTE
LAYCOCK	A.	18054	PTE
LAYCOCK	BENJAMIN FRANKLING	17898	PTE
LAYCOCK	NORMAN	23280	PTE
LAYTHAM	FRANK	23145	PTE
LEACH	FRED	33829	PTE
LEACH	T. A.	15274	PTE
LEAP	J.	15535	PTE
LEATHER	HARRY	40823	PTE
LEATHER	STANLEY	27021	PTE
LEATHERD	RICHARD	33977	PTE
LEAVER	ALFRED	240185	A/CPL
LEAVER	JAMES MICHAEL	22138	PTE
LEDIGO	GEORGE HENRY	17307	PTE

Surname	Forename(s)	Number	Rank
LEDWICK	J.	18030	PTE
LEE	ALEXANDER	32040	PTE
LEE	CLIFFORD	27315	PTE
LEE	ERNEST	36927	PTE
LEE	GEORGE	7440	WOII
LEE	HAROLD	31440	PTE
LEECH	JAMES	38818	PTE
LEEMING	ARTHUR	15183	WOII
LEEMING	FRED	15774	PTE
LEEMING	JAMES KING	15286	PTE
LEEMING	JOHN	15287	PTE
LEEMING	THOMAS	22165	CPL
LEES	ALFRED	16248	PTE
LEES	JOHN	37862	PTE
LEESE	GEORGE	29310	PTE
LEGON	ROBERT	49481	PTE
LEIGH	HARRY	10879	PTE
LEIGH	J. R.	15625	PTE
LEO	JOHN	15000	PTE
LEONARD	THOMAS	15659	PTE
LESSITER	SYDNEY ALBERT	7409	PTE
LESTER	JOHN EDWARD	30066	PTE
LETTERD	J.	15288	PTE
LEVY	EMANUEL	32147	PTE
LEWIS	CHARLES	41035	PTE
LEWIS	ERNEST CHARLES	33846	PTE
LEWIS	FRANCIS	17909	PTE
LEWIS	FREDERICK	31403	PTE
LEWIS	HARRY	34427	PTE
LEWIS	HARRY ILLIFFE	17764	PTE
LEWIS	RICHARD	32146	PTE
LEWIS	THOMAS JAMES	32092	PTE
LEWIS	WILLIAM	15917	PTE
LEYLAND	ARTHUR	202482	PTE
LIGGINS	THOMAS	27065	CPL
LIGHTBOWN	GEORGE	37827	PTE
LIGHTFOOT	NORMAN	15026	PTE
LINDSAY	FRED	15815	PTE
LINDSAY	WILLIAM CUNNINGHAM	30518	PTE
LINDUS	WILLIAM EDWARD	21593	PTE
LITTLE	JAMES ROBERT	19597	L/CPL
LIVESEY	ALBERT	20071	PTE
LIVESEY	HARRY	37056	PTE
LIVESEY	HERBERT	37859	PTE
LIVESEY	JAMES EDWARD	15937	PTE
LIVESEY	MILTON	35703	PTE
LIVESEY	RICHARD	16519	SGT
LIVINGSTONE	JAMES	16447	PTE
LLOYD	GEORGE NELSON	30719	PTE
LLOYD	GEORGE RICHARD	29311	PTE
LLOYD	JOSEPH	23297	PTE
LLOYD	THOMAS JOHN	236248	PTE
LOCHERTY	JOSEPH	30474	PTE
LOCKETT	J.	15724	PTE
LOCKETT	JOHN	15574	PTE
LOCKETT	JOSEPH	27712	SGT
LOCKWOOD	JOSEPH HENRY	31402	PTE
LOGAN	FRED	32038	PTE
LOMAS	HERBERT	38907	PTE
LOMAX	ABEL	17877	PTE
LOMAX	ERIC	31439	CPL
LOMAX	JOHN	20815	PTE
LOMAX	JOHN	204107	PTE
LONG	CHARLES HUTCHINSON	15918	PTE
LONG	JAMES WALLACE	34920	PTE
LONGDON	SAMUEL	235143	PTE
LONGWORTH	WILLIAM HENRY	24127	PTE
LONSDALE	GEORGE	20091	PTE
LONSDALE	HARRY	25495	PTE
LONSDALE	RICHARD	15585	PTE
LORD	ALFRED	22191	A/CPL
LORD	ALFRED HOPKINSON	16015	PTE
LORD	CHARLES ALFRED	31085	PTE
LORD	EDWARD	37716	PTE
LORD	ERNEST	36995	PTE
LORD	HAWORTH	22333	PTE
LORD	HENRY CHADWICK	20830	PTE
LORD	J. R.	18274	PTE
LORD	JOHN	32148	PTE
LORD	JOSEPH	25015	PTE
LORD	SAMUEL	17860	PTE
LORD	T.	15750	PTE
LORD	WILLIAM	20989	PTE
LOUGHLIN	JOHN	29368	PTE
LOUGHNEY	JOHN	34757	PTE
LOWCOCK	JOHN	7234	SGT
LOWE	GEORGE	33822	PTE
LOWE	GEORGE WILLIAM	40075	PTE
LOWE	JAMES	15660	PTE
LOWE	MAURICE GEORGE	235118	PTE
LOWE	ROBERT	12198	PTE
LOWE	SAMUEL	33838	PTE
LOWTHER	WILLIAM	22125	PTE
LUCAS }	JOHN	15859	CPL
LUCAS }	JOHN	35437	CPL
LUCKWELL	WALTER	40809	PTE
LUND	GILES	15025	L/CPL
LUND	HERBERT	36987	PTE
LUND	PERCY	15694	PTE
LUND	WILLIAM	241139	A/COL/SC
LUNT	ARTHUR	15244	PTE
LUPTON	HERCHALL	37835	PTE
LYNCH	JOSEPH CHARLES	30638	PTE
LYON	HARRY	41027	PTE
LYON	JAMES	15027	SGT
LYON	JOHN	33908	PTE
LYONS	HERBERT	241276	CPL
LYONS	JOHN	32495	PTE
LYTHE	ERNEST	15936	PTE
MACDONALD	GEORGE	22524	CPL
MACKAY	PETER JOSEPH	33401	PTE
MACLEAN	DONALD	26771	PTE
MADDEN	MICHAEL	40689	PTE
MADEN	JAMES HENRY	26685	PTE
MAGNALL	GEORGE	22253	PTE
MAGRATH	ANDREW	15860	PTE
MAINWARING	JOHN DAVIDSON	26872	PTE
MAITLAND	ARTHUR	242071	PTE
MAKEMSON	WILLIAM	236245	PTE
MAKIN	CLIFFORD	32043	PTE
MAKIN	WALTER	15128	PTE
MAKIN	WILLIAM	17905	PTE
MAKINSON	JAMES	15960	PTE
MALANEY	JOHN FRANK	203079	PTE
MALLINSON	C.	24798	PTE
MALONE	H.	15029	PTE
MALONE	JOHN RICHARD	18040	CPL
MALONE	WILLIAM	31441	PTE
MALTBY	SAMUEL	27316	PTE
MANLOVE	JAMES	15513	PTE
MANN	GEORGE	16522	PTE
MANN	SIDNEY	235255	PTE
MANNION	JAMES	12883	PTE
MANTLE	JOSEPH HENRY	19338	CPL
MARCROFT	RICHARD STANLEY	10827	PTE
MARGINSON	PERCY	30643	PTE
MARKHAM	JACK	15457	SGT
MARKHAM	JOSEPH	23316	PTE
MARMONT	STANLEY ARTHUR	29384	PTE
MARSDEN	EDWARD	35639	PTE
MARSDEN	FRANK	15938	SGT
MARSDEN	FRANK	32042	PTE

Surname	Forename	Number	Rank
MARSDEN	MARK WILLIAM	15626	PTE
MARSDEN	RICHARD HENRY	40970	PTE
MARSDEN	WILLIAM	15537	PTE
MARSH	ABSALOM	15356	CPL
MARSHALL	CECIL THOMAS	15901	PTE
MARSHALL	JOSEPH	10294	CPL
MARSHALL	JOSEPH	24228	PTE
MARSHALL	JOSEPH	40159	PTE
MARSHALL	JOSEPH	15369	PTE
MARSHALL	WILL	15597	PTE
MARSLAND	EDMUND	39631	PTE
MARSLAND	GEORGE THOMAS	40899	PTE
MARSLAND	JOHN	39930	PTE
MARSTON	ALBERT WILLIAM RICHARD	26867	PTE
MARTIN	BEN	20705	PTE
MARTIN	J. T.	200529	PTE
MARTIN	KNOWLES	17969	PTE
MARTIN	PERCY	31534	PTE
MARTIN	THOMAS ROBERT	27009	PTE
MASKELL	ALBERT	36369	PTE
MASLEN	JAMES OLIVER	35702	PTE
MASON	JAMES	15725	PTE
MASON	WILLIAM	38822	PTE
MASSER	HORACE	31537	PTE
MATHERS	WILLIAM	19853	PTE
MATTHEW	WILFRED	241735	PTE
MATTHEWS	CYRIL	35700	PTE
MATTHEWS	GEORGE	40852	PTE
MATTHEWS	NOAH	27111	PTE
MAUDE	WILLIAM	36481	SGT
MAUGHAM	THOMAS	17949	PTE
MAWDSLEY	JAMES HENRY	12456	PTE
MAWHOOD	JOSEPH	33933	PTE
MAXWELL	WILLIAM	33794	PTE
MAY	ARTHUR ARCHIBALD	32044	PTE
MAY	CHRISTOPHER	39376	A/CPL
MAYHEW	REGINALD WILLIAM	40853	PTE
MAYNARD	HENRY GEORGE	36602	PTE
MAYNARD	JOHN	30647	PTE
MAYOH	HARRY	30472	PTE
MCCABE	JAMES	15245	CPL
MCCALL	SAMUEL	242643	CPL
MCCALL	SAMUEL	33504	PTE
MCCANN	JOSEPH	15575	PTE
MCCARRICK	JOHN	16290	PTE
MCCARTHY	THOMAS	32104	PTE
MCCLELLAN	JOHN	32093	PTE
MCCORMICK	JAMES	39012	PTE
MCCREA	ROBERT	20964	PTE
MCDERMOTT	J.	37194	PTE
MCDERMOTT	JOHN	35640	PTE
MCDERMOTT	PATRICK	31540	PTE
MCDONALD	WILLIAM	15130	PTE
MCDONOUGH	JAMES	30713	PTE
MCDONUGH	WILLIAM	49342	PTE
MCEWAN	JAMES	31538	PTE
MCFADDEN	HENRY	33847	PTE
MCGARRITY	DAVID	17744	PTE
MCGOLDRICK	CHARLES	30506	PTE
MCGOWAN	JOHN	39918	PTE
MCGRATH	JOSEPH	39009	PTE
MCGREGOR	ROBERT BRUCE	36771	PTE
MCGUILL	JOHN JAMES	240891	PTE
MCGUIRE	HENRY	15370	PTE
MCGUIRE	REUBEN	31459	PTE
MCHALE	JOSEPH	17883	PTE
MCHUGH	J.	5968	PTE
MCHUGH	THOMAS	31536	PTE
MCINTOSH	ALEXANDER	35701	PTE
MCINTYRE	HERBERT	36180	PTE
MCKEE	ALBERT	5919	SGT
MCKENNA	PATRICK		
MCKENNA	WILLIAM	15028	PTE
MCKERNAN	FRANCIS JOSEPH	31535	PTE
MCKINLEY	HERBERT EDWARD	36359	PTE
MCKNIGHT	IRVIN	36356	PTE
MCKONE	JAMES	201610	PTE
MCLOUGHLIN	J.	15514	PTE
MCLOUGHLIN	JAMES	35444	PTE
MCMINNUS	HERBERT	240203	PTE
MCMURRAY	CHARLES	17786	PTE
MCNALLY	WILFRED	203450	PTE
MCNAMARA	GILBERT JOHN	39919	PTE
MCNEILL	JOSEPH	38911	PTE
MCNEILL	SAMUEL	5634	CPL
MCQUILLIAM	FREDERICK	235194	PTE
MCSPIRIT	JOHN	30650	PTE
MCVEIGH	PETER	242424	PTE
MCWHINNEY	THOMAS	26811	PTE
MEADE	JOHN	33824	PTE
MEDLEY	F.	15751	PTE
MEEHAM	MICHAEL	29125	PTE
MELIA	THOMAS	24044	PTE
MELLELIEU	FRED	15419	PTE
MELLEN	PETER	40101	PTE
MERCER	ALBERT	15085	PTE
MERCER	FRANK	29461	PTE
MERCER	JOHN	10512	PTE
MERCER	ROBERT	15775	CPL
MERCER	SAMUEL	18290	PTE
MEREDITH	GEORGE SIMON	33827	PTE
METCALF	JOHN	17851	PTE
METCALFE	GEORGE	33968	PTE
METEER	DAVID	49266	PTE
MIDDLEMASS	WESTON	33909	PTE
MIDGLEY	ENOCH	27414	PTE
MIDWOOD	ASHTON	30352	PTE
MILLAR	SAMUEL WAY	16450	PTE
MILLAR	WILLIAM	30480	PTE
MILLER	JOHN	200621	SGT
MILLER	ROBERT	40718	PTE
MILLICHIP	WILLIAM CHARLES	39013	PTE
MILLINGTON	GEORGE	15420	PTE
MILLINGTON	WILLIAM	29414	PTE
MILLS	ALFRED JAMES	38835	PTE
MILLS	CHARLIE	30438	PTE
MILLS	HARRY	29565	PTE
MILLS	RAYMOND ARTHUR	32288	PTE
MILNER	DANIEL	11890	PTE
MILNER	JOHN HOLDEN	35563	PTE
MILTON	GEORGE	15538	PTE
MILTON	JOHN HENRY LEE	15816	PTE
MILTON	WILLIAM	20943	PTE
MITCHELL	DAVID	30649	PTE
MITCHELL	F. W.	15617	L/CPL
MITCHELL	FRANCIS	40092	PTE
MITCHELL	HARRY	242772	PTE
MITCHELL	JAMES	35641	PTE
MITCHELL	JOHN	15333	PTE
MITCHELL	JOHN WILLIAM	203241	PTE
MITCHELL	REGINALD	33793	PTE
MITCHELL	WILLIAM	31528	PTE
MITCHINSON	RICHARD	31527	PTE
MITTON	HARRY	22260	PTE
MOLLOY	JOHN	15941	PTE
MONAGHAN	JOHN	15466	SGT
MONK	HARRY	33788	PTE
MOON	HARRY	36326	PTE
MOORCROFT	ALBERT	15662	PTE
MOORE	ARTHUR	27277	PTE
MOORE	ERNEST	30651	PTE
MOORE	ERNEST	39252	PTE
MOORE	HAROLD	36603	PTE

MOORE	J. J.	16013	CPL	NEALE	JOHN HENRY	30070	PTE
MOORE	JAMES	35458	A/CPL	NEARY	WILLIAM	8264	PTE
MOORE	JAMES OLIVER	29542	PTE	NEEDLE	SAM WILLIAM	15875	PTE
MOORE	RICHARD	22160	PTE	NELMES	JOHN WORGAN	30023	PTE
MOORFIELD	PETER	23931	PTE	NELSON	FRANK	37065	PTE
MOORHOUSE	JAMES	26680	PTE	NELSON	GEORGE HENRY	15820	PTE
MOORHOUSE	PERCY	17537	PTE	NELSON	THOMAS	30652	PTE
MORAN	JOSEPH	13450	CPL	NEVILLE	HARRY	39698	CPL
MORAN	WILLIAM	17344	PTE	NEWHAM	HARRY	15940	PTE
MORATH	WILLIAM LEO	33403	PTE	NEWMAN	JOHN	33911	PTE
MORGAN	ALOYSIUS	37306	PTE	NEWSHAM	J. W.	15030	PTE
MORGAN	CHARLES	38731	PTE	NEWTON	GEORGE	39650	SGT
MORGAN	JOHN	29544	PTE	NICHOLL	HARRY	32050	PTE
MORGAN	MICHAEL	20959	PTE	NICHOLSON	FRED	49265	PTE
MORONEY	F.	15249	PTE	NICHOLSON	JOSEPH	32047	PTE
MORRIS	GEORGE	23933	PTE	NICHOLSON	WILLIAM	17726	PTE
MORRIS	JAMES	13023	A/SGT	NICKSON	EDWARD	15334	A/SGT
MORRIS	JAMES	15727	PTE	NICOLLS	MICHAEL HENRY	33506	PTE
MORRIS	JAMES ROBERT	12373	SGT	NIELD	WILLIAM	200428	PTE
MORRIS	JOHN HARVEY	10790	SGT	NIGHTINGALE	JOHN	200155	PTE
MORRIS	JOSEPH CYRIL	32046	PTE	NIGHTINGALE	JOSEPH	15447	PTE
MORRIS	PERCY	31533	PTE	NIXON	ALBERT	15729	SGT
MORRISON	FRANCIS	35642	PTE	NIXON	JOHN	34568	PTE
MORTIMER	DAVID	32594	PTE	NOBLE	JOHN WILLIAM	15371	PTE
MORTIMER	WILLIE	21861	PTE	NOBLE	LAURENCE	17923	PTE
MOSCOVITCH	LAZARUS	29766	PTE	NOLAN	JOSEPH	32049	PTE
MOSELEY	WILLIAM FEELEY	29545	PTE	NOON	MARTIN	32094	PTE
MOSS	CORNELIUS	37290	PTE	NOON	THOMAS	33404	PTE
MOSS	DAVID	38758	PTE	NORRIS	ERNEST	32048	PTE
MOSS	EDWARD SYDNEY	31532	PTE	NORRIS	HAROLD	31460	PTE
MOSS	PERCY	33400	PTE	NORRIS	PATRICK	13494	PTE
MOSS	THOMAS	39270	PTE	NOWELL	CHARLES	15821	PTE
MOSS	THOMAS	40114	PTE	NOWELL	ESMUND	15961	PTE
MOULDING	JAMES	15992	PTE	NOWELL	JOHN	200716	PTE
MOULTON	SAMUEL	32045	PTE	NUTT	CHARLES EDWIN	31542	PTE
MOUSDELL	MOSES	31458	PTE	NUTTALL	ARTHUR	24169	PTE
MOZLEY	WILLIAM	26539	PTE	NUTTALL	GEORGE	201752	PTE
MUCHMORE	THOMAS WALTER	31124	PTE	NUTTALL	JOHN	36350	PTE
MULHALL	ALBERT	15818	PTE	NUTTALL	SAM	19329	PTE
MULHALL	JAMES	17838	PTE	NUTTALL	WALTER	15031	PTE
MULHALL	THOMAS	15817	PTE	NUTTALL	WILLIAM	24809	PTE
MULLANEY	JOHN	26710	PTE	NUTTER	ARTHUR	16043	PTE
MULLANEY	WILLIAM	33945	PTE	NUTTER	FRED	27109	PTE
MULLANY	THOMAS	33853	PTE	NUTTER	HARRY	15920	PTE
MULLENDER	HAROLD	24157	PTE	O'BRIEN	JAMES	12619	PTE
MULLIN	FRANK	33888	PTE	O'CONNELL	CHARLES WILLIAM	30426	PTE
MULLINS	HENRY JOHN	9585	PTE	O'CONNOR	ARTHUR PATRICK	15903	PTE
MULVANEY	JAMES	33402	PTE	O'CONNOR	EDWARD	39015	PTE
MUNDY	RICHARD HENRY	17868	PTE	O'CONNOR	JOHN	18035	PTE
MURPHY	J. T.	15392	PTE	O'CONNOR	JOHN FRANCIS	31442	SGT
MURPHY	JAMES	16014	SGT	O'CONNOR	PATRICK	8267	PTE
MURPHY	JOHN	15902	PTE	O'DONNELL	HERBERT	36862	PTE
MURPHY	THOMAS	25182	PTE	O'HARE	D.	15075	PTE
MURRAY	HENRY	32183	PTE	O'HARE	WILLIAM	15134	PTE
MURRAY	JOHN RUPERT	33910	PTE	O'MARA	J.	15558	SGT
MUSGROVE	JOHN ROBERT TURNER	25079	PTE	O'NEILL	JOSEPH	241263	WOII
MUSGROVE	TOM	202145	PTE	O'NEILL	PATRICK	9408	PTE
MYERS	ALBERT	30648	PTE	O'NEILL	PATRICK	27120	PTE
MYERS	FRANK	26695	PTE	O'NEILL	RICHARD	4936	PTE
MYERS	JOHN THOMAS	40167	PTE	O'ROURKE	FREDERICK	20945	PTE
MYERSCOUGH	WILLIAM	17926	PTE	O'SHEA	JOHN	11053	PTE
MYFORD	PERCY VINCENT	33831	CPL	O'TOOLE	ANTHONY	5094	PTE
NADIN	ARTHUR	15819	PTE	OATES	JAMES	18253	PTE
NADIN	HAROLD	16928	PTE	OCKENDEN	GEORGE ENOS	33877	PTE
NADIN	JACK	27097	PTE	OGDEN	JOHN	39432	PTE
NAIRN	JOHN	6178	PTE	OGISON	JOHN PETER	33914	PTE
NAUGHTON	HENRY	35120	PTE	OKELL	EDWARD	33913	PTE
NAYLOR	ALBERT	18018	A/SGT	OLDHAM	FRED	39409	PTE
NAYLOR	JOHN RICHARD	20781	CPL	OLDHAM	JOSEPH	35683	PTE
NAYLOR	THOMAS	8601	PTE	OLIVER	JOHN JAMES	33912	PTE
NEAL	FRANK	31541	PTE	OLIVER	MATTHEW	33966	PTE

Surname	Given Names	Number	Rank		Surname	Given Names	Number	Rank
OLLETT	JOHN ROBERT	37763	PTE		PEILL	LEONARD	202098	PTE
OLLETT	SAMUEL PULLMAN	22097	PTE		PEMBERTON	FRED	27039	PTE
ONIONS	ROBERT	31544	PTE		PEMBERTON	HAROLD	15137	PTE
ONIONS	THOMAS	38723	PTE		PEMBERTON	HAROLD	201135	PTE
OPENSHAW	ARTHUR	37863	PTE		PEMBERTON	P.	15664	PTE
ORAM	RICHARD JAMES	29464	PTE		PEMBERTON	THALBERG	18022	PTE
ORMAN	JACOB	10093	PTE		PENDLEBURY	JAMES	15861	PTE
ORME	FREDERICK WILLIAM	19575	PTE		PENDLEBURY	RICHARD	15448	PTE
ORMEROD	ARTHUR	24821	PTE		PENDLETON	WILLIAM JOHN	32161	CPL
ORMEROD	FRANK	24161	CPL		PENLINGTON	GEORGE WILFRED	17271	PTE
ORMEROD	RICHARD	15173	CPL		PENNINGTON	ELIAS	12699	PTE
ORMEROD	WILLIAM ARTHUR	15388	A/CPL		PEPPER	SYDNEY	19818	PTE
ORMESHER	SETH	32229	PTE		PERCIVAL	WILFRED	29426	PTE
ORRELL	JOE	35644	PTE		PERIGO	JOHN WILLIAM	16182	PTE
OSBALDESTON	G.	15777	PTE		PERRY	CHARLES WILLIAM	29395	PTE
OSBORNE	HENRY CHARLES	10979	PTE		PERRY	JOHN WILLIAM	13053	PTE
OSTLER	REGINALD GEORGE	33934	PTE		PETTIE	JOHN PHILIP	15138	SGT
OWEN	ERNEST FREDERICK	5651	SGT		PETTIFER	PERCY CONROY	30658	PTE
OWEN	GEORGE	27317	PTE		PETTY	FRED HARRIS	240342	PTE
OWENS	CHARLES	17976	PTE		PEVERALL	AUGUSTUS JAMES	27075	PTE
PAGE	JAMES FRANK	49279	PTE		PICKERING	ARTHUR	15697	PTE
PALMER	JOHN	17903	PTE		PICKERING	JOHN	27081	PTE
PALMER	JOHN	27996	PTE		PICKERING	ROBERT	15942	PTE
PAPWORTH	CHARLES	26604	PTE		PICKERING	WILLIAM JAMES	16027	PTE
PARKER	CHARLES EDWIN	40862	PTE		PICKLES	FRED KAY	35596	PTE
PARKER	HAROLD	18939	PTE		PICKLES	HERBERT	17161	PTE
PARKER	HAROLD	29469	PTE		PICKLES	RICHARD	25386	PTE
PARKER	HERBERT	15065	PTE		PICKLES	ROBERT FOULDS	23149	PTE
PARKER	HERBERT	23890	PTE		PICKLES	SYDNEY	242384	PTE
PARKER	THOMAS	32096	PTE		PICKLES	WILLIAM	12513	PTE
PARKER	W.	15962	PTE		PICKUP	EDWARD ROGERS	33883	PTE
PARKER	WILLIAM AARON	36615	PTE		PICKUP	FRANK TAYLOR	26831	PTE
PARKES	T.	15135	SGT		PICKUP	FREDERICK	15594	PTE
PARKINGTON	FRED	15822	PTE		PICKUP	GEORGE	15552	PTE
PARKINSON	EDWARD	15421	PTE		PICKUP	J. R.	18008	PTE
PARKINSON	FRED	15102	PTE		PICKUP	JOHN	17875	PTE
PARKINSON	THOMAS	36955	PTE		PICKUP	JOHN RENNIE	38356	PTE
PARKINSON	THOMAS	37311	PTE		PICKUP	SAMUEL	35705	PTE
PARKINSON	WILLIAM HENRY	15925	PTE		PICKUP	WILLIAM	15034	PTE
PARLOUR	CHARLES	240461	SGT		PICKUP	WILLIAM	28729	PTE
PARR	JONATHAN	32053	PTE		PICKVANCE	JOSEPH	37539	PTE
PARRY	RICHARD	13547	PTE		PIGGOTT	ALBERT	33958	PTE
PARRY	THOMAS	15539	PTE		PIKE	ARTHUR JOHN	242879	PTE
PARRY	THOMAS	18397	PTE		PILKINGTON	GEORGE WILLIAM	15862	PTE
PARTINGTON	ADAM	20954	PTE		PILKINGTON	HARRY	30657	PTE
PARTINGTON	JOSEPH IRVING	49232	PTE		PILKINGTON	HARRY	236247	PTE
PARTRIDGE	CHARLES WILLIAM	49338	PTE		PILKINGTON	J.	15035	SGT
PASS	JAMES	33871	PTE		PILKINGTON	JAMES ALBERT	31545	PTE
PASSMORE	T.	15995	PTE		PILKINGTON	JOSEPH	15166	PTE
PATE	BURROWS	34162	PTE		PILKINGTON	WILLIAM	15823	SGT
PATE	HUGH WINTERBOTTOM	28748	PTE		PILKINGTON	WILLIAM	32055	PTE
PATE	WILLIAM	15576	PTE		PILLING	SAMUEL	21872	PTE
PATES	WILLIAM HENRY	30538	PTE		PILLINGER	HENRY	33890	PTE
PAUL	FREDERICK	32185	PTE		PINCHIN	HARRY	16950	PTE
PAUL	LUKE	240287	PTE		PINCOTT	GEORGE STANLEY	39259	PTE
PAWSON	WILLIAM	29466	PTE		PINDER	WILLIAM THORPE	33406	PTE
PAYNE	GILBERT ALLAN	202125	PTE		PIPER	WALTER	37700	PTE
PEACH	ROWLAND	24527	CPL		PITMAN	WILLIAM	23936	CPL
PEARCE	R.	17857	PTE		PLACE	ERNEST	15036	PTE
PEARSON	ARTHUR JAMES GODFREY	32279	PTE		PLACE	THOMAS	35651	PTE
PEARSON	HERBERT	27752	SGT		PLANT	JAMES	30470	PTE
PEARSON	JOHN	30564	PTE		PLIMLEY	HERBERT	30654	PTE
PEARSON	JOHN	37618	PTE		PLIMMER	JAMES STANLEY	27319	CPL
PEARSON	JOHN WILFRID	49242	PTE		PLOWRIGHT	WILLIAM HENRY	27753	PTE
PEARSON	THOMAS	21252	PTE		PLUMMER	THOMAS	21625	PTE
PEARSON	WILLIAM	18074	PTE		PODD	BENJAMIN GEORGE	22823	PTE
PEART	WALTER	15066	PTE		PODMORE	GEORGE	15766	PTE
PEAT	WILLIAM	17503	PTE		POLLARD	ARTHUR	241261	PTE
PEDLEY	ERNEST	27052	PTE		POLLARD	BELL	15729	PTE
PEEL	HAROLD	12548	PTE		POLLARD	GEORGE	15139	PTE
PEEL	HERBERT SINGLETON	20990	PTE		POLLARD	GEORGE	37703	PTE
PEET	JOHN FELIX	30992	PTE					

POLLARD	JOHN	15824	PTE
POLLARD	THOMAS HENRY	202156	PTE
POLLARD	VICTOR	33790	PTE
POLLARD	WILLIE	15467	PTE
POLLITT	JAMES HENRY	15067	PTE
POLLITT	JOHN HENRY	40649	PTE
POMFRET	HENRY	241723	PTE
POOLE	WILLIAM JESSE	49315	PTE
POOLEY	JOHN	26313	PTE
POORE	ALBERT	32187	PTE
POPE	ANGELO	15518	PTE
POPPLE	WALTER HENRY	204042	PTE
PORTER	HAROLD	26821	PTE
PORTER	WILLIAM	49237	PTE
PORTER	WILLIAM	49287	PTE
PORTLOOK	FRANCIS JOHN	29396	PTE
POSTLETHWAITE	WILLIAM	30662	PTE
POTTER	FRANK	32054	PTE
POUNDER	ALBERT	240294	PTE
POUNDER	NORMAN	20932	PTE
POWDRILL	ERNEST JOHN	18027	PTE
POWELL	ERNEST	16547	PTE
POWELL	T.	15295	PTE
POWELL	WALTER JAMES	49245	PTE
POWER	HENRY	15393	PTE
POWER	J.	17999	PTE
POWER	JAMES	35455	PTE
POYNTON	NORMAN	35645	PTE
PRECIOUS	WALTER	40234	PTE
PRENDERGAST	JOHN WILLIAM	35650	PTE
PRESCOTT	ERIC ERNEST	39748	SGT
PRESCOTT	FRED	33405	PTE
PRESSLER	ARTHUR	20963	PTE
PRESTON	FLEMING	15394	PTE
PRESTON	GEORGE	25380	PTE
PRESTON	JAMES	27754	PTE
PRESTON	JOHN JOSEPH	31443	CPL
PRICE	CHARLES	40872	PTE
PRICE	FRANCIS	30655	PTE
PRICE	LEONARD GEORGE	39888	PTE
PRICE	ROBERT	33848	PTE
PRICE	THOMAS WILLIAM	17373	PTE
PRIEST	ALFRED	20287	PTE
PRIESTLEY	JOHN HENRY	24289	PTE
PRITCHARD	THOMAS	20760	PTE
PROCTER	THOMAS	200239	SGT
PROCTOR	F.	17895	PTE
PROCTOR	F. E.	17895	PTE
PROCTOR	HARRY	15469	PTE
PROCTOR	HUBERT	15470	SGT
PROCTOR	JAMES HENRY	29470	PTE
PROTHERO	THOMAS	49223	PTE
PUCKRIN	FRANCIS JOSEPH	30461	PTE
PULL	WALTER	15337	CPL
PUNCHARD	HARRY	29613	PTE
PURCHASE	ERNEST	33915	PTE
PURSGLOVE	BEN	37870	PTE
PURSGLOVE	HARRY	15767	SGT
PURSLOW	VICTOR	203172	PTE
PYE	ANDREW	27434	PTE
PYE	JOSEPH	29467	PTE
QUINN	FRANK	11927	PTE
QUINN	FRANK	33825	PTE
QUINN	JAMES	9423	L/CPL
QUINTON	WALTER	25494	PTE
RABY	T. H.	15338	PTE
RADCLIFFE	FREDERICK WILLIAM	15730	PTE
RADMORE	LEWIS	15087	CPL
RADMORE	WILLIAM	26798	CPL
RAINFORD	HERBERT	16018	PTE
RAINFORD	RALPH	15863	CPL
RALPH	JOSEPH JAMES	17929	PTE
RAMSBOTTOM	ERNEST	15825	PTE
RAMSBOTTOM	JOHN JAMES	36339	PTE
RANDALL	ALFRED	15826	PTE
RANKIN	ARTHUR WILLIAM	32058	PTE
RATCLIFFE	FRED	16019	SGT
RATCLIFFE	JOHN	26263	CPL
RATCLIFFE	WILLIAM	15540	PTE
RAWCLIFFE	GEORGE	201618	A/SGT
RAWCLIFFE	HERBERT	17936	PTE
RAWCLIFFE	JOHN	15297	PTE
RAWCLIFFE	RILEY	15140	PTE
RAWLINSON	THORNTON	40622	PTE
RAWLINSON	WILLIAM	36624	PTE
RAWNSLEY	AMBROSE	17990	PTE
RAWSON	HERBERT	40669	PTE
RAYNER	ALBERT	17273	CPL
RAYTON	HENRY	17966	PTE
RAYWORTH	T. A.	33407	PTE
READETT	GEORGE	203191	PTE
READY	JAMES	39868	PTE
REAVEY	EDWARD	33917	PTE
REDHEAD	JOHN HENRY	27026	PTE
REDMAYNE	ROBERT	240832	PTE
REDMOND	DANIEL	31404	PTE
REDMOND	HENRY	33409	PTE
REDPATH	ANDREW	22336	PTE
REDSHAW	JOSEPH	33410	PTE
REES	JOHN EDWARD	31548	PTE
REEVES	FRANK STOKER	30511	PTE
REEVES	THOMAS	17231	PTE
REEVES	WILLIAM JOHN	30197	PTE
REGAN	WILLIAM	13935	PTE
RENSHAW	WILLIAM	26603	PTE
RENSHAW	WILLIAM ARNOLD	27321	SGT
RENTON }	JAMES	20907	CPL
RENTON }	JAMES	35401	CPL
RENTON	RICHARD	15339	PTE
REYNOLDS	ARTHUR	49289	PTE
REYNOLDS	RICHARD	29471	PTE
REYNOLDS	ROBERT	17668	PTE
REYNOLDS	THOMAS JOHN	33408	PTE
RHODES	ALBERT	22309	PTE
RHODES	ARTHUR	5177	PTE
RICHARDS	JOHN GEORGE	29397	PTE
RICHARDS	WILLIAM HENRY	37378	PTE
RICHARDSON	ARTHUR	235617	PTE
RICHARDSON	BERTIE SAMUEL	31444	PTE
RICHARDSON	D.	18059	PTE
RICHARDSON	MATTHEW	49259	PTE
RICHARDSON	REGINALD FRANCIS	30549	PTE
RICHARDSON	WILLIAM	40351	PTE
RIDDICK	EDWARD	49236	PTE
RIDEHALGH	HENRY	36182	PTE
RIDGE	GEORGE	29340	CPL
RIDGE	WILLIAM HENRY	15752	CPL
RIDGWAY	JAMES	32057	PTE
RIDING	WILLIAM	15943	PTE
RIDING	WILLIAM	16996	PTE
RIDING	WILLIAM	35706	PTE
RIGBY	ARTHUR	240802	PTE
RIGBY	ERNEST	15864	PTE
RIGBY	FREDERICK	39921	PTE
RIGBY	HENRY	17940	PTE
RIGBY	JAMES	15587	SGT
RIGBY	ROBERT WORTHINGTON	15629	PTE
RIGG	ALBERT	15038	PTE
RILEY	ARTHUR	20972	PTE
RILEY	ERNEST	15586	PTE
RILEY	GEORGE THOMAS	27119	PTE
RILEY	HAROLD	17208	PTE

Surname	Forename	Number	Rank
RILEY	JOHN	235053	PTE
RILEY	JOHN WILLIAM	17854	PTE
RILEY	JOSEPH	17840	PTE
RILEY	M.	16452	PTE
RILEY	PATRICK	15310	PTE
RILEY	R.	16021	PTE
RILEY	VERNON	26494	PTE
RILEY	WILFRID	35653	PTE
RILEY	WILLIE	15731	PTE
RIMMER	ALFRED	23448	PTE
RIMMER	J.	15541	PTE
RIMMER	NATHAN	32097	PTE
RIMMER	OLIVER	15397	CPL
RISHTON	EDWARD	22141	PTE
RITCHINGS	ALFRED EDWARD	17866	PTE
RITCHINGS	WILLIAM HENRY	17865	PTE
ROBERTS	ALFRED EDWARD	31546	PTE
ROBERTS	ARTHUR LESLIE	242540	PTE
ROBERTS	CHARLES GILBERT	32060	PTE
ROBERTS	FREDERICK	24175	PTE
ROBERTS	HARRY	24227	PTE
ROBERTS	HARRY	235147	PTE
ROBERTS	ISAAC THOMAS	33839	PTE
ROBERTS	J. W.	15184	PTE
ROBERTS	JAMES HENRY	35439	A/SGT
ROBERTS	JAMES NORVAL	30576	PTE
ROBERTS	JOSEPH	39438	PTE
ROBERTS	LESLIE	17057	PTE
ROBERTS	P.	16020	L/CPL
ROBERTS	THOMAS TATTERSALL	35654	PTE
ROBERTSHAW	RAWSON	31140	PTE
ROBINS	A.	15904	PTE
ROBINSON	ALLEN	13829	PTE
ROBINSON	ALPH	31181	PTE
ROBINSON	ARTHUR	15997	PTE
ROBINSON	ARTHUR	23355	PTE
ROBINSON	CHARLES	33517	A/SGT
ROBINSON	EDGAR JOHN	29398	PTE
ROBINSON	EDGAR JOSEPH	24871	PTE
ROBINSON	HAROLD	21543	PTE
ROBINSON	HARRY	40443	PTE
ROBINSON	JAMES	15667	PTE
ROBINSON	JAMES	29087	PTE
ROBINSON	JAMES	240455	PTE
ROBINSON	JOHN	21675	PTE
ROBINSON	JOHN ROBERT	23048	PTE
ROBINSON	JOHN THOMAS	35449	PTE
ROBINSON	JOHN WILLIAM	15252	PTE
ROBINSON	JOSEPH	15963	PTE
ROBINSON	SYDNEY	27272	SGT
ROBINSON	THOMAS	15449	PTE
ROBINSON	THOMAS	20084	PTE
ROBINSON	THOMAS	22084	PTE
ROBINSON	THOMAS	26738	PTE
ROBINSON	THOMAS EDMUND	29353	PTE
ROBINSON	TOM	10416	PTE
ROBINSON	WILLIAM	24651	PTE
ROBINSON	WILLIAM	31405	PTE
ROBINSON	WILLIAM	39172	PTE
ROBINSON	WILLIAM PETER	33411	PTE
ROBINSON	WILLIE	15103	PTE
RODDY	THOMAS	36700	PTE
RODEN	J.	15668	PTE
RODEN	JOHN	35450	A/CPL
RODGERS	ALFRED EDWARD	32061	PTE
RODGERS	HAROLD	32098	PTE
RODWELL	GEORGE	12729	PTE
RODWELL	HARRY	27294	A/CPL
ROEBUCK	GEORGE THOMAS	23862	PTE
ROEBUCK	HENRY	29430	PTE
ROGERS	ALBERT EDWARD	17980	CPL
ROGERS	ALBERT VICTOR	22303	PTE
ROGERS	FREDERICK ERNEST	27323	PTE
ROGERS	GEORGE	31445	CPL
ROGERS	JOHN EDWARD	30665	PTE
ROGERS	JOHN WILLIE	22168	CPL
ROGERSON	EDWARD	25453	PTE
ROLLINS	SETH	15964	PTE
ROLLINSON	GEORGE CHARLES	32059	PTE
ROONEY	MATTHEW	31413	PTE
ROSCOE	GEORGE	36867	PTE
ROSCOE	JAMES JOSEPH	12810	PTE
ROSE	ALBERT	241667	PTE
ROSE	RALPH	27042	PTE
ROSE	THOMAS	26919	PTE
ROSS	FREDERICK BRUCE	20718	PTE
ROSS	J.	24890	PTE
ROSSALL	JOSEPH	29367	PTE
ROSSALL	WILLIAM	25140	SGT
ROSSALL	WILLIAM	30161	PTE
ROSTRON	ARTHUR STANLEY	24086	PTE
ROSTRON	FRED WHITTAKER	25492	PTE
ROSTRON	GEORGE	21941	PTE
ROSTRON	JOSEPH	15965	PTE
ROTHWELL	EDWARD	10070	SGT
ROTHWELL	HAROLD	27138	PTE
ROTHWELL	JOHN	26557	PTE
ROUTH	HARRY	15733	PTE
ROUTH	HARRY	15753	PTE
ROUTH	HERBERT	16044	PTE
ROUTH	THOMAS	36378	PTE
ROWCROFT	JAMES	33930	PTE
ROWE	FRANK	31547	PTE
ROWELL	ARTHUR JOHN	9373	CPL
ROWLANDS	ROBERT ARTHUR	39370	PTE
ROWNTREE	JOSEPH HIGGINSON	15290	PTE
ROWSELL	ERNEST	40865	PTE
ROYAL	CHARLES JOHN	38825	PTE
ROYALL	THOMAS	49310	PTE
ROYDEN	JOHN SAMUEL	31461	PTE
ROYLE	GEORGE HENRY	29832	PTE
ROYLE	JOHN	32062	PTE
RULE	JOHN ERNEST	27278	PTE
RUSHTON	ALBERT	23311	PTE
RUSHTON	HARRY BARTON	19023	PTE
RUSHTON	JONATHAN	26776	PTE
RUSHTON	JOSEPH	15921	PTE
RUSHTON	JOSHUA	40121	PTE
RUSHTON	RICHARD LAWRENCE	40603	PTE
RUSHTON	THOMAS	25251	PTE
RUSS	WILLIAM JOSEPH	235202	PTE
RUSSEL	JAMES	23833	PTE
RUSSELL	JOHN	15088	PTE
RUSSELL	JOHN HENRY	15373	PTE
RYAN	THOMAS WHITTAKER	18070	WOII
RYCROFT	JAMES	242362	PTE
SAGAR	ROBERT HENRY	26078	PTE
SAGAR	ROBERT HINDLE	35708	PTE
SALE	THOMAS	33835	PTE
SALISBURY	WILLIAM	242237	PTE
SALKELD	WILLIAM	37530	PTE
SALMON	WALTER YATES	235624	PTE
SALT	RONALD FEATHERSTONE	32063	PTE
SAMPSON	ERNEST	49278	PTE
SANDERS	GEORGE	27254	PTE
SANDERS	JOSEPH	49243	PTE
SANDERSON	CHARLES	242545	PTE
SANDERSON	DOUGLAS	235981	WOII
SANDERSON	HARRY	31448	CPL
SANDERSON	ROBERT FISHER	39429	PTE
SANDEY	FREDERICK HERBERT	30670	SGT
SANDIFORD	JOHN WILLIAM JONES	40616	PTE

SAUNDERS	LEONARD	15966	PTE
SAWYER	JACK	32068	PTE
SAXTON	GEORGE CHARLES	33974	PTE
SAYER	FREDERICK	15971	PTE
SAYER	ROBERT SUMNER	21751	PTE
SCANLON	JOHN HENRY	30568	PTE
SCHOFIELD	J. H.	15754	L/CPL
SCHOFIELD	THOMAS	26470	PTE
SCHOLEFIELD	GEORGE HAROLD	25264	PTE
SCHOLES	JAMES ALBERT	17893	PTE
SCHOLES	RICHARD	26957	PTE
SCOTT	FRED	49290	PTE
SCOTT	FREDERICK ERNEST	32421	PTE
SCOTT	HENRY WALTER	31183	PTE
SCOTT	JOHN	49269	PTE
SCOTT	SYLVESTER	16023	PTE
SCOTT	WALTER	29059	PTE
SEAGREAVES	RICHARD	16124	PTE
SEARLE	CHARLES	21529	PTE
SEARS	EDMUND JOHN	10554	PTE
SECKER	FREDERICK WILLIAM	15422	CPL
SEDMAN	GEORGE	20940	PTE
SELBY	GEORGE EPHRAIM	27273	PTE
SELLARS	SAMUEL HENRY	12265	PTE
SENIOR	JOHN HAWKINS	30468	PTE
SEWARD	JOHN	39389	PTE
SHACKLETON	FRED	23180	PTE
SHACKLETON	GEORGE FRANCIS	35126	PTE
SHACKLETON	JAMES WILLIAM	33852	PTE
SHACKLETON	THOMAS	22180	PTE
SHAMBROOK	ARTHUR	39256	PTE
SHARMAN	CHRISTOPHER	202031	SGT
SHARMAN	FRANK	36684	PTE
SHARP	ERNEST	25183	PTE
SHARPE	WILLIAM	15908	PTE
SHARPLES	EDWARD	15039	PTE
SHARPLES	JOHN	15458	PTE
SHARPLES	JOSEPH	15542	PTE
SHARPLES	TOM	33886	PTE
SHARRATT	ALFRED	235071	PTE
SHARROCK	H.	16063	PTE
SHARROCK	HENRY	16065	PTE
SHAW	CROWTHER	15559	PTE
SHAW	EDWARD	9940	PTE
SHAW	EDWIN	14599	PTE
SHAW	JAMES	35522	PTE
SHAW	JAMES	200875	PTE
SHAW	JOHN WILLIAM	13064	PTE
SHAW	MATTHEW	25258	PTE
SHAW	REGINALD	33892	PTE
SHAW	SAMUEL	27325	PTE
SHAW	THOMAS	23452	PTE
SHAW	WILBERT	22305	PTE
SHAWYER	WILLIAM ARTHUR	30445	PTE
SHEATH	CHARLES JOSEPH	29423	PTE
SHEDDEN	DAVID	15340	A/SGT
SHEFFIELD	FRANK	15484	PTE
SHEPHERD	FREDERICK	15423	PTE
SHEPHERD	JOHN ARTHUR	15291	CPL
SHERBURN	ABEL	15756	PTE
SHERBURN	ARTHUR COLLINGE	203220	PTE
SHERBURNE	EDWARD	17938	PTE
SHERBURNE	JOSEPH	22182	PTE
SHERRINGTON	JAMES	15672	PTE
SHEVLIN	PATRICK	49482	PTE
SHIRT	WILLIAM	27297	PTE
SHORES	FRANK	27327	PTE
SHORROCK	JOSEPH	17910	PTE
SHORROCKS	WILLIAM	7425	WOI
SHORT	ELI JAMES	35663	PTE
SHORT	WILLIAM	27328	PTE
SHUTTLEWORTH	EDWARD	15632	PTE
SHUTTLEWORTH	H.	15521	PTE
SHUTTLEWORTH	HENRY MITCHELL	15292	PTE
SHUTTLEWORTH	JOHN	15343	PTE
SIDDALL	JOHN	13044	PTE
SILCOCK	ROBERT	40909	PTE
SILVER	REGINALD	33416	PTE
SIMISTER	JAMES WILLIAM	22354	PTE
SIMM	WILLIAM	30675	PTE
SIMMONS	HAROLD	32118	PTE
SIMMS	JAMES	17169	PTE
SIMPER	SYDNEY JOSEPH	235265	PTE
SIMPSON	HARRY	24141	PTE
SIMPSON	JOHN	15424	PTE
SIMS	DAVID	40857	PTE
SINFIELD	FRANK	203719	PTE
SINGLETON	EDWARD	15041	PTE
SINGLETON	FREDERICK	29363	PTE
SINGLETON	GEORGE	15174	PTE
SINGLETON	LAWRENCE	16064	CPL
SINGLETON	ROGER	15922	PTE
SINGLETON	RUDOLPH	23183	PTE
SINGLETON	WALTER	29416	PTE
SINGLETON	WILLIAM	22108	PTE
SKIMMING	JOHN	49241	PTE
SKINNER	JOHN	28175	CPL
SLATER	ALBERT	15341	PTE
SLATER	GEORGE	37213	PTE
SLATER	HERBERT	15520	PTE
SLATER	HERBERT	33860	PTE
SLATER	JAMES	28569	PTE
SLATER	JAMES	35665	PTE
SLATER	JOHN	15967	PTE
SLATER	JOSEPH	22836	PTE
SLATER	JOSEPH	29356	PTE
SLATER	RICHARD	240447	PTE
SLATER	THOMAS	15828	CPL
SLATER	THOMAS	29379	PTE
SMALL	JOHN	202361	PTE
SMALLEY	H.	18240	PTE
SMALLPAGE	REUBEN	33857	PTE
SMALLSHAW	JACK	15148	PTE
SMALLSHAW	PERCY	15699	PTE
SMELLIE	FRED	23328	CPL
SMITH	ALBAN	36363	PTE
SMITH	ALBERT	23151	PTE
SMITH	ALBERT	32119	PTE
SMITH	ALBERT	33864	PTE
SMITH	ALBERT	40502	PTE
SMITH	ARTHUR HENRY	30514	PTE
SMITH	ARTHUR HENRY	31406	PTE
SMITH	BENJAMIN	5837	PTE
SMITH	CORNELIUS	15877	PTE
SMITH	EDWARD	32064	PTE
SMITH	ERNEST	235149	PTE
SMITH	FRANK	15253	CPL
SMITH	FRED	23136	PTE
SMITH	GEORGE EDWARD	5744	PTE
SMITH	GILBERT	16594	CPL
SMITH	HARRY	15305	CPL
SMITH	J. W.	17437	PTE
SMITH	JAMES	35657	PTE
SMITH	JAMES	200028	PTE
SMITH	JAMES HENRY	202699	PTE
SMITH	JAMES WATSON	30455	SGT
SMITH	JOHN	15425	PTE
SMITH	JOHN	22976	PTE
SMITH	JOHN	37725	PTE
SMITH	JOHN BERTRAM	31408	PTE
SMITH	JOHN HERBERT	33413	PTE
SMITH	JOSEPH	28571	PTE

Surname	Forename(s)	Number	Rank
SMITH	JOSEPH	200911	PTE
SMITH	RICHARD	15188	SGT
SMITH	RICHARD PERCIVAL	30554	CPL
SMITH	ROBERT	35655	PTE
SMITH	SAMUEL	15254	CPL
SMITH	SAMUEL	19630	PTE
SMITH	STEPHEN	31549	PTE
SMITH	SYDNEY	18799	PTE
SMITH	THOMAS	13034	PTE
SMITH	THOMAS	38361	PTE
SMITH	THOMAS	240617	PTE
SMITH	THOMAS HAWORTH	15380	PTE
SMITH	WALTER	15945	PTE
SMITH	WALTER	18311	PTE
SMITH	WILLIAM	15829	PTE
SMITH	WILLIAM	31407	PTE
SMITH	WILLIAM	33833	PTE
SMITH	WILLIAM	201016	PTE
SMITH	WILLIE	27130	PTE
SMITHERAM	WILFRED GEORGE	38669	PTE
SMITHERS	LOUIS	202706	PTE
SMITHIES	ROBERT	15311	PTE
SMITHSON	ROBERT	24962	PTE
SMOLENSKI	CHARLES	33412	PTE
SNAILHAM	JAMES	15349	PTE
SNAPE	EDWARD	26844	PTE
SNAPE	RICHARD STAINES	20970	PTE
SNAPE	WILLIAM	17581	PTE
SNELLING	WILLIAM GEORGE	49314	PTE
SNOWDEN	FRED	27148	PTE
SOLLOWAY	JOHN LAWRENCE	30678	PTE
SOLOMAN	MARCUS	33855	PTE
SOUTER	THOMAS	33795	PTE
SOUTHALL	ROBERT	16184	PTE
SOUTHERN	CHARLES	29362	PTE
SOUTHWELL	TOM	32065	PTE
SOUTHWORTH	G.	16000	PTE
SOUTHWORTH	HARRY	23124	PTE
SOUTHWORTH	R.	17991	PTE
SOUTHWORTH	THOMAS	15426	SGT
SOWERBUTTS	JOHN JAMES	28683	PTE
SPARKS	GEORGE WILLIAM	37072	PTE
SPEAK	ARTHUR	241750	PTE
SPEAK	DAVID JAMES	18101	PTE
SPEAK	HOLFORD	24139	PTE
SPEAK	THOMAS	15450	SGT
SPEAKMAN	JAMES	15673	PTE
SPEAR	FRANK	15580	PTE
SPEDDING	THOMAS	15757	PTE
SPEIGHT	HUGH	40564	PTE
SPENCER	ALFRED	28866	PTE
SPENCER	ERNEST	25497	PTE
SPENCER	FRANK	24092	PTE
SPENCER	J. A.	15377	PTE
SPENCER	WILLIAM JAMES	16048	PTE
SPIGHT	EDMUND WALKER	30435	PTE
SPRUCE	JOHN WILLIAM	29407	PTE
SQUIRES	JAMES	18060	PTE
STACEY	JOHN	241107	PTE
STANDING	ARTHUR JAMES	33953	PTE
STANDRING	THOMAS	31409	PTE
STANGER	ADOLPHUS	27249	PTE
STANNARD	JAMES	24955	PTE
STANSFIELD	ARTHUR	18510	PTE
STANWORTH	BENJAMIN	9880	A/WOI
STAPLETON	WILLIAM	16273	PTE
STARK	WILLIAM HEIGHTON	25369	PTE
STARKIE	ALBERT	34928	PTE
STARKIE	ARTHUR	29474	PTE
STARKIE	ARTHUR	34572	CPL
STARKIE	EARL	24262	PTE
STARKIE	EDWARD	29477	PTE
STARKIE	ROBERT	15522	PTE
STARNES	ERNEST WALTER	17671	CPL
STATTER	ARNOLD KAY	16589	PTE
STEAD	LEONARD	31550	PTE
STEELE	HARRY	29472	PTE
STEELE	ROBERT	235887	PTE
STENDALL	PETER EDGAR	29155	PTE
STEPHENSON	JOSEPH	203539	PTE
STEVENS	JAMES	202393	PTE
STEVENS	JAMES RICHARD	32066	PTE
STEVENSON	GEORGE THOMAS	201324	PTE
STEVENSON	JOHN	21480	PTE
STEVENTON	A. T.	15256	QM
STEWART	JOHN	49228	PTE
STILL	GILBERT	33826	PTE
STINCHON	THOMAS	18991	PTE
STIRZAKER	GEORGE	40657	PTE
STOCKDALE	JOHN	26585	PTE
STOKES	HORACE NEVILLE	31463	PTE
STONALL	JAMES RICHARD	32067	PTE
STONES	JAMES	40762	PTE
STONES	JOHN WILLIAM	33836	PTE
STONES	JOSEPH	18023	CPL
STONES	JOSEPH	30556	PTE
STOREY	AARON	15089	SGT
STOREY	BERTRAM JAMES	31125	PTE
STOREY	HERBERT	38357	PTE
STOTT	ALFRED	15472	PTE
STOTT	FREDERICK	15582	PTE
STOTT	HERBERT CECIL	24658	CPL
STOTT	WILLIAM	30674	PTE
STREATER	FRANK	39721	A/SGT
STREET	ALBERT	15342	PTE
STRINGFELLOW	GILBERT	16024	CPL
STRINGFELLOW	GILBERT	35459	L/CPL
STROUD	FRANCIS HERBERT	242051	PTE
STROWGER	PETER	235270	PTE
STUART	WILLIAM ALEXANDER	15732	PTE
STUBBINS	GEORGE	15381	PTE
STUTTARD	GEORGE	15427	PTE
STUTTARD	WILLIAM	15581	PTE
STUTTARD	WILLIAM	35435	PTE
SUDDERS	JAMES CHARLES	35664	PTE
SULLIVAN	DANIEL	21132	PTE
SULLIVAN	DANIEL	35658	PTE
SULLIVAN	JAMES	15733	SGT
SULLIVAN	JAMES	32111	PTE
SULLIVAN	WILLIAM	31462	PTE
SULLIVAN	WILLIAM	33414	PTE
SUMBLAND	THOMAS	40919	PTE
SUMMERLY	THOMAS	33918	PTE
SUMNER	JOHN	37291	PTE
SUMNER	REGINALD	18711	PTE
SUNDERLAND	ROBERT	24495	PTE
SUNDERLAND	THOMAS	23985	PTE
SUNLEY	WALTER	27298	PTE
SUTCLIFFE	JAMES RICHARD	15042	PTE
SUTCLIFFE	WALTER	24074	PTE
SUTCLIFFE	WILLIE	29475	PTE
SUTTON	JOSEPH	15350	PTE
SWAIN	WALTER	30482	A/CPL
SWALES	JOHN	23945	PTE
SWALLOW	WILLIAM	15588	WOII
SWEENEY	HUGH	31446	SGT
SWEENEY	THOMAS	13437	PTE
SWINDELLS	JOHN	31447	PTE
SWINDLEHURST	THOMAS	15149	PTE
SWITHENBANK	THOMAS CORNELIUS	203718	PTE
SWORDS	MAURICE THOMAS	21266	PTE
SYKES	JOSHUA	235623	PTE

TABERN	THOMAS	35671	PTE
TALBOT	EDMUND	15972	PTE
TALBOT	FREDERICK	20046	CPL
TALBOT	JOSEPH THOMAS	24076	PTE
TANSER	ISAAC	235110	PTE
TANSEY	THOMAS	241083	PTE
TATE	ALFRED	39236	PTE
TATHAM	WILLIAM HENRY	23163	PTE
TATTERSALL	H.	15374	PTE
TATTERSALL	SAMUEL LOWE	37075	PTE
TATTERSALL	WALTER	37226	PTE
TAYLERSON	RICHARD HENRY	242551	PTE
TAYLOR	ALBERT	40918	PTE
TAYLOR	ALBERT WILLIAM	32428	PTE
TAYLOR	BERTRAM	27313	PTE
TAYLOR	EDGAR	29479	PTE
TAYLOR	EDWARD	35669	A/CPL
TAYLOR	EDWIN LOMAX	19356	CPL
TAYLOR	ELIAS	29357	PTE
TAYLOR	FRANK	24793	PTE
TAYLOR	FRED	39398	PTE
TAYLOR	GAVIN	40219	PTE
TAYLOR	GEORGE	33419	PTE
TAYLOR	GEORGE ARTHUR	200520	PTE
TAYLOR	GUY RAWSTRON	27004	CPL
TAYLOR	HENRY	15150	PTE
TAYLOR	HERBERT	15395	CPL
TAYLOR	J. W.	15258	PTE
TAYLOR	JAMES	5271	PTE
TAYLOR	JAMES BRADLEY	35667	PTE
TAYLOR	JOHN	33418	PTE
TAYLOR	JOHN	40430	PTE
TAYLOR	JOHN WILLIAM	37686	PTE
TAYLOR	JOSEPH LAWRENCE	32109	PTE
TAYLOR	LEWIS BRAMWELL	54410	PTE
TAYLOR	ROBERT	36998	PTE
TAYLOR	ROLAND	39893	PTE
TAYLOR	THOMAS	24787	PTE
TAYLOR	THOMAS GRAHAM	32566	PTE
TAYLOR	WALTER	22255	PTE
TAYLOR	WILLIAM	16148	PTE
TAYLOR	WILLIAM ARKWRIGHT	15878	PTE
TEAGUE	FREDERICK RICHARD	49283	PTE
TEE	FRANK	30449	SGT
TELFORD	WILLIAM HOLROYD	30419	PTE
TERO	ALBERT EDWARD	33956	PTE
TERRY	J.	15973	PTE
TETHERTON	SYDNEY GEORGE	33841	PTE
THATCHER	EDWARD JAMES	29399	PTE
THELWELL	WILFRED	32069	PTE
THEOBALD	GEORGE	33961	PTE
THEXTON	JOHN	13399	PTE
THEXTON	WILFRED GREAVES	30688	PTE
THISTLETHWAITE	F.L.	15451	L/CPL
THOMAS	ARTHUR CHARLES	27256	PTE
THOMAS	CHARLES LLOYD	32100	PTE
THOMAS	DAVID	14715	PTE
THOMAS	DAVID GEORGE	40867	PTE
THOMAS }	FRANCIS JOSEPH	15045	CPL
THOMAS }	FRANCIS JOSEPH	35410	CPL
THOMAS	JOHN	30684	PTE
THOMAS	JOHN HENRY	34645	CPL
THOMAS	NOAH	40848	PTE
THOMAS	STEPHEN	15703	CPL
THOMASON	JOHN WILLIAM	15785	PTE
THOMPSN	CYRIL	30685	PTE
THOMPSON	ALBERT	15830	CPL
THOMPSON	ALFRED	242256	PTE
THOMPSON	ARTHUR	27142	PTE
THOMPSON	ARTHUR JOSEPH	54445	PTE
THOMPSON	EDWIN	17845	PTE
THOMPSON	EDWIN	28750	PTE
THOMPSON	ERNEST EDGAR	200725	PTE
THOMPSON	H.	18273	PTE
THOMPSON	HARRY	241411	PTE
THOMPSON	ISAAC	29406	PTE
THOMPSON	J. A.	15675	CPL
THOMPSON	JAMES	30687	PTE
THOMPSON	JAMES FAIRCLOUGH	22146	PTE
THOMPSON	JERRY	15755	CPL
THOMPSON	JOHN	15046	COL.SGT
THOMPSON	JOHN	24570	PTE
THOMPSON	JOSEPH	27299	SGT
THOMPSON	JOSEPH	37010	PTE
THOMPSON	JOSEPH ALEXANDER	18971	PTE
THOMPSON	RICHARD WILLIAM	36957	PTE
THOMPSON	ROBERT	23281	PTE
THOMPSON	SAMUEL	29425	PTE
THOMPSON	THOMAS	201328	PTE
THOMPSON	WILLIAM	49240	PTE
THORNBER	JOHN	18938	PTE
THORNBER	W.	15185	SGT
THORNBORROW	THOMAS HENRY	49230	PTE
THORNE	ALBERT EDWARD	49312	PTE
THORNLEY	RALPH HULME	15429	PTE
THORNLEY	RICHARD	242225	SGT
THORNTON	CLAUDE	27296	PTE
THORNTON	HENRY	35583	PTE
THORNTON	IRVING	40641	PTE
THORNTON	JOHN ARTHUR	37830	PTE
THORNTON	JOSEPH	25307	PTE
THORNTON	RICHARD	35668	PTE
THORPE	JOHN	23305	PTE
THORPE	JOHN BRAMWELL	15201	PTE
THORPE	JOSHUA	235627	PTE
TIBBLES	WALTER JOHN	29385	PTE
TIDSWELL	ERNEST	203014	PTE
TIERNEY	THOMAS	31552	PTE
TILLEY	JAMES SAMUEL ALFRED	33502	PTE
TIMILTY	BERNARD	30689	SGT
TIMMINS	HERBERT	29602	PTE
TIMMS	HAROLD FREDERICK	31477	CPL
TINNION	ALBERT	25257	PTE
TINNION	E.	18723	PTE
TITLEY	CHARLES	15879	PTE
TITMUS	ARTHUR THEODORE	40907	PTE
TITTERTON	SAMUEL ARTHUR	36702	PTE
TKACHUK	KIRILL	51307	PTE
TOBIN	THOMAS FRANCIS	33417	PTE
TODD	ALBERT	33984	PTE
TODD	WALTER COUNCELL	15259	SGT
TOLLEY	GEORGE WILLIAM	241683	PTE
TOMLINSON	JOHN WILLIAM	9807	PTE
TOMLINSON	THOMAS WALTER	15389	PTE
TOMLINSON	WILLIAM	15635	CPL
TOOMBS	CHARLES WILLIAM	32120	PTE
TOONE	BENJAMIN	33840	PTE
TOOTELL	FRED	37202	PTE
TOOTELL	WILLIAM	15676	PTE
TOPLEY	FREDERICK GEORGE	9325	PTE
TOPPING	JOHN JAMES	15946	PTE
TORKINGTON	EDWIN EUSTACE	29483	PTE
TORKINGTON	ROWLAND	241424	CPL
TOWERS	THOMAS	15545	PTE
TOWLER	ALBERT	29480	PTE
TOWNSEND	BENJAMIN HAIGH	40640	PTE
TOWNSEND	F. C.	15344	L/CPL
TOWNSEND	RICHARD HENRY	202158	PTE

TOWNSEND	THOMAS	15313	PTE
TOWNSON	R.	18061	PTE
TRAVIS	CHARLES AMBROSE	29120	PTE
TREGARTHA	EDWIN CHARLES	18055	PTE
TREGARTHA	HERBERT	203750	PTE
TREGEMBA	WILLIAM THOMAS	32427	PTE
TREGURTHA	FRED	28782	PTE
TREGURTHA	REGINALD	17952	PTE
TRIBBLE	HARRY	54395	CPL
TRICKETT	JOHN JAMES	35666	PTE
TRISTRAM	EDWARD	30686	PTE
TUHEY	JAMES	15734	PTE
TURNER	ALEXANDER	33866	PTE
TURNER	CHARLES	31464	PTE
TURNER	FRED	30711	PTE
TURNER	FRED JOHN	39311	PTE
TURNER	GEORGE	5088	PTE
TURNER	GEORGE BARKWITH	31410	PTE
TURNER	HARRY	36382	PTE
TURNER	JAMES	32099	PTE
TURNER	JOHN WILLIAM	30682	PTE
TURNER	JOSEPH	202350	PTE
TURNER	JOSEPH	242172	PTE
TURNER	ROBERT	235625	PTE
TURNER	THOMAS	202304	PTE
TUTON	JOHN HENRY	27300	PTE
TWEEDALE	FRANK	27073	PTE
TWELVETREES	BERNARD	15977	SGT
TYRER	ALBERT	39324	PTE
TYRER	JOHN	19249	PTE
TYRER	NATHAN	24135	PTE
TYSON	ARTHUR	16055	PTE
UNSWORTH	HERBERT	15866	PTE
UPTON	ADIN	201182	PTE
UPTON	HENRY	38724	PTE
URQUHART	THOMAS	33967	PTE
USHER	ALBERT EDWARD	236246	PTE
UTTLEY	JONATHAN	15974	PTE
UTTLEY	RICHARD	15832	PTE
VAREY	ALFRED	201157	PTE
VARLEY	J.	15091	PTE
VARLEY	JOHN THOMAS	23157	PTE
VARLEY	NEVILLE	18245	PTE
VARLEY	WILLIAM	27613	PTE
VARLEY	WILLIAM	49341	PTE
VARLEY	WILLIAM HENRY	22369	PTE
VEACH	THOMAS	49244	PTE
VEEVERS	HAROLD	24512	PTE
VENABLES	SIDNEY RICHARD	49286	PTE
VERNEY	JAMES AUGUSTUS	35456	PTE
VERNON	FRANK	31478	CPL
VERNON	PERCY EDWARD	33949	PTE
VICKERS	HENRY	30691	PTE
VICKERS	JACOB	32070	PTE
VICKERS	MATHIAS	31450	CPL
WADDICOR	ERNEST	201754	PTE
WADDINGTON	F.	16049	PTE
WADDINGTON	HARRY	15209	A/WOII
WADDINGTON	JOHN	29371	PTE
WADDINGTON	WILLIAM	35676	PTE
WADE	FREDERICK ROWLAND	27302	PTE
WADSWORTH	JOHN BRAMHAM	29489	PTE
WAGER	THOMAS WILLIAM	15598	CPL
WAINE	PERCY	18970	PTE
WAITE	JAMES	202912	PTE
WALKDEN	J. W.	17260	PTE
WALKDEN	WILLIAM	16461	PTE
WALKER	ALBERT	40758	PTE
WALKER	JAMES	15069	COL.SGT
WALKER	JOHN ARTHUR	31021	PTE

WALKER	THOMAS WILLIAM	30698	PTE
WALKER	WILLIAM	29350	PTE
WALKER	WILLIAM FREDERICK	29910	PTE
WALLACE	GEORGE STEWART	32073	PTE
WALLBANK	JOHN HAROLD	29139	PTE
WALLBANK	WILSON	40609	PTE
WALLEY	CHARLES	27083	PTE
WALLS	HARRY	35672	PTE
WALMSLEY		15210	CSM
WALMSLEY	ARTHUR	36354	PTE
WALMSLEY	E.	15865	PTE
WALMSLEY	FREDERICK ALBERT	15260	SGT
WALMSLEY	JAMES	15047	PTE
WALMSLEY	ROBERT	29485	CPL
WALMSLEY	TOM	15459	PTE
WALNE	JAMES	203242	PTE
WALSH	FREDERICK	36343	PTE
WALSH	JAMES	15151	PTE
WALSH	JAMES	16356	PTE
WALSH	JAMES	18956	PTE
WALSH	JAMES	201820	PTE
WALSH	JOHN	16235	PTE
WALSH	PATRICK	200524	PTE
WALSH	ROBERT	29366	PTE
WALSH	THOMAS HOYLE	27003	PTE
WALSH	WILLIAM	203745	PTE
WALSH	WILLIAM HODGSON	37834	PTE
WALTON	ALBERT	34573	PTE
WALTON	EZRA	27303	PTE
WALTON	JOHN	18618	PTE
WALTON	JOHN ARTHUR	16046	PTE
WALTON	JOSEPH	37872	PTE
WALTON	TOM	5954	PTE
WARBURTON	CHARLES	40027	PTE
WARBURTON	EASTWOOD PICKUP	27043	PTE
WARBURTON	HARRY	24130	PTE
WARBURTON	JAMES ALBERT	37335	PTE
WARBURTON	JOHN	27304	PTE
WARBURTON	JOHN	39092	PTE
WARBURTON	WILLIAM	17922	PTE
WARBURTON	WILLIAM HENRY	32357	PTE
WARD	JAMES	16001	PTE
WARD	JAMES	26961	PTE
WARD	JAMES	35677	PTE
WARD	JOHN EDWARD	15351	PTE
WARD	SYDNEY BOWEN	31479	CPL
WARD	THOMAS	26262	PTE
WARD	THOMAS	242058	PTE
WARD	WALTER	21921	CPL
WARD	WILFRED NORMAN	32071	PTE
WARDALL	THOMAS ARTHUR	27146	PTE
WARDLEWORTH	VINCENT EDWARD	15152	PTE
WARDLEY	A.	18774	PTE
WAREING	D.	15677	L/CPL
WAREING	THOMAS	20634	PTE
WARING	ROBERT	31557	PTE
WARING	WILLIAM	15678	PTE
WARING	WILLIAM	26960	PTE
WARREN	CROXELL ALFRED	33876	PTE
WARREN	RICHARD HERBERT	19837	PTE
WARRENER	FREDERICK DANIEL	27118	PTE
WARWICK	GEORGE	30130	PTE
WARWICK	HARRY	15460	PTE
WATERHOUSE	ARTHUR BAYLEY	32241	PTE
WATERS	CHARLES BENSON	32072	PTE
WATMOUGH	RICHARD	15968	PTE
WATMOUGH	RICHARD	35423	PTE
WATSON	CECIL	33992	CPL
WATSON	DAVID	33885	PTE
WATSON	FRED	21427	PTE

WATSON	HARRY	24887	PTE
WATSON	HARRY	27293	PTE
WATSON	JACK RUSHTON	34447	PTE
WATSON	JAMES ALLAN	24797	PTE
WATSON	SYDNEY	25166	PTE
WATSON	WALTER	29380	CPL
WATTS	JOHN THOMAS	15636	PTE
WATTS	THOMAS	32496	PTE
WEARDEN	WILLIAM	22362	PTE
WEATHERBY	CHARLES	8811	SGT
WEBB	CHARLES	34795	PTE
WEBB	FREDERICK	24153	PTE
WEBBER	ARTHUR	15176	SGT
WEBSTER	HENRY	18062	PTE
WEBSTER	JOHN THOMAS	15579	PTE
WEIR	DAVID ANDREW	33789	PTE
WELCH	CHARLES ERNEST	38999	PTE
WELLS	FRED	31452	CPL
WERBISKY	JOSEPH	32244	PTE
WEST	ERNEST	15831	PTE
WEST	ERNEST	242614	PTE
WEST	WILLIAM	30693	PTE
WESTAWAY	GEORGE STANBURY	30420	PTE
WESTERN	JOHN	30363	PTE
WESTHEAD	WILFRED	15679	PTE
WESTON	WILLIAM HAROLD	21991	PTE
WESTWELL	FRED	22235	PTE
WESTWELL	J. T.	17842	PTE
WESTWELL	RICHARD	36991	PTE
WESTWOOD	HARRY HAMMOND	15947	PTE
WETTON	JAMES	7387	PTE
WHALLEY	JOSEPH	15488	PTE
WHALLEY	T.	16130	PTE
WHARTON	PETER	235982	PTE
WHATMOUGH	WILLIAM	15948	PTE
WHELAN	DENIS	15396	PTE
WHELAN	JOHN	26306	PTE
WHEWELL	FRED	17918	PTE
WHEWELL	FRED	35419	PTE
WHEWELL	HERBERT	15834	PTE
WHEWELL	SHEPHERD	15833	PTE
WHIPP	HARRY	34738	PTE
WHITBOURN	HARRY	6778	WOCLII
WHITBY	WILLIAM HENRY	32075	PTE
WHITCHELO	ROBERT WILLIAM	31126	PTE
WHITE	EDWARD WILLIAM	39024	PTE
WHITE	GEORGE	31475	SGT
WHITE	HARRY	33868	PTE
WHITE	HARRY	202532	PTE
WHITE	MARK	241917	PTE
WHITE	WILFRED	16201	SGT
WHITEHEAD	ALBERT	16003	PTE
WHITEHEAD	ALFRED HENRY	31555	PTE
WHITEHEAD	HAROLD	32259	PTE
WHITEHEAD	HARRY	36345	PTE
WHITEHEAD	J.	17853	PTE
WHITEHEAD	JOHN WILLIAM	26696	PTE
WHITEHEAD	RICHARD	39354	PTE
WHITEHEAD	ROBERT	26697	PTE
WHITELAW	JAMES	33919	PTE
WHITELEY	HAROLD	34797	PTE
WHITESIDE	EDWARD	16554	SGT
WHITESMITH	FRED	20939	PTE
WHITFIELD	GEORGE	39226	PTE
WHITFORD	HENRY	33874	PTE
WHITLEY	WILLIAM HENRY	23944	PTE
WHITLOCK	PERCY	30828	PTE
WHITMORE	HERBERT	40817	PTE
WHITTAKER	ALBERT	24416	PTE
WHITTAKER	CLARENCE	18891	PTE
WHITTAKER	EARL	15735	CPL
WHITTAKER	HARRY	17919	PTE
WHITTAKER	HARRY	40687	PTE
WHITTAKER	J.	18704	PTE
WHITTAKER	JACOB	20993	PTE
WHITTAKER	JAMES	26769	PTE
WHITTAKER	RICHARD WALKDEN	37362	PTE
WHITTAKER	THOMAS	15949	PTE
WHITTAKER	TOM	25381	PTE
WHITTAKER	WILFRED	18063	PTE
WHITTAKER	WILLIAM	21802	PTE
WHITTAKER	WILLIAM	34357	PTE
WHITTAKER	WILLIAM	36947	PTE
WHITTAM	ROBERT	202144	PTE
WHITTLE	H.	16025	PTE
WHITTLE	WILLIAM	39360	PTE
WHITWORTH	FRED	33935	PTE
WHITWORTH	JOSEPH HENRY	22144	SGT
WIDDALL	RNEST	31465	PTE
WIDDOP	CLARENCE	15453	PTE
WIGFIELD	HARRY	27306	PTE
WIGGAN	JOHN JAMES	16047	PTE
WIGGANS	MCINTYRE	15167	PTE
WIGNALL	HENRY	38937	PTE
WIGNALL	JAMES	24429	PTE
WILCOCK	THOMAS	242640	PTE
WILCOX	HARRY	33422	PTE
WILD	CHARLES	241491	PTE
WILD	JAMES EDWARD	14705	A/CPL
WILDE	RICHARD	29427	PTE
WILDE	WILLIAM	33837	PTE
WILDING	HERBERT	15681	PTE
WILDING	JACK	15454	PTE
WILDING	SETH HOLT	23158	PTE
WILDING	THOMAS	16067	PTE
WILDMAN	CECIL	240198	PTE
WILKEN	EDMUND HERBERT	29490	PTE
WILKINSON	ALBERT	18496	PTE
WILKINSON	ARTHUR	26671	PTE
WILKINSON	EDWARD	241195	PTE
WILKINSON	ERNEST	203625	PTE
WILKINSON	FRED	20946	PTE
WILKINSON	GEORGE	25003	PTE
WILKINSON	HAROLD	25068	PTE
WILKINSON	HAROLD	201227	PTE
WILKINSON	HARRY	17982	PTE
WILKINSON	HERBERT	26577	PTE
WILKINSON	JAMES ORMEROD	27121	PTE
WILKINSON	JOHN	15382	CPL
WILKINSON	JOHN	24511	PTE
WILKINSON	JOHN JOSEPH	40870	PTE
WILKINSON	RICHARD	17881	PTE
WILKINSON	ROBERT	22366	PTE
WILKINSON	ROBERT	37070	PTE
WILKINSON	WILLIAM	23140	PTE
WILKINSON	WILLIAM	27090	PTE
WILKINSON	WILLIAM	203711	PTE
WILKINSON	WILLIAM HENRY	38726	PTE
WILKS	ARTHUR	31468	PTE
WILLACY	THOMAS	26874	A/CPL
WILLANS	HAROLD STANLEY	15912	PTE
WILLIAMS	DAVID JOHN	32103	PTE
WILLIAMS	ELWIN TUDOR	20728	PTE
WILLIAMS	EZER	49313	PTE
WILLIAMS	FREDERICK HENRY	31127	PTE
WILLIAMS	HENRY	49331	PTE
WILLIAMS	JAMES	31558	PTE
WILLIAMS	LEONARD	40825	PTE
WILLIAMS	PETER	33849	PTE
WILLIAMS	RICHARD	11027	CPL
WILLIAMS	THOMAS	14789	PTE
WILLIAMS	WILLIAM HENRY	17648	PTE

Surname	Forename(s)	Number	Rank
WILLIS	ARTHUR	20933	PTE
WILLIS	GEORGE ROBERT	30536	CPL
WILLIS	JOHN	16737	SGT
WILMINGTON	E.	17965	PTE
WILMINGTON	LUKE	17993	PTE
WILMINGTON	TOM	15153	PTE
WILSON	ALFRED	39419	PTE
WILSON	EDWIN GEORGE	30692	PTE
WILSON	H.	15726	SGT
WILSON	HENRY	7434	PTE
WILSON	HENRY	15736	SGT
WILSON	JAMES EDWARD	17821	PTE
WILSON	JOHN	18058	PTE
WILSON	RENNIE	202174	PTE
WILSON	ROBIN	39245	PTE
WILSON	THOMAS	15683	CPL
WILSON	THOMAS	30712	PTE
WILSON	THOMAS	31467	PTE
WILSON	WALTER	12112	SGT
WILSON	WILLIAM	19816	PTE
WILSON	WILLIAM AITKEN	15202	PTE
WINCHESTER	T. W.	17904	PTE
WINCHESTER	THOMAS WILFRED	17994	PTE
WINDLE	HARRY	15051	PTE
WINDLE	THOMAS	23330	PTE
WINFIELD	GEORGE ALFRED	235153	PTE
WINTER	H.	15154	PTE
WINTER	JOHN	24514	PTE
WISEMAN	EDWARD	18204	PTE
WIXTED	JAMES CLARENCE	15835	PTE
WIXTED	JOHN	15778	PTE
WIXTED	WILLIAM	15639	PTE
WOLFENDEN	JAMES	25236	PTE
WOLSTENCROFT	JOSEPH	15105	PTE
WOOD	ALFRED	12323	PTE
WOOD	FRED	35674	PTE
WOOD	GEORGE HERBERT	7428	SGT
WOOD	HENRY	28695	PTE
WOOD	HERBERT	17917	PTE
WOOD	HERBERT	27308	PTE
WOOD	JOHN	25451	PTE
WOOD	RICHARD	26868	PTE
WOOD	RICHARD	32102	PTE
WOOD	THOMAS	16556	PTE
WOOD	WILLIAM	202064	CPL
WOOD	WILLIAM HENRY	22193	T/WOT
WOODALL	WALTER	24088	PTE
WOODBINE	FRED	17462	PTE
WOODIER	ARTHUR	31553	PTE
WOODMAN	GEORGE HENRY	10908	CPL
WOODRUFF	WILLIAM	201509	PTE
WOODS	ALFRED	15546	PTE
WOODS	HARRY	15704	PTE
WOODS	HENRY	24870	PTE
WOODS	JAMES HENRY	15684	A/SGT
WOODS	JAMES HENRY	23016	PTE
WOODS	ROBERT	26462	PTE
WOODS	STEPHEN	15547	PTE
WOODS	WILLIAM	33420	PTE
WOODS	WILLIAM	33424	PTE
WOODVINE	WILLIAM	17658	PTE
WOODWARD	GEORGE	38414	PTE
WOODWARD	PETER HAMPSON	36784	A/CPL
WOOF	THOMAS METCALF	30699	PTE
WOOLEY	SAMUEL	40653	PTE
WOOLFSON	NUSSON	49340	PTE
WORDEN	CHARLES	33423	PTE
WORKMAN	GEORGE ALBERT	29121	PTE
WORSLEY	GEORGE BARTON	15431	PTE
WORTHINGTON	DANIEL	15837	PTE
WORTHINGTON	FRED	30517	PTE
WOTTON	JOHN FRANCIS	241408	PTE
WRAY	ROBERT	17347	PTE
WRAY	WILLIAM GEORGE	24903	PTE
WREGLESWORTH	FRED	30762	PTE
WRENCH	WILLIAM	30122	PTE
WRIGHT	ALBERT	29372	PTE
WRIGHT	BENJAMIN	38362	PTE
WRIGHT	CLIFFORD	38695	PTE
WRIGHT	DAVID	200341	PTE
WRIGHT	GEORGE FREDERICK	32074	PTE
WRIGHT	HAROLD JOSEPH	33929	PTE
WRIGHT	HARRY	19880	PTE
WRIGHT	HARRY	29854	PTE
WRIGHT	JOHN	7080	PTE
WRIGHT	JOHN	15345	PTE
WRIGHT	MILTON	29486	PTE
WRIGHT	REGINALD	31451	SGT
WRIGHT	T.	15911	PTE
WRIGHT	THOMAS LINGARD	30229	CPL
WRIGHT	WILLIAM	15104	A/SGT
WRIGHT }	WILLIAM	15191	PTE
WRIGHT }	WILLIAM	35405	PTE
WRIGLEY	EDGAR DAVIES	32101	PTE
WRIGLEY	FRITH	40773	PTE
WRIGLEY	HAROLD	29769	PTE
WROE	WILLIAM	16655	PTE
WYNNE	JOHN FRANCIS GEOFFREY	49233	PTE
YARD	WILLIAM	33875	PTE
YARDLEY	DAVID ERNEST	29361	PTE
YARRANTON	CHARLES	15924	PTE
YATES	GEORGE ADDISON	15346	A/COL/SGT
YATES	JAMES	203903	PTE
YATES	MOSES	16463	PTE
YATES	THOMAS	15432	PTE
YATES	THOMAS HENRY	17863	PTE
YATES	WILLIAM	25487	SGT
YEO	WILLIAM	32508	PTE
YORK	PERCY	33938	CPL
YOUNG	DAVID	15952	PTE
YOUNG	GEORGE FREDERICK	40816	PTE
YOUNG	JAMES	15097	A/CPL
YOUNG	JOHN	17884	PTE
YOUNG	REGINALD	30700	PTE
YOUNG	WILLIAM LESLIE	21428	PTE
YOUNGS	ERNEST ARTHUR	33858	PTE

The orginal Pals and their fate

KEY * = Died as a result of the offensive operations 1.7.1916 - 5.7.1916. Only those where a positive link to the July Somme attack can be proved, usually by local newspapers, have been so marked.
W = Wounded, as above.
+ = Died during the war (all causes). Brackets indicate the unit and/or battalion, where this was not the 11th East Lancs.

Marks	No.	Name
	15000	LEO
+W	15002	BENTLEY
	15003	BLEASDALE
*	15005	CHAPMAN
W	15006	COWGILL
*	15007	CUNLIFFE
W	15008	DOHERTY
	15010	FELL
W	15011	FIFIELD
	15012	GIBSON
W	15013	GLOVER
W	15015	HARRINGTON
	15017	HINDLE
	15019	HOLDEN
W	15020	INGHAM
(7th Btn. +)	15021	ISHERWOOD
	15023	KIRKHAM
W	15024	KITCHENER
*	15025	LUND
*	15026	LIGHTFOOT
*	15027	LYON
*	15028	MCKENNA
	15029	MALONE
	15030	NEWSHAM
	15031	NUTTALL
	15034	PICKUP
W	15035	PILKINGTON
*	15036	PLACE
*	15038	RIGG
W	15039	SHARPLES
	15041	SINGLETON
+	15042	SUTCLIFFE
W	15045	THOMAS
	15046	THOMPSON
	15047	WALMSLEY
	15051	WINDLE
	15054	CHALLEN
W	15057	BENNETT
W	15059	DOWNEY
	15060	HEATON
+W	15061	HOWARTH
W	15062	HOWARTH
+	15065	PARKER
W	15066	PEART
*	15067	POLLITT
	15069	WALKER
*	15071	FLETCHER
	15074	HINDLE
	15075	O'HARE
	15076	BOWERS
*	15077	CLAYTON
W	15078	COLGAN
+	15079	COWBURN
	15080	DOBSON
*	15082	EDGE
W	15083	HARGREAVES
*	15085	MERCER
	15087	RADMORE
*	15088	RUSSELL
	15089	STOREY
W	15091	VARLEY
	15097	YOUNG
	15098	BERRY
+W	15100	HOLDEN
	15102	PARKINSON
*	15103	ROBINSON
	15104	WRIGHT
(1st Btn. +)	15105	WOLSTENCROFT
*	15107	BAINES
	15108	BATH
+	15109	BIRTWISTLE
(7th Btn. +)W	15111	BROADLEY
W	15112	CHADWICK
W	15116	DUFFY
W	15119	ENGLISH
(8th Btn. +)	15121	GRIMSHAW
W	15123	HEY
*	15124	HINDLE
	15125	HOLDEN
	15126	KERMEEN
W	15128	MAKIN
W	15130	MCDONOUGH
*	15134	O'HARE
W	15135	PARKES
	15137	PEMBERTON
+	15138	PETTIE
	15139	POLLARD
	15140	RAWCLIFFE
	15148	SMALLSHAW
	15149	SWINDLEHURST
W	15150	TAYLOR
*	15151	WALSH
(7th Btn.+)W	15152	WARDLEWORTH
	15153	WILMINGTON
	15154	WINTER
+W	15156	AINSWORTH
	15157	BARKER
W	15158	BRADY
*	15159	BRINDLE
	15160	CANNON
+	15161	COLLIER
	15162	GASKELL
*	15164	GREEN
	15165	HULL
	15166	PILKINGTON
	15167	WIGGANS
*	15173	ORMEROD
W	15174	SINGLETON
	15176	WEBBER
W	15177	BODEN
	15178	ANDREW
*	15179	ASHWORTH
	15181	HIGGIN
W	15183	LEEMING
W	15184	ROBERTS
W	15185	THORNBER
	15188	SMITH
	15189	HARRISON
W	15191	WRIGHT
W	15193	CLARKE
*	15194	CONWAY
W	15197	HEYWOOD
*	15199	KENNEDY
W	15200	LANDON
+W	15201	THORPE
	15202	WILSON
	15206	CLEGG
	15207	DUNKLEY
	15208	GILMARTIN
+	15209	WADDINGTON
W	15210	WALMSLEY
	15211	GRIMSHAW
+	15213	ARCHER
	15214	BACHE
+	15215	BAILEY
*	15216	BANKS
*	15217	BARNES
	15218	BEARD
(8th Btn. +)	15219	BEST
W	15220	BIRD
	15221	BLACKLEDGE
W	15222	BRENNAND
*	15223	BRIGGS
*	15224	BURY
	15225	BURY
W	15226	CHADWICK
W	15227	CHADWICK
(8th Btn. +)W	15230	DEWHURST
+	15231	DOWNES
	15233	EDDLESTON
	15235	FELL
	15237	GRIFFITHS
*	15238	HARLING
	15240	HINDLE
	15241	HODGSON
W	15242	HOPE
W	15244	LUNT
W	15245	MCCALL
	15249	MORONEY
W	15252	ROBINSON
W	15253	SMITH
*	15254	SMITH
	15256	STEVENTON
	15258	TAYLOR
*	15259	TODD
	15260	WALMSLEY
W	15261	GREAVES
W	15262	BARNES
W	15264	CATTERALL
W	15265	CLITHEROE
+	15267	ELLISON
	15269	FINAN
W	15273	HUNTON

W	15274	LEACH
W	15277	DAKIN
	15278	DUCKWORTH
	15279	FORREST
	15280	GALLAGHER
*	15283	HAYDOCK
	15285	JACKSON
	15286	LEEMING
	15287	LEEMING
W	15288	LETTERD
W	15290	ROWNTREE
	15291	SHEPHERD
W	15292	SHUTTLEWORTH
W	15293	BRITTLEBANK
	15294	COLLINGE
W	15295	POWELL
	15296	DUTSON
	15297	RAWCLIFFE
W	15300	BARLOW
W	15301	BARNES
	15302	GREAVES
*	15303	HOWLEY
*	15304	JACKSON
	15305	SMITH
W	15306	CUNLIFFE
	15307	EAGLES
	15310	RILEY
*	15311	SMITHIES
	15313	TOWNSEND
	15314	BARNES
W	15315	BARON
*	15316	BEAGHAN
	15317	BIRTWELL
W	15322	DUERDEN
	15323	FARRELL
	15327	HARGREAVES
*	15328	HOLLAND
	15329	JEFFERSON
	15333	MITCHELL
*	15334	NICKSON
+	15337	PULL
	15338	RABY
W	15339	RENTON
	15340	SHEDDEN
W	15341	SLATER
	15342	STREET
(7th Btn. +)	15343	SHUTTLEWORTH
W	15344	TOWNSEND
	15345	WRIGHT
	15346	YATES
W	15348	HUNT
W	15349	SNAILHAM
	15350	SUTTON
*	15351	WARD
+	15356	MARSH
*	15361	BRECKELL
*	15362	DENT
W	15363	HEAP
	15364	HOLT
	15365	HOLT
W	15366	HOWARTH
	15367	HUMPHREYS
*	15368	INGHAM
W	15369	MARSHALL
	15370	MCGUIRE
*	15371	NOBLE
	15373	RUSSELL
W	15374	TATTERSALL
	15376	DAVIES
W	15377	SPENCER
	15378	DODD

	15379	HINDLE
W	15380	SMITH
	15381	STUBBINS
	15382	WILKINSON
	15383	ALMOND
+	15384	ASPINALL
	15385	BRIDGE
W	15387	GREEN
*	15388	ORMEROD
	15389	TOMLINSON
W	15391	DEAN
	15392	MURPHY
+	15393	POWER
W	15394	PRESTON
W	15395	TAYLOR
W	15396	WHELAN
*	15397	RIMMER
W	15398	ASHWORTH
*	15399	ATKINSON
	15400	BRADSHAW
	15401	BRYCE
	15402	BURY
	15403	COADY
	15404	COX
	15405	CRAWFORD
	15407	BRICE
	15408	DARLINGTON
	15409	ENTWISTLE
*	15412	HARGREAVES
	15413	HEAP
	15414	HEATON
W	15417	GREEN
+	15418	LANE
W	15419	MELLELIEU
W	15420	MILLINGTON
*	15421	PARKINSON
W	15422	SECKER
W	15423	SHEPHERD
W	15424	SIMPSON
*	15425	SMITH
	15426	SOUTHWORTH
*	15427	STUTTARD
*	15429	THORNLEY
	15431	WORSLEY
+	15432	YATES
*	15433	ASTLEY
	15436	DERBYSHIRE
*	15437	ENTWISTLE
*	15438	GASKELL
W	15439	HALL
(8th King's Own +)	15440	HART
W	15441	HAYES
W	15442	HAYES
	15443	HIGHAM
W	15444	HILTON
W	15445	IDDON
W	15447	NIGHTINGALE
*	15448	PENDLEBURY
*	15449	ROBINSON
	15450	SPEAK
W	15451	THISTLETHWAITE
*	15453	WIDDOP
	15454	WILDING
W	15455	BENSON
	15456	BROWN
	15457	MARKHAM
	15458	SHARPLES
W	15459	WALMSLEY
	15460	WARWICK
W	15461	CLARK
W	15462	GORST

W	15463	HALE
*	15465	INGHAM
	15466	MONAGHAN
	15467	POLLARD
*	15469	PROCTOR
	15470	PROCTOR
W	15472	STOTT
	15473	ABBOTT
W	15475	HOLLAND
*	15476	FRANCIS
+	15478	BARON
*	15479	BARNES
+	15484	SHEFFIELD
	15485	COSGROVE
*	15486	HERSEY
	15487	KENYON
*	15488	WHALLEY
W	15491	BENTLEY
*	15493	BURY
*	15494	CAREY
W	15497	COLCLOUGH
(M.G.C. +)	15499	DEMPSEY
	15500	EVANS
*	15501	GIBSON
W	15502	GIBSON
	15503	HAGGERTY
*	15504	HARDMAN
+	15505	HARGREAVES
	15506	HOLROYD
	15507	HOLMES
W	15508	ILLINGWORTH
	15509	JOHNSON
W	15510	KAY
W	15511	KIRKHAM
W	15513	MANLOVE
W	15514	MCLOUGHLIN
	15518	POPE
	15520	SLATER
	15521	SHUTTLEWORTH
	15522	STARKIE
	15524	ALLSUP
W	15525	ALLSUP
*	15526	BERRY
	15527	BROWN
W	15528	BUCKLEY
W	15529	GENT
	15530	HARRISON
	15531	HALTON
W	15532	HEATON
W	15535	LEAP
	15537	MARSDEN
+	15538	MILTON
*	15539	PARRY
*	15540	RATCLIFFE
W	15541	RIMMER
	15542	SHARPLES
W	15545	TOWERS
	15546	WOODS
W	15547	WOODS
+	15550	HALLIWELL
*	15552	PICKUP
	15555	COOK
*	15556	DUST
	15558	O MARA
*	15559	SHAW
*	15560	BAXTER
+	15561	BURROWS
	15562	CHRISTIAN
W	15563	DICKINSON
W	15566	FLETCHER
*	15567	HALSTEAD

	No.	Name		No.	Name		No.	Name
W	15569	HALTON	W	15667	ROBINSON		15767	PURSGLOVE
W	15570	HARGREAVES	W	15668	RODEN		15768	BANNISTER
W	15571	HEAP		15672	SHERRINGTON	*	15769	BARNES
W	15572	INGHAM	*	15673	SPEAKMAN		15770	BEAGHAN
	15573	KNOWLES	W	15675	THOMPSON		15771	DUCKWORTH
*	15574	LOCKETT	*	15676	TOOTELL		15772	HINDLE
W	15575	MCCARRICK	W	15677	WAREING	W	15773	HUGHES
(2/4th Btn. +) W	15576	PATE		15678	WARING	+	15774	LEEMING
W	15579	WEBSTER		15679	WESTHEAD		15775	MERCER
W	15580	SPEAR		15681	WILDING		15777	OSBALDESTON
W	15581	STUTTARD	W	15683	WILSON	*	15778	WIXTED
*	15582	STOTT		15684	WOODS	(M.G.C. +)	15780	ASPINALL
+	15584	HACKING		15687	BARRETT		15781	BALDWIN
+	15585	LONSDALE	*	15689	DIXON		15782	CALVERLEY
*	15586	RILEY	*	15690	HALEWOOD	+ W	15783	HASLEM
W	15587	RIGBY		15694	LUND	+ W	15785	THOMASON
W	15588	SWALLOW		15697	PICKERING	*	15788	BARNES
	15589	ASHTON	W	15699	SMALLSHAW	*	15790	BOWERS
	15591	GREENHALGH	W	15703	THOMAS		15791	BOOTH
+ W	15592	HOWARTH		15704	WOODS		15793	COLLINSON
*	15593	HOLDEN		15707	BROWN	*	15794	CHADWICK
*	15594	PICKUP	*	15708	BULLEN	W	15795	CULLEY
	15595	DAVIES		15709	BYRNE		15797	DUCKWORTH
*	15597	MARSLAND	*	15711	CLAYTON	W	15798	BARNES
W	15598	WAGER	W	15712	COOK		15801	FIELDING
W	15599	ALSTON		15713	COOKSON	+	15807	HOYLE
W	15600	ALSTON		15714	CRABTREE		15808	HORSEFIELD
+	15602	BALDWIN	*	15715	DAVIES	*	15809	HODSON
	15603	BANNISTER	W	15716	ENWRIGHT	W	15810	HUDSON
	15604	BAXTER	W	15717	FLETCHER	*	15811	ILEY
W	15605	BERESFORD	+	15718	HARTLEY		15814	KENDAL
W	15606	BIRD	W	15719	HOWARD	+	15815	LINDSAY
	15608	BULLOCK		15722	JACKSON	W	15816	MILTON
	15610	COLECLOUGH	W	15723	KENDALL	*	15817	MULHALL
W	15614	HAINING	W	15724	LOCKETT	*	15818	MULHALL
+	15615	FOGG	W	15725	MASON		15819	NADIN
	15616	GREENWOOD	W	15726	WILSON	W	15820	NELSON
W	15617	MITCHELL		15727	MORRIS	W	15821	NOWELL
	15619	HINDLE		15729 ?	NIXON	*	15822	PARKINGTON
	15620	HUGHES		15729 ?	POLLARD		15823	PILKINGTON
W	15621	HULME	*	15730	RADCLIFFE	*	15824	POLLARD
W	15623	KENT	*	15731	RILEY	+	15825	RAMSBOTTOM
	15624	LAMBERT	W	15732	STUART		15826	RANDALL
	15625	LEIGH		15733 ?	ROUTH	+	15828	SLATER
W	15626	MARSDEN		15733 ?	SULLIVAN	+ W	15829	SMITH
	15629	RIGBY	*	15734	TUHEY		15830	THOMPSON
*	15632	SHUTTLEWORTH	+ W	15735	WHITTAKER		15831	WEST
*	15635	TOMLINSON		15736	WILSON	*	15832	UTTLEY
	15636	WATTS		15737	BELL	W	15833	WHEWELL
	15637	HUMPHREY	*	15738	BRUNSKILL	*	15834	WHEWELL
W	15639	WIXTED	*	15739	CAMM	+	15835	WIXTED
*	15641	BOLTON	W	15740	CROSSLEY		15837	WORTHINGTON
W	15642	CLAYTON	W	15741	DAVEY		15838	BIRTWELL
W	15643	CORNWELL	W	15742	DICKINSON	W	15839	AINSCOUGH
*	15644	COWELL	W	15744	HANSLIP	W	15841	BARROW
W	15645	CUTLER	W	15746	JOHNS		15842	BERRY
*	15646	ENDERBY	*	15747	JOLLY	W	15843	CALDERBANK
	15647	FRANCE		15749	KENYON		15845	CALDERBANK
W	15649	HODSON	W	15750	LORD	W	15848	CRITCHLEY
W	15650	HOLGATE	W	15751	MEDLEY	W	15849	CULSHAW
+ W	15651	HUNTER	W	15752	RIDGE		15850	CUERDEN
+ W	15652	HURST	W	15753	ROUTH		15851	DERBYSHIRE
	15653	HASTINGS	W	15754	SCHOFIELD	+ W	15854	GREENWOOD
	15655	KENNEDY	*	15755	THOMPSON	*	15855	HARDMAN
+ W	15656	LANCASTER	W	15756	SHERBURN		15856	HOLDING
*	15657	LANG	*	15757	SPEDDING	*	15857	HULL
*	15658	LAWRENSON	+	15760	HEYS		15859	LUCAS
	15659	LEONARD	W	15762	DAVIS	+	15860	MAGRATH
+ W	15660	LOWE		15764	HATTON	*	15861	PENDLEBURY
W	15662	MOORCROFT		15765	IRELAND	(8th Btn. +) W	15862	PILKINGTON
W	15664	PEMBERTON	W	15766	PODMORE	W	15863	RAINFORD

	No.	Surname
W	15864	RIGBY
W	15865	WALMSLEY
*	15866	UNSWORTH
W	15869	CLOUGH
	15870	COUPE
	15871	DAKIN
*	15872	DENNEY
W	15873	HARRISON
	15874	HODGSON
	15875	NEEDLE
W	15877	SMITH
*	15878	TAYLOR
W	15879	TITLEY
	15883	ADAMS
W	15885	BOTTOMLEY
*	15886	CALVERT
	15888	COOK
+ W	15889	CLIFFE
	15890	CRYER
W	15891	EDWARDS
+	15892	HOLMES
W	15893	HODSON
W	15894	INGHAM
	15897	HAWORTH
W	15898	HADFIELD
W	15899	KENDAL
	15901	MARSHALL
*	15902	MURPHY
	15903	O'CONNOR
W	15904	ROBINS
*	15908	SHARPE
	15911	WRIGHT
(8th Btn. +) W	15912	WILLANS
	15913	ATKINSON
	15914	BARON
*	15915	COOK
	15916	HINDLE
	15917	LEWIS
	15918	LONG
*	15920	NUTTER
+	15921	RUSHTON
W	15922	SINGLETON
W	15924	YARRANTON
*	15925	PARKINSON
	15926	BOOTH
*	15927	COX
+	15928	CRABTREE
+	15929	CASSIDY
	15930	DEAN
+	15932	FAWCETT
	15933	HARKIN
+	15935	JACKSON
W	15936	LYTHE
	15937	LIVESEY
*	15938	MARSDEN
W	15940	NEWHAM
*	15941	MOLLOY
+	15942	PICKERING
W	15943	RIDING
	15945	SMITH
*	15946	TOPPING
	15947	WESTWOOD
	15948	WHATMOUGH
+	15949	WHITTAKER
+	15952	YOUNG
	15953	BENNETT
	15955	BRYERS
*	15956	CLARKSON
*	15957	DICKENSON
(1st Btn. +) W	15958	FADDEN
	15959	HAILWOOD

	No.	Surname
*	15960	MAKINSON
	15961	NOWELL
W	15962	PARKER
	15963	ROBINSON
*	15964	ROLLINS
	15965	ROSTRON
*	15966	SAUNDERS
	15967	SLATER
	15968	WATMOUGH
W	15970	HESELTINE
W	15971	SAYER
	15972	TALBOT
W	15973	TERRY
	15974	UTTLEY
	15976	KILNER
	15977	TWELVETREES
	15979	DIXON
W	15980	ANDERSON
	15981	ASHWORTH
+	15982	BUCKLEY
+	15984	DUCKWORTH
	15986	EVANS
W	15987	FOLAN
*	15989	HOLDEN
W	15992	MOULDING
	15993	HAYNES
W	15995	PASSMORE
	15997	ROBINSON
	16000	SOUTHWORTH
*	16001	WARD
(7th Btn. +)	16003	WHITEHEAD
W	16004	BROMLEY
	16005	BROWN
*	16006	CARR
	16009	DRINKWATER
*	16011	GRIMSHAW
	16012	HORROCKS
	16013	MOORE
W	16014	MURPHY
*	16015	LORD
W	16018	RAINFORD
	16019	RATCLIFFE
W	16020	ROBERTS
+	16021	RILEY
	16023	SCOTT
W	16024	STRINGFELLOW
W	16025	WHITTLE
*	16027	PICKERING
W	16030	BATESON
W	16031	BRADLEY
W	16032	HARGREAVES
+	16033	CLARK
	16034	COWPE
*	16035	DOUGHERTY
W	16036	FAIREY
	16037	FODEN
W	16038	HARRISON
	16039	HEYWORTH
W	16041	KAY
+	16043	NUTTER
W	16044	ROUTH
W	16046	WALTON
	16047	WIGGAN
W	16048	SPENCER
	16049	WADDINGTON
	16050	BARROW
	16052	HARGREAVES
*	16055	TYSON
	16056	BARRON
*	16057	BLACKSTONE
W	16058	BULLEN

	No.	Surname
*	16059	IDDON
	16060	DALTON
W	16061	ELLIS
W	16063	SHARROCK
	16064	SINGLETON
	16065	SHARROCK
W	16066	HOLDSWORTH
	16067	WILDING
	16068	CLAYTON
*	16070	BRETHERTON
*	17830	HOLDEN
W	17831	COTTER
+ W	17833	HOLGATE
*	17834	GRIMSHAW
	17836	GRAHAM
W	17837	BREAKS
*	17838	MULHALL
*	17839	BROADLEY
	17840	RILEY
	17842	WESTWELL
W	17843	BIRCH
W	17844	COTTOM
W	17845	THOMPSON
W	17846	AINSWORTH
	17848	CORNWALL
W	17849	GRICE
W	17850	CHAMBERS
*	17851	METCALF
	17852	CUNNINGHAM
	17853	WHITEHEAD
W	17854	RILEY
	17855	FLYNN
W	17857	PEARCE
	17858	BROUGHTON
	17859	CLARKE
*	17860	LORD
	17861	BAILEY
*	17862	CHARNLEY
*	17863	YATES
+	17864	BIRTWISTLE
	17865	RITCHINGS
	17866	RITCHINGS
*	17868	MUNDY
W	17869	HAWORTH
*	17870	DUERDEN
+	17875	PICKUP
W	17876	CHAPMAN
+	17877	LOMAX
W	17879	HAWORTH
	17881	WILKINSON
*	17882	BELL
W	17883	MCHUGH
*	17884	YOUNG
	17885	DOOLEY
	17886	KENYON
W	17887	HINDLE
*	17889	FINNEY
	17890	DEWHURST
	17892	BOARDMAN
W	17893	SCHOLES
	17895	PROCTOR
	17895	PROCTOR
+ W	17896	HAWORTH
W	17897	HAWORTH
*	17898	LAYCOCK
*	17901	INGHAM
	17902	JOHNSON
W	17903	PALMER
	17904	WINCHESTER
(2/5th Btn +) W	17905	MAKIN
	17909	LEWIS

		17910	SHORROCK
	W	17914	GREENWOOD
(9th Btn +)	W	17916	CLOUGH
	*	17917	WOOD
	W	17918	WHEWELL
		17919	WHITTAKER
	*	17920	GRIMSHAW
	W	17922	WARBURTON
		17923	NOBLE
	W	17925	BENTLEY
	*	17926	MYERSCOUGH
		17927	HINDLE
	W	17928	ACKRILL
		17929	RALPH
	W	17932	COCKER
	*	17936	RAWCLIFFE
		17938	SHERBURNE
	W	17939	GRAYSON
	W	17940	RIGBY
		17941	DRIVER
		17942	BARNES
	*	17943	HOULKER
	+	17944	HUDSON
		17945	DYSON
	W	17946	CLARKE
	*	17949	MAWDSLEY
	+	17950	BRADY
		17952	TREGURTHA
	W	17953	HOLDING
	*	17957	HOLDING
	*	17963	IRVINE
		17965	WILMINGTON
	*	17966	RAYTON
		17967	BARON
		17969	MARTIN
	W	17971	BENTLEY
	*	17972	JACKSON
		17976	OWENS
		17977	DAWSON
	*	17980	ROGERS
	W	17982	WILKINSON
	*	17983	CLEGG
		17984	COLL
	W	17986	DAVIS
	*	17987	DAVIS
(2nd Btn +)	W	17990	RAWNSLEY
	W	17991	SOUTHWORTH
		17993	WILMINGTON
	+	17994	WINCHESTER
	W	17995	BURY
		17996	BIRCH
	W	17997	CHADWICK
	*	17998	LAMBERT
	W	17999	POWER
	*	18003	ALLEN
		18004	HAWORTH
		18007	HINDLE
	W	18008	PICKUP
	W	18009	JAQUES
	*	18011	COADY
		18012	AMOS
	+	18013	FOSTER
		18014	BURY
	*	18017	DIX
	W	18018	NAYLOR
	W	18020	KENNY
	W	18022	PEMBERTON
		18023	STONES
		18024	BOARDMAN
	W	18025	HEYES
	W	18027	POWDRILL
	W	18029	GRUNDY
	W	18030	LEDWICK
	*	18031	CLARK
	W	18034	ISHERWOOD
	*	18035	O'CONNOR
		18036	GRAHAM
	+	18037	KENYON
		18039	EBORN
		18040	MALONE
	*	18041	HAIGH
		18042	HART
		18043	KENYON
	+	18044	BOOTH
		18046	BAILEY
	W	18047	BLOOR
	W	18048	BEWSHER
		18049	BULLOCK
	W	18054	LAYCOCK
	W	18055	TREGARTHA
		18057	COOPER
	+	18058	WILSON
		18059	RICHARDSON
	*	18060	SQUIRES
	W	18061	TOWNSON
	*	18062	WEBSTER
		18063	WHITTAKER
		18069	ATKINSON
		18070	RYAN
		18071	KENNEDY
	*	18072	HOGAN
		18074	PEARSON
	W	18077	AMES
	W	18078	CULLEN

Decorations 1916—1918 11th East Lancs

Compiled by Fergus Read

LG = London Gazette

The list is hopefully correct in its details, but may be incomplete. Corrections and additions will be gratefully received by the compiler. Mentions in Despatches have not been included.

Where a place name is shown in brackets these are reproduced as they appear in the London Gazette. They may indicate place of birth, enlistment or residence.

ATKINSON, Stranger
Military Medal
LG 23.2.1918 Pte. 23835 (Anfield Plain, Durham) (Atkinson was killed in action 12.9.1918).

BAILEY, Herbert
Distinguished Service Order
For conspicuous gallantry and devotion to duty. Owing to the heavy going the two rear battalions were late arriving on the starting tapes. Shortly before zero hour he, whose battalion was only covering the right half of the brigade front, grasped the situation and deployed across the whole front just in time to follow the leading battalion behind the barrage. When severely wounded later, he showed a high example of courage when in great pain. LG 26.11.1917 Capt. (A/Maj.)

BECKETT, Walter
Distinguished Conduct Medal
For conspicuous gallantry and devotion to duty. When in charge of a Lewis gun team got into position to frustrate a flank attack, and enfiladed the enemy, who were collecting in an orchard. He kept the gun in action after all the team had become casualties, and prevented any sorties from the orchard. When ordered to withdraw he brought the gun back, having used all his ammunition. LG 3.9.1918 Cpl. 27029 (Sabden).

BENTLEY, George William Henry
Military Cross
For conspicuous gallantry and devotion to duty when in command of a company in several critical phases, especially in holding on to a very extended front for five hours when heavily attacked, and keeping his men well in hand when withdrawing. LG 26.7.1918 T/Capt.

BEWSHER, Stanley M.
Military Medal
LG 16.11.1916 Pte 18048 (An award for 1st July, 1916).

BLACKLEY, Thomas
Distinguished Conduct Medal
For conspicuous gallantry and devotion to duty. This N.C.O. was sent with ten men to discover the situation in a village. Finding it occupied by the enemy he attacked and drove them out, holding the village until relieved. During the action he located an enemy machine gun position which was causing trouble, and silenced it. LG 3.9.1918 Sgt. 16353 (Wigan).

BLENKINSOP, James Walter
Military Medal
LG 14.5.1919 Sgt. 27262 (Stillington).

BRADSHAW, Russell
Military Medal
(The recommendation for this award reads as follows. No citations for the Military Medal were printed in the LG at this date, and such details survive infrequently in the records today).
This N.C.O. was in charge of the Battalion signallers during the operations of June 28th, 1918 East of NIEPPE FOREST. Immediately the objective had been taken he went out to establish communication with the forward companies. There was considerable difficulty in getting connection further forward than the support company but this N.C.O. made repeated efforts under heavy machine gun and artillery fire and ultimately succeeded in establishing and maintaining communication. The conduct of this N.C.O. during the whole operation was a magnificent example to his men. He worked continuously for 8 hours and in spite of constant shell fire he succeeded in maintaining connection with the front line throughout the operation. LG 21.10.1918 Cpl. 15400 (Accrington).

BUCKLEY, Frank
Military Medal
LG 14.5.1919 Pte. (L/Cpl). 15528 (Chorley).

BURY, Harry
Military Medal
LG 20.8.1919 Cpl. 15402 (Accrington).

CATLOW, Thomas
Military Medal
(Details from the 'Accrington Observer & Times' 29.6.1918).
Awarded the Military Medal for taking an important message under heavy shellfire on 27th March, 1918. Whilst engaged in this risky errand he was wounded and has been in hospital at Prescot ever since. He was presented with the Military Medal at Liverpool. LG 16.7.1918 Pte. 17475 (Oswaldtwistle).

CHADDOCK, Richard Stanton
Military Cross
For conspicuous gallantry and devotion to duty. When all his officers had become casualties, he took command, and led his men to their objective with remarkable ability and coolness. Although his left flank was in constant danger of being enveloped by fresh enemy troops, he made such dispositions that, when finally compelled to withdraw, he was able to do so with complete success. LG 9.1.1918 T/2nd Lieut.

DIXON, Frank Bradley
Distinguished Conduct Medal
For conspicuous gallantry and devotion to duty. During an attack this man, who was carrying Lewis Gun ammunition, saw the No. 1 of a team become a casualty. He immediately picked up the gun and carried it forward. Eventually he was the only one of his team who was not a casualty, but in spite of the heavy load of eight pans of ammunition and his own rifle, he carried the Lewis gun through very heavy hostile machine gun fire up to the objective, where he established it in a favourable position. He opened a flanking fire on a party of the enemy, who still resisted, and caused them many casualties and the post was captured. It was a fine example of resolution and gallant devotion to duty. LG 30.10.1918 Pte. 37849 (Clayton-le-Moors).

DRIVER, Robert
Military Medal
(Details from the 'Accrington Observer & Times' 27.10.1917).
For good initiative and gallant conduct whilst out in No Man's land with a wiring party on the night of September 28th, 1917. LG 4.2.1918 Sgt. (A/C.S.M.) 200579 (Clitheroe). (Driver was originally numbered 17941, and came from Oswaldtwistle).

DUFF, John Shire
Military Cross
For conspicuous gallantry and devotion to duty. During a retirement, though slightly wounded in the arm, this officer continued in command of his company and carried out an order which he received, in spite of machine gun and point-blank artillery fire. Later, he brought his company out in good order and took up a position allotted to him, when he had to be evacuated through loss of blood, after a fine example of endurance at a critical time. LG 16.9.1918 Lieut (T/Capt.)

EASTWOOD, William
Military Medal
LG 16.7.1918 Pte. 30600 (Nelson)

FLEISCHER, Spencer Richard
Military Cross
For conspicuous gallantry and devotion to duty. On several occasions his courage and determination enabled his company to delay the enemy's advance, and eventually to take up fresh positions driving off strong attacks. LG 16.9.1918 Lieut. (T/Capt.).
Distinguished Service Order
For conspicuous gallantry and devotion to duty. He led his company against a strongly fortified position, which he captured in spite of determined resistance, inflicting severe casualties on the enemy, taking field guns, trench mortars and large numbers of heavy and light machine guns. He personally rushed one of the guns that was delaying our advance. His capture of this important position undoubtedly made subsequent success possible. LG 15.10.1918 Lieut. (T/Capt.). M.C.

FULLER, John Norman
Military Cross
During an attack this officer was in command of the right platoon of his company. On reaching the enemy front line he rushed and captured an enemy machine gun, killing the detachment. Shortly afterwards he and his serjeant rushed another machine gun. The serjeant was killed, but 2nd Lt. Fuller shot the enemy gunner with his revolver and captured the gun. Throughout the attack he led his platoon with great gallantry and determination, and they captured two minenwerfer and six machine guns. He set a fine example of courage and leadership. LG 15.10.1918 T/2nd Lieut.

GEORGE, John Ieuan
Military Medal
LG 9.7.1917 Sgt. 34526 (George was killed in action on 14.7.1918).

GELLING, James
Military Medal
LG 14.5.1919 Pte. (L/Cpl.) 18411 (Nelson).

HANSON, Joseph Edwin
Military Medal
(Details from the 'Accrington Observer & Times' 19.10.1918).
For gallantry connected with transport work under heavy fire on 29th September, 1918. Pte. Hanson joined the 11th East Lancs. in early 1917. LG 14.5.1919 Pte. 36346 (Great Harwood).

HARSTON, John Charles
Military Medal
LG 14.5.1919 Cpl. 27287 (Barnsley).

HORSFALL, Basil Arthur
Victoria Cross

For most conspicuous bravery and devotion to duty. Second Lieut. Horsfall was in command of the centre platoon during an attack on our position. When the enemy first attacked his three forward sections were driven back and he was wounded in the head. Nevertheless, he immediately organised the remainder of his men and made a counter attack which recovered his original positions. On hearing that out of the remaining three officers of his company two were killed and one wounded, he refused to go to the dressing station, although his wound was severe. Later his platoon had to be withdrawn to escape very heavy shell fire, but immediately the shelling lifted he made a second counter attack and again recovered his positions. When the order to withdraw was given he was the last to leave his position, and although exhausted, said he could have held on if it had been necessary. His conduct was a splendid example to his men, and he showed throughout the utmost disregard of danger. This very gallant officer was killed when retiring to positions in the rear. LG 22.5.1918 2nd Lieut. (Horsfall was killed in action 27.3.1918).

HOWARTH, W.E.
Military Medal
LG 20.8.1919 Cpl. (A/R.S.M.) 29585 (Chorlton-cum-Hardy).

IRELAND, Roger
Military Medal
LG 11.2.1919 Sgt. 240852 (Padiham).

KAY, Ernest David
Military Cross
For conspicuous gallantry and devotion to duty. This officer in charge of a platoon, acted as rearguard to withdrawing troops the whole of one day, and was the last to leave each successive position. He continually rallied stragglers and re-organised the line on his flanks. The following day, seeing the enemy massing in a hollow, he took three Lewis guns forward 150 yards to a position from which he could effectively enfilade them. He was always in the open, watching for the enemy's movements or controlling the fire of his men. LG 16.9.1918 2nd Lieut. (The only 'Pal' to return to the Battalion after gaining a commission. Kay was formerly Sgt. 16041).

KERSHAW, John Victor
Distinguished Service Order
LG 1.1.1918 T/Maj.

LACEY, Cornelius
Distinguished Conduct Medal
For conspicuous gallantry and devotion to duty. When a platoon which had lost both its officers and serjeant was retiring, this warrant officer, leaving his trench, ran about 70 yards across the open under intense machine gun and rifle fire, and rallied the men, leading them to a fresh position to protect the flank, which was threatened. LG 3.9.1918 C.S.M. 23893 (Plumstead). (Lacey was killed in action on 12.4.1918).

LANG, Austin
Military Medal
LG 19.2.1917 Sgt. 15657. (An award for 1st July, 1916). (Lang is listed as being killed in action 2.7.1916).

LAYCOCK, Herbert Cecil
Military Cross
For conspicuous gallantry and devotion to duty. He was the senior officer of his battalion in the front line, in command of the centre platoon. He kept the line intact, although for three hours his flanks were enfiladed. During the withdrawal he covered the retirement of the wounded and M.O.'s staff, by taking up a position with two Lewis guns in front of the aid post. LG 26.7.1918 T/2nd Lieut.

LEEMING, Arthur
Distinguished Conduct Medal
For conspicuous gallantry in action. When all his officers became casualties, he took command and, though severely wounded, handled his company with great coolness and skill. LG 20.10.1916 C.S.M. 15183. (An award for 1st July, 1916).

LEWIS, F.
Military Medal
LG 14.5.1919 Pte. (A/L Cpl.) 31403 (Manchester)

LEWIS, H.
Military Medal
LG 14.5.1919 Pte. (L/Cpl.) 34427 (Burnley).

LEWIS, Lewis Hewitt
Military Cross
For conspicuous gallantry and devotion to duty when in command of a reconnoitring patrol. On the right preceding an attack he reconnoitred the enemy front line under heavy artillery and machine gun fire, and brought back valuable information. LG 20.10.1916 T/Capt.
Distinguished Service Order
For conspicuous gallantry and devotion to duty. On many occasions, while in command of the rearguard during two days' hard fighting the conspicuous services of this officer were of the utmost value. His organisation of patrols undoubtedly saved a very difficult situation. On one occasion the non-commissioned officer and two runners who were with him having become casualties, he was left alone, but with great determination, he was able to carry out the orders given to him. Later on, under heavy machine gun fire, he was able by his energy and fine example to arrest a retirement that might have assumed serious proportions, but with great courage in spite of difficulties, he rallied the men, collecting the stragglers, he put them into good positions, which he consolidated, and thus restored a very critical situation. LG 16.9.1918 T/Maj. M.C.

LONSDALE, William Farrer
Military Cross
For conspicuous gallantry and devotion to duty whilst leading his platoon to the enemy's trench which he seized and consolidated, superintending the work, and encouraging his men for some time after being severely wounded in the wrist. He continued to set the same fine example of pluck and determination until finally compelled to give in owing to the effects of the wound. LG 17.9.1917 2nd Lieut.

LOTT, John Cyprian
Military Cross
For conspicuous gallantry and devotion to duty in leading his company to their objective with great dash and ability. During consolidation he set a splendid example of coolness and disregard of danger, moving about on the top and encouraging his men. On several occasions he has shown exceptional gallantry, within three days personally leading three bombing attacks against a strongly wired enemy position. LG 17.9.1917 2nd Lieut. (Lott was killed in action 13.4.1918).

LUCAS, John
Distinguished Conduct Medal
On the 28th September, 1918, during the attack north of Ploegsteert, he was in charge of portions of his platoon which had become detached. He surrounded a pill box, causing the surrender of one officer and eight men. Although both his flanks were exposed, he continued to hold on to his position until ordered to withdraw. LG 11.3.1920 Cpl. 35437 (Chorley).

MACALPINE, Francis G.
Military Cross
For conspicuous gallantry and devotion to duty. By his fine example and personal courage he saved a very critical situation, collecting stragglers and consolidating a position under close fire from the enemy. LG 16.9.1918 T/Capt.

McKENZIE, Cyril
Distinguished Service Order
For conspicuous gallantry and devotion to duty in leading his company from position to position with uniform success. Five times attacked, he maintained his position until the end. He three times counter-attacked and gained his objective. LG 26.7.1918 T/Lieut. (A/Capt.).
Military Cross
After very heavy fighting, in which all his other officers were killed or wounded, he reached the objective and captured the position with only thirty one men left out of the whole company. The position he had taken was subjected to an intense and continuous bombardment for forty eight hours, in spite of which he continued the difficult work of consolidation with remnants of the company, inspiring them by his cheerfulness and courage. LG 15.10.1918 T/Lieut. (A/Capt.) D.S.O.

McLOUGHLIN, James
Military Medal
LG 29.8.1918 Pte. 35444 (Accrington).

MILLS, Harry
Military Medal
LG 29.8.1918 Pte. 29565 (Birkenhead).

MOORE, J. J.
Military Medal
LG 16.7.1918 Pte. (L/Cpl.) 16013 (Chorley).

MORRIS, Percy
Military Medal
LG 14.5.1919 Pte. 31533 (Mottram).

MOZLEY, William
Military Medal
LG 11.2.1919 Pte. 26539 (Colne).

NEVILLE, Harry
Military Medal
LG 11.2.1919 Pte. (L/Cpl.) 39698 (Warrenpoint).

NOWELL, Esmond
Distinguished Conduct Medal
For conspicuous gallantry in attack. Being sent by his company Commander to deliver a message he performed this duty, although wounded, under heavy fire; and subsequently returned to his company. LG 22.9.1916 L/Cpl. 15961 (Chorley). (An award for 1st July, 1916).

NUTT, Charles Edwin
Military Medal
LG 29.8.1918 Pte. 31542 (West Gorton). (Nutt was killed in action 17.5.1918).

PALMER, John Charles
Military Cross
LG 3.6.1918 T/Lieut.

PARLOUR, Charles
Military Medal
LG 14.5.1919 Sgt. 240461 (Burnley).

PILKINGTON, William
Distinguished Conduct Medal
For conspicuous gallantry and devotion to duty. On one occasion, when in spite of intense shelling by heavy artillery, he kept his trench mortar in action, although he had to dig it out several times when it had been buried by shells. He did excellent work on many occasions. LG 17.4.1918 Sgt. 15823 (Accrington).

PURSGLOVE, Harry
Distinguished Conduct Medal
On 4th October, 1918, near Warneton, he carried out a very successful daylight patrol. He crossed the River Lys by means of a half demolished bridge, and in broad daylight patrolled the enemy bank of the river, bringing back important information regarding positions and movement. While both crossing and recrossing the river the patrol was subject to considerable hostile trench mortar and machine gun fire. LG 11.3.1920 Sgt. 15767 (Oswaldtwistle).

RAWCLIFFE, Thomas William
Military Cross
For conspicuous gallantry and devotion to duty in bringing four trench mortars into position through a very heavy barrage. By determination and coolness he got his guns into position. LG 20.10.1916 T/Lieut. (An award for 1st July, 1916).

RAYWORTH, T. A.
Military Medal
LG 14.5.1919 Pte. 33407 (Sketty).

RICKMAN, Arthur Wilmot
Distinguished Service Order
LG 1.1.1917 Maj. (T/Lieut. Col.).
Bar to the Distinguished Service Order
This officer commanded his battalion covering the retirement of the brigade to a new position after both flanks had been turned. He displayed great courage and judgement. The following day he held an extended front against three determined attacks, and when the troops on his right flank were driven in he rallied them under close fire, and formed a defensive flank with them. LG 16.9.1918 Maj. (T/Lieut. Col.).

RIGBY, JAMES
Military Medal
(Details from the 'Accrington Observer & Times' 9.11.1918).
In May 1916 he was asked by his captain to go out single handed and trap three snipers who were sending grenades into the British trench and doing a great amount of damage. The place was called 'Suicide Corner'. (This was the first award to the Battalion — see Page 125). LG 9.11.1916 L/Cpl. 15587.

RITCHINGS, Albert Edward
Military Medal
LG 14.5.1919 Pte. 17866 (Accrington)

SHAW, James
Military Medal
LG 7.10.1918 Pte. 200875 (Blackburn).

SMITH, Fred
Military Medal
LG 16.7.1918 Pte. 23136 (Blackburn).

SNOWDEN, Fred
Military Medal
LG 13.11.1918 Pte. 27148 (Padiham).

SOUTHWORTH, Thomas
Distinguished Conduct Medal
For conspicuous gallantry and devotion to duty during an attack on enemy trenches. Having followed his officer into the enemy lines he killed three of the enemy, and when his officer was wounded took command, leading his platoon ably during the subsequent operations. He did splendid work in consolidating the position and his personal example had much to do with the success of the attack. LG 17.9.1917 Sgt. 15426 (Accrington). (An award for the action on 28.6.1917).
Croix de Guerre (Belgium)
LG 12.7.1918 Sgt. 15426 (Accrington).

SPEAK, Holford
Military Medal
(Details from the 'Burnley Express' 19.8.1916 and the 'Burnley News' 13.9.1916).
Pte. Speak sought the protection of a shell hole from heavy fire from the enemy. Shortly after reaching the place, he heard a comrade over the top crying for help. Though he himself was suffering from a bullet wound in the hand, he returned to the open field to the assistance of his comrade, there to sustain a further knockout blow — this time from shrapnel. Private Speak received dangerous wounds on the left side of the body. He was taken to hospital at Boulogne, and afterwards transferred to England. Happily he is stated to be progressing favourably. LG 1.9.1916 Pte. 24139 (An award for 1st July 1916).

STRINGFELLOW, Gilbert
Military Medal
(Details from the 'Chorley Guardian' 19.5.1917). Awarded for capturing nine Germans single handed on Easter Monday (1917). LG 9.7.1917 L. Cpl. 16024/35459.

STUART, William Alexander
Military Medal
(Details from the 'Accrington Observer & Times' 20.7.1918). For specially fine work under heavy artillery and machine gun fire on April 12-13 at his forward lines between Battalion H.Q. and Company H.Q. He salvaged sufficient wire to establish communication and though the line was constantly broken he never failed to repair it thereby maintaining communication between Battalion H.Q. to Company H.Q. throughout the engagement. He showed a fine example of devotion to duty and his efforts undoubtedly contributed to the success of the defence. LG 29.8.1918 L/Cpl. 15732 (Caergiole).

SWALLOW, William
Military Medal
LG 13.3.1919 C.S.M. 15588 (Accrington).

TAYLOR, Guy Rawstron
Military Medal
LG 11.2.1919 Cpl. (L/Sgt.) 27004 (Haslingden). (Taylor was killed in action 5.9.1918).

THOMPSON, Isaac
Military Medal
LG 16.7.1918 Pte. 29406 (Blackpool). (Thompson was killed in action 28.9.1918).

TIMILTY, B.
Military Medal
LG 11.2.1919 Sgt. 30689 (Seedley).

WALMSLEY, Robert
Military Medal
LG 11.2.1919 Cpl. 29485 (Turton). (Walmsley was killed in action 28.9.1918).

WARBURTON, W.
Distinguished Conduct Medal
For conspicuous courage and gallantry in attacking single handed an enemy bombing party. He killed the officer, wounded others and caused the remainder to retire. LG 22.9.1916 Pte. 17922. (An award for 1st July, 1916).

WHEELDON, Frederick Lawrence
Distinguished Service Order
For conspicuous gallantry and devotion to duty in leading his platoon to the attack under very heavy fire. He was the first to reach and to push into the enemy's trench, where he was opposed by four of the enemy, all of whom he killed single handed, although severely wounded in both arms and legs by a bomb which one of them threw at him. He continued on until eight men were left out of his platoon. This alone shows what a splendid example of leadership he displayed during the operations. LG 17.9.1917 T/2nd Lieut. (An award for the action on 28.6.1917).

WILKINSON, Harold
Military Medal
LG 14.5.1919 Pte. (L/Cpl.) 201227 (Darwen).

WHITE, Wilfred
Military Medal
Sgt. 16201. (White was killed in action 28.6.1918).

WILTON, Harold
Military Cross
For conspicuous gallantry and devotion to duty. When the whole of the troops in front had retired through the battalion this officer was ordered to prolong the line to the left with his company. This he proceeded to do under point blank artillery and machine gun fire, and although his flank was exposed he held on so effectively that he delayed the enemy by forcing them to consolidate. On three occasions when troops retired through his command he quietly held on until ordered to retire, and in one position he was attacked three times, repelling the enemy each time. LG 16.9.1918 T/Lieut. (A. Capt.).

Decorations to former 'Pals' and to those linked to the raising of the battalion

BROADLEY, Phillip J.
Officer of the Order of the British Empire (O.B.E.).
LG 1.1.1919 Capt. (An award 'for services rendered during the war'. Broadley was a former officer in the 'Pals', later engaged on National Service in Yorkshire.

CHALLEN, Stephen Benjamin
Military Cross
LG 12.12.1919 T/Lieut. att'd 9th South Lancs. (Challen served as a private in 'C' Company, 15054, on 1.7.1916. Later commissioned, he gained this M.C. for services in Salonika).

MILTON, James Clymo
Member of the Order of the British Empire (M.B.E.)
LG 3.6.1919 Maj. (Probably an award for work as Provost-Marshall in Ireland at a time of Seinn Fein activity).
Officer of the Order of the British Empire (O.B.E.)
LG 1.1.1923 T/Lieut. Col. M.B.E.

NOWELL, Esmond
Military Medal
LG 21.10.1916 L/Cpl. 15961 att'd 2nd East Lancs. (Nowell had previously won the D.C.M. serving with the 'Pals' on 1st July, 1916).

PELTZER, Anton
Distinguished Service Order
LG 3.6.1919 T./Maj. (A/Lieut. Col.) 9th East Lancs.

THOMAS, Francis Joseph
Military Medal
LG 9.7.1917 Pte. 35410 8th East Lancs. (Thomas had previously served as Cpl. 15045 with 'A' Company, and subsequently served again with the battalion).

11th (Service) Battalion. (Accrington)
MONTHLY ARMY LIST

September 1915

In Command
RICKMAN, A. W., *Major*

Majors
SLINGER, G. N.
ROSS, R.
MILTON, J. C.

Captains
BROADLEY, P. J.
WATSON, A. G.
CHENEY, W. H.
LIVESEY, H
PELTZER, A., *Adjutant*
RILEY, H. D.
TOUGH, A. B.
ROBERTS, W. R.
KERSHAW, J. V.
RAMSBOTTOM, J.

Lieutenants
HARWOOD, T. Y.
HEYS, F. A.
MACALPINE, F. G.
BAILEY, F.
RUTTLE, J. H.
RYDEN, L.
BURY, H.
RAWCLIFFE, T. W.
MITCHELL, H. H.
RIGBY, W. G. M.
KENNY, T. J.
WILLIAMS G. G.
STONEHOUSE C.

2nd Lieutenants
HAYWOOD, S.
WHITTAKER, H. E.
SLINGER, W.
BIRTWISTLE, F.
ASHWORTH, H.
JONES, E.
STORROCK, J. C.
HAYWOOD, C. D.
ASHWELL, E.
BRABIN, H.
FAULKNER, W.
BEAUMONT, G. J.
HELSON G.
LEWINO, W. A.
ROBINSON, N. C.
KOHN, W. A.
SIMS, B. W.
PALMER, J. C.
RITCHIE, E. E.
WATSON G.

Adjutant
PELTZER, A., *Captain*

Quarter-Master
LAY, G., *Hon. Captain*

September 1916

In Command
RICKMAN, A. W., *Major*

2nd in Command
REISS, E. L. *Captain*

Majors
ROSS, R.
MILTON, J. C. *Officer Cadet Bn*

Captains
BROADLEY P. J.
PELTZER, A., *Adjutant.*
KERSHAW, J. V.
RAMSBOTTOM, J.
HEYS, F. A.
MACALPINE, F. G.
GORST, G. T., *Lt. Bn.*

Lieutenants
BAILEY, F.
RUTTLE, J. H.
RYDEN, L.
RAWCLIFFE, T. W.
WILLIAMS, G. G.
SHORROCK, J. C.
ASHWELL, E.
WILLIAMS T. H.
BEAUMONT G. J.

2nd Lieutenants
GORDON, R. S.
McKENZIE, C.
BOUSFIELD, J. S.
MALLINSON, C. H.
ASHWORTH H.
CLIFFORD, S.
BRABIN, H.
LEWINO, W. A.
BATTERSBY, R. St. J. B.
ENDEAN, B.
CLEGG, H.
THOMPSON, H. W.
JAMES, R. W.
PALMER, J. C.
WATSON, G.
STANSFIELD, A. H. B.
CLARKE, L. W.
BOWLS, W.
LETT, A. R. C.
RAEBURN, G. P.
WILD, F. J.
DUFF, J. S.

Adjutant
PELTZER, A., *Captain*

Quarter-Master
SMITH, T. *Hon. Lt.*

July 1917

In Command
RICKMAN, A. W., *(D.S.O.) Major*

Majors
WAUHOPE, G. B.

Captains
PELTZER, A.
KERSHAW, J. V.
RAMSBOTTOM, J.
LEWIS, L. H.
HEYS, F. A.
MACALPINE, F. G.
DOBSON, F. K.

Lieutenants
WILLIAMS, G. G.
DUFF, J. S.
GORDON, R. S.
WILTON, H.

2nd Lieutenants
HOGAN, R. V. J. S.
McKENZIE, C.
BOUSFIELD, J. S.
MALLINSON, C. H.
LAUDERDALE, W. A.
LEWINO, W. A.
SMITH, O. T.
GOLCHER, G. B. W.
BATTERSBY, R. St. J. B.
ENDEAN, B.
CLEGG, H.
SIMS, B. W.
PALMER, J. C.
STANSFIELD, A. H. B.
BOWLES, W.
LETT, A. R. C.
WILD, F. J.
INMAN, R. H.
EVANS, A. H. C.
TAYLOR, S.
MILTON, E. L.
MAUDSLEY, J. T.
LEWIS-JONES, D.
RICHARDSON, H. C.
LOTT, J. C.
PENDERGAST, L.
BENDALL, G. M.
WHEELDON, F. L.
LONSDALE, W. F.

Quarter-Master
SMITH, T., *Hon. Lt.*

November 1918

In Command
RICKMAN, A. W. *(D.S.O.) Major*

2nd in Command
KERSHAW, J. V. *(D.S.O.)*

Majors
LEWIS, L. H. *(D.S.O., M.C.)*

Captains
HEYS, F. A.
MACALPINE, F. G. *(M.C.)*
DUFF, J. S. *(M.C.)*
BENTLEY, G. W. H. *(M.C.)*
FLEISCHER, S. R. *(D.S.O., M.C.)*

Lieutenants
WILTON, H. *(M.C.)*
LEWIS-JONES, D.
MALLINSON, C. H.
STANSFIELD, A. H. B.
McKENZIE, C. *(D.S.O., M.C.)*
BOUSFIELD, J. S.
PIGOTT, E. W.
GOLCHER, G. B. W.
BATTERSBY, R. St. J. B.
ENDEAN, B.
KING, T. H. P.
BOWLES, W.
RICHARDSON, H. C.
BENDALL, G. M.

2nd Lieutenants
CHADDOCK, R. S. *(M.C.)*
SMITH, W.
GRIMSHAW, J. E.
JAMES, S. F.
KAY, E. D. *(M.C.)*
CARRUTHERS, A. R.
GURNER, E. D.
TYER, E.
WOOD, R.
BROWNE, J. L.
PERKINS, D. L.
DEAN, A. E. E.
DROMGOOLE, F. W.
FORGIE, J. A.
GREENHILL, J. H. G.
HOLT, H.
ODDY, M.
BYGRAVE, A.
CRAVEN, C. A.
RICHARDS, G. P.
COMPTON, F. J.
SMITH, W.
PORTER, W.
PINK, C. H. G.
GAINES, R. B.
FULLER, J. N. *(M.C.)*

Quarter-Master
SMITH, T. *Lt.*

AN INDEX OF PRINCIPAL PERSONS MENTIONED IN THE TEXT

ANDERSON, PTE. H. 148, 155-6.
ASHWORTH, LT. H. 101, 105, 127.
ASQUITH, RT. HON. H.H., 12, 92.
BAKER, RT. HON. H., 12, 20.
BELL, PTE. J., 89, 160.
BEWSHER, PTE. S., 141, 150, 151, 170.
BIRCH, PTE. (W COY), 176.
BIRCH, PTE. (X COY), 81.
BLOOR, PTE. H., 156, 187, 189.
BRADSHAW, CPL. R., 93, 98, 114, 117, 124, 127, 129, 149, 157-8.
BROADLEY, CAPT. P., 20, 24, 44, 65, 72, 130.
BURY, L/CPL. H., 149, 157-8.
BURY, LT. H., 49, 94, 115, 125.
CAREY, PTE. T., 117, 156.
CARTER-CAMPBELL, BR./GEN. G.T.C., 99, 128, 177.
CHEETHAM, PTE. A., 180.
CLARK, PTE. S., 129, 140, 151, 187.
CLARKE, PTE. W., 139-40, 141-2, 154-5, 170.
COADY, PTE. T., 70, 81, 117, 130, 132, 141, 177.
COCKSHUTT, LT., 37, 47.
COWELL, PTE. W., 73, 104, 106, 115, 117, 121, 130, 131, 160.
DERBY, LORD, 18, 92, 116.
DICKSON, MAJ./GEN. E.T., 57, 74.
DRISCOLL, COL. D.P., 21, 22.
DUERDEN, PTE. O., 149-50.
EDWARDS, I., 70, 71, 132.
FISHER, PTE. R., 95, 148, 155.
GIDLOW-JACKSON, 2/LT. C.W., 49, 74.
GLOVER, PTE. C., 59, 93, 99, 146, 150, 175, 178.
GOUGH, LT./GEN. SIR H., 174, 177.
GREAVES, PTE. W., 129, 159.
GREY, SIR, E., 12.
HAIG, GEN. SIR, D., 130, 132, 173-4.
HALE, CPL. H., 149-50.
HARWOOD, J., 19-22, 24, 29, 31, 34, 37, 40-41, 45, 51, 53, 57, 61, 73-4, 83, 87, 89-91, 100-101, 115, 127-8, 132, 176, 185-6, 188.

HEY, C.S.M. F. 129, 141, 151.
HEYS, LTD. F.A., 46, 159, 176.
HINDLE, AQMS. J.A., 81, 117, 188.
HINDLE, PTE. J., 139.
HOLT, CAPT. N., 31, 33.
HUNTER-WESTON, LT./GEN. SIR A.G., 119, 126, 132, 137, 169, 173, 174.
INGHAM, SGT. B., 29, 143, 160.
KAISER, U/O. F., 146.
KAY, SGT. E., 47, 81, 142, 154, 178, 188.
KAY, PTE. H., 113, 123, 126, 129, 131, 139, 148-9, 156, 159.
KITCHENER, F/M. LORD H., 14-16, 18-22, 25, 31, 34, 37, 40, 53, 106, 116.
KNIGHT, MISS K., 51, 52, 118-119, 186-7.
LIVESEY, CAPT. H., 140, 142, 146, 150, 177.
LLOYD GEORGE, RT. HON. D., 65, 87.
NUTTER, PTE., H. 'KID', 70, 132.
MACALPINE, CAPT. A.G., 122, 142, 150.
MACKINNON, GEN. SIR, W., 24.
MCKENZIE, BR./GEN., 57, 73.
MARSHALL, L./CPL. W., 29, 66, 68, 81, 92-3, 105, 111, 113, 116, 117, 123, 131, 139, 143, 145, 154, 159-60.
MILTON, CAPT. J.C., 21, 24, 29, 31, 33, 34, 37, 41, 44, 49, 51, 66, 100, 125.
MORRELL, RT. HON. P. M.P., 50.
MURRAY, GEN. SIR, A., 94, 104, 106.
PELTZER, CAPT. A., 65, 68, 124, 142.
PILKINGTON, SGT. J., 159.
PLACE, PTE. E., 26, 66, 129, 130, 138, 159.
POLLARD, PTE. G., 25-6, 39, 66, 68, 71, 73, 89, 105, 109, 113, 117, 121, 123-4, 126-7, 129-30, 131, 132, 137, 138, 159.
POLLITT, PTE. J., 181.
RAWCLIFFE, LT. T.W., 37, 48, 49, 57, 59, 67-8, 71-2, 89, 94, 98, 104, 123, 129, 130, 145, 150, 158-9.
RAWLINSON, GEN. SIR, H., 119, 174.
REES, BR./GEN. H.C., 127, 128, 140, 150, 153, 169, 173.
REISS, MAJ. E.L., 98, 142, 157.

RICKMAN, LT./COL. A.W., 67, 68, 69, 71, 73, 74, 75, 83, 85, 87, 89, 90, 91, 92, 94, 98, 100, 101, 105-6, 107, 115, 117, 124, 128, 132, 137, 139, 140, 142, 145, 148, 150, 151, 153, 157, 160, 176, 181, 182, 185, 188.
RIGBY, DR., 33, 34, 187.
RIGBY, SGT. J., 125, 150, 188.
RIGBY, 2/LT. W.G.M., 49, 62, 98.
RILEY, CAPT. H.D., 28, 46, 131, 137-8, 140, 142, 160.
RILEY, Q.M.S. 24, 28.
ROBINSON, CAPT. (TERR. FORCE), 21, 24, 27, 28, 37, 47.
ROBINSON, LT., 71-72.
ROSS, CAPT., R., 28, 29, 44, 47, 51, 55, 62, 67, 75, 116, 117, 125, 159, 188.
RUTTLE, LT. J., 53, 98, 125.
SAYER, PTE. F., 95-6, 115, 117, 122, 124-5, 131, 137-8, 140, 152, 158, 159, 160, 178-9.
SCHLOSS, U/O., 146.
SHARPLES, COL. R., 16, 20, 24, 29, 31, 33, 37, 40, 44, 45, 48, 49, 55, 63, 67, 188.
SLINGER, CAPT. G.N., 20, 44, 48, 49, 61, 66-7, 68, 75, 188.
SMITH, CPL. S., 123, 159.
SNAILHAM, L./CPL. J., 33, 67, 73, 99, 107, 126, 129, 149, 152, 156-7, 170.
SPENGLER, U/O., 151.
STANTON, R.E., 62.
STUTTARD, PTE. G., 131, 176.
TODD, CPL. W., 104, 160.
TOUGH, CAPT. A.B., 140, 141, 145.
TUDWAY, COL. R.J., 48.
WANLESS O'GOWAN, MAJ./GEN. R., 94.
WATSON, CAPT. A.G., 13, 20, 22, 24, 44, 117, 125.
WHITTAKER, CPL. E., 169, 170, 178, 180.
WHITTAKER, LT. M.E., 53, 59.
WILKINSON, PTE. H., 129, 159.
WILLIAMS, LT. G.G., 53, 98, 140, 177.

Photo postscript

Above: Mr. Will Marshall, ex-Lance Corporal, 'Z' (Burnley) Company, now (1987) lives quietly in Burnley. Still quite active, he likes to play the odd game of bowls in the nearby park. Mr. Marshall's recorded voice, describing his experiences on 1st July, 1916, is a feature of a reconstructed section of World War One trench and dug-out on permanent display in the Lancashire County and Regimental Museum, Stanley Street, Preston.

Right: Pte. Will Marshall, 'Z' (Burnley) Company, poses proudly for this studio portrait in May 1915.

249

Far right: Mr. Ralph Thornley of Church, visits the grave of his uncle, Corporal Ralph Thornley at Euston Road Cemetery Colincamps. His uncle was killed in action, 1st July, 1916.

Right: Pte. George Pollard, age sixteen years, five months in a studio photograph taken for Christmas 1914.

Below: In 1985 George returned to the Somme battlefield for the first time since July 1916. He served in the Amiens area in 1917/18 in the R.F.C./R.A.F. acting for a time as armourer to Major Bill McCudden V.C. In Euston Road Cemetery, Colincamps, George pauses for a few moments before the grave of Corporal Sam Smith, his section corporal from September 1914 to July 1916. He was killed in action on 1st July, 1916.

Above: Three ex-Pals meet in 1985. Many reminiscences were exchanged in the visit of Stanley Bewsher (centre) to the home in Accrington of Harry Kay (left). Although George Pollard (right) was a close friend of Harry Kay's and saw him frequently, they met Stanley for the first time.

Left: James Snailham, in his home in Yorkshire with his wife and the author in 1985.

Below: Each year on the Sunday nearest July 1st, the Queen's Lancashire Regiment commemorates Somme Sunday at Blackburn Cathedral. In 1985 Russell Bradshaw (left) travelled from his home on the south coast to attend and to meet, for the first time, George Pollard (third left). The author and his wife, Ruth, accompanied them at the service.

SELECTED BIBLIOGRAPHY

(Published In London Except Where Stated)

KEEGAN, Paul
'An Officer', The New Army in the Making
(Trench & Tubner, 1915)

BLAKE, R. (Editor)
The Private Papers of Douglas Haig 1914-1919
(Eyre & Spottiswoode, 1952)

BORASTON, J.
Sir Douglas Haig's Despatches
(Dent, 1919)

BROPHY, J. & PARTRIDGE E.
The Long Trail: What the British Soldier sang and said in the Great War of 1914-1918
(Andre Deutsch, 1965)

BROWN, M.
Tommy goes to War
(Dent, 1978).

CAMPBELL, R.
The Ebb and Flow of Battle
(Hamish Hamilton, 1977)

CONAN DOYLE, Arthur
The British Campaign in France and Flanders
(Hodder & Stoughton, 1918)

COOMBES, Rose E.
Before Endeavours Fade
(After the Battle Mag., 1979)

CROSSLEY, R.
A History of the Accrington Pals, unpublished manuscript
(No date)

CHARTERIS J.
At G.H.Q.
(Cassell, 1931)

ELGOOD, P. G.
Egypt and the Army
(O.U.P., 1924)

ELLIS, J.
Eye Deep in Hell — Life in the Trenches 1914-1918
(Croom Helm, 1976)

FARRAR-HOCKLEY, A.
The Somme
(Batsford, 1964)

FUSSELL, Paul
The Great War and Modern Memory
(O.U.P., 1979)

GARDNER, Brian
The Big Push
(Cassell, 1961)

GERMAINS, Victor, W.
The Kitchener Armies
(Peter Davies, 1930)

GILES, John
The Somme, then and now
(Bailey Bros., 1977)

GLADDEN, Norman
The Somme 1916
(W. Kimber, 1974)

GRAVES, Robert
Goodbye to all That
(Penguin, 1960)

GREEN, H.
The British Army in the First World War (The Regulars, Territorials and Kitcheners' Army)
(Treherne & Co., 1968)

GOUGH, Sir Herbert
The Fifth Army
(Hodder & Stoughton, 1931)

HARRIS, John
Covenant with Death
(Hutchinson, 1961 (Fiction))

HARRIS, J.
The Somme: Death of a Generation
(White Lion Publications, 1975)

HAY, Ian
The First Hundred Thousand
(Blackwood, 1915)

HOULTON, M.
World War One: Trench Warfare
(Ward Locke, 1974)

JAMES, E. A. Brigadier
British Regiments 1914-1918
Samson Books, 1978)

KEEGAN, John
The Face of Battle
(Penguin, 1978)

MACDONALD, Lyn
Somme
(Michael Joseph, 1983)

MAGNUS, Philip
Kitchener: Portrait of an Imperialist
(John Murray, 1958)

MESSENGER, C.
Trench Fighting
(Pan Books, 1973)

MIDDLEBROOK, M.
The First Day on the Somme
(Allen Lane, 1981)

MYATT, F.
The British Infantry 1660-1945
(Blandford Press, Poole, 1983)

NICHOLSON, Major General Sir N. (Editor)
The History of the East Lancashire Regiment in the Great War 1914-1919
(Littlebury Bros., (Liverpool), 1936)

SIR G. McMUNN & Cyril FALLS (Editors)
Official History of the Great War, Military Operations, Egypt and Palestine Volume 1 and Appendices
(H.M.S.O., 1928)

C. F. A. OGLANDER (Editor)
Official History of the Great War, Military Operations, Gallipoli. Volume 2 (Maps & Appendices)
Heinneman, 1932)

Lt. Colonel EDMONDS (Editor)
Official History of the Great War, Military Operations, France & Belgium, 1916 (Sir Douglas Haigs command to 1st July: Battle of the Somme)
Macmillan, 1932)

Capt. W. MILES (Editor)
Official History of the Grat War, Military Operations, France & Belgium, 1916 (2nd July to the end of the Battles of the Somme) Appendices & Maps
(Macmillan, 1938)

Major BECKE (Editor)
Official History of the Great War, Orders of Battle of Divisions Parts 3A and 3B (New Army)
H.M.S.O., 1945)

Major BECKE (Editor)
Official History of the Great War Part 4, The Army Council, G.H.Q.'s Armies and Corps 1914-1918
(H.M.S.O., 1945)

PALMER, F. K.
With the New Army on the Somme
(John Murray, 1917)

SAYER, F. & CRABTREE, P.
'The History of 'Z' Company'
(Published privately (Burnley), 1938)

SPARLING, R. A.
The History of the 12th (Service) Battalion York & Lancaster Regiment
(J. W. Northend, Sheffield, 1920)

TERRAINE, John
Douglas Haig: The Educated Soldier
(Hutchinson, 1963)

TERRAINE, John
Impacts of War
(Hutchinson, 1970)

THOMPSON, P. A.
Lions led by Donkeys
(Werner Laurie, 1927)

TURNER, L. C. F.
Origins of the First World War
(Edward Arnold, 1970)

WALLACE, Edgar
Kitchener's Army and the Territorials
(George Newnes, 1916)

WHITEHOUSE, C. J. & IBBOTSON, G. P.
Great War Camps on Cannock Chase
(Published Privately, Brocton, 1978)

Other Works

Infantry Training Manual (4 Company Organisation) General Staff
H.M.S.O., 1914)

Operational Orders 16/6/16 94 Brigade, 31 Division

Battle Report 1/7/16 12th Service Battalion, York & Lancaster Regiment
(By courtesy of York and Lancaster Regimental Museum)

The First of July, a reunion dinner speech to the survivors of the Sheffield Battalion given at Sheffield, 18th December, 1920 by Lieutenant-General Sir Aylmer Hunter-Weston K.C.B., D.S.O., M.P.
(Souvenir Booklet)

11th East Lancashire Battalion, War Diary 1915-1919

VIII Corps reports to General Staff H.Q. 1/7/16-3/7/16
(Courtesy of the PRO)

Special Order of the Day 28/6/16 94 Brigade
(Courtesy of the IWM)

A Personal Record of the War 1915, 1916, 1917 by Brigadier General H. C. Rees D.S.O.
(Courtesy of the IWM)

Army Book 136, 'My Experience of the Army in England', by Sergeant J. Bridge
(Courtesy Mr. A. Trengove)

Soldiers who died in the Great War 1914-1919 Volume 35 (East Lancs Regiment)
(H.M.S.O., 1921)

Commonwealth War Graves Commission Registers

Newspapers

Accrington Gazette
Accrington Observer and Times
Bacup Times
Blackburn Times
Burnley Express
Burnley News
Caernarvon and Denbigh Herald
Chorley Guardian
Chorley Weekly News
Darwen News
Haslingden Gazette
Nelson Leader
Northern Daily Telegraph
Oldham Chronicle
Rossendale Free Press
The Times

Acknowledgments

In writing this book I have received the most generous help from many people. It would have been impossible for me to tell the story of the 11th Service (Accrington) East Lancashire Regiment without the help of the Battalion veterans and their families, and those families whose thoughts — for some, over seventy years later — are ever with the menfolk they lost. Without exception I was welcomed into their homes with kindness and courtesy. They shared with me family recollections and without hesitation gladly lent me — a comparative stranger — their precious photographs and personal mementoes. Time after time I became the anxious holder for a week or so, for copying, of the only photograph of 'Father', 'Brother' or 'Husband' which a family possessed. Always I was told, 'If it will help you in your research, take it.' Such is the openheartedness of East Lancashire people. I am honoured indeed to count them as my friends.

I will always be deeply moved by the courage and fortitude of the veterans who endured the catastrophe of the 'Great War'. I am especially indebted to the following for their patience in answering my many questions, and forbearance when I inadvertently re-awakened memories best forgotten:

Pte. H. Anderson; Pte. R. Barrow; Pte. S. Bewsher, M.M.; Cpl. R. Bradshaw, M.M.; Pte. A. Cheetham; Pte. S. Clark; Pte. R. Fisher; Pte. F. Foote; Capt. R. Glenn (York & Lancaster Regiment); Pte. H. Jones; Pte. H. Kay; Major T. P. King; L/Cpl. W. Marshall; Major T. W. Rawcliffe, M.C.; Cpl. F. Sayer; L/Cpl. J. Snailham; with especial thanks to my good friend, Pte. G. Pollard.

To the families of the following 'Pals', my special thanks for their time and hospitality, and for their generosity in allowing me a look into their own family history.

Pte. J. Ames; Sgt. W. Ashmead; Pte. W. Baines; Pte. J. Baldwin; Cpl. F. Bath; Pte. F. Baxendale; Pte. C. Birtwell; Pte. W. Breaks; Cpl. G. Breakell; L/Cpl. W. Briggs; Capt. P. J. Broadley, O.B.E.; Pte. R. Buckley; Pte. T. Carey; Pte. H. Chadwick; Cpl. (later Lt.) S. B. Challen; Pte. W. Clarke; Sgt. S. Clegg; Pte. W. Clegg; Sgt. L. Coldclough; Pte. P. Crabtree; Pte. J. Cocker; Pte. W. Cowell; Ptes. J. and S. Cullen; Pte. E. Culley; Pte. J. Davy; Pte. O. T. Duerden; Sgt. I. Edge; Pte. A. S. Edwards; Sgt. A. K. Entwistle; Pte. O. Fairweather; Pte. W. T. Fielding; Pte. W. Fifield; Pte. A. S. Gibson; L/Cpl.

C. Glover; Pte. W. Greaves; Pte. J. Grimshaw; Capt. T. Y. Harwood; C.S.M. Hey; A.Q.M.S. J. Hindle; Pte. W. Holmes; Pte. C. E. Humphreys; Pte. R. Ingham; Pte. E. Kenyon; Pte. J. Laffy; Pte. W. Landon; Pte. F. Leeming; Pte. T. Lord; Cpl. S. McCall; Capt. F. G. MacAlpine, D.S.O.; Pte. P. Martin; Pte. J. Molloy; Cpl. A. Naylor; Pte. H. Nutter; Pte. W. O'Hare; Pte. W. Parkinson; Pte. T. Passmore; Pte. W. Peart; Pte. H. Peel; Capt. (later Lt. Col.) A. Peltzer, D.S.O.; Pte. J. Perry; Pte. H. Power; Sgt. H. Pursglove, D.C.M.; Pte. (later Lt.) H. Platt, M.C.; Lt. Col. A. S. Rickman, D.S.O. + bar; Sgt. J. Rigby, M.M.; Pte. A. Riley; Ptes. W. and A. E. Ritchings, M.M.; Pte. S. Rollins; Sgt. J. Rowntree; Lt. J. Ruttle; L/Cpl. L. Saunders; Major G. N. Slinger; Pte. C. Smith; Sgt. T. Southworth, D.C.M.; Pte. J. Thomas; L/Cpl. R. Thornley; Pte. J. Topping; Pte. W. Varley; Pte. J. Walton; Pte. V. Wardleworth; Major A. G. Watson, O.B.E.; Cpl. E. Whittaker; Pte. H. Wilding; Pte. H. Wilkinson; Pte. T. Wilmington; Ptes. J. and W. Wixted; Sgt. J. A. Woods and Pte. S. Woods; Pte. C. Yarranton.

I owe a special obligation to my good friends John Bailey of Brentwood, Essex, and Professor Frank J. Merli of the Department of History, Queens College, City University of New York. John's unsurpassed knowledge of all aspects of W.W.1, combined with Frank's 'Strunking' of my earliest efforts in writing, helped me beyond words. I acknowledge with gratitude their interest and constructive criticism.

To Dermot Healey of the Manchester Studies Unit, Manchester Polytechnic, I am most grateful, for his advice and encouragement in my earliest researches and 'starting me off'.

Writing this book would have been impossible without the help of the Librarians and staff of the Lancashire Library Service. For their constant helpfulness and patience during my many enquiries, I particularly thank Mr. Brian Ashton, Mrs. Josie Green, Mrs. Helen Barratt and Mrs. Barbara Reade at Accrington, Miss Jean Siddall and Miss Janice Bell at Burnley, Mr. Jim Heyes at Chorley and Miss Diana Winterbotham at Library Headquarters, Preston. I also thank Mr. Jim Fielding of Oldham Library Local Studies Unit; Anne Venables, Archivist to Gwynedd County Court Record Office, Caernarfon, Gwynedd; Maryann Gomes and Marion Hewitt of the North West Film Archive at Manchester Polytechnic for their generous help in providing stills

254

from archive film and the staffs of Manchester Central Library and Hull Central Library.

I am deeply indebted to all those who, in a spirit of friendship and generosity, gave me so much of their time and knowledge in correspondence and my personal visits. These include:

Jack Bottomley (Leader of Burnley Boys Club) of Burnley; George Broadhurst of Accrington; Ken Davy of Ontario, Canada; Tony Eaton of Northallerton; Ralph Gibson of Sheffield; George Harwood, formerly of Blaydon, Tyne and Wear; Mrs. Carol Hill of Chorley; Mrs. June Huntingdon of Accrington; Walter and Percy Holmes of Accrington; David Ingham of Sabden; Mrs. E. Leach of Chorley; Geoff Lund of Clayton-le-Moors; Dr. A. Peacock of York; George Quinn of Ontario, Canada; M. Georges Rachaine of St. Genevieve des Bois, Paris; Malcolm Shearer of Camberley; and Mr. A. Trengove of Rishton.

I wish to express my gratitude to Liz and Dave Driver of Hemel Hempstead, with particular thanks to Dave for 'Will Cowell' and 'T. E. Francis'. My thanks also to John Garwood of Chorley for 'Seth Rollins' and for his gift of photographs.

To Judith and Trevor Adams for their assistance and photographic expertise; to John Cartmell and his fellow-members of the East Lancashire Medal and Militaria Society for their expert advice; to Mr. Richard Crossley of the 'Accrington Observer and Times' for his ever-willing assistance and constant support; to Philip Healy of the University of Sheffield, Division of Continuing Education, for his help and advice; to Major G. Rickman for his many kindnesses and enthusiastic support; to Major S. Tipping, Regimental H.Q. The Queen's Lancashire Regiment, for all his help; to Kathleen and Jack Broderick for their help as friends, and their expert knowledge as local historians in tracing local families: to all these I extend my warmest thanks.

The lists of medal and award winners, nominal rolls and extracts from the Army Lists are the results of a huge amount of detailed research by Mr. Fergus Read, the Curator of the Lancashire County and Regimental Museum, Preston. The value of these lists to veterans and their families, to expert and amateur historians alike, and to medal collectors and researchers is inestimable. Fergus, with his professional expertise coupled with an exuberant enthusiasm, has made a superb contribution to the story of the Accrington Pals. I am deeply grateful.

My thanks are due to Mr. Martin Middlebrook for his kind permission to use material relating to Pte. H. Bury in Chapter 7. Thanks also to Mr. Richard Baumgartner for the loan of photographs from his collection.

I am extremely grateful to Herr Raab of the Generallandesarchiv, Karlsruhe, West Germany for permission to use 169 Infantry Regiment archive material.

Thanks also the staffs of the Public Record Office, Kew, the Trustees of the Imperial War Museum, London S.E.1, particularly Mr. Clive Hughes, and the Commonwealth War Graves Commission, Maidenhead, Berks., for their help and for permission to use documentary material. For her perseverance and skill in transcribing my scrawl into impeccable typing, I thank Maureen Evans.

I am grateful indeed to Jon Cooksey author of Pals (Barnsley) for his enthusiastic help and particularly for his generous loan of German archive material.

For her help with additional typing and for her generous loan of precious family material relating to L/Cpl. Briggs, I sincerely thank Mrs. Enid Briggs of Accrington.

During the compilation of this book I had the privilege of working closely with Roni, Wes and Alan of the Graphics and Features Department of the Barnsley Chronicle. Their first-rate professionalism and expertise is self evident in the quality of the maps, photographs and typography. I am delighted also that our team-work blossomed into friendship.

Most of all, my thanks to Ruth and Lois for their support, tolerance and endless patience, whilst I 'burnt the midnight oil'.

Where applicable the source of photographs is acknowledged in abbreviated form e.g. A.O.& T. — Accrington Observer and Times, L.L.B.D. — Lancashire Library, Burnley District etc. Photographs not credited are from the authors collection.

Photographs which are held by the Imperial War Museum appear by kind permission of the Trustees of the Imperial War Museum.

Whilst every effort has been made to trace copyright holders of all photographs, the publishers would be pleased to hear from any copyright holders not mentioned in the preceding acknowledgments.

Bill Turner is fifty-six (1987), married with one daughter. Although not a native of Accrington (he was born in Haslingden, four miles away) he has lived in the town for thirty years. For most of his working life he was employed in the electricity supply industry, most recently as a Principal Assistant in Management Services. In 1981 he gained a B.A. degree after six years part-time study with the Open University. He has been a Justice of the Peace since 1968.

He has long been interested in local history and has lectured on the subject throughout East Lancashire. He has published several articles in local newspapers and in magazines for the local history and military history enthusiast.

He started his researches into the Accrington Pals after discovering that the history books described only in the vaguest of terms what happened to the Battalion in World War One.

There are tear-dimmed eyes in the town to-day,
There are lips to be no more kissed,
There are bosoms that swell with an aching heart,
When they think of a dear one missed.
But time will prove their heartfelt grief;
Of their sons they will proudly tell,
How in the gallant charge in this world-wide war,
As "Pals" they fought and fell!

Will Marshall, August 1916.